9 Story & Art by

Maki Enjoji

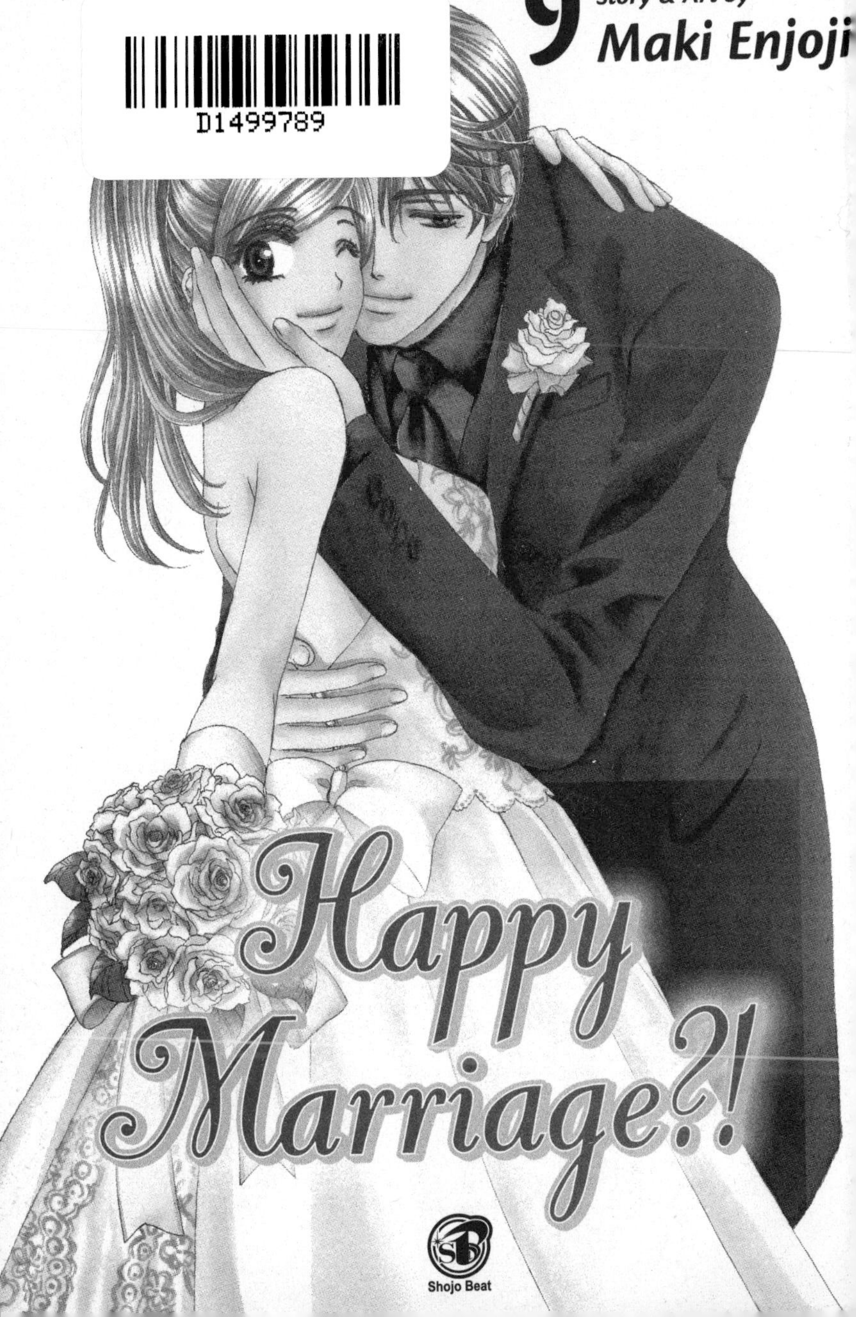

Happy Marriage?!

Shojo Beat

Happy Marriage?!

Characters

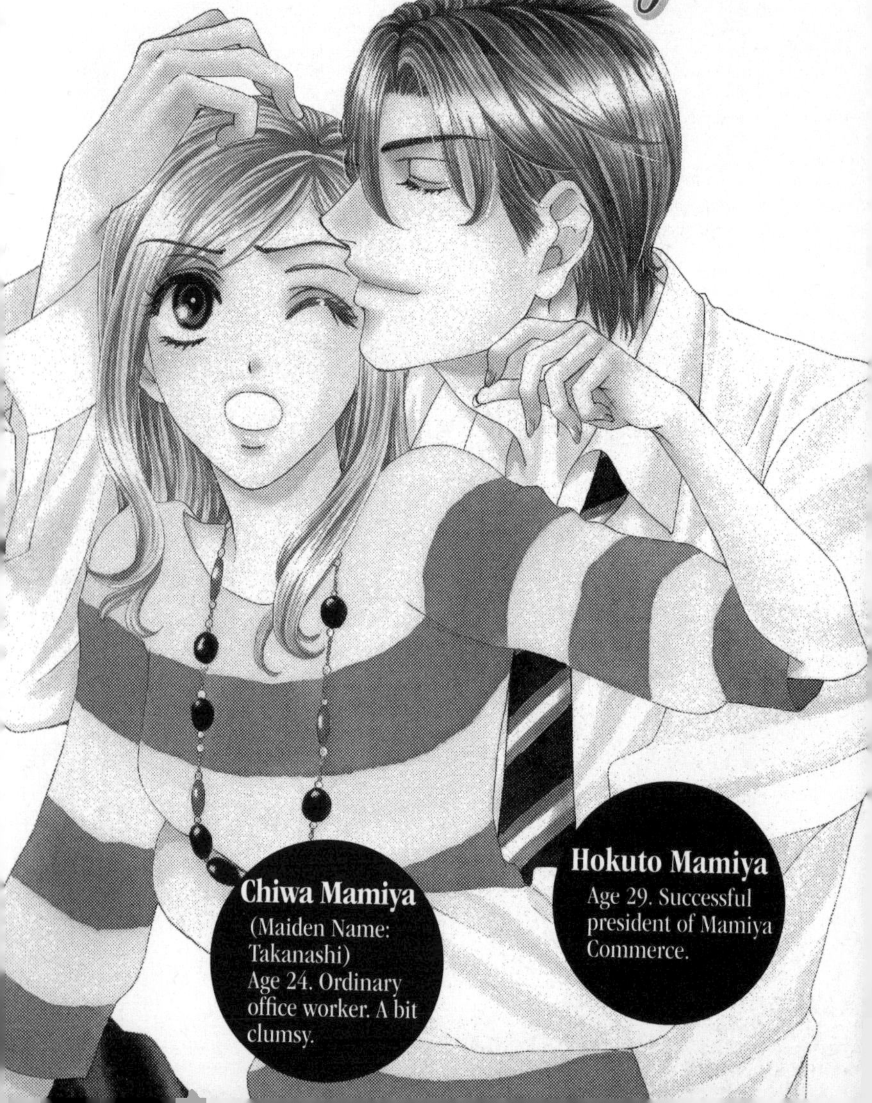
Hokuto Mamiya
Age 29. Successful president of Mamiya Commerce.
Chiwa Mamiya
(Maiden Name: Takanashi)
Age 24. Ordinary office worker. A bit clumsy.

Misaki Shitara

President of a famous brand. In the past she was in a relationship with Hokuto...?

Kaname Asahina

Two years older than Chiwa, he was an upperclassman at her university. He is now her boss at work.

Story

Chiwa Takanashi has no girlish fantasies about finding Prince Charming, and she wanted nothing but to lead a normal life until she found herself marrying company president Hokuto to pay off her father's debts. Though the marriage is in name only, Chiwa has fallen in love with her husband. The two make love for the first time, consummating their marriage.

Hokuto and Chiwa's life starts to get hectic after Hokuto's job change, and strange incidents keep happening around Chiwa. Realizing that someone is out to get her, she starts investigating to find out who is behind it...

Happy Marriage?!

Contents

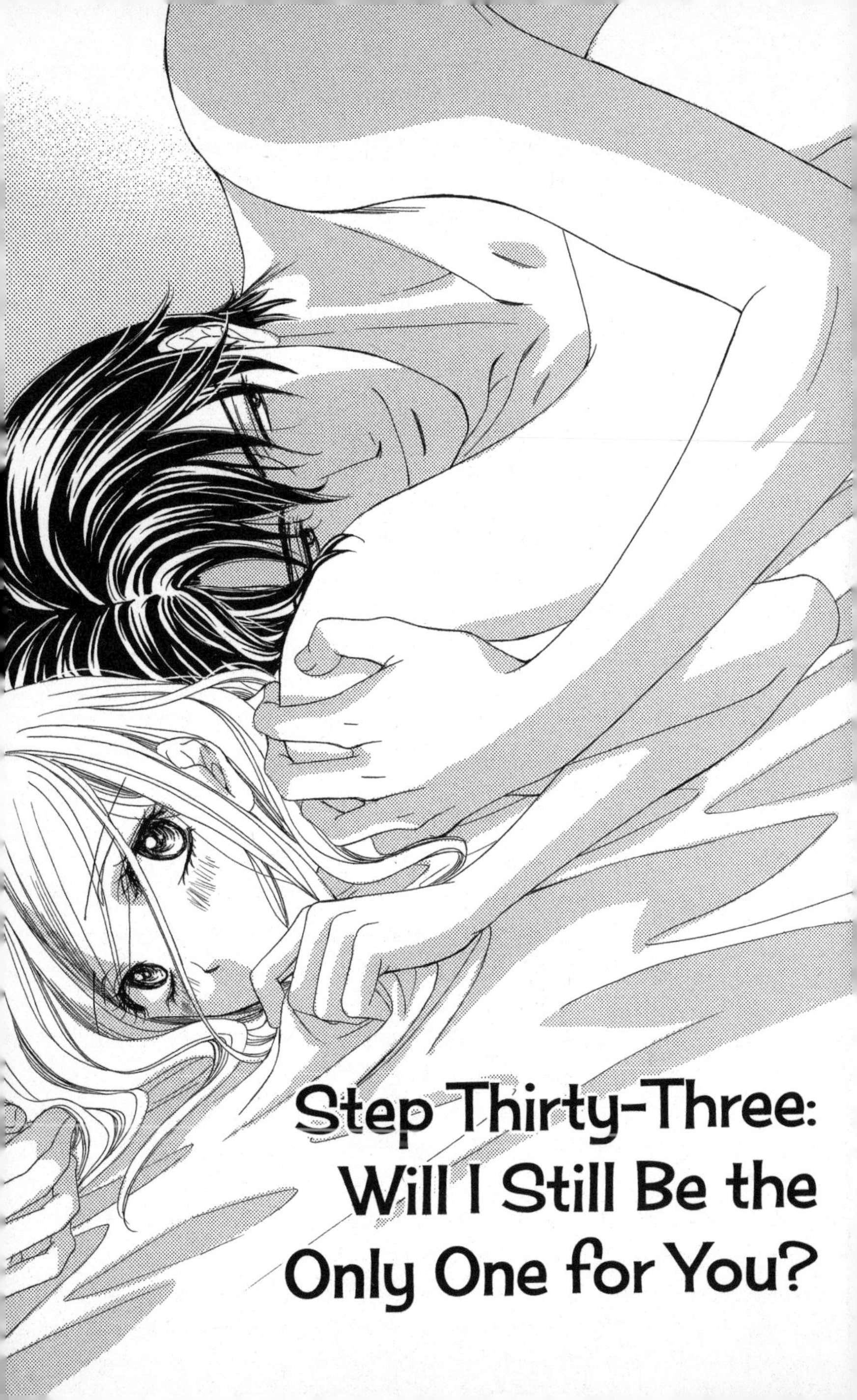

Step Thirty-Three: Will I Still Be the Only One for You?

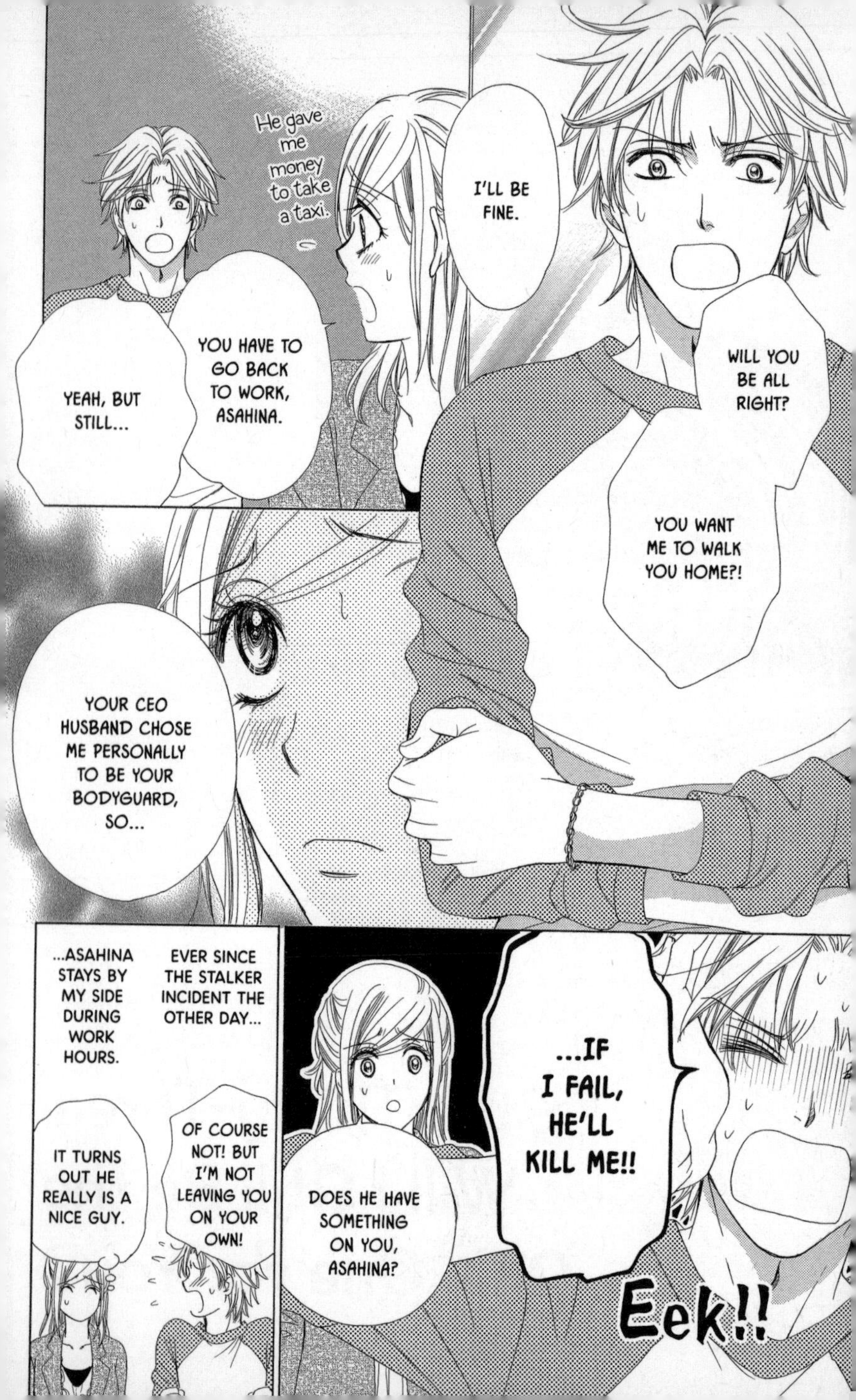
WILL YOU BE ALL RIGHT?
YOU WANT ME TO WALK YOU HOME?!
I'LL BE FINE.
He gave me money to take a taxi.
YOU HAVE TO GO BACK TO WORK, ASAHINA.
YEAH, BUT STILL...
YOUR CEO HUSBAND CHOSE ME PERSONALLY TO BE YOUR BODYGUARD, SO...
DOES HE HAVE SOMETHING ON YOU, ASAHINA?
...IF I FAIL, HE'LL KILL ME!!
Eek!!
EVER SINCE THE STALKER INCIDENT THE OTHER DAY...
...ASAHINA STAYS BY MY SIDE DURING WORK HOURS.
OF COURSE NOT! BUT I'M NOT LEAVING YOU ON YOUR OWN!
IT TURNS OUT HE REALLY IS A NICE GUY.

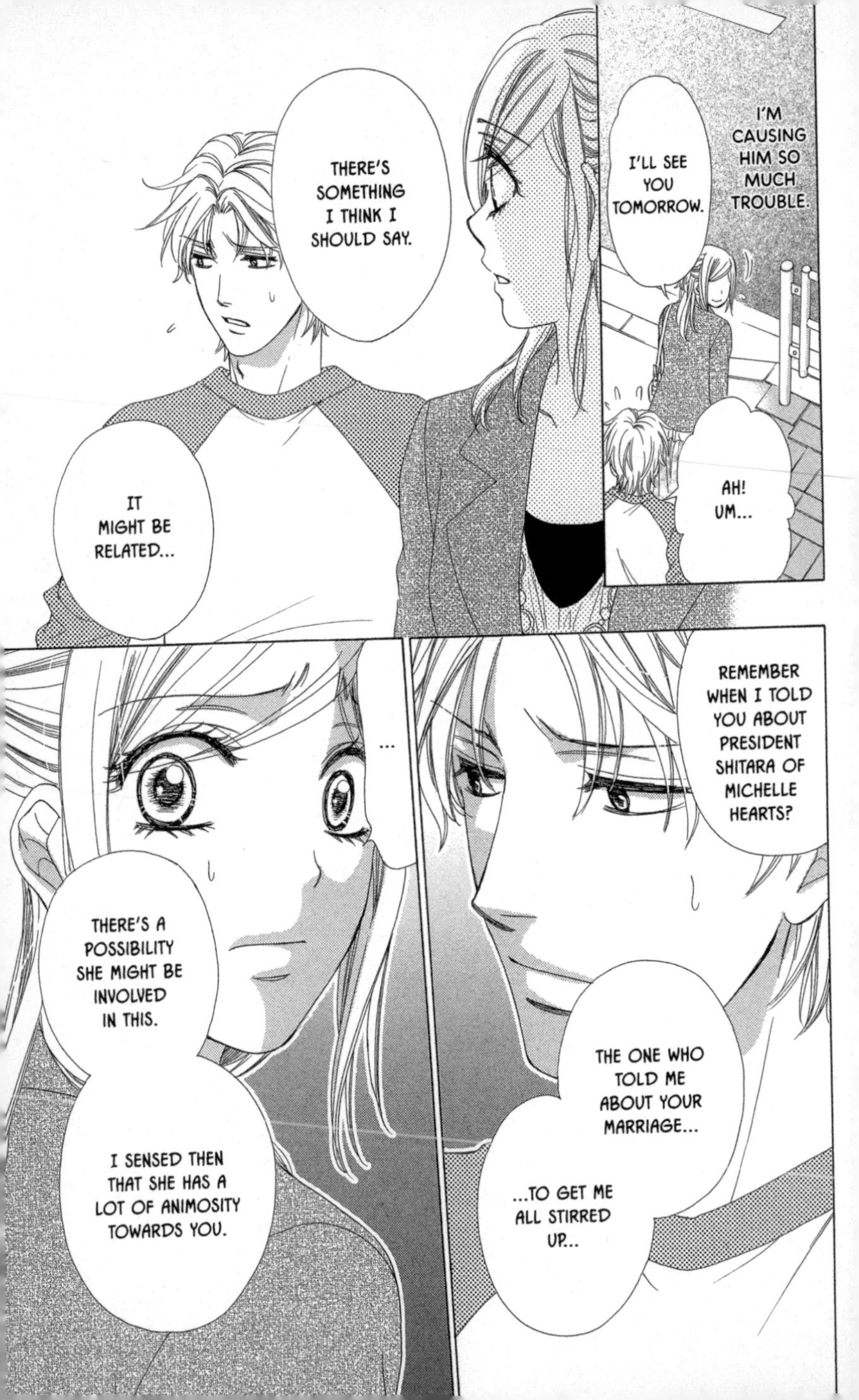
I'M CAUSING HIM SO MUCH TROUBLE.
I'LL SEE YOU TOMORROW.
AH! UM...
THERE'S SOMETHING I THINK I SHOULD SAY.
IT MIGHT BE RELATED...
REMEMBER WHEN I TOLD YOU ABOUT PRESIDENT SHITARA OF MICHELLE HEARTS?
THE ONE WHO TOLD ME ABOUT YOUR MARRIAGE...
...TO GET ME ALL STIRRED UP...
...
THERE'S A POSSIBILITY SHE MIGHT BE INVOLVED IN THIS.
I SENSED THEN THAT SHE HAS A LOT OF ANIMOSITY TOWARDS YOU.

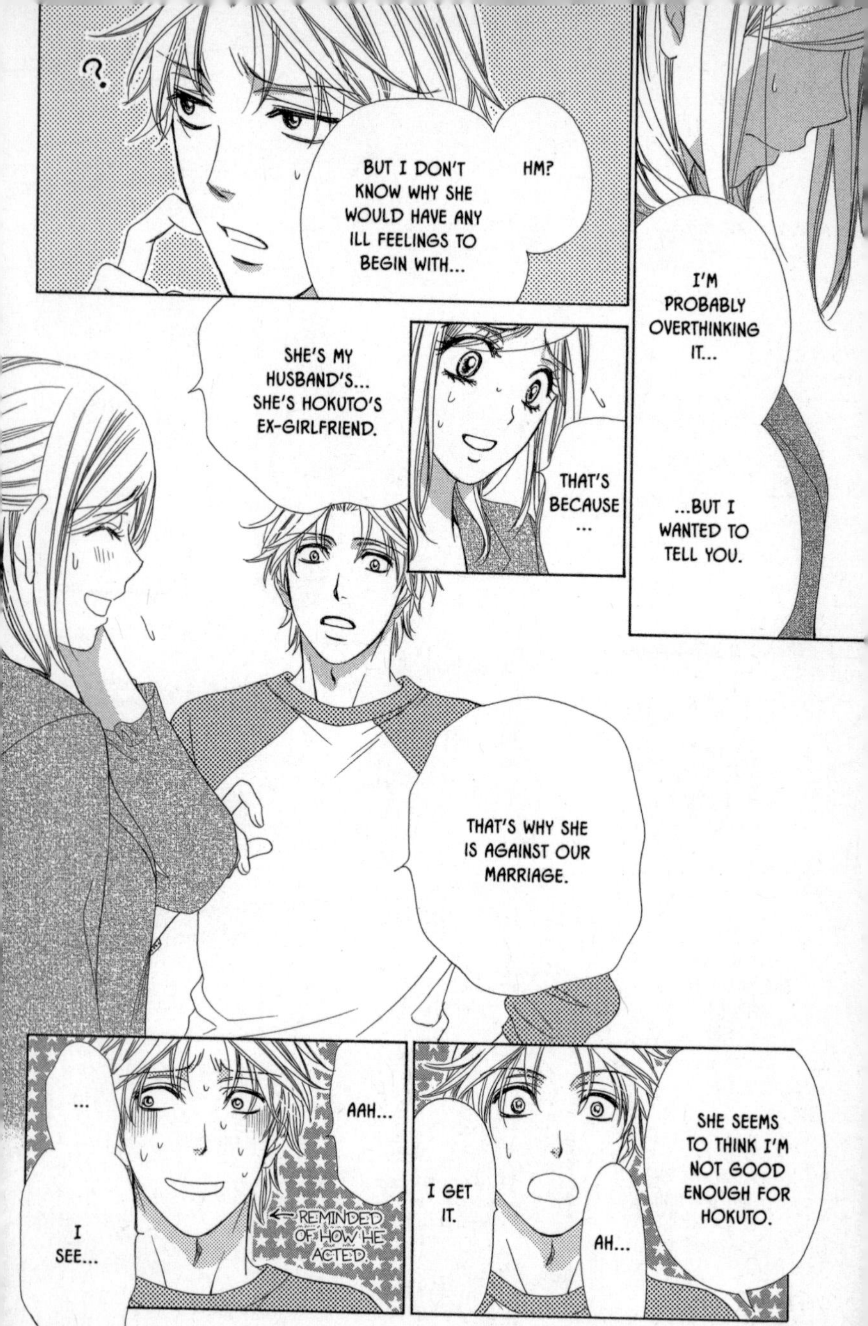
I'M PROBABLY OVERTHINKING IT...
...BUT I WANTED TO TELL YOU.
?
HM?
BUT I DON'T KNOW WHY SHE WOULD HAVE ANY ILL FEELINGS TO BEGIN WITH...
THAT'S BECAUSE ...
SHE'S MY HUSBAND'S... SHE'S HOKUTO'S EX-GIRLFRIEND.
THAT'S WHY SHE IS AGAINST OUR MARRIAGE.
SHE SEEMS TO THINK I'M NOT GOOD ENOUGH FOR HOKUTO.
AH...
I GET IT.
AAH...
REMINDED OF HOW HE ACTED.
...
I SEE...

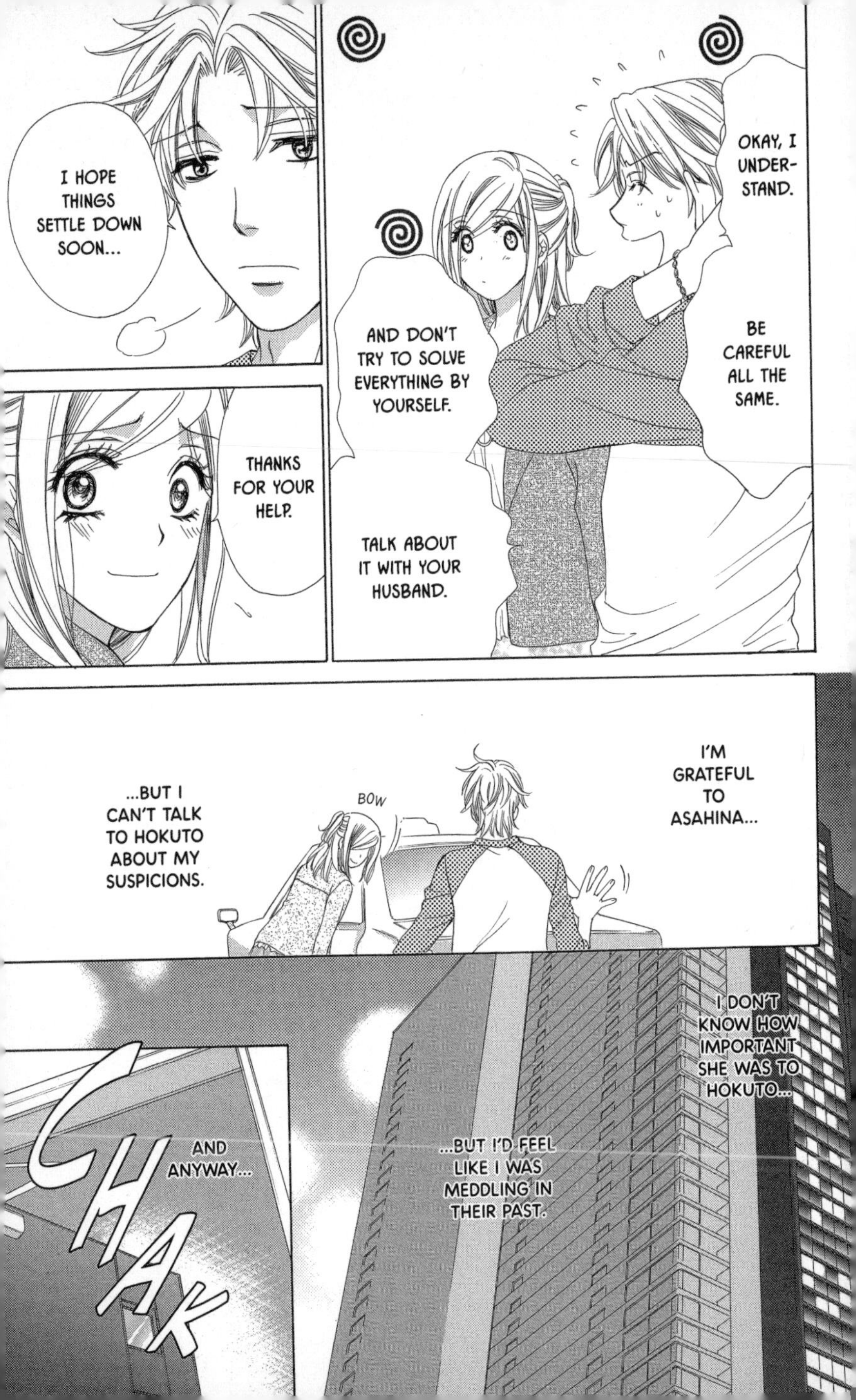
OKAY, I UNDERSTAND.
BE CAREFUL ALL THE SAME.
AND DON'T TRY TO SOLVE EVERYTHING BY YOURSELF.
TALK ABOUT IT WITH YOUR HUSBAND.
I HOPE THINGS SETTLE DOWN SOON...
THANKS FOR YOUR HELP.
I'M GRATEFUL TO ASAHINA...
BOW
...BUT I CAN'T TALK TO HOKUTO ABOUT MY SUSPICIONS.
I DON'T KNOW HOW IMPORTANT SHE WAS TO HOKUTO...
...BUT I'D FEEL LIKE I WAS MEDDLING IN THEIR PAST.
AND ANYWAY...
CHAK

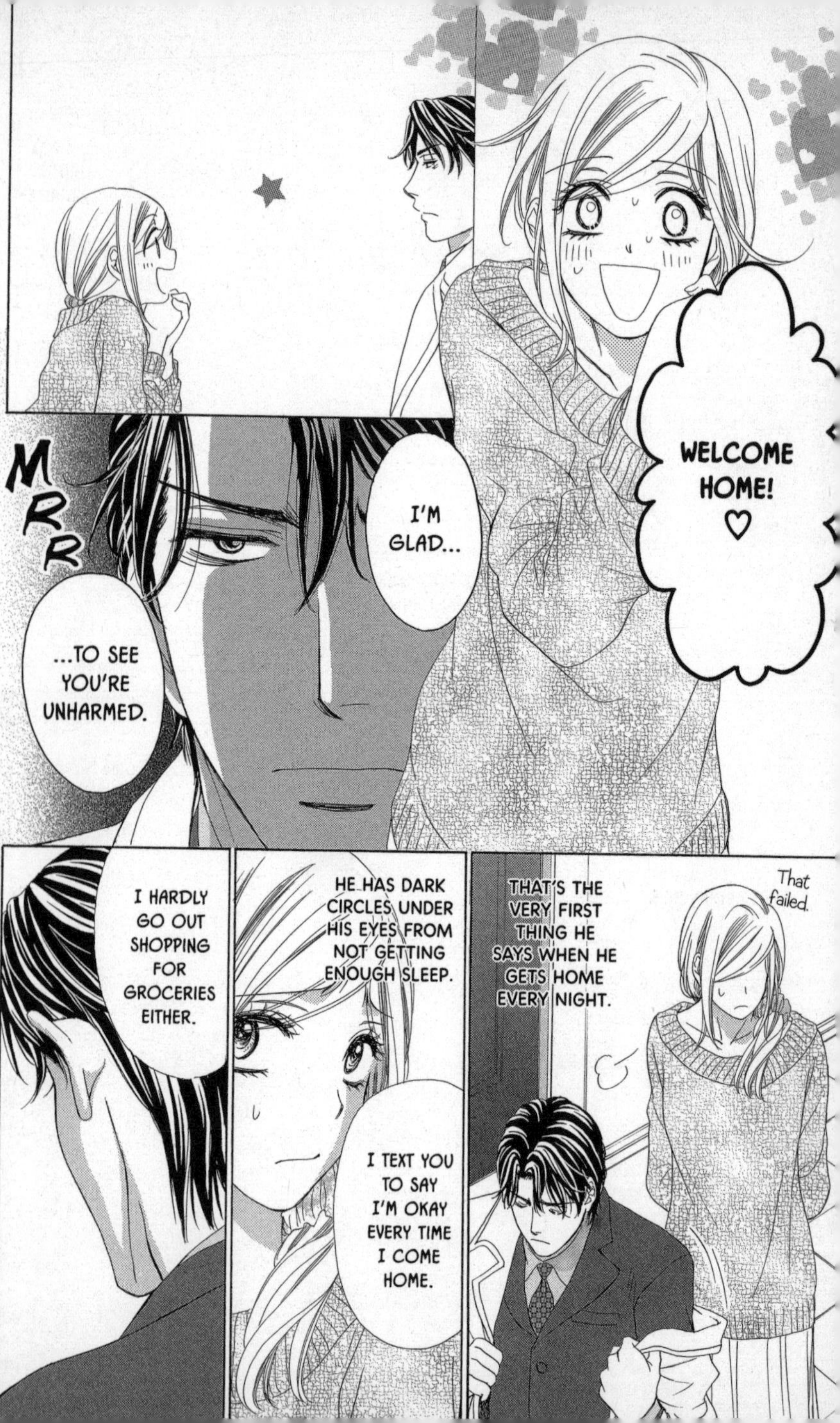
WELCOME HOME! ♡
MRR
I'M GLAD...
...TO SEE YOU'RE UNHARMED.
That failed.
THAT'S THE VERY FIRST THING HE SAYS WHEN HE GETS HOME EVERY NIGHT.
HE HAS DARK CIRCLES UNDER HIS EYES FROM NOT GETTING ENOUGH SLEEP.
I TEXT YOU TO SAY I'M OKAY EVERY TIME I COME HOME.
I HARDLY GO OUT SHOPPING FOR GROCERIES EITHER.

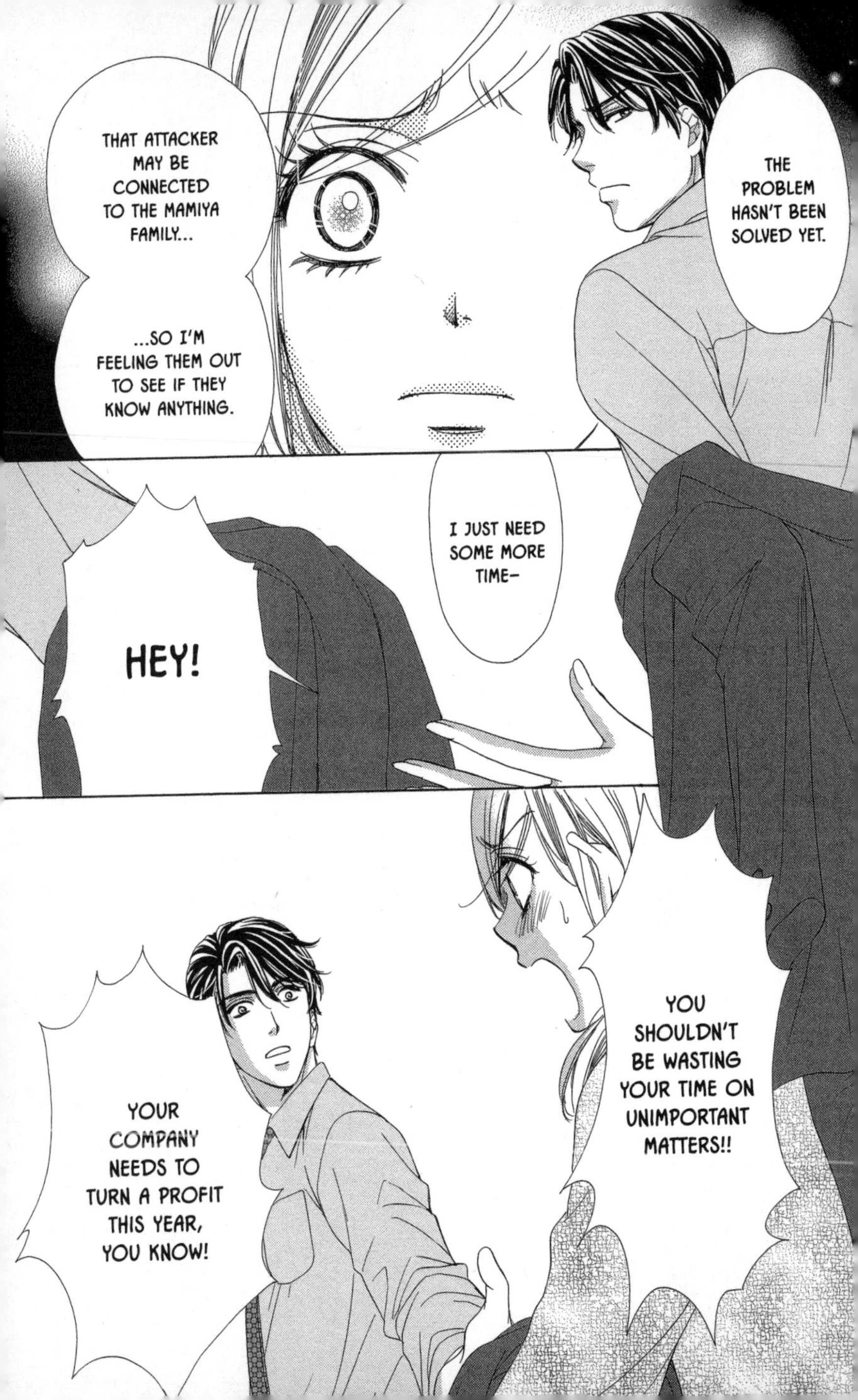
THE PROBLEM HASN'T BEEN SOLVED YET.
THAT ATTACKER MAY BE CONNECTED TO THE MAMIYA FAMILY...
...SO I'M FEELING THEM OUT TO SEE IF THEY KNOW ANYTHING.
I JUST NEED SOME MORE TIME–
HEY!
YOU SHOULDN'T BE WASTING YOUR TIME ON UNIMPORTANT MATTERS!!
YOUR COMPANY NEEDS TO TURN A PROFIT THIS YEAR, YOU KNOW!

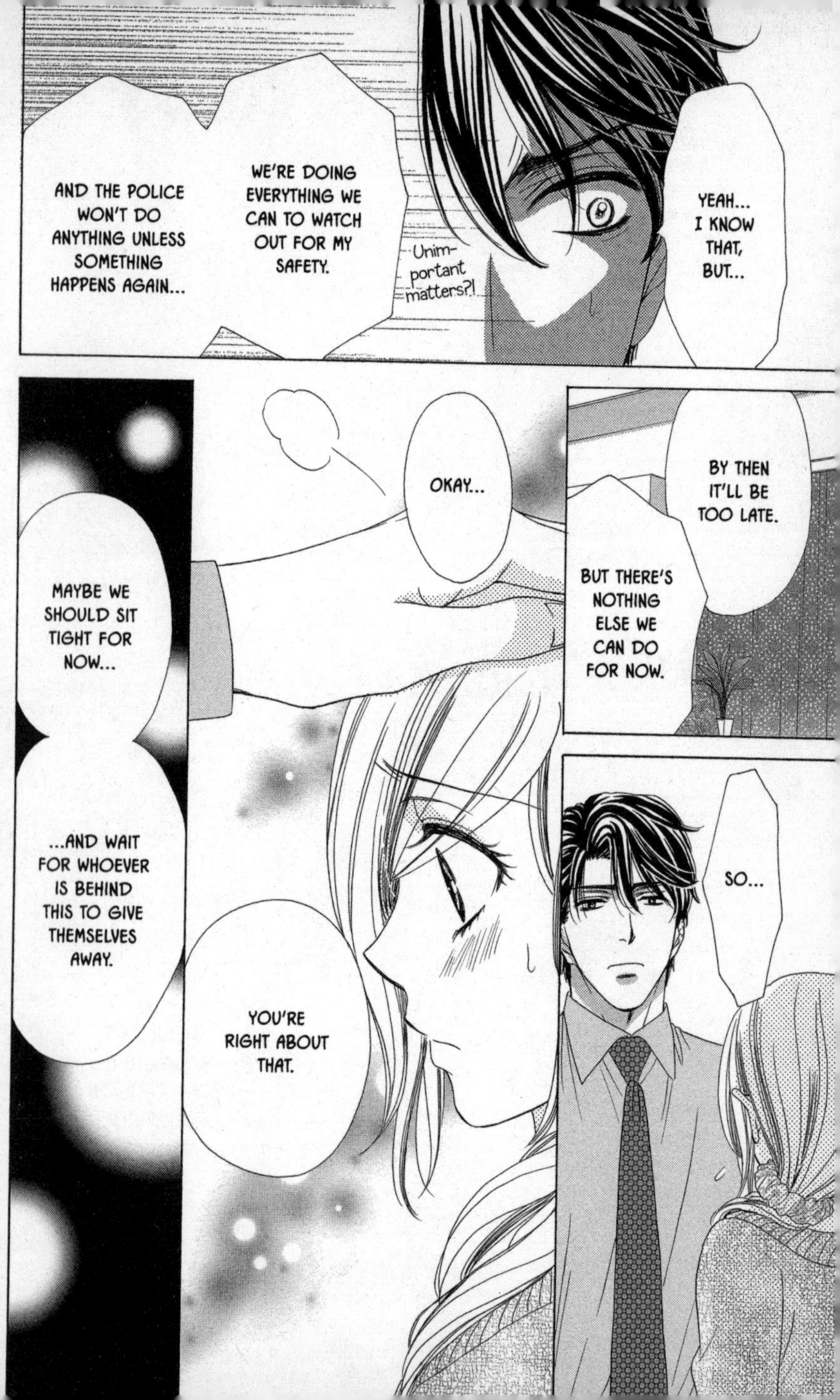
YEAH... I KNOW THAT, BUT...
Unimportant matters?!
WE'RE DOING EVERYTHING WE CAN TO WATCH OUT FOR MY SAFETY.
AND THE POLICE WON'T DO ANYTHING UNLESS SOMETHING HAPPENS AGAIN...
BY THEN IT'LL BE TOO LATE.
BUT THERE'S NOTHING ELSE WE CAN DO FOR NOW.
SO...
OKAY...
MAYBE WE SHOULD SIT TIGHT FOR NOW...
...AND WAIT FOR WHOEVER IS BEHIND THIS TO GIVE THEMSELVES AWAY.
YOU'RE RIGHT ABOUT THAT.

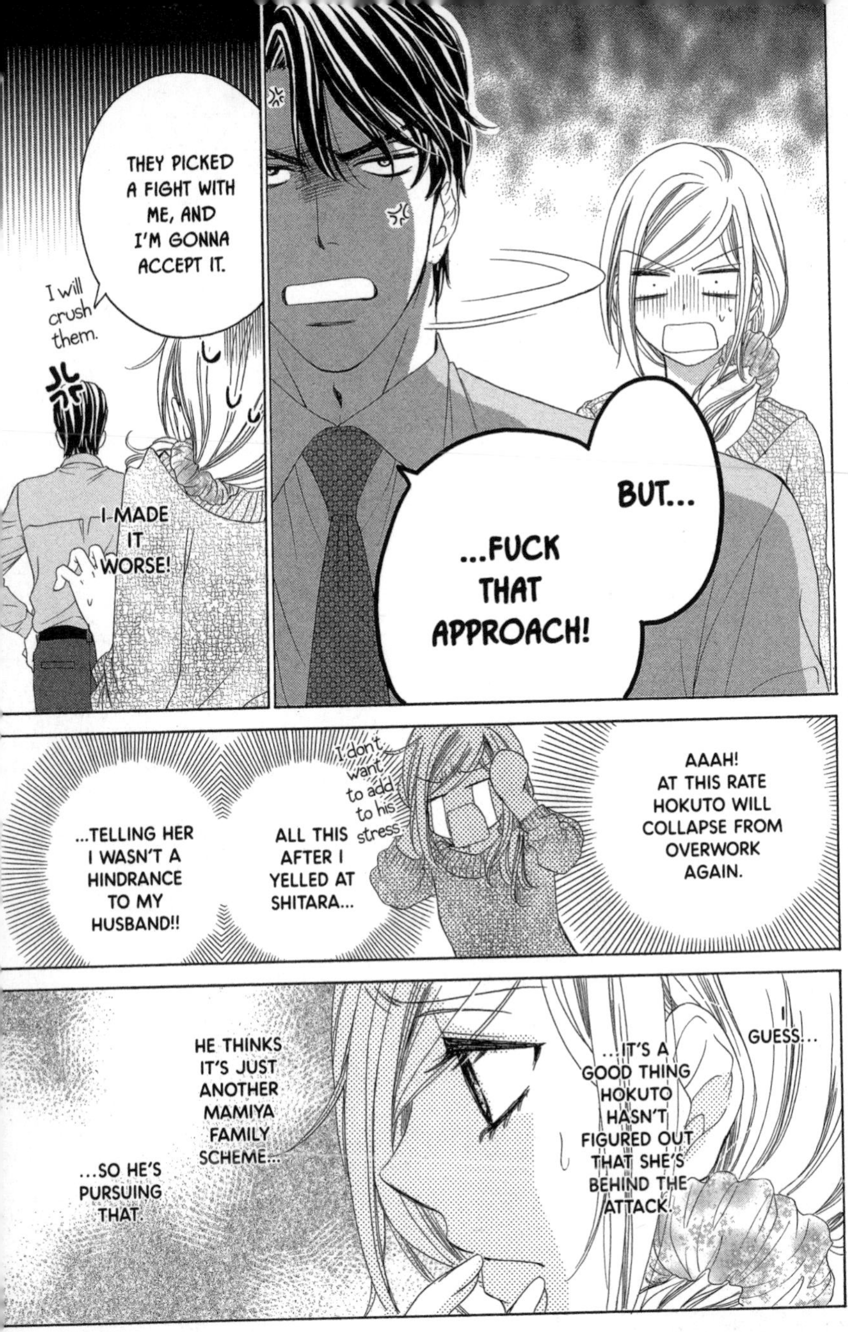
BUT... ...FUCK THAT APPROACH!
THEY PICKED A FIGHT WITH ME, AND I'M GONNA ACCEPT IT.
I will crush them.
I MADE IT WORSE!
AAAH! AT THIS RATE HOKUTO WILL COLLAPSE FROM OVERWORK AGAIN.
I don't want to add to his stress.
ALL THIS AFTER I YELLED AT SHITARA...
...TELLING HER I WASN'T A HINDRANCE TO MY HUSBAND!!
I GUESS...
...IT'S A GOOD THING HOKUTO HASN'T FIGURED OUT THAT SHE'S BEHIND THE ATTACK.
HE THINKS IT'S JUST ANOTHER MAMIYA FAMILY SCHEME...
...SO HE'S PURSUING THAT.

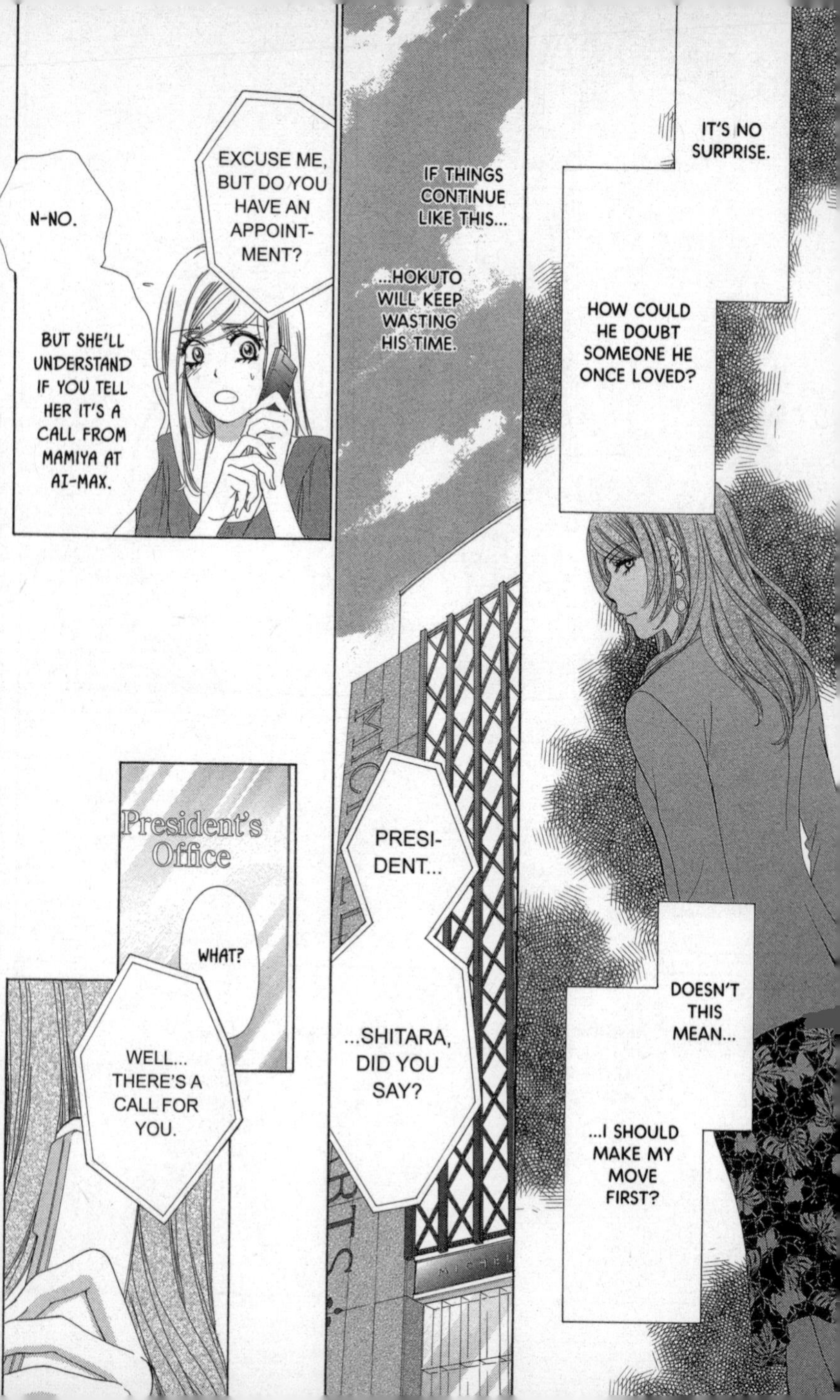
IT'S NO SURPRISE.
HOW COULD HE DOUBT SOMEONE HE ONCE LOVED?
DOESN'T THIS MEAN...
...I SHOULD MAKE MY MOVE FIRST?
IF THINGS CONTINUE LIKE THIS...
...HOKUTO WILL KEEP WASTING HIS TIME.
PRESI-DENT...
...SHITARA, DID YOU SAY?
EXCUSE ME, BUT DO YOU HAVE AN APPOINT-MENT?
N-NO.
BUT SHE'LL UNDERSTAND IF YOU TELL HER IT'S A CALL FROM MAMIYA AT AI-MAX.
President's Office
WHAT?
WELL... THERE'S A CALL FOR YOU.

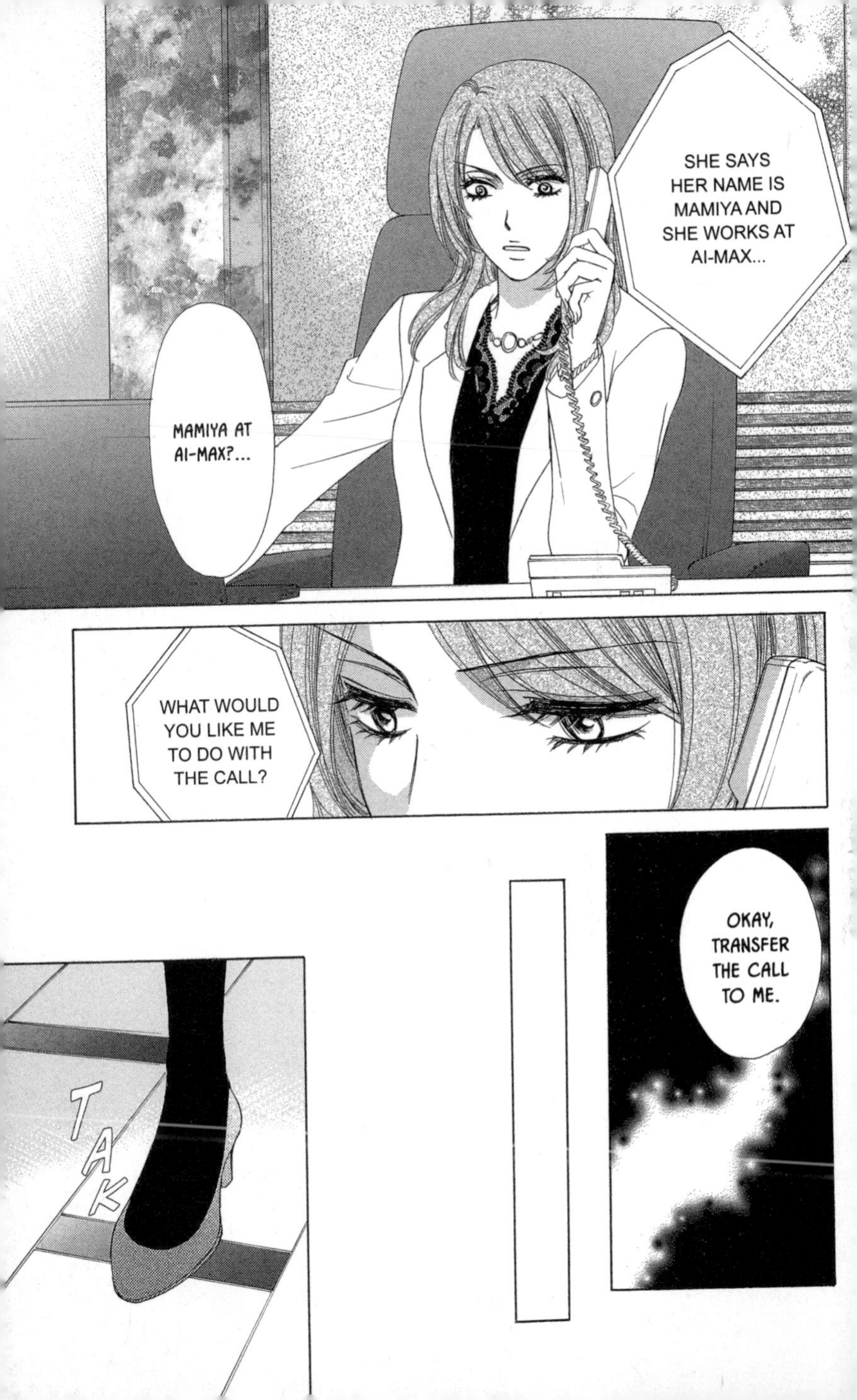
SHE SAYS HER NAME IS MAMIYA AND SHE WORKS AT AI-MAX...
MAMIYA AT AI-MAX?...
WHAT WOULD YOU LIKE ME TO DO WITH THE CALL?
OKAY, TRANSFER THE CALL TO ME.
TAK

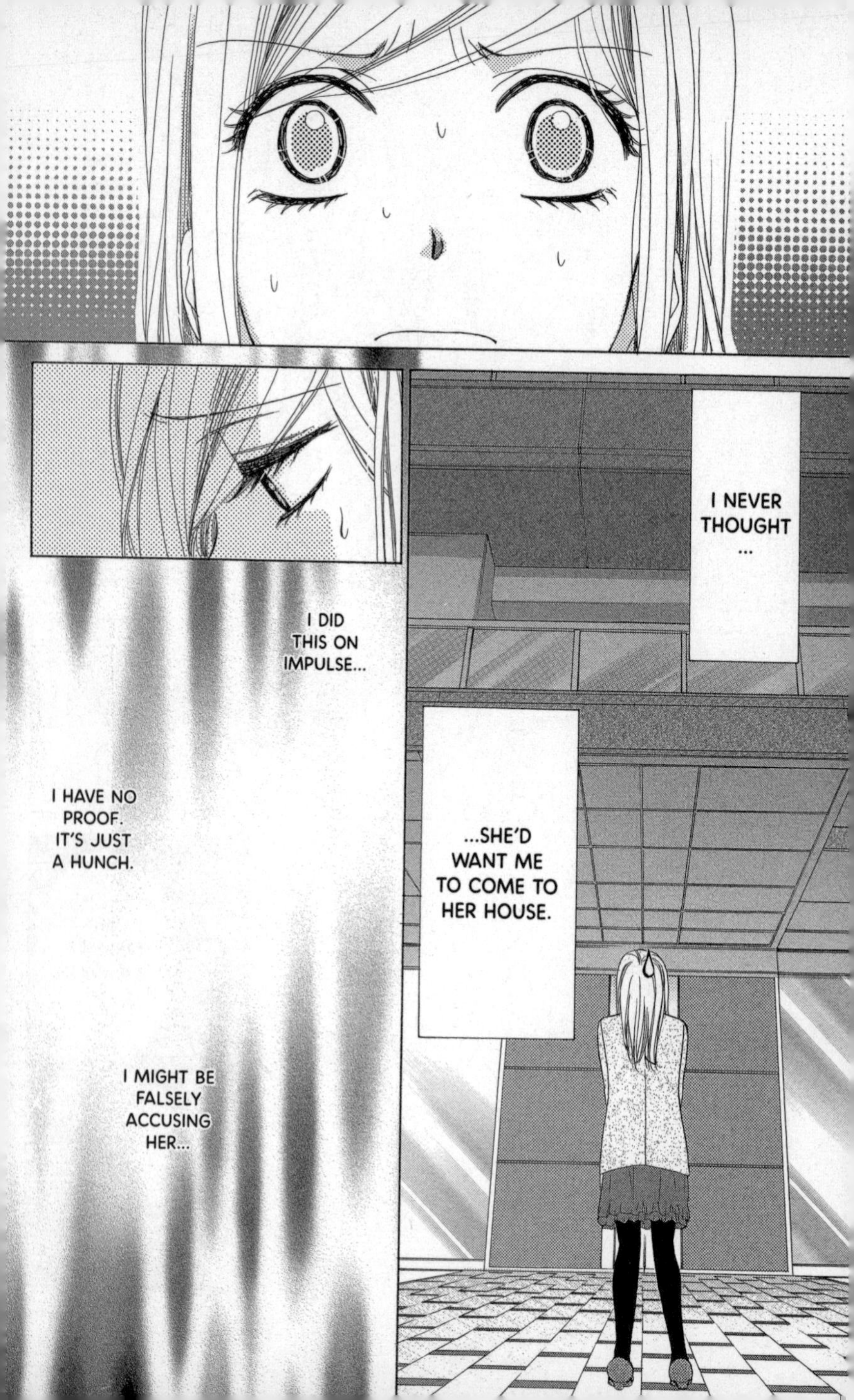
I NEVER THOUGHT...
...SHE'D WANT ME TO COME TO HER HOUSE.
I DID THIS ON IMPULSE...
I HAVE NO PROOF. IT'S JUST A HUNCH.
I MIGHT BE FALSELY ACCUSING HER...

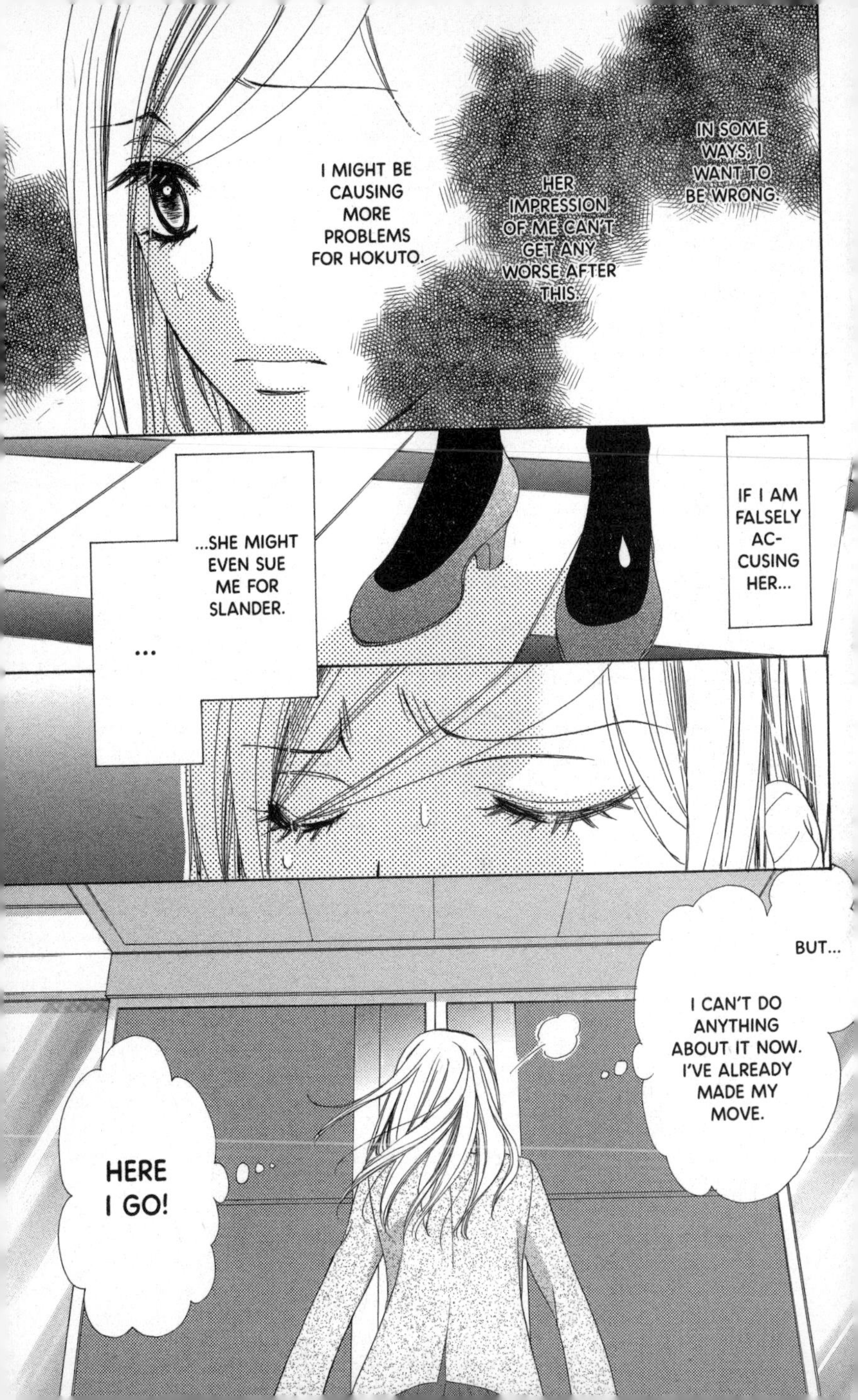
IN SOME WAYS, I WANT TO BE WRONG.
HER IMPRESSION OF ME CAN'T GET ANY WORSE AFTER THIS.
I MIGHT BE CAUSING MORE PROBLEMS FOR HOKUTO.
IF I AM FALSELY AC-CUSING HER...
...SHE MIGHT EVEN SUE ME FOR SLANDER.
...
BUT...
I CAN'T DO ANYTHING ABOUT IT NOW. I'VE ALREADY MADE MY MOVE.
HERE I GO!

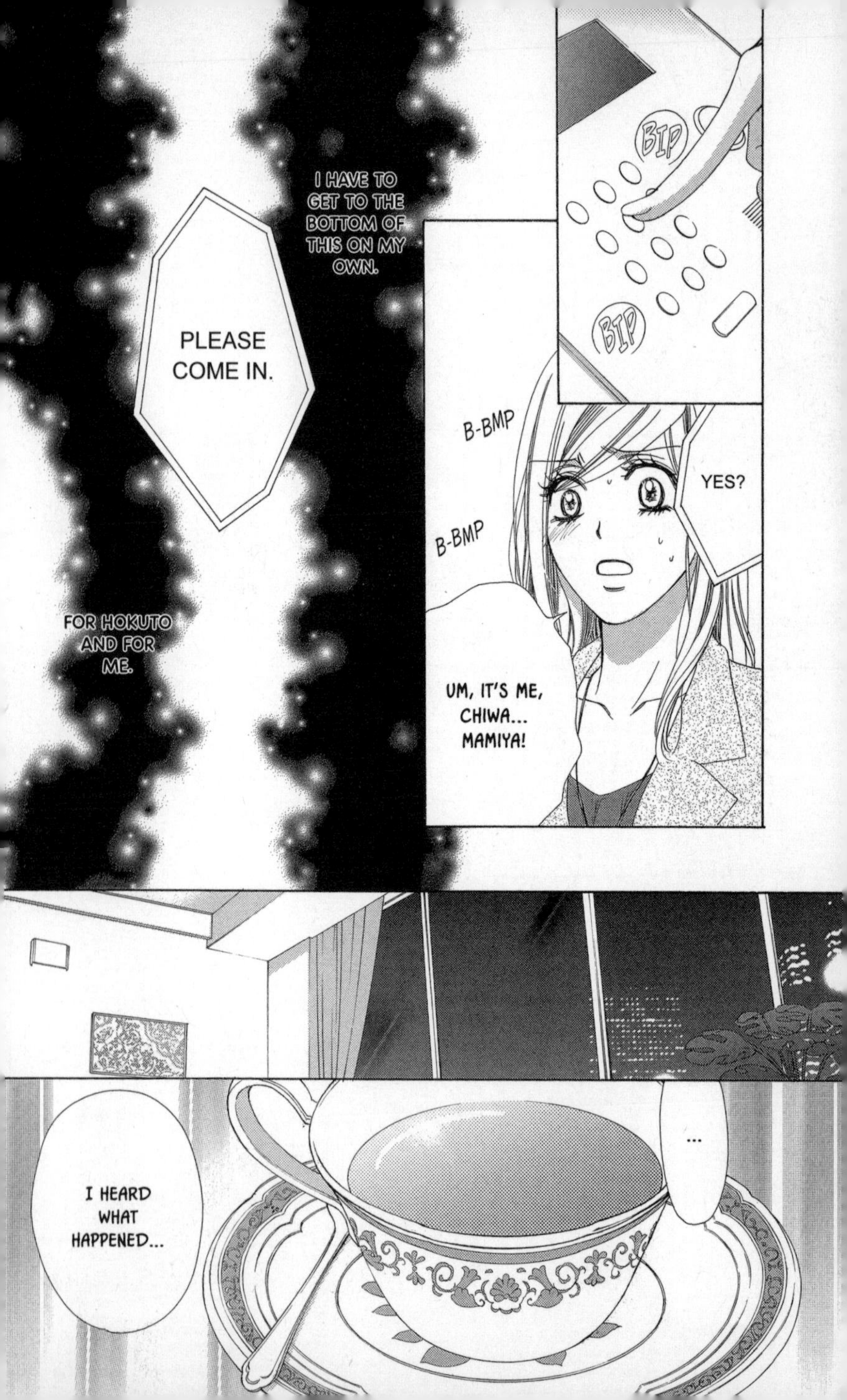
BIP
BIP
YES?
B-BMP
B-BMP
UM, IT'S ME, CHIWA... MAMIYA!
I HAVE TO GET TO THE BOTTOM OF THIS ON MY OWN.
PLEASE COME IN.
FOR HOKUTO AND FOR ME.
...
I HEARD WHAT HAPPENED...

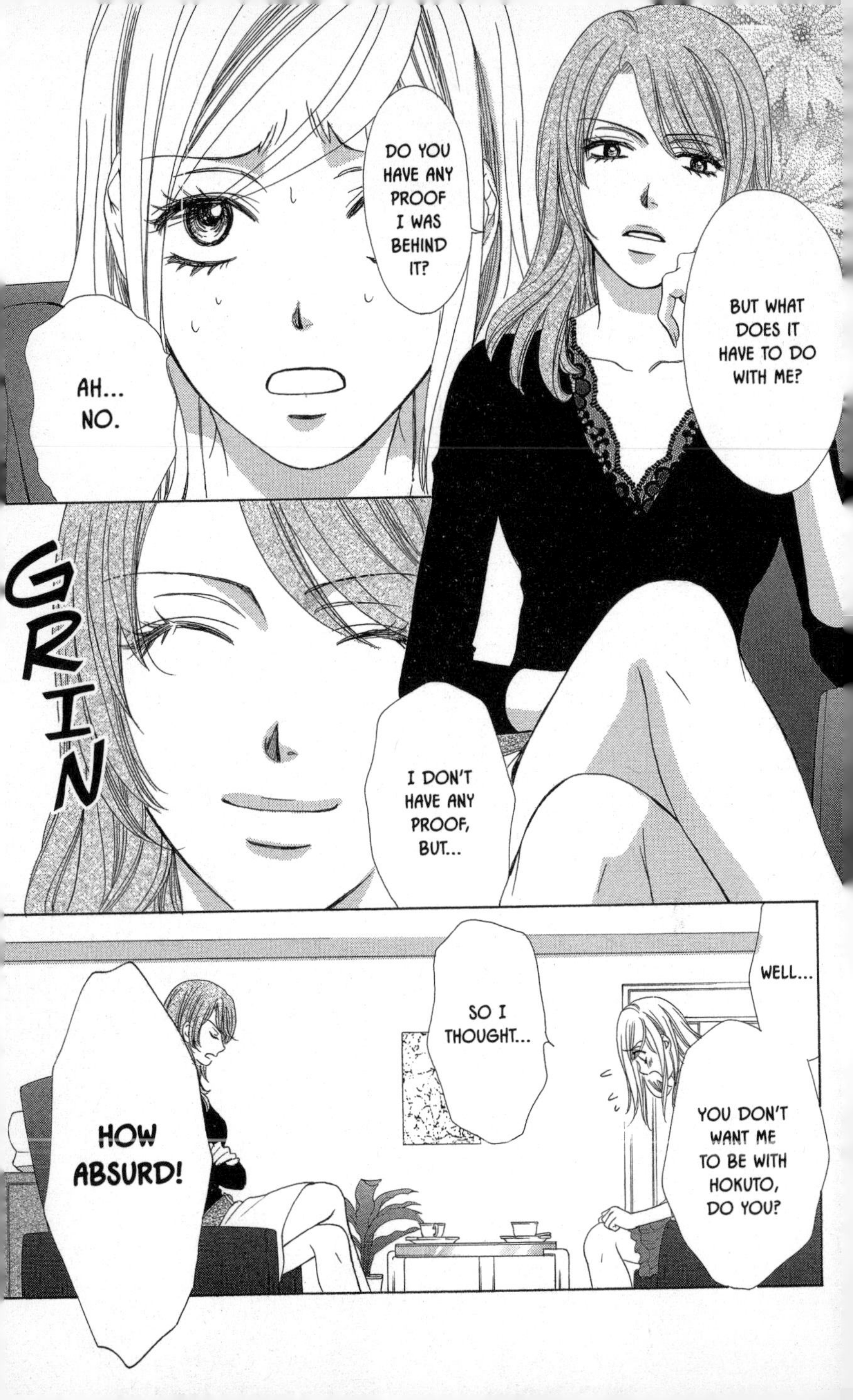
BUT WHAT DOES IT HAVE TO DO WITH ME?
DO YOU HAVE ANY PROOF I WAS BEHIND IT?
AH... NO.
GRIN
I DON'T HAVE ANY PROOF, BUT...
WELL...
SO I THOUGHT...
YOU DON'T WANT ME TO BE WITH HOKUTO, DO YOU?
HOW ABSURD!

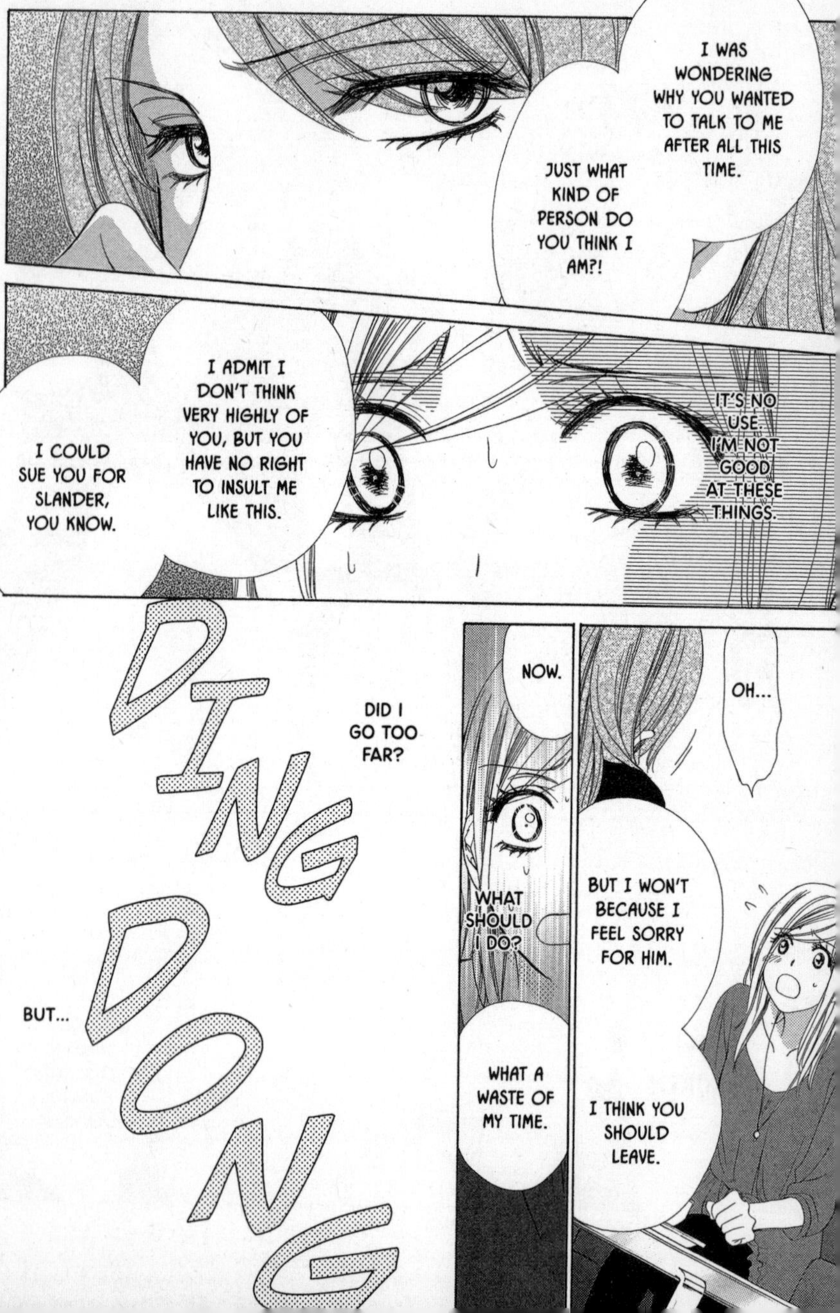
I WAS WONDERING WHY YOU WANTED TO TALK TO ME AFTER ALL THIS TIME.
JUST WHAT KIND OF PERSON DO YOU THINK I AM?!
IT'S NO USE. I'M NOT GOOD AT THESE THINGS.
I ADMIT I DON'T THINK VERY HIGHLY OF YOU, BUT YOU HAVE NO RIGHT TO INSULT ME LIKE THIS.
I COULD SUE YOU FOR SLANDER, YOU KNOW.
OH...
BUT I WON'T BECAUSE I FEEL SORRY FOR HIM.
I THINK YOU SHOULD LEAVE.
NOW.
WHAT SHOULD I DO?
WHAT A WASTE OF MY TIME.
DID I GO TOO FAR?
DING DONG
BUT...

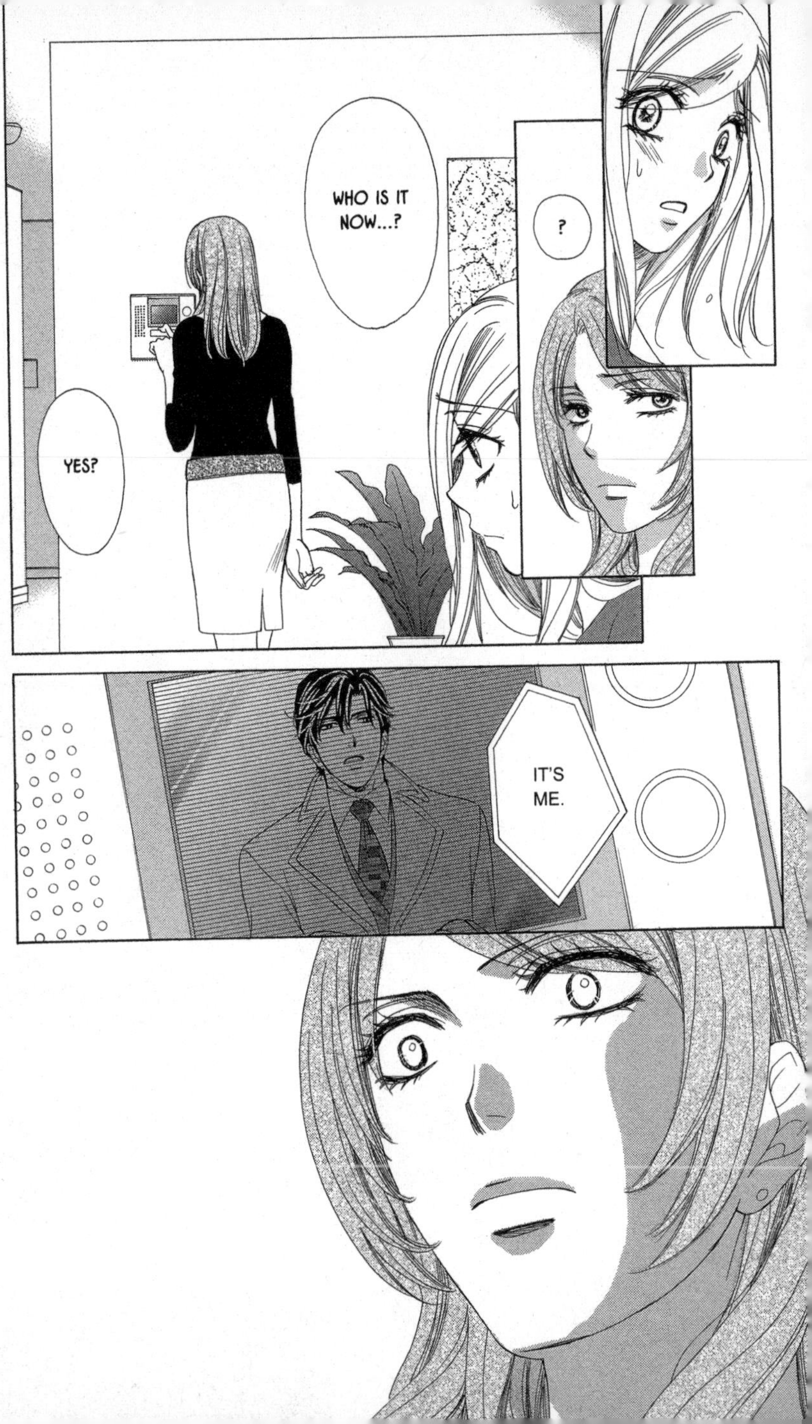
?
WHO IS IT NOW...?
YES?
IT'S ME.

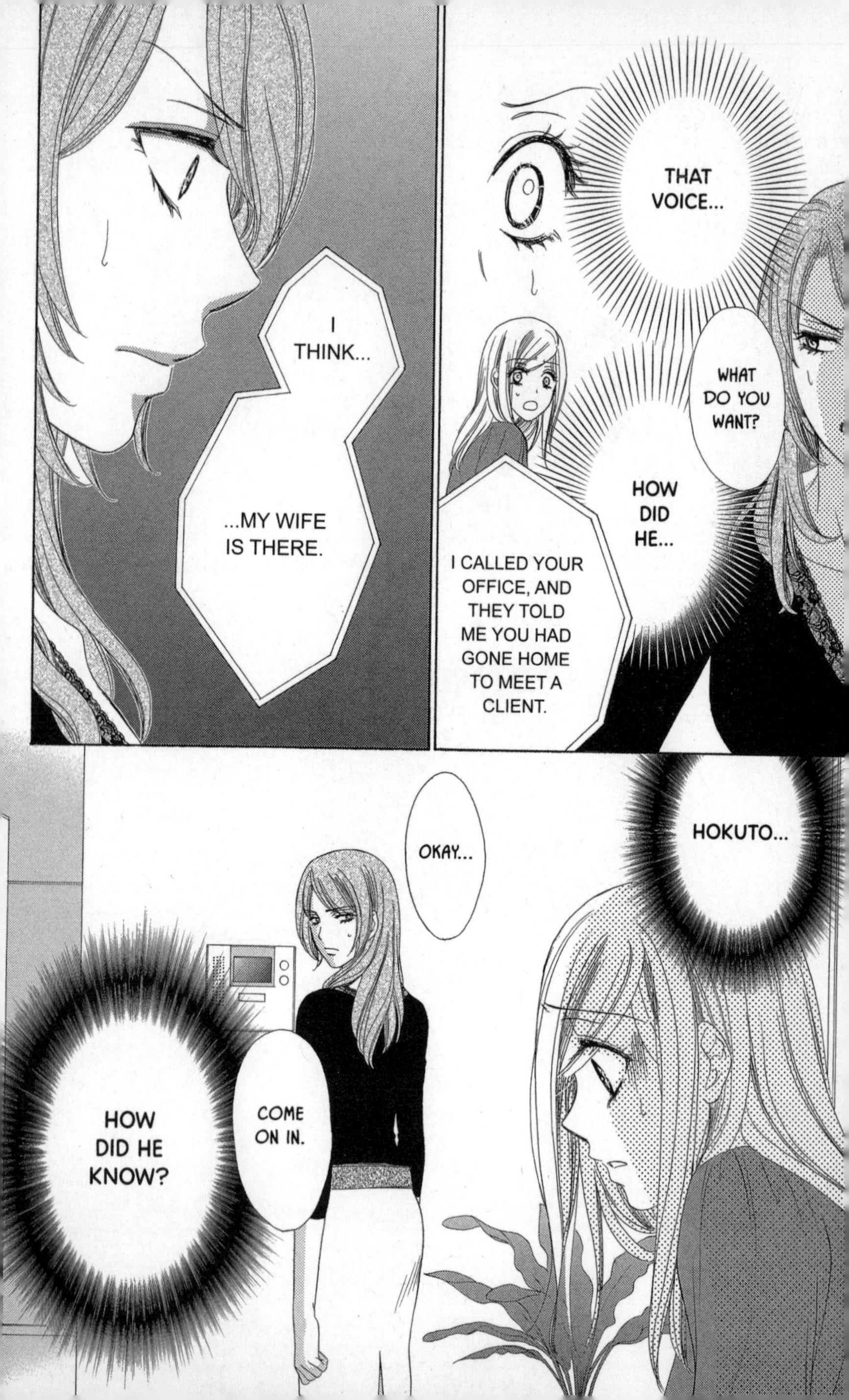
THAT VOICE...
WHAT DO YOU WANT?
HOW DID HE...
I CALLED YOUR OFFICE, AND THEY TOLD ME YOU HAD GONE HOME TO MEET A CLIENT.
I THINK...
...MY WIFE IS THERE.
HOKUTO...
OKAY...
COME ON IN.
HOW DID HE KNOW?

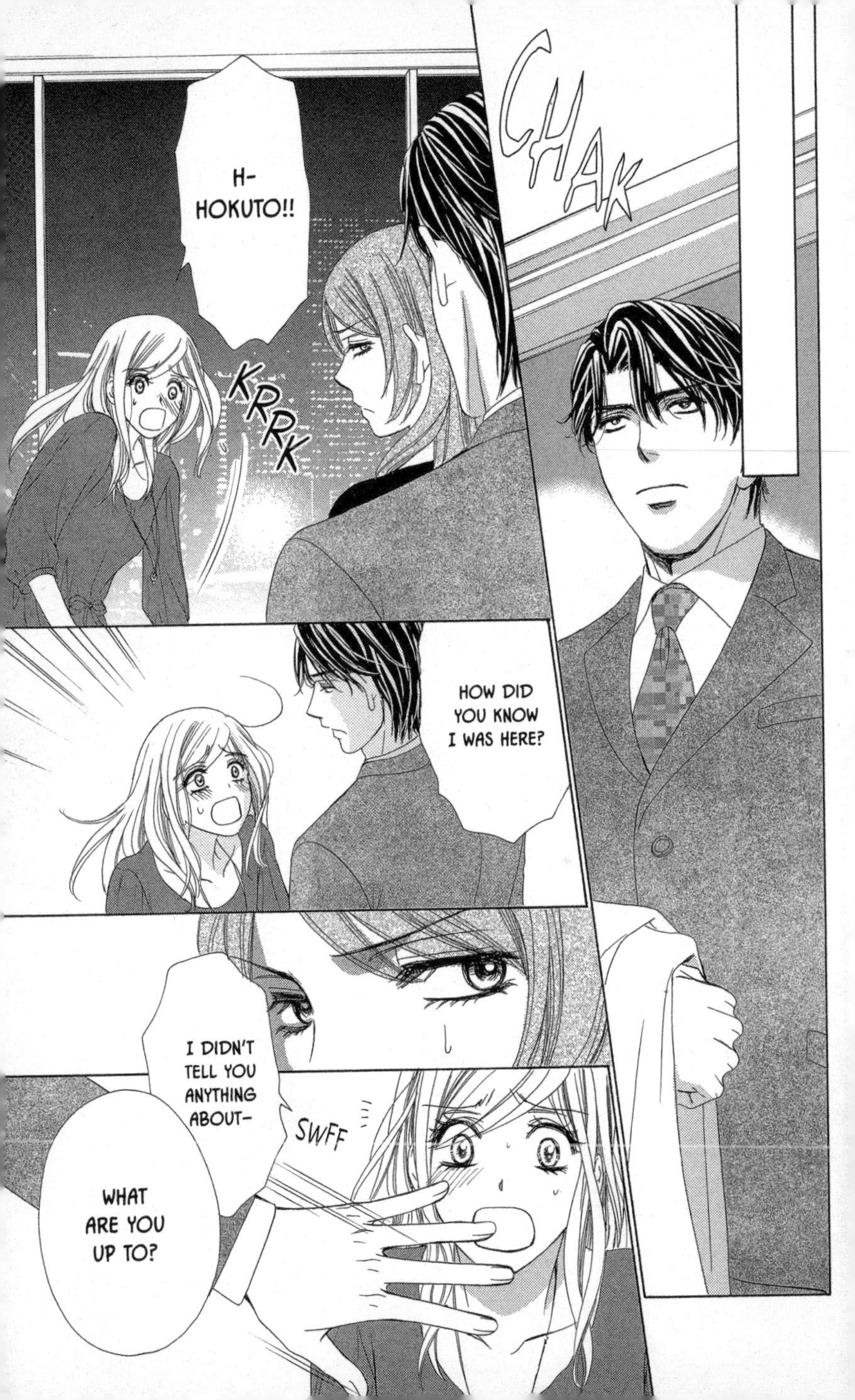
CHAK
H-HOKUTO!!
KRRK
HOW DID YOU KNOW I WAS HERE?
I DIDN'T TELL YOU ANYTHING ABOUT-
SWFF
WHAT ARE YOU UP TO?

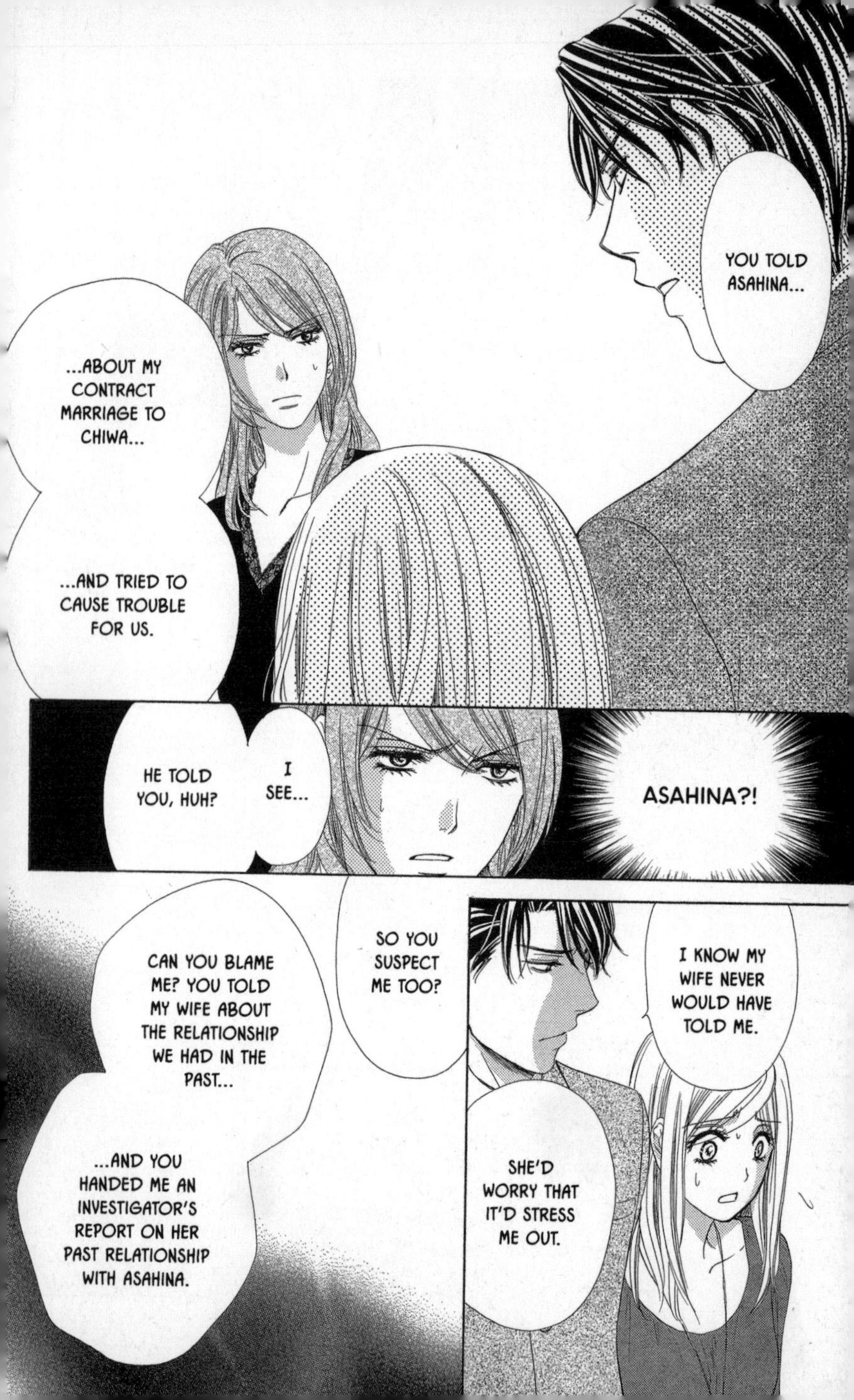
YOU TOLD ASAHINA...
...ABOUT MY CONTRACT MARRIAGE TO CHIWA...
...AND TRIED TO CAUSE TROUBLE FOR US.
ASAHINA?!
I SEE...
HE TOLD YOU, HUH?
I KNOW MY WIFE NEVER WOULD HAVE TOLD ME.
SHE'D WORRY THAT IT'D STRESS ME OUT.
SO YOU SUSPECT ME TOO?
CAN YOU BLAME ME? YOU TOLD MY WIFE ABOUT THE RELATIONSHIP WE HAD IN THE PAST...
...AND YOU HANDED ME AN INVESTIGATOR'S REPORT ON HER PAST RELATIONSHIP WITH ASAHINA.

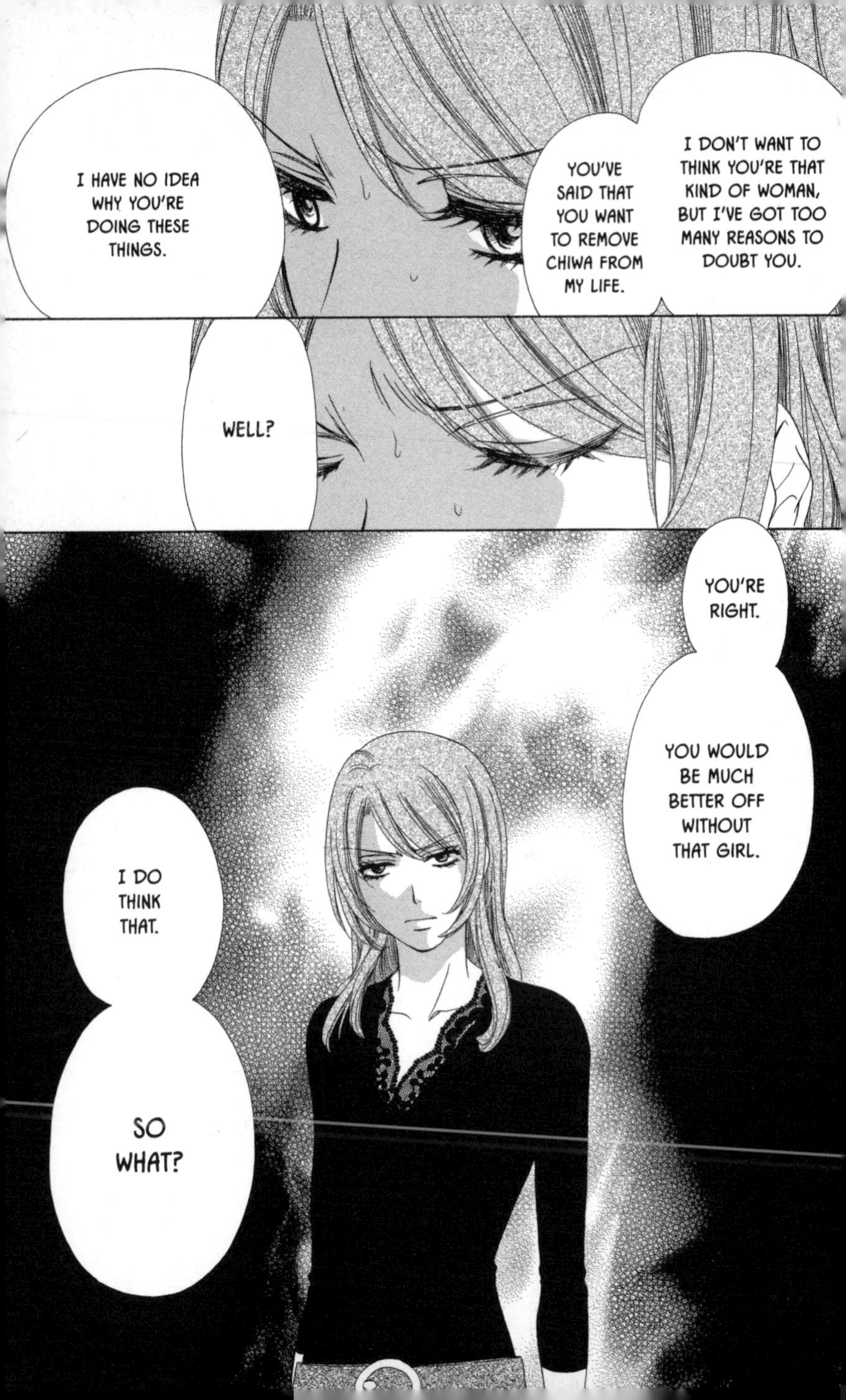
I DON'T WANT TO THINK YOU'RE THAT KIND OF WOMAN, BUT I'VE GOT TOO MANY REASONS TO DOUBT YOU.
YOU'VE SAID THAT YOU WANT TO REMOVE CHIWA FROM MY LIFE.
I HAVE NO IDEA WHY YOU'RE DOING THESE THINGS.
WELL?
YOU'RE RIGHT.
YOU WOULD BE MUCH BETTER OFF WITHOUT THAT GIRL.
I DO THINK THAT.
SO WHAT?

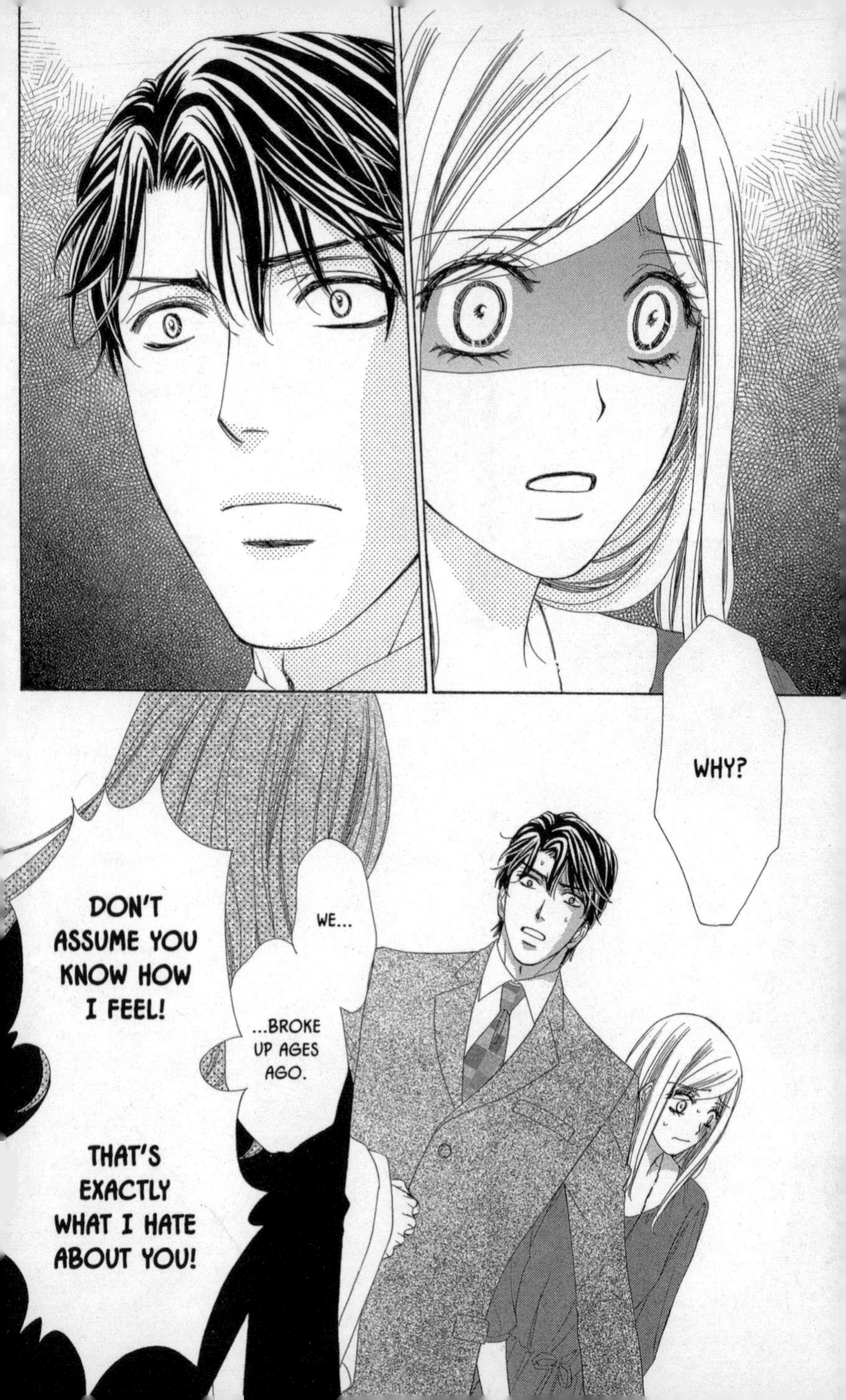
WHY?
WE...
...BROKE UP AGES AGO.
DON'T ASSUME YOU KNOW HOW I FEEL!
THAT'S EXACTLY WHAT I HATE ABOUT YOU!

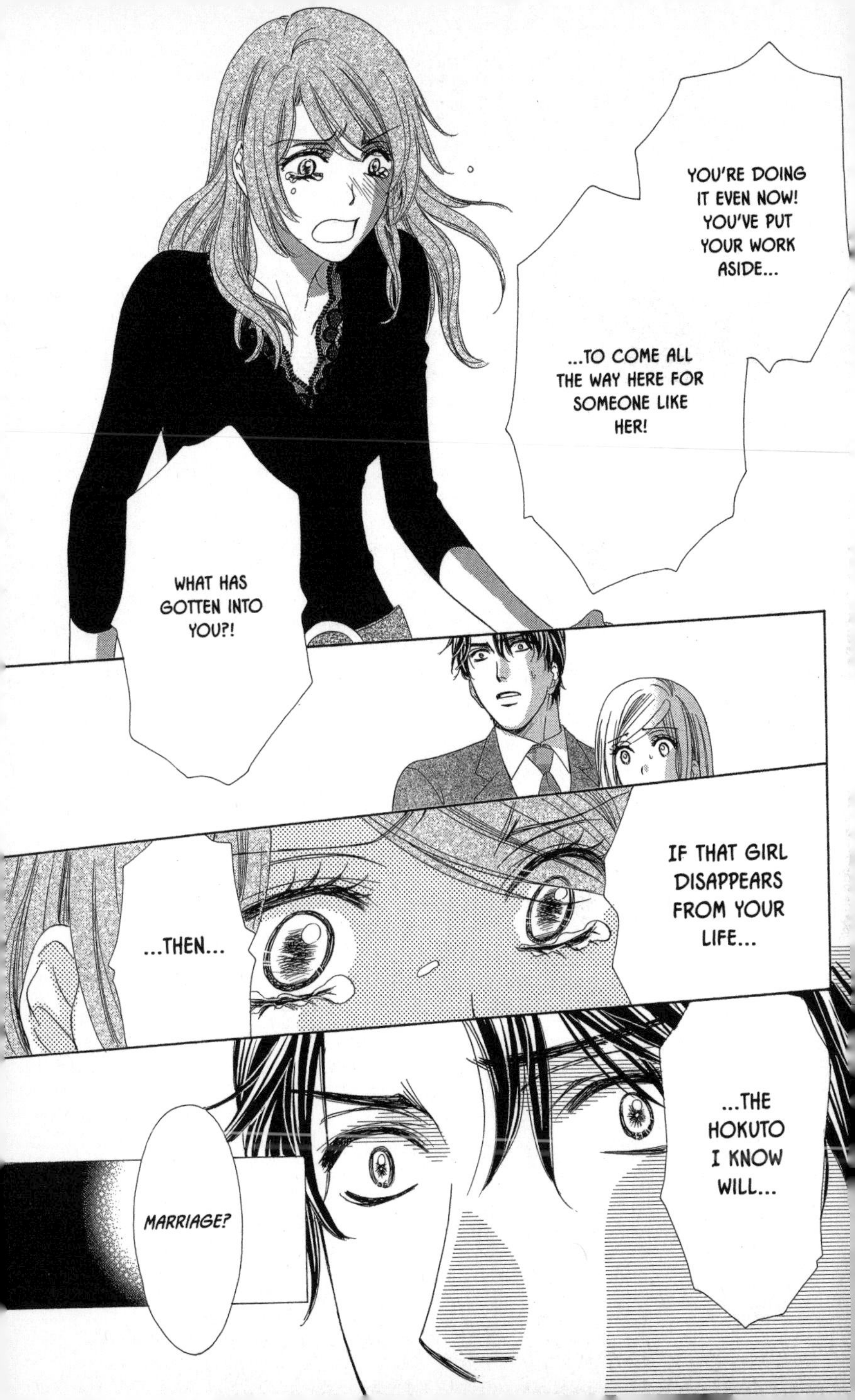
YOU'RE DOING IT EVEN NOW! YOU'VE PUT YOUR WORK ASIDE...
...TO COME ALL THE WAY HERE FOR SOMEONE LIKE HER!
WHAT HAS GOTTEN INTO YOU?!
IF THAT GIRL DISAPPEARS FROM YOUR LIFE...
...THEN...
...THE HOKUTO I KNOW WILL...
MARRIAGE?

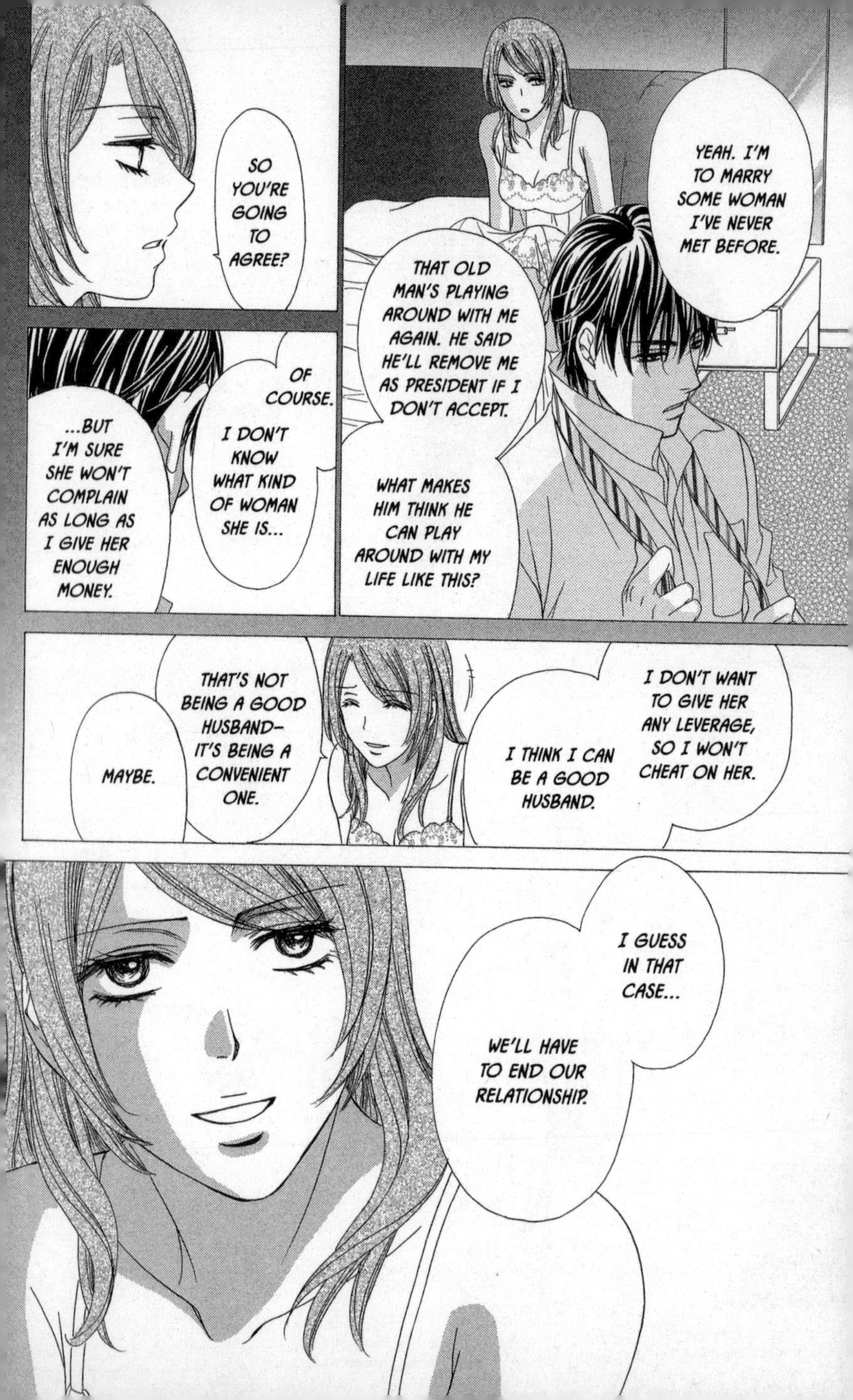
YEAH. I'M TO MARRY SOME WOMAN I'VE NEVER MET BEFORE.
THAT OLD MAN'S PLAYING AROUND WITH ME AGAIN. HE SAID HE'LL REMOVE ME AS PRESIDENT IF I DON'T ACCEPT.
WHAT MAKES HIM THINK HE CAN PLAY AROUND WITH MY LIFE LIKE THIS?
SO YOU'RE GOING TO AGREE?
OF COURSE.
I DON'T KNOW WHAT KIND OF WOMAN SHE IS...
...BUT I'M SURE SHE WON'T COMPLAIN AS LONG AS I GIVE HER ENOUGH MONEY.
I DON'T WANT TO GIVE HER ANY LEVERAGE, SO I WON'T CHEAT ON HER.
I THINK I CAN BE A GOOD HUSBAND.
THAT'S NOT BEING A GOOD HUSBAND– IT'S BEING A CONVENIENT ONE.
MAYBE.
I GUESS IN THAT CASE...
WE'LL HAVE TO END OUR RELATIONSHIP.

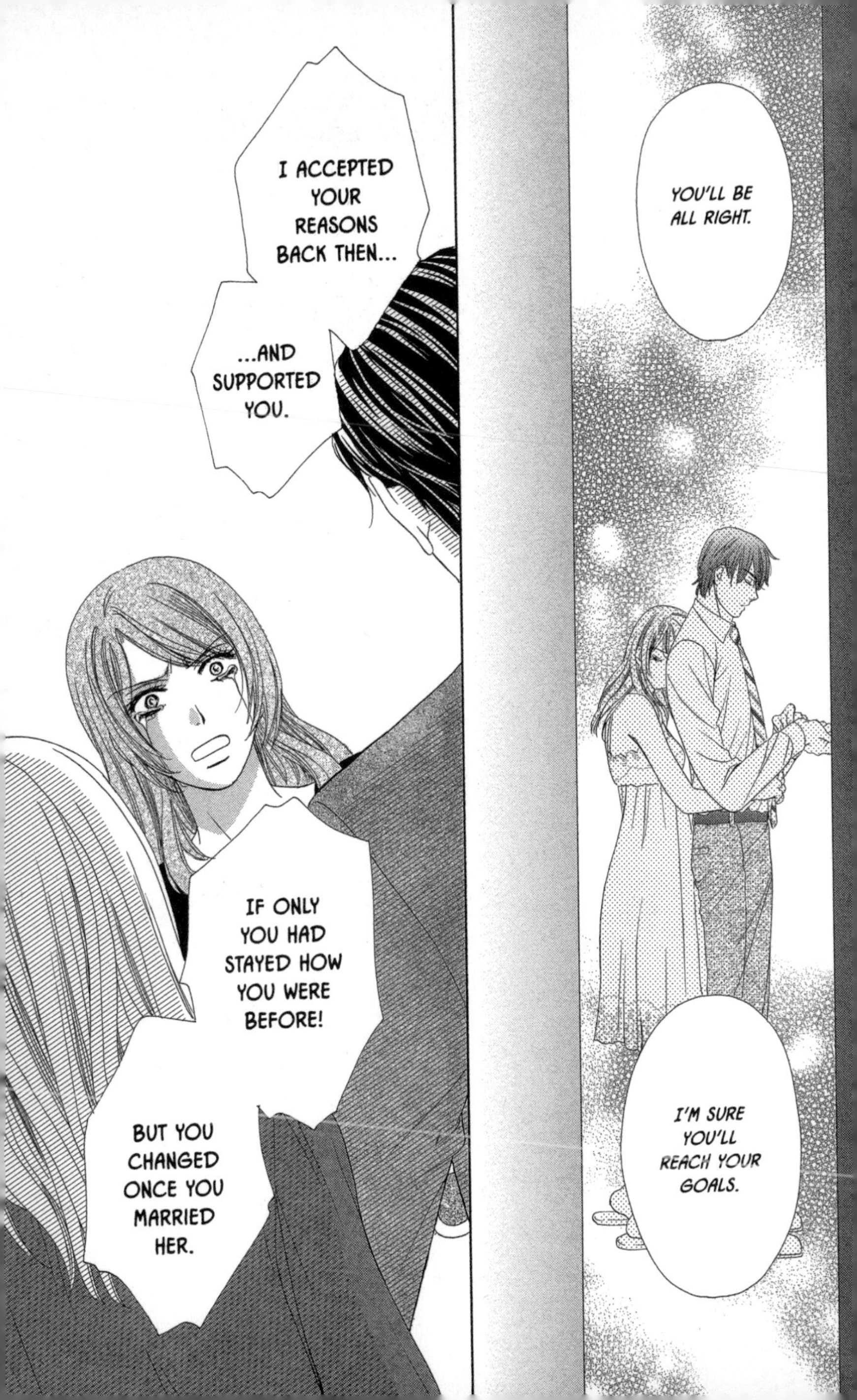
YOU'LL BE ALL RIGHT.
I'M SURE YOU'LL REACH YOUR GOALS.
I ACCEPTED YOUR REASONS BACK THEN...
...AND SUPPORTED YOU.
IF ONLY YOU HAD STAYED HOW YOU WERE BEFORE!
BUT YOU CHANGED ONCE YOU MARRIED HER.

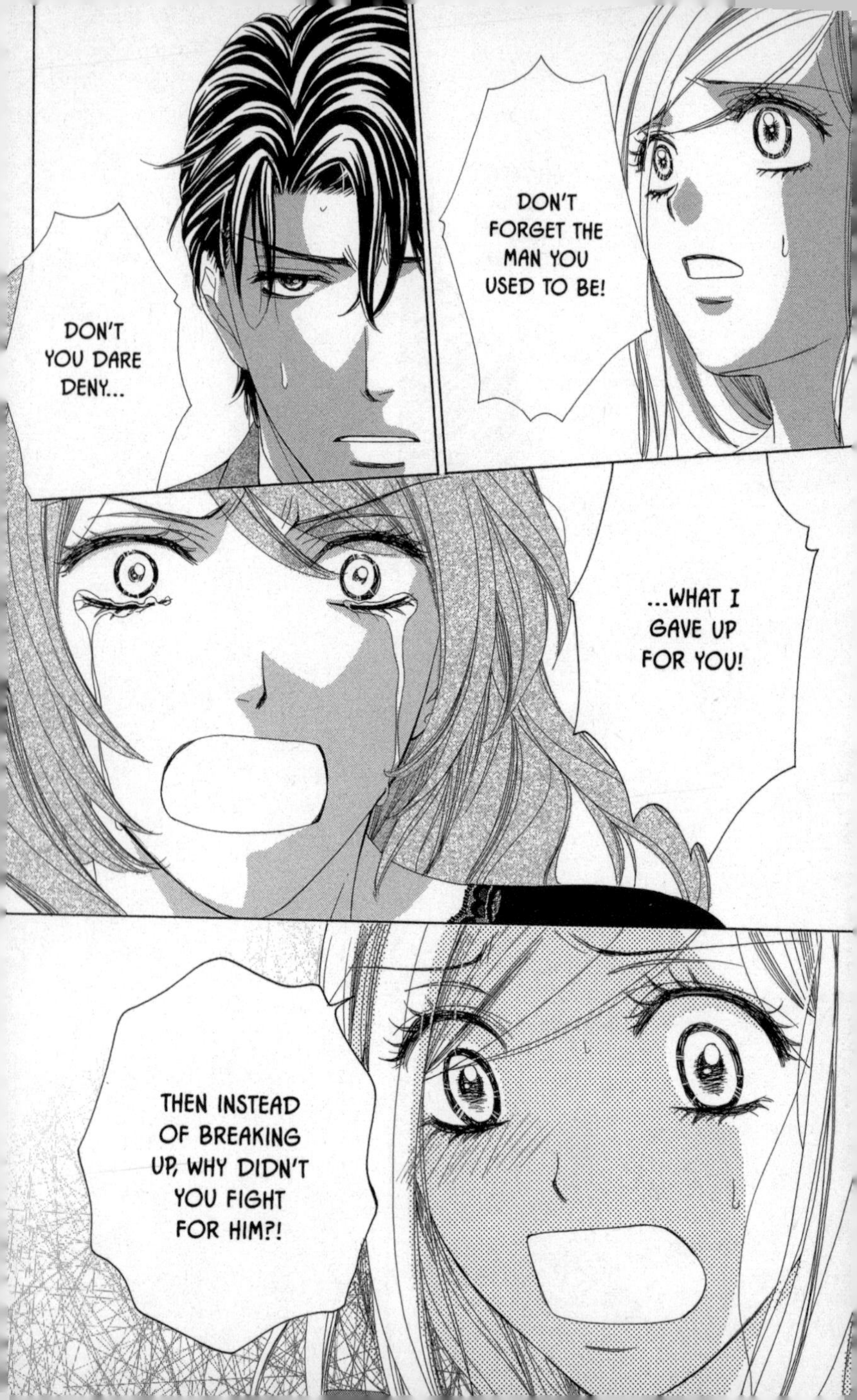
DON'T FORGET THE MAN YOU USED TO BE!
DON'T YOU DARE DENY...
...WHAT I GAVE UP FOR YOU!
THEN INSTEAD OF BREAKING UP, WHY DIDN'T YOU FIGHT FOR HIM?!

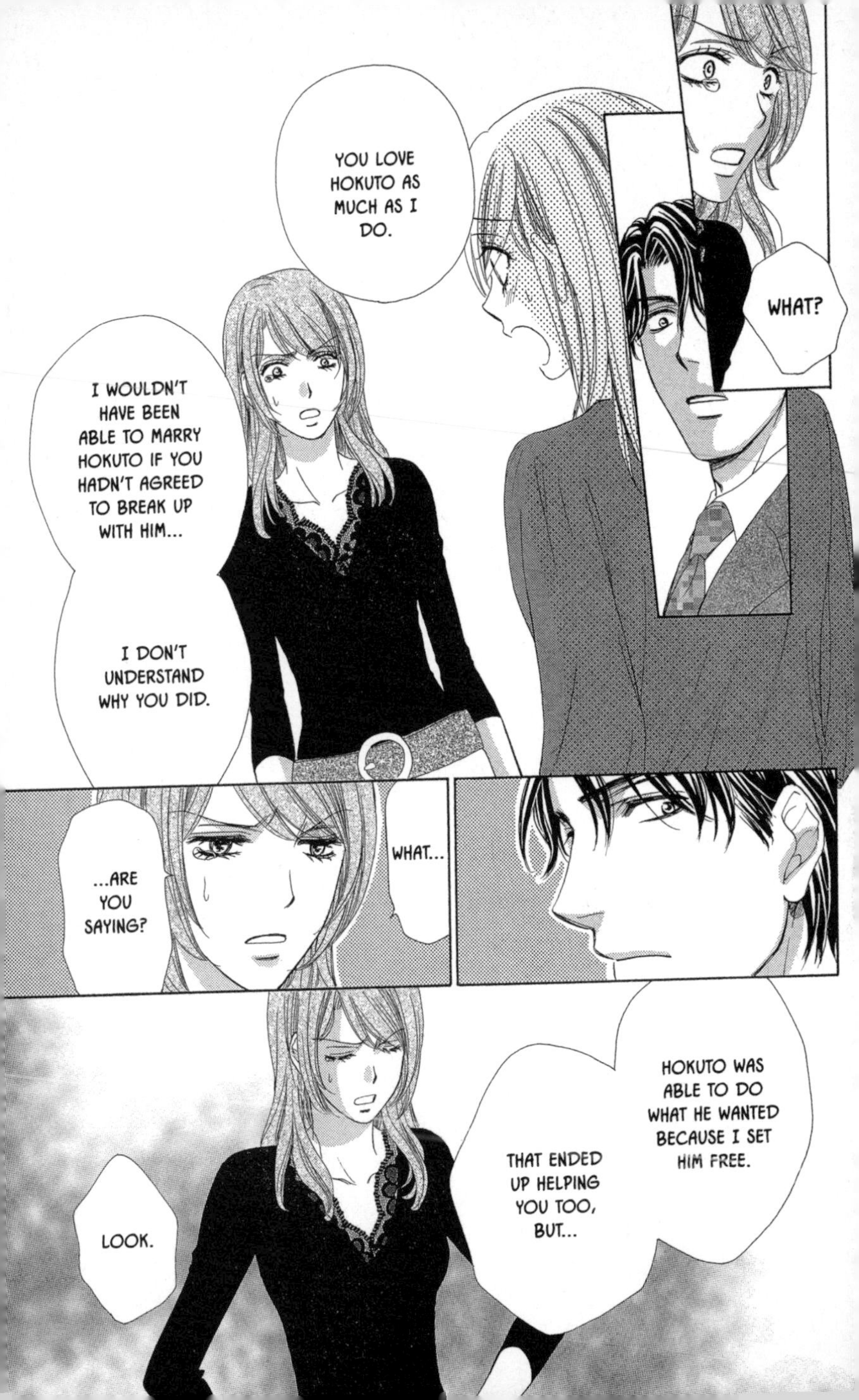
YOU LOVE HOKUTO AS MUCH AS I DO.
WHAT?
I WOULDN'T HAVE BEEN ABLE TO MARRY HOKUTO IF YOU HADN'T AGREED TO BREAK UP WITH HIM...
I DON'T UNDERSTAND WHY YOU DID.
WHAT...
...ARE YOU SAYING?
HOKUTO WAS ABLE TO DO WHAT HE WANTED BECAUSE I SET HIM FREE.
THAT ENDED UP HELPING YOU TOO, BUT...
LOOK.

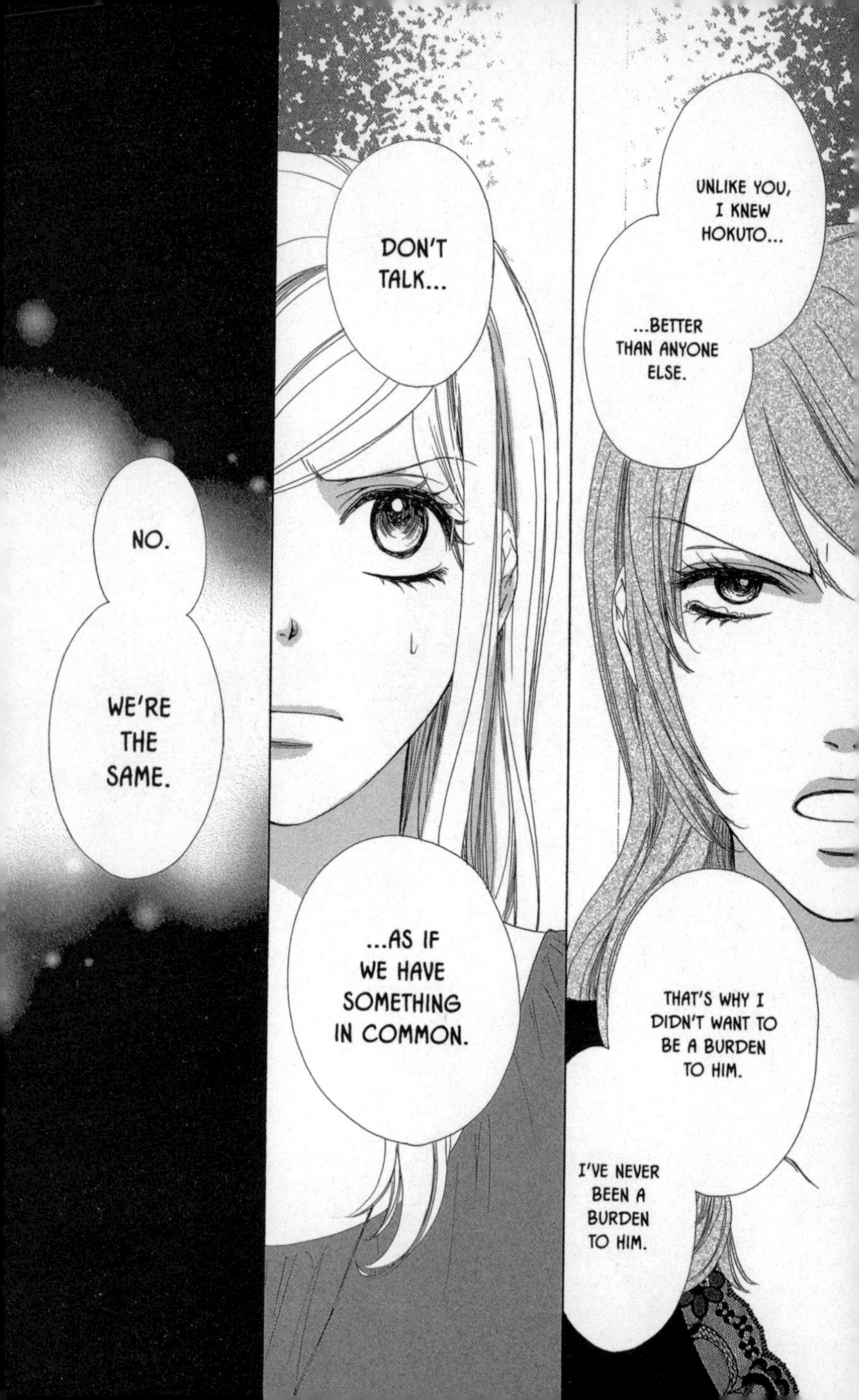
UNLIKE YOU, I KNEW HOKUTO...
...BETTER THAN ANYONE ELSE.
THAT'S WHY I DIDN'T WANT TO BE A BURDEN TO HIM.
I'VE NEVER BEEN A BURDEN TO HIM.
DON'T TALK...
...AS IF WE HAVE SOMETHING IN COMMON.
NO.
WE'RE THE SAME.

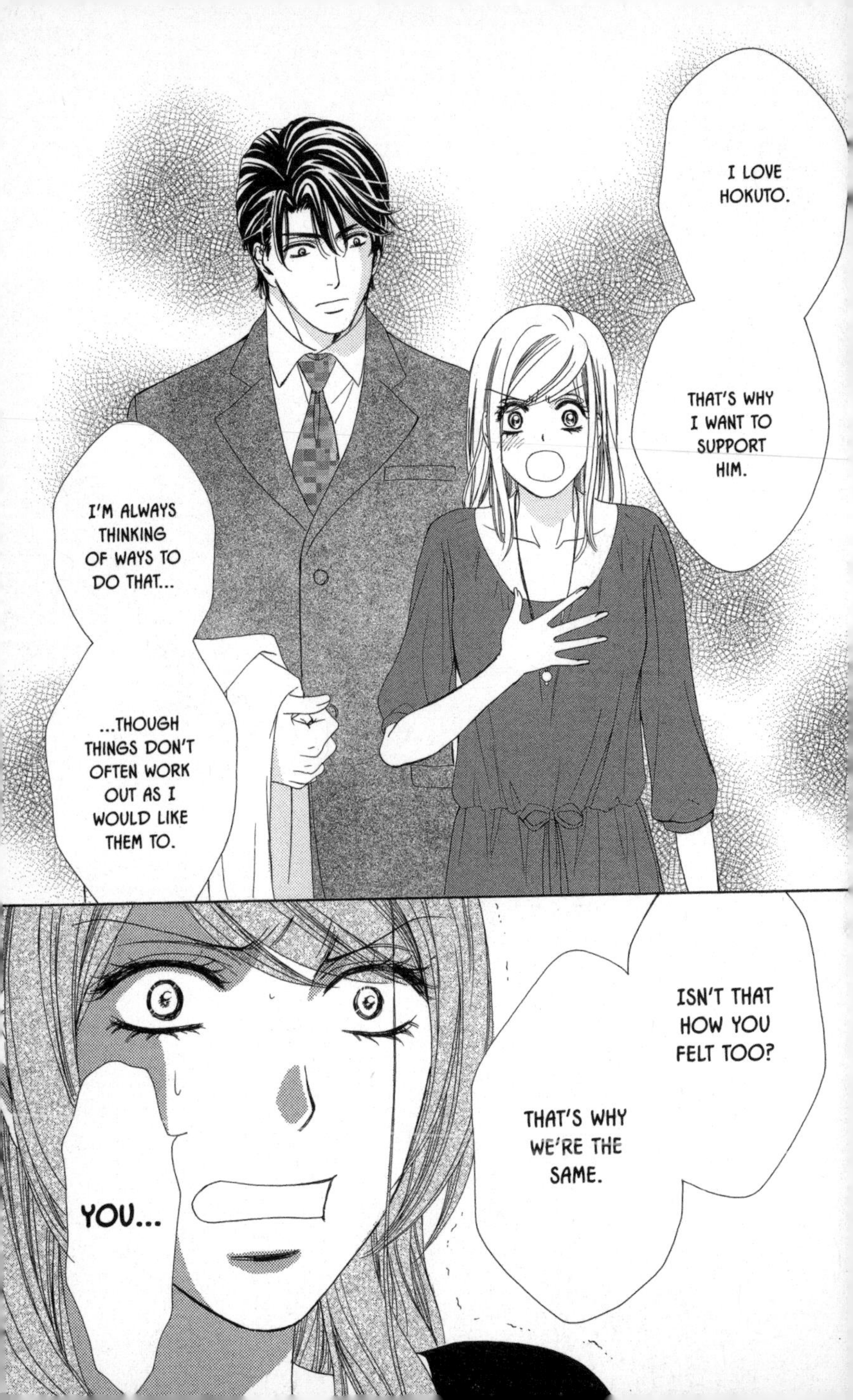

I LOVE HOKUTO.
THAT'S WHY I WANT TO SUPPORT HIM.
I'M ALWAYS THINKING OF WAYS TO DO THAT...
...THOUGH THINGS DON'T OFTEN WORK OUT AS I WOULD LIKE THEM TO.
ISN'T THAT HOW YOU FELT TOO?
THAT'S WHY WE'RE THE SAME.
YOU...

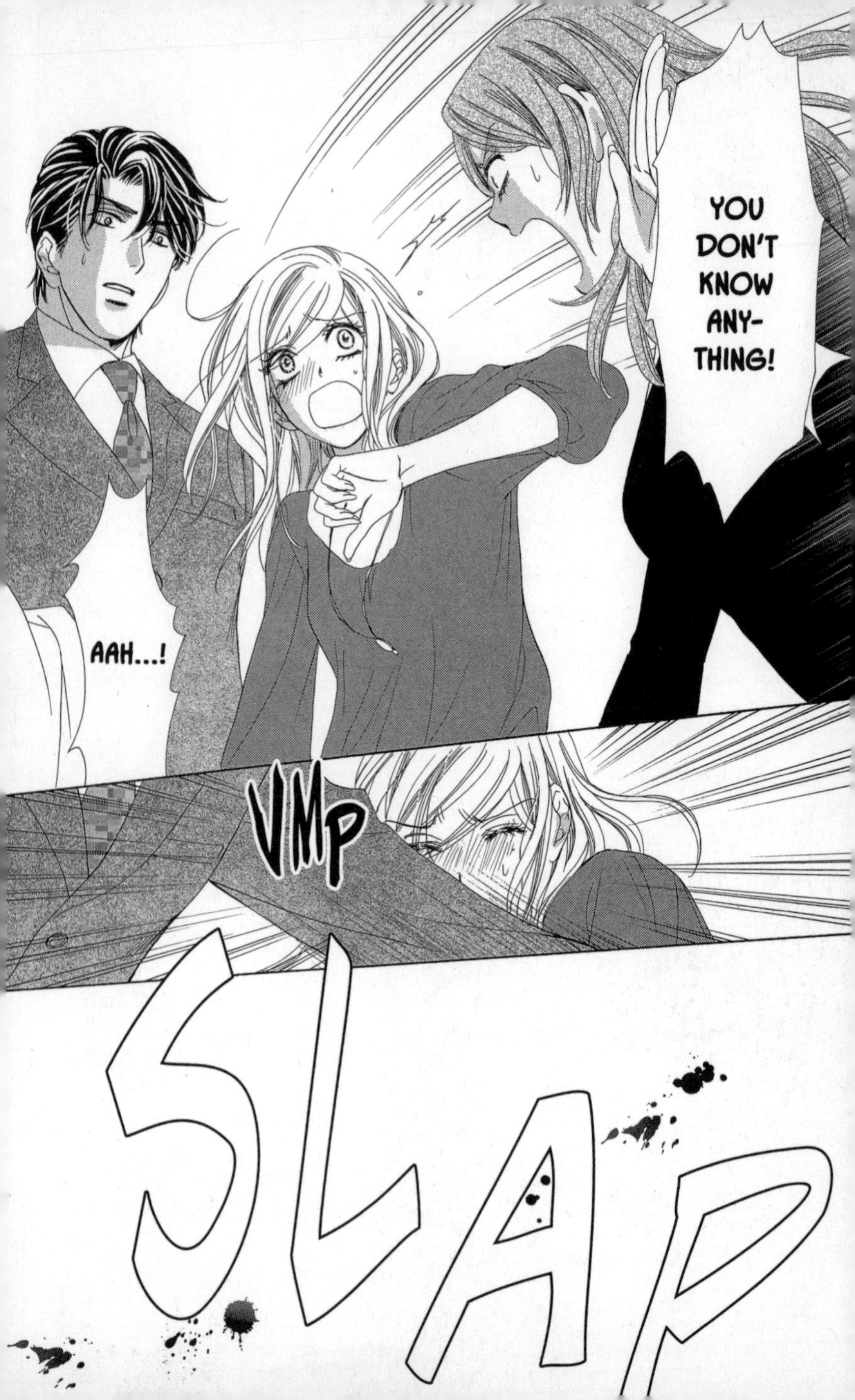
YOU DON'T KNOW ANY-THING!
AAH...!
VMP
SLAP

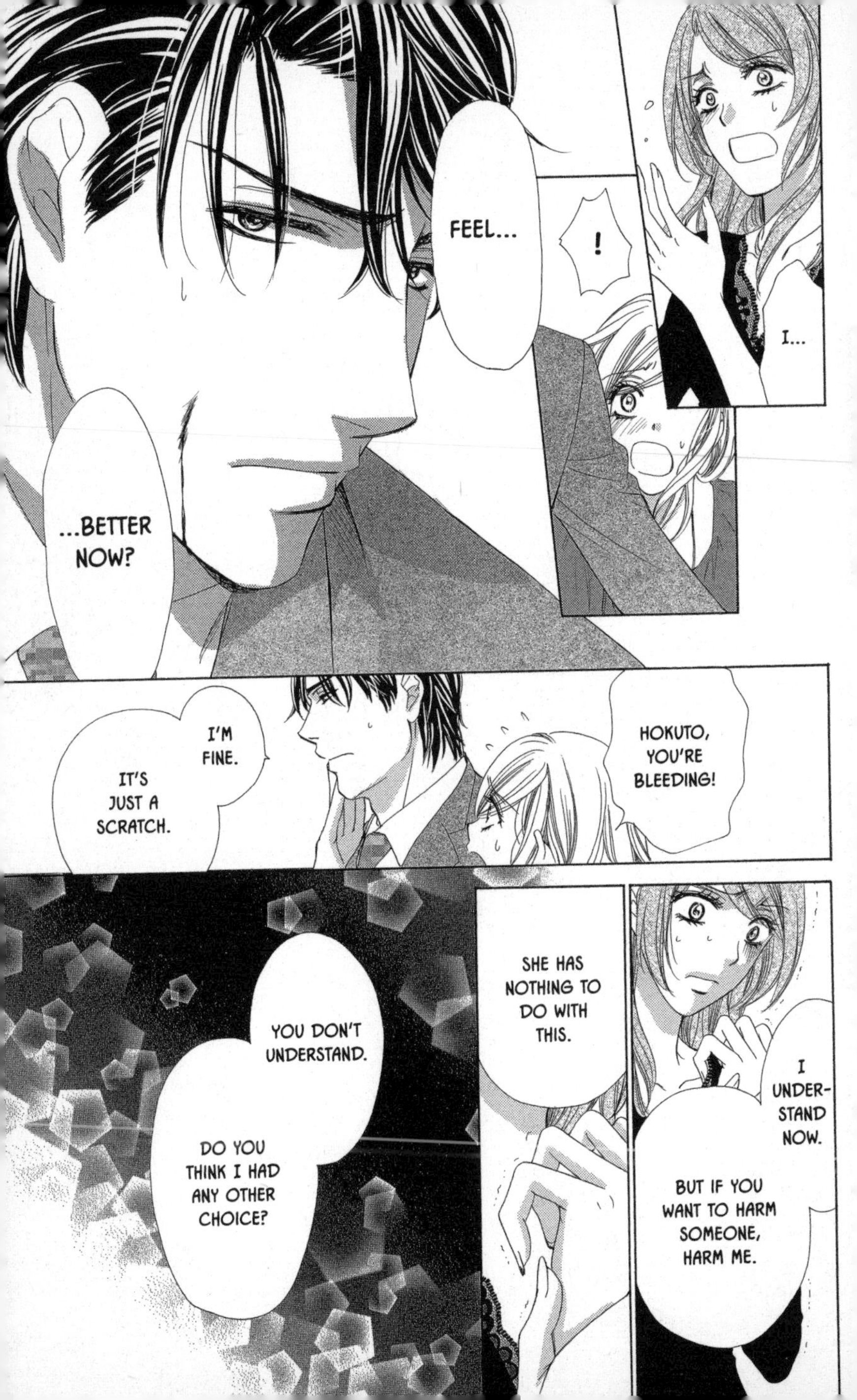
I...
!
FEEL...
...BETTER NOW?
HOKUTO, YOU'RE BLEEDING!
I'M FINE.
IT'S JUST A SCRATCH.
I UNDER-STAND NOW.
BUT IF YOU WANT TO HARM SOMEONE, HARM ME.
SHE HAS NOTHING TO DO WITH THIS.
YOU DON'T UNDERSTAND.
DO YOU THINK I HAD ANY OTHER CHOICE?

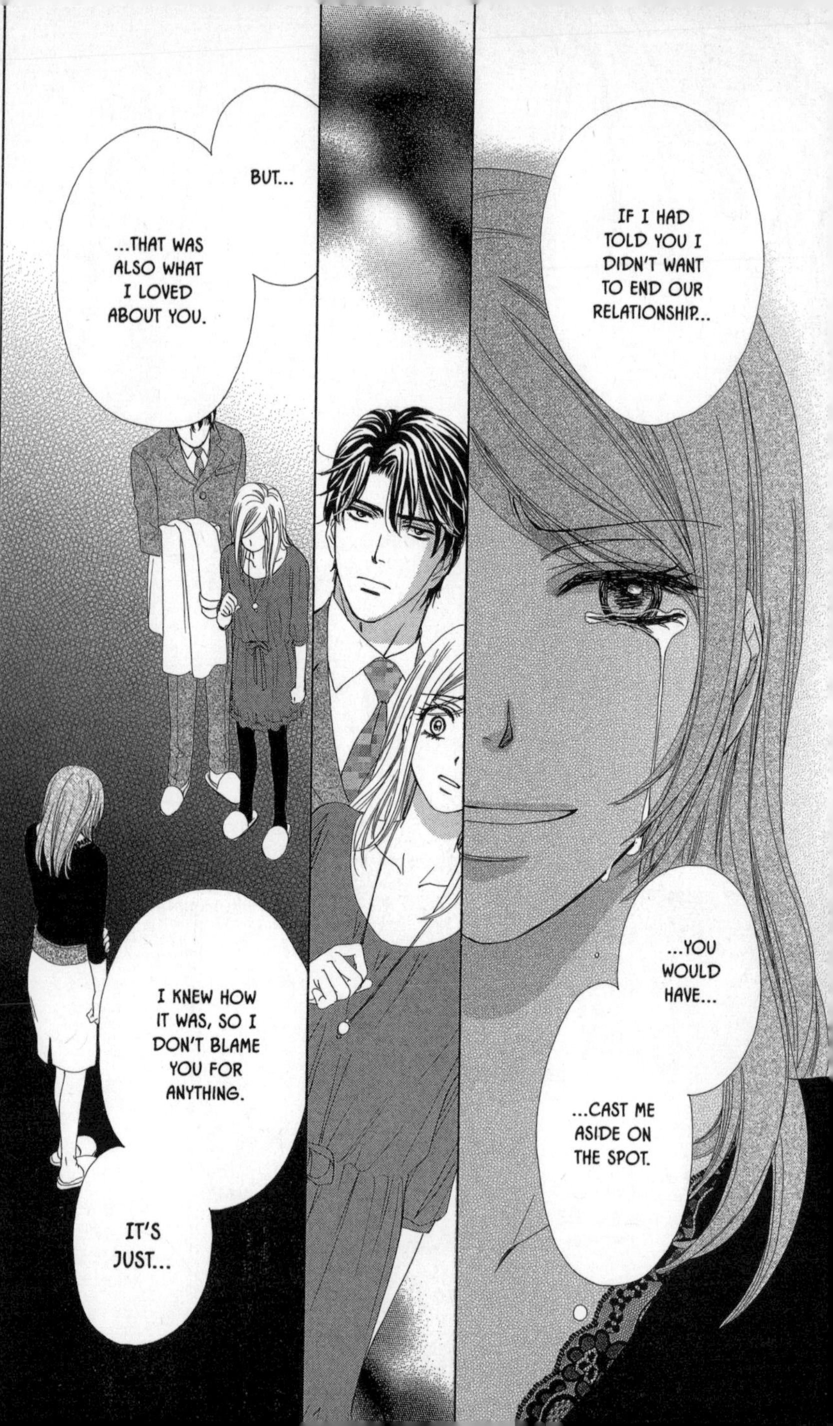
IF I HAD TOLD YOU I DIDN'T WANT TO END OUR RELATIONSHIP...
...YOU WOULD HAVE...
...CAST ME ASIDE ON THE SPOT.
BUT...
...THAT WAS ALSO WHAT I LOVED ABOUT YOU.
I KNEW HOW IT WAS, SO I DON'T BLAME YOU FOR ANYTHING.
IT'S JUST...

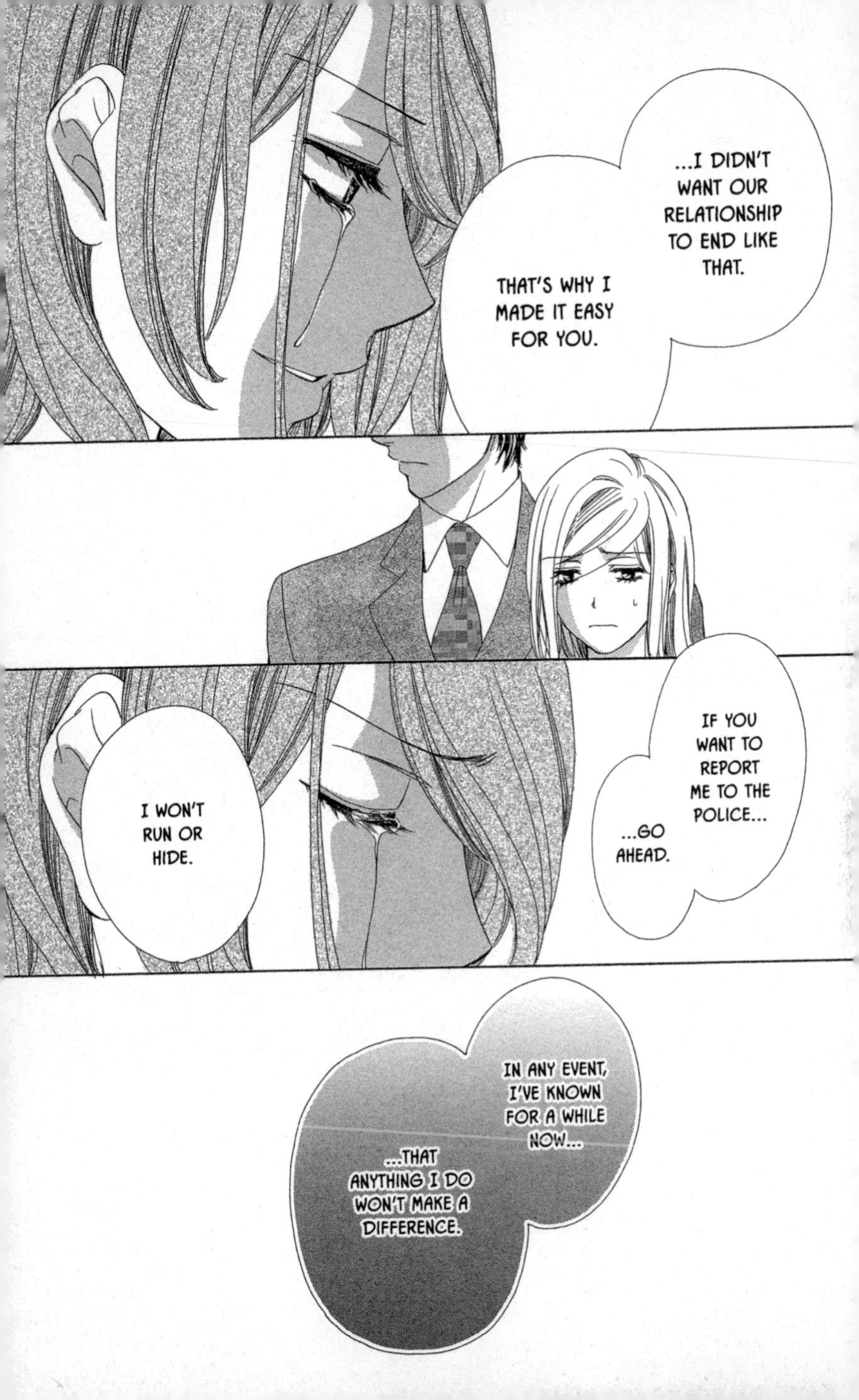
...I DIDN'T WANT OUR RELATIONSHIP TO END LIKE THAT.
THAT'S WHY I MADE IT EASY FOR YOU.
IF YOU WANT TO REPORT ME TO THE POLICE...
...GO AHEAD.
I WON'T RUN OR HIDE.
IN ANY EVENT, I'VE KNOWN FOR A WHILE NOW...
...THAT ANYTHING I DO WON'T MAKE A DIFFERENCE.

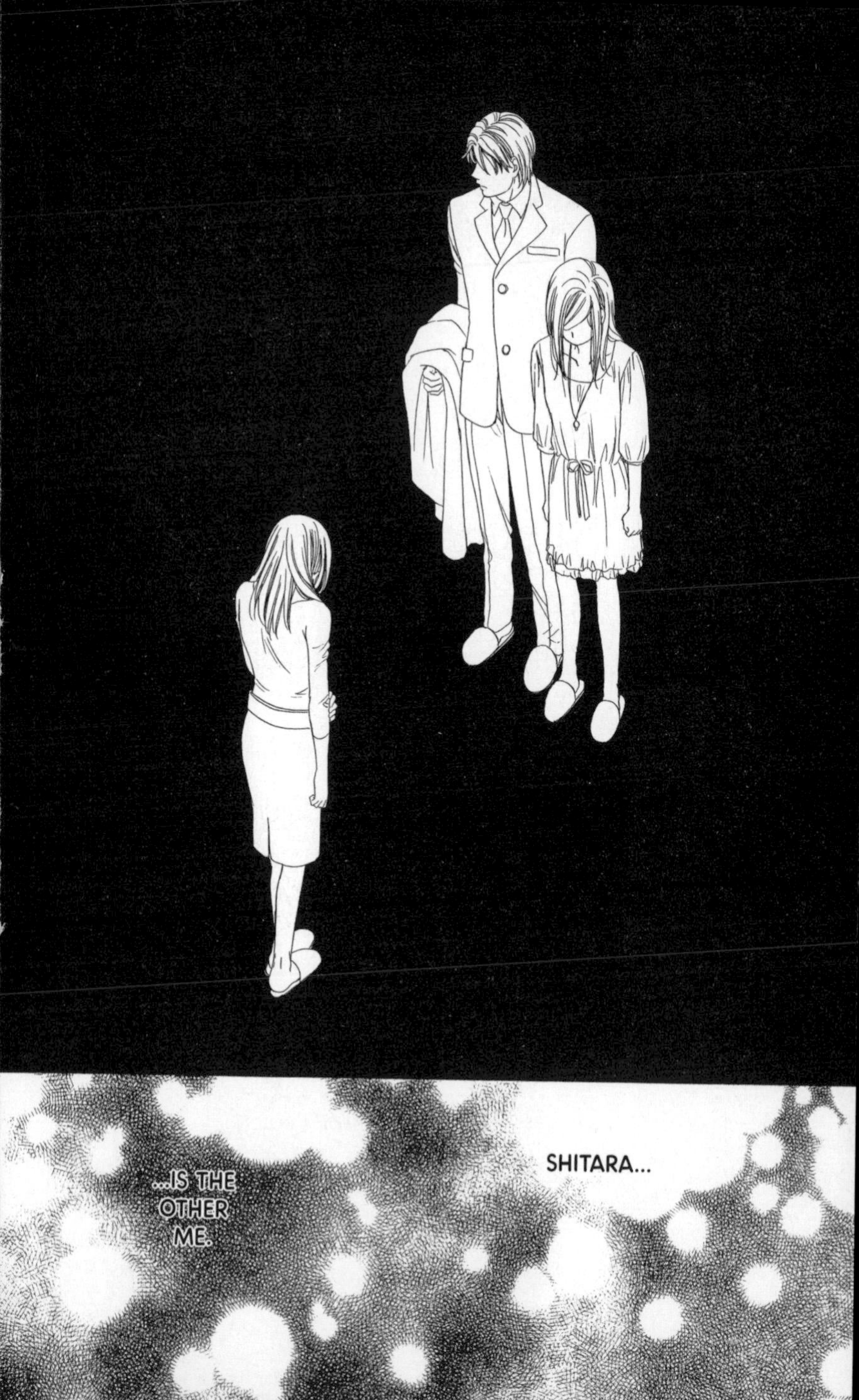
SHITARA...
...IS THE OTHER ME.

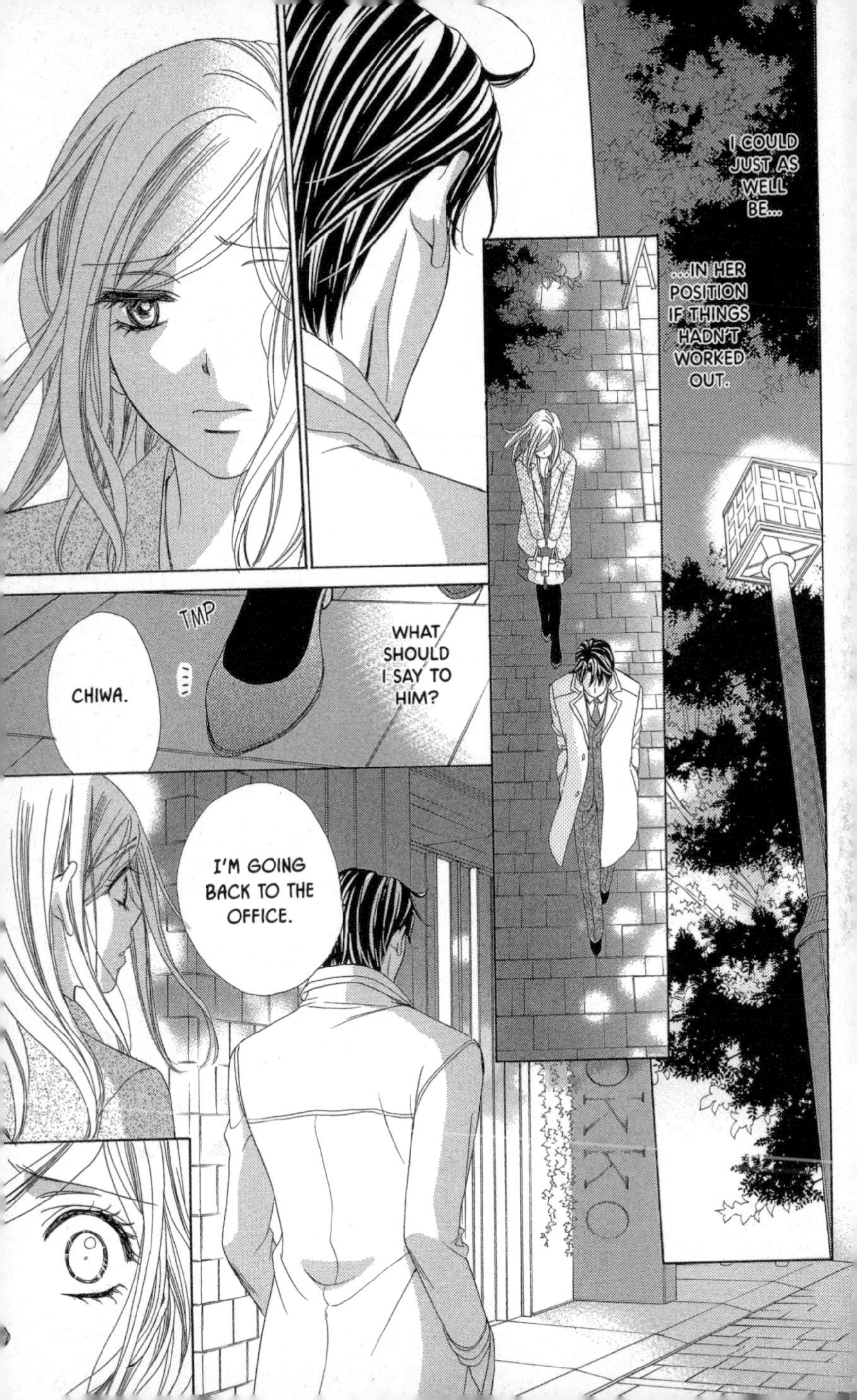
I COULD JUST AS WELL BE...
...IN HER POSITION IF THINGS HADN'T WORKED OUT.
WHAT SHOULD I SAY TO HIM?
TMP
!
CHIWA.
I'M GOING BACK TO THE OFFICE.

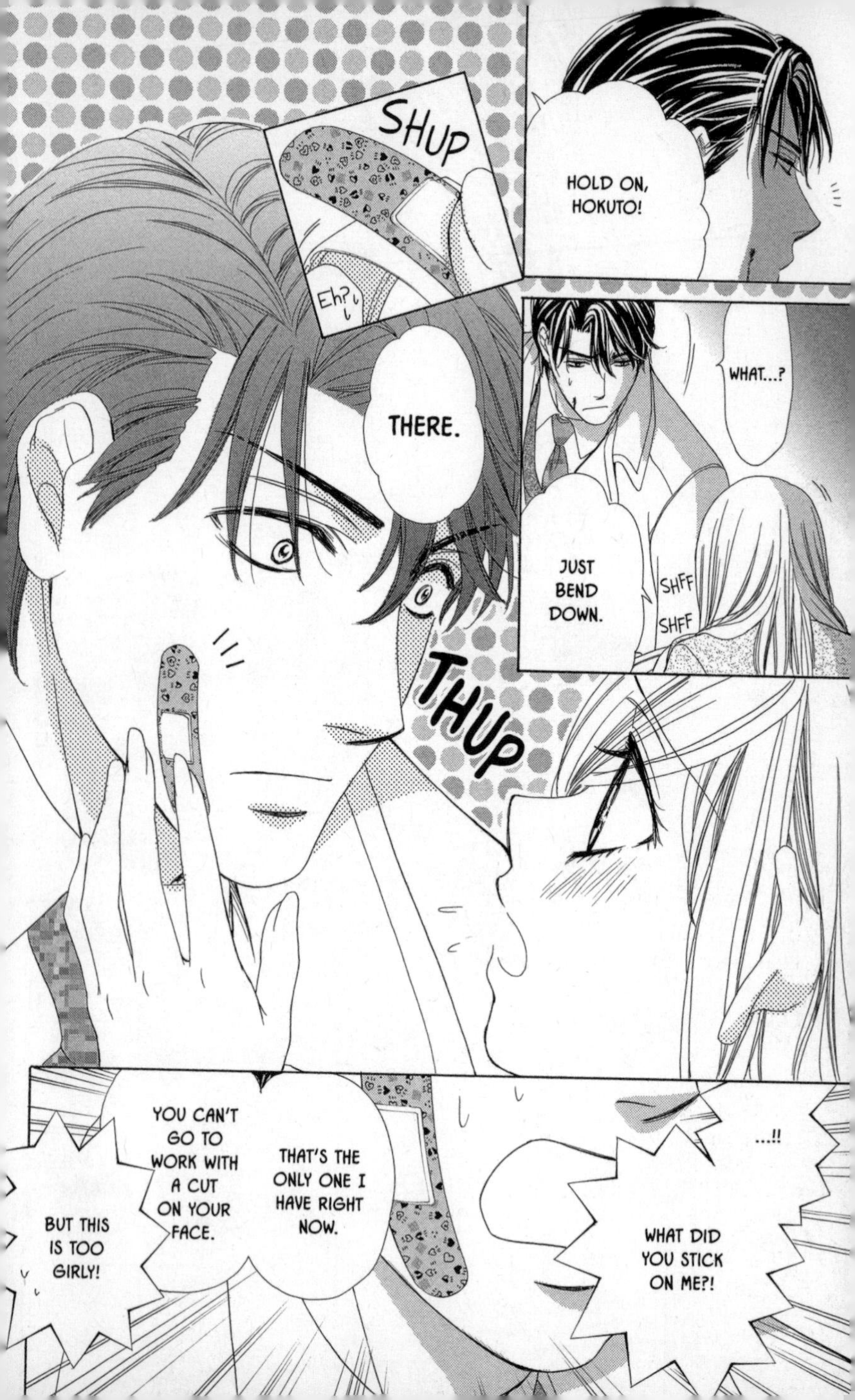
HOLD ON, HOKUTO!
WHAT...?
JUST BEND DOWN.
SHFF
SHFF
SHUP
Eh?
THERE.
THUP
...!!
WHAT DID YOU STICK ON ME?!
YOU CAN'T GO TO WORK WITH A CUT ON YOUR FACE.
THAT'S THE ONLY ONE I HAVE RIGHT NOW.
BUT THIS IS TOO GIRLY!

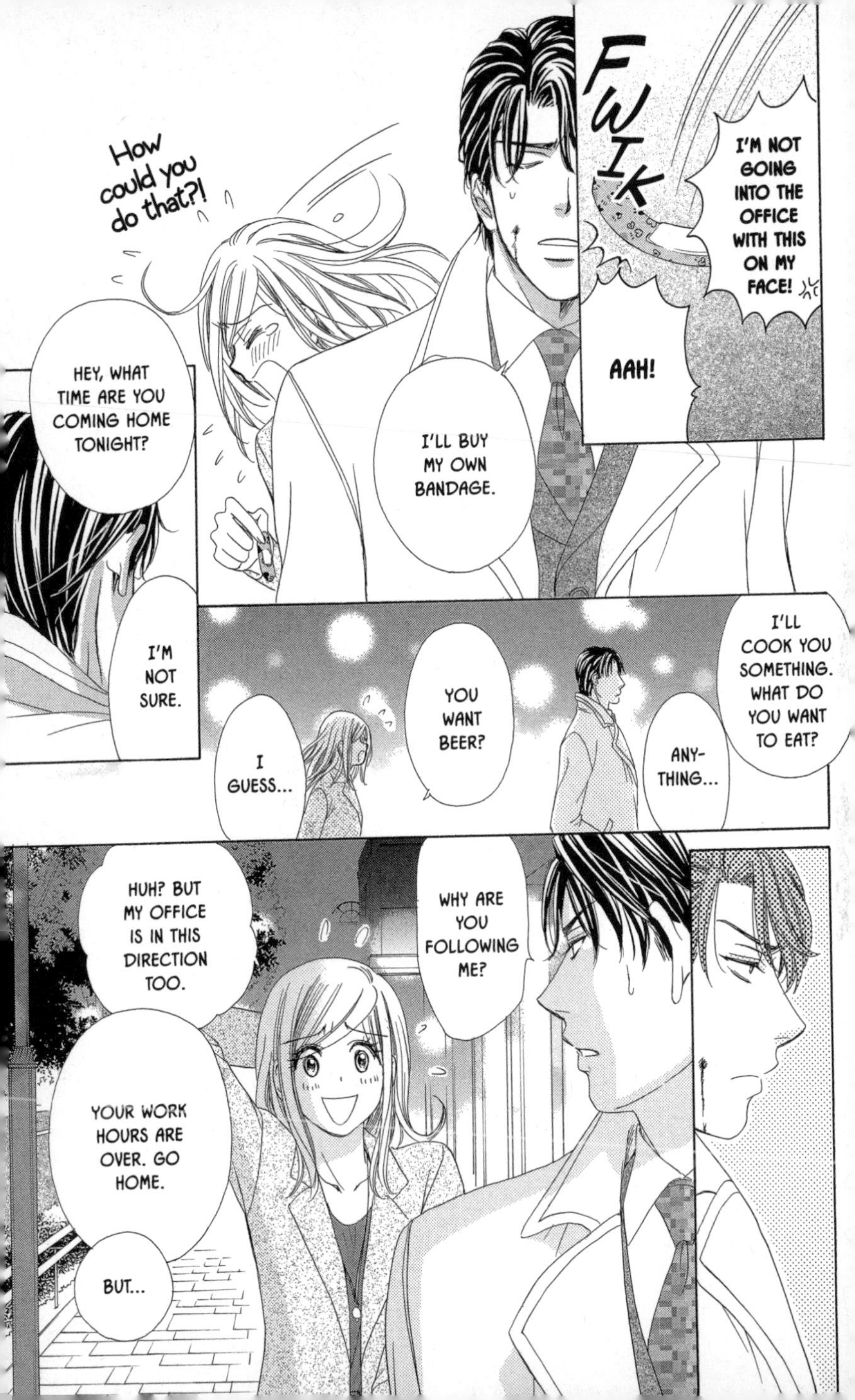
FWIK
I'M NOT GOING INTO THE OFFICE WITH THIS ON MY FACE!
AAH!
How could you do that?!
I'LL BUY MY OWN BANDAGE.
I'LL COOK YOU SOMETHING. WHAT DO YOU WANT TO EAT?
ANY-THING...
YOU WANT BEER?
I GUESS...
HEY, WHAT TIME ARE YOU COMING HOME TONIGHT?
I'M NOT SURE.
WHY ARE YOU FOLLOWING ME?
HUH? BUT MY OFFICE IS IN THIS DIRECTION TOO.
YOUR WORK HOURS ARE OVER. GO HOME.
BUT...

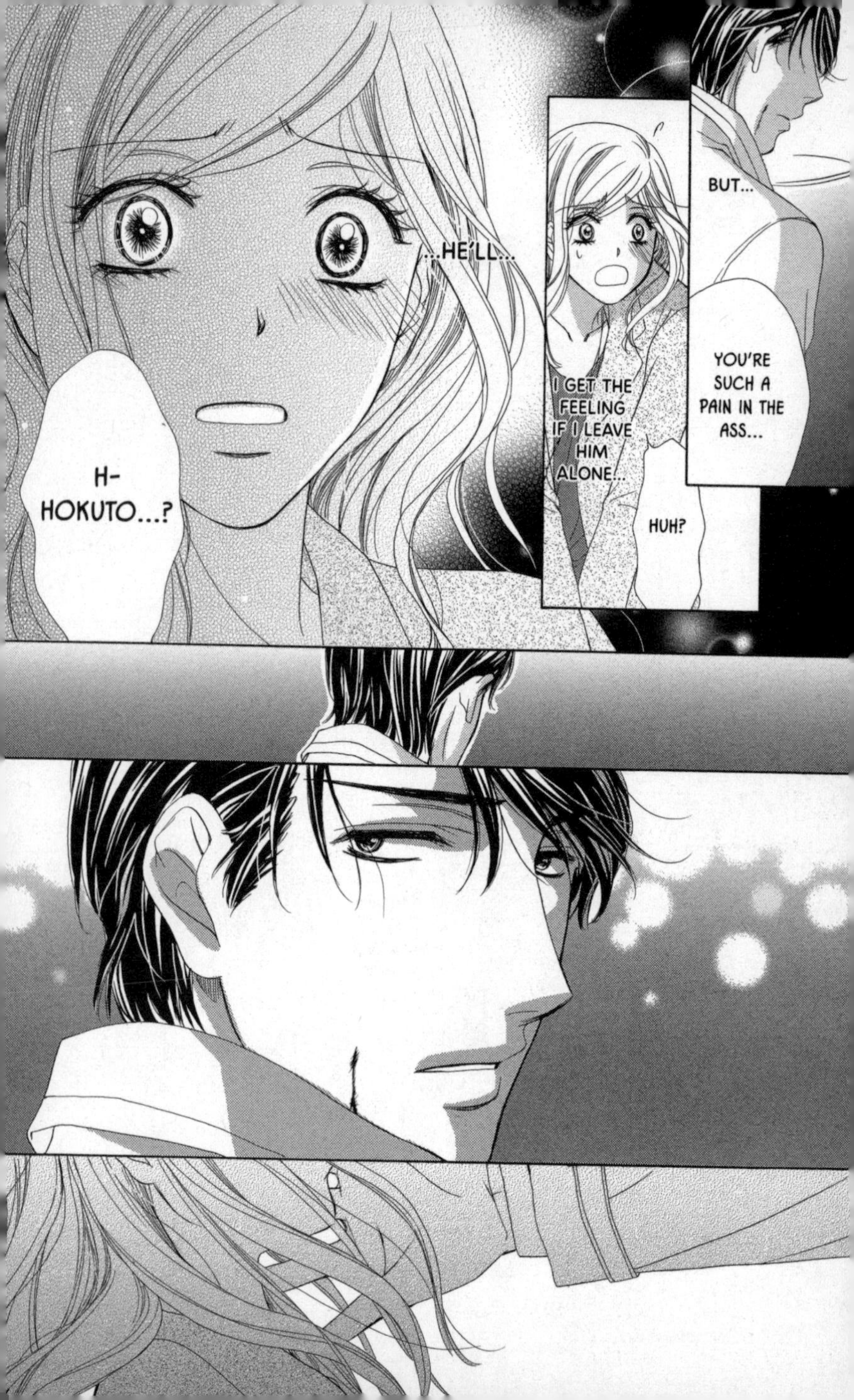
BUT...
YOU'RE SUCH A PAIN IN THE ASS...
HUH?
I GET THE FEELING IF I LEAVE HIM ALONE...
...HE'LL...
H-HOKUTO...?

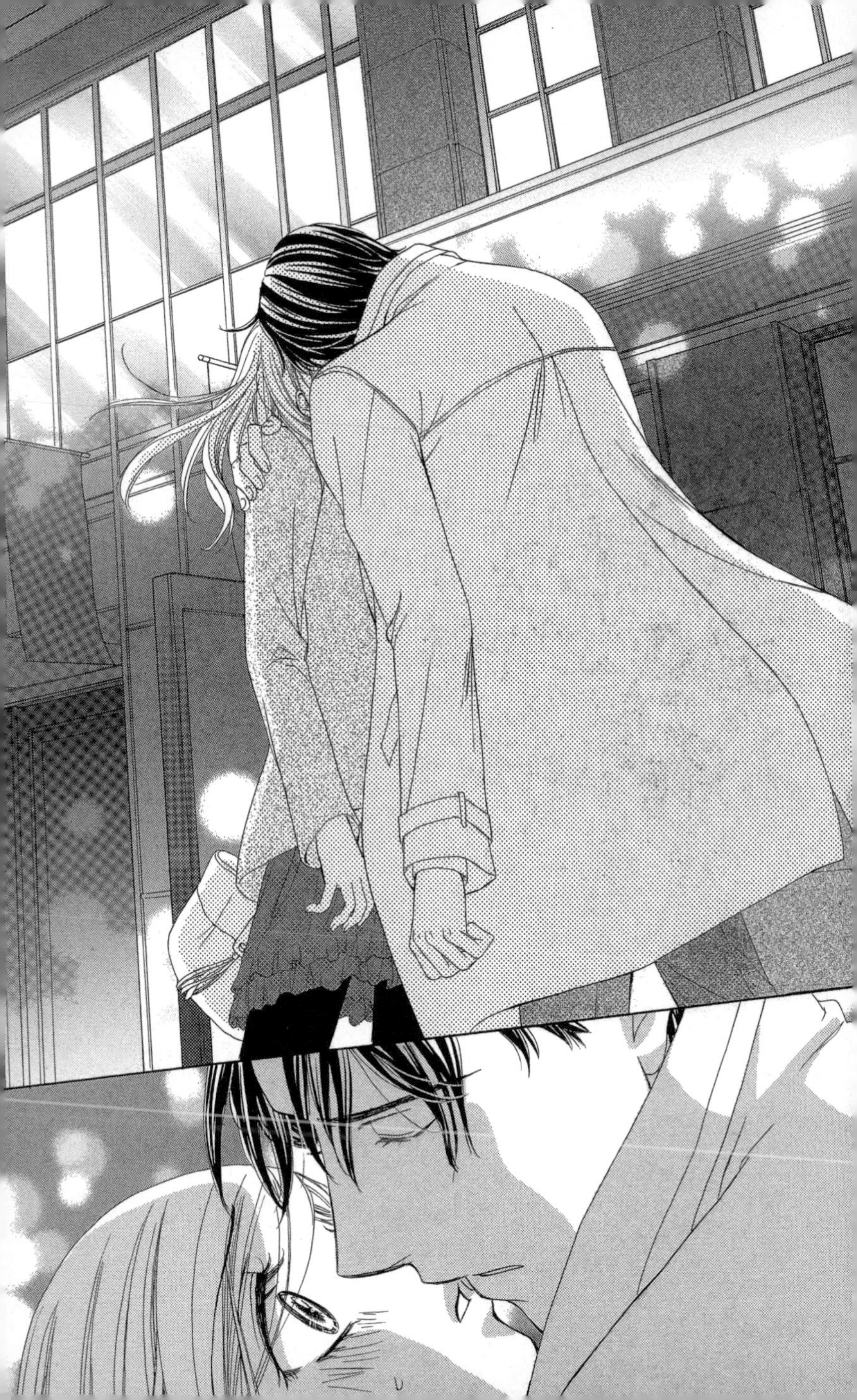

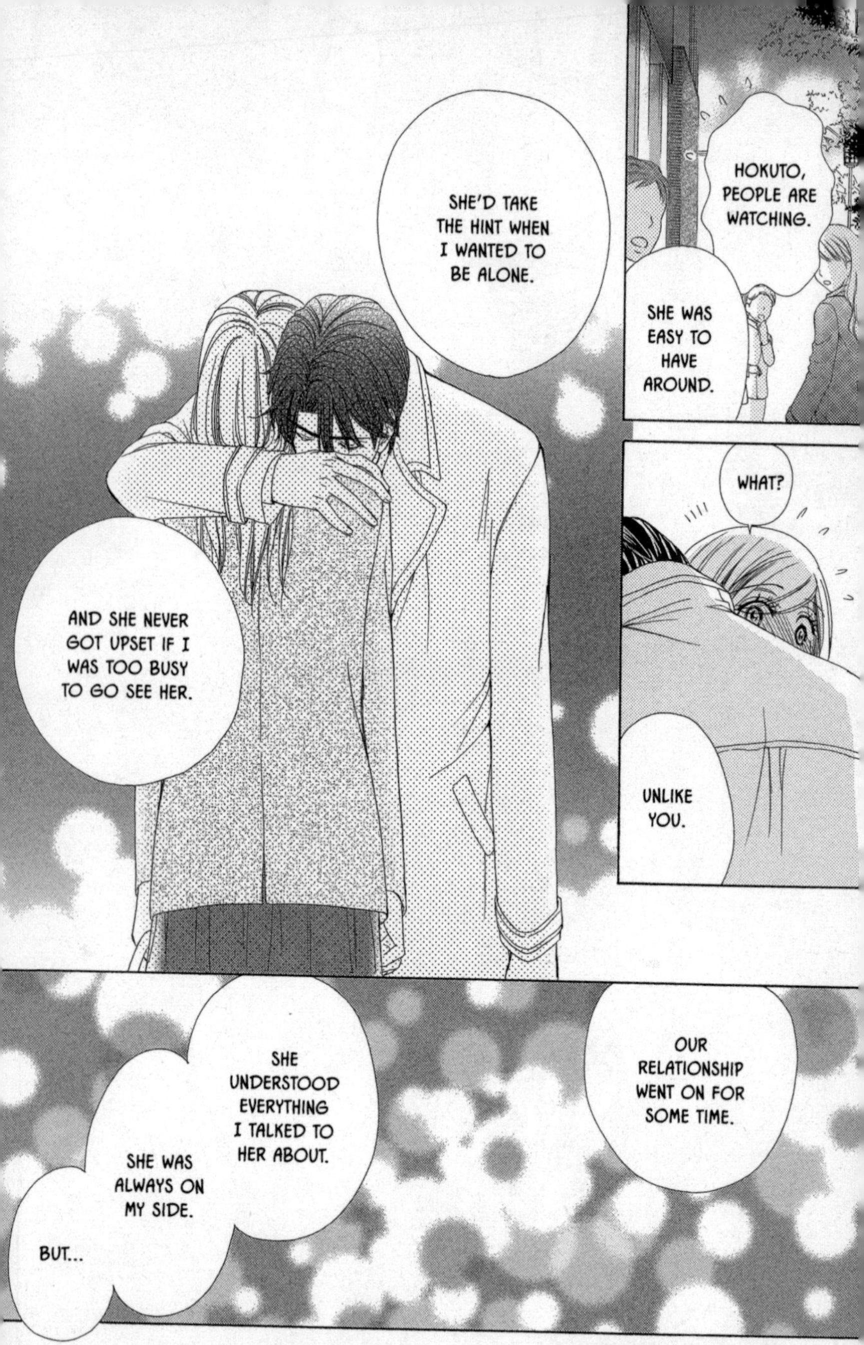
HOKUTO, PEOPLE ARE WATCHING.
SHE WAS EASY TO HAVE AROUND.
WHAT?
UNLIKE YOU.
SHE'D TAKE THE HINT WHEN I WANTED TO BE ALONE.
AND SHE NEVER GOT UPSET IF I WAS TOO BUSY TO GO SEE HER.
OUR RELATIONSHIP WENT ON FOR SOME TIME.
SHE UNDERSTOOD EVERYTHING I TALKED TO HER ABOUT.
SHE WAS ALWAYS ON MY SIDE.
BUT...

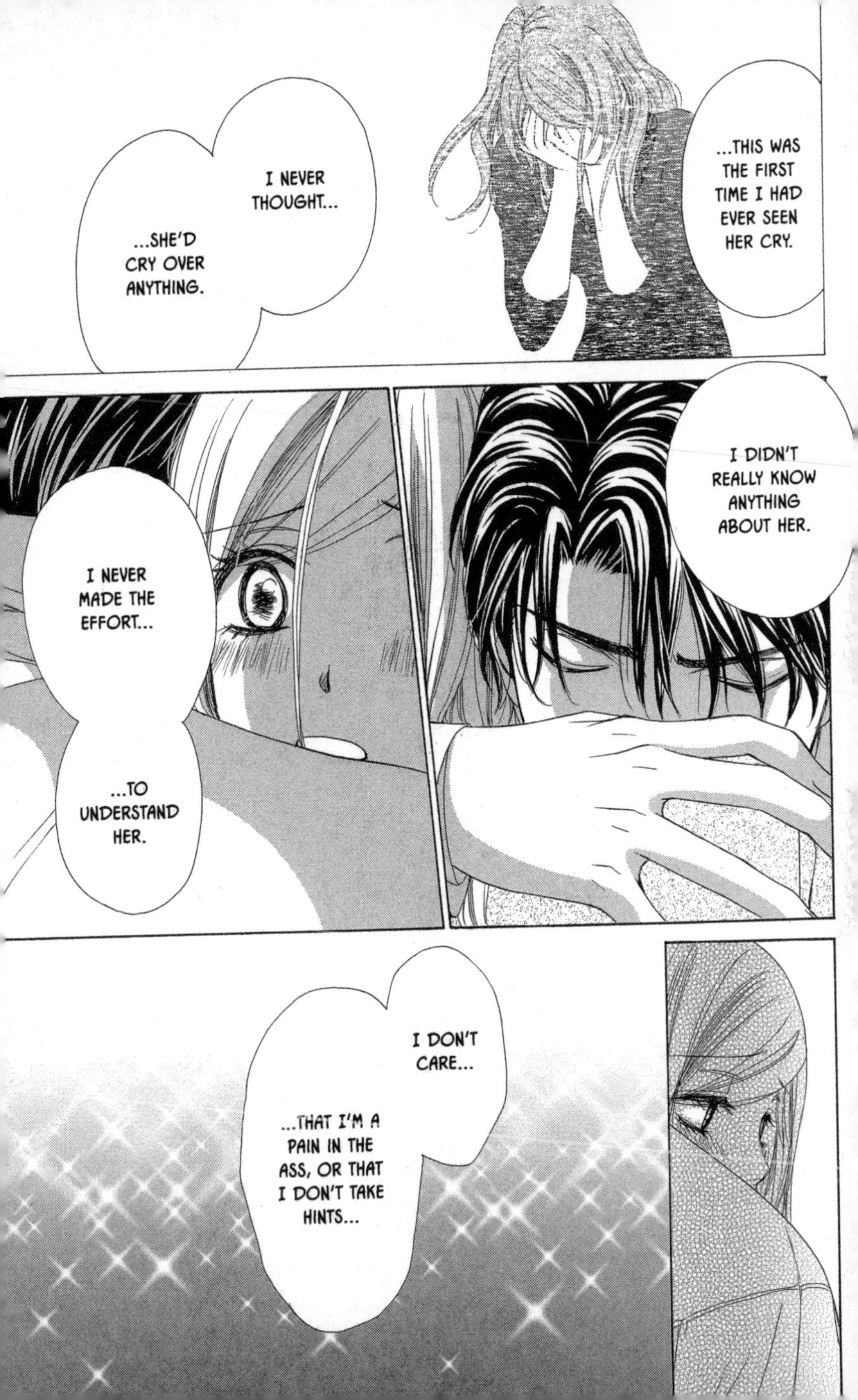
...THIS WAS THE FIRST TIME I HAD EVER SEEN HER CRY.
I NEVER THOUGHT...
...SHE'D CRY OVER ANYTHING.
I DIDN'T REALLY KNOW ANYTHING ABOUT HER.
I NEVER MADE THE EFFORT...
...TO UNDERSTAND HER.
I DON'T CARE...
...THAT I'M A PAIN IN THE ASS, OR THAT I DON'T TAKE HINTS...

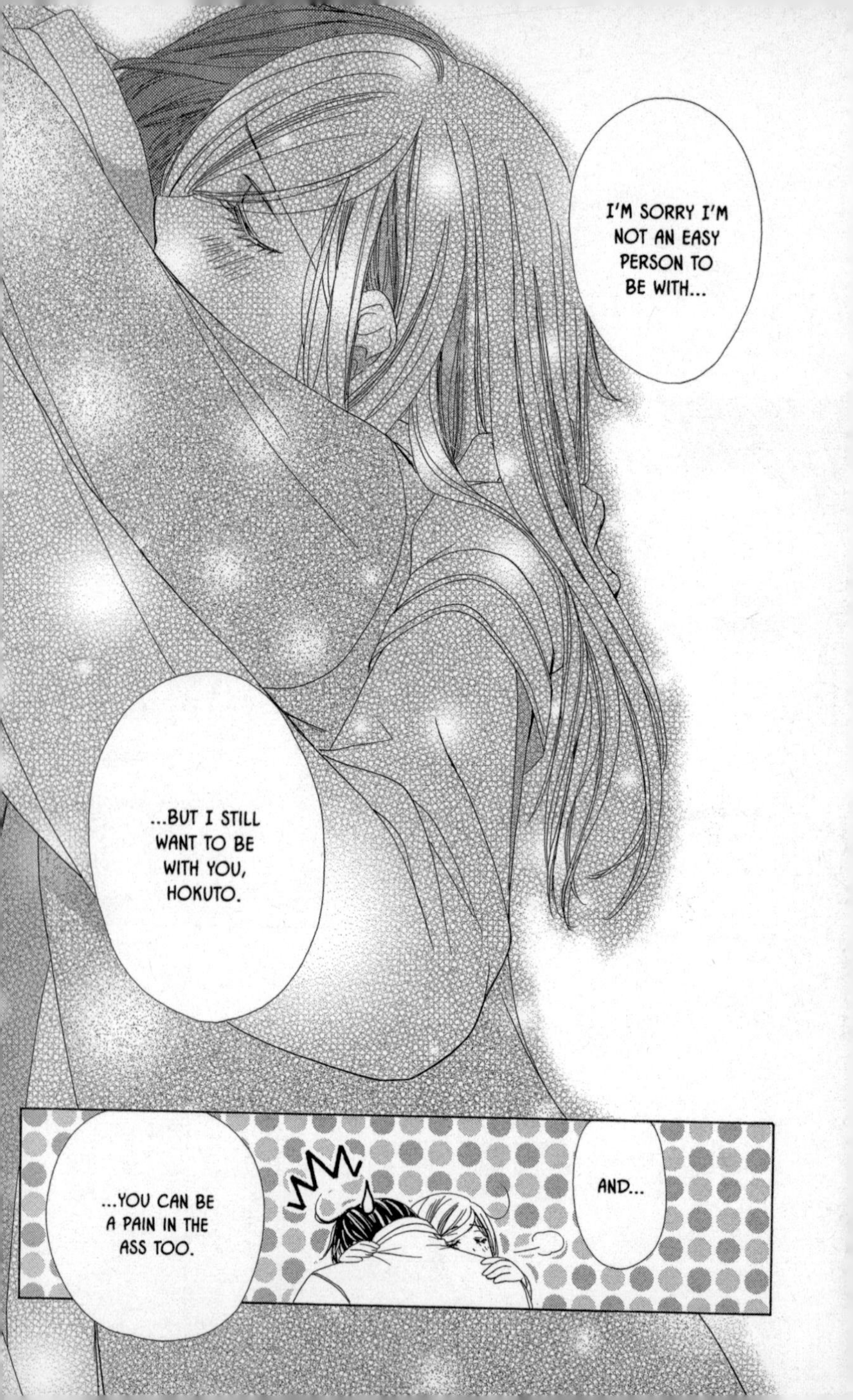
I'M SORRY I'M NOT AN EASY PERSON TO BE WITH...
...BUT I STILL WANT TO BE WITH YOU, HOKUTO.
AND...
...YOU CAN BE A PAIN IN THE ASS TOO.

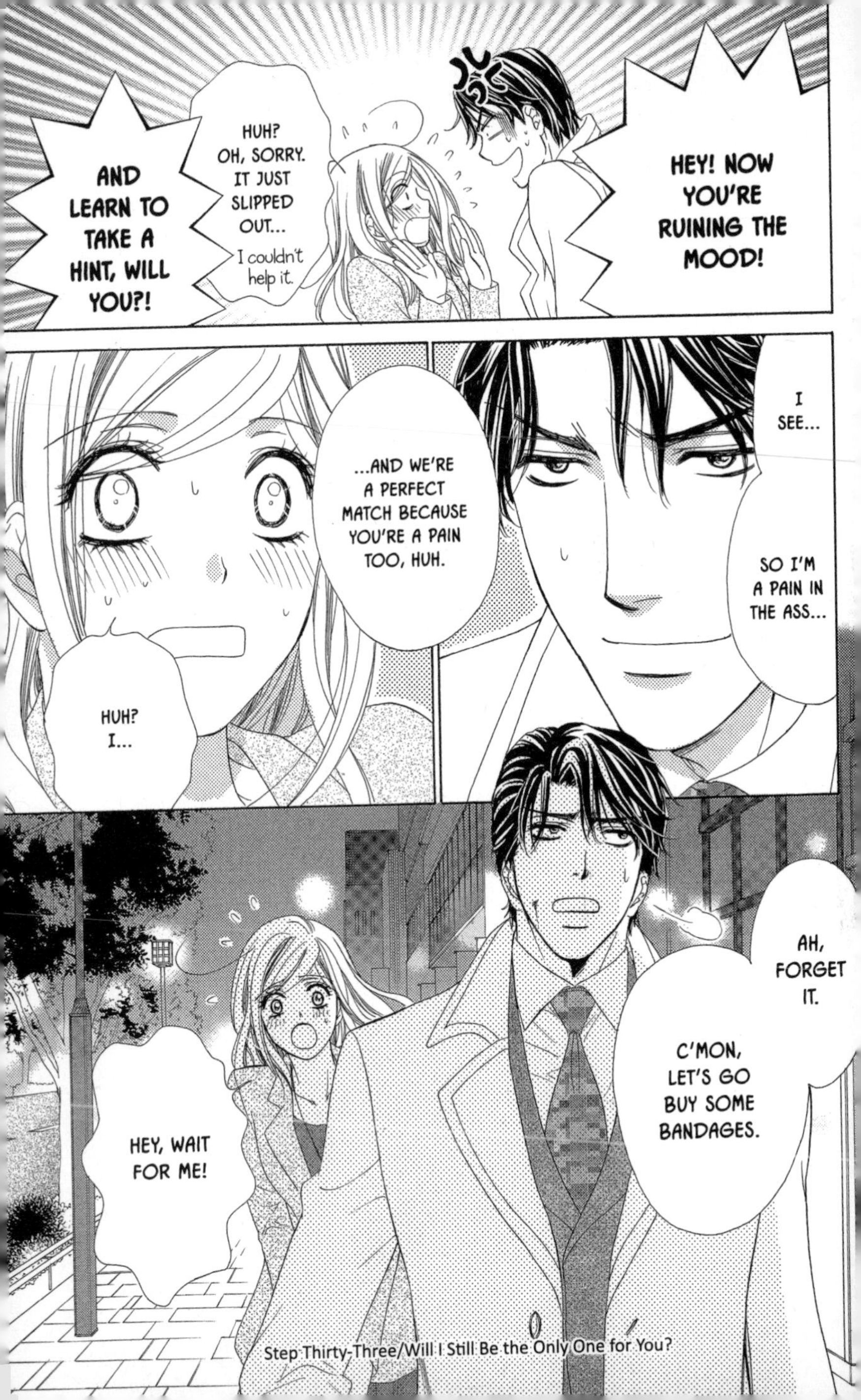
HEY! NOW YOU'RE RUINING THE MOOD!
HUH? OH, SORRY. IT JUST SLIPPED OUT...
I couldn't help it.
AND LEARN TO TAKE A HINT, WILL YOU?!
I SEE...
SO I'M A PAIN IN THE ASS...
...AND WE'RE A PERFECT MATCH BECAUSE YOU'RE A PAIN TOO, HUH.
HUH? I...
AH, FORGET IT.
C'MON, LET'S GO BUY SOME BANDAGES.
HEY, WAIT FOR ME!

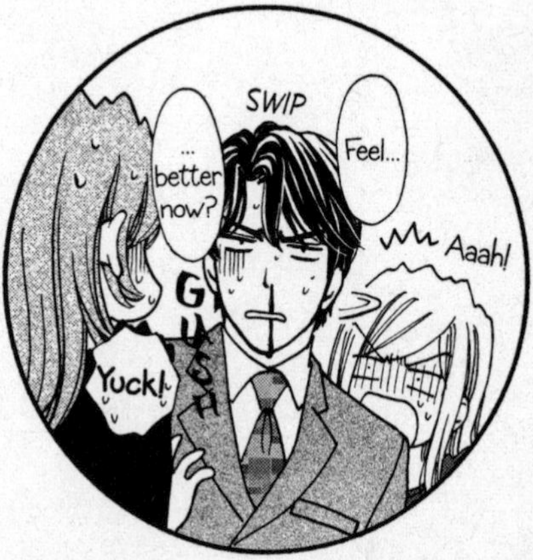

Feel...
SWIP
... better now?
Aaah!
GUSH
Yuck!

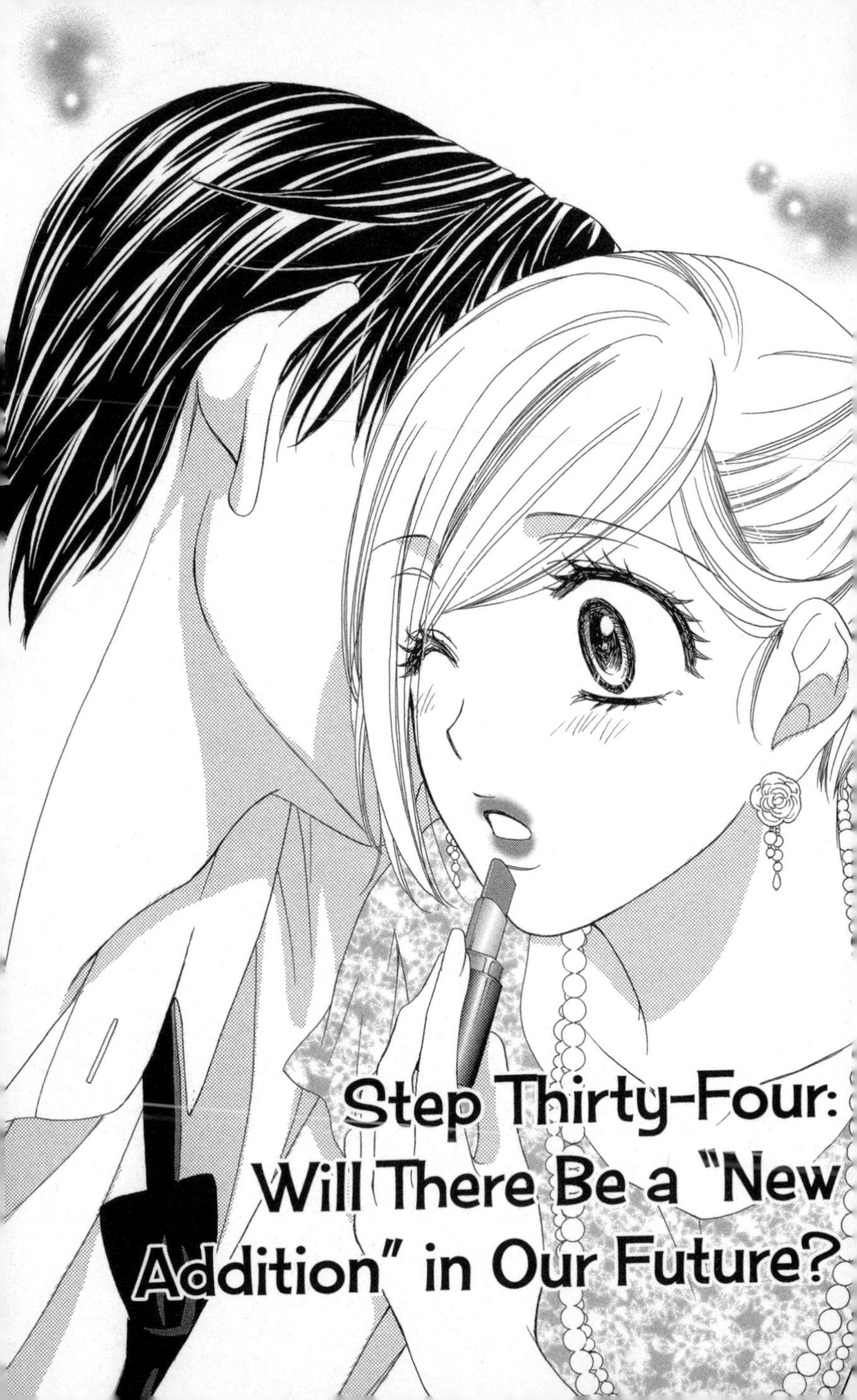
Step Thirty-Four:
Will There Be a "New
Addition" in Our Future?

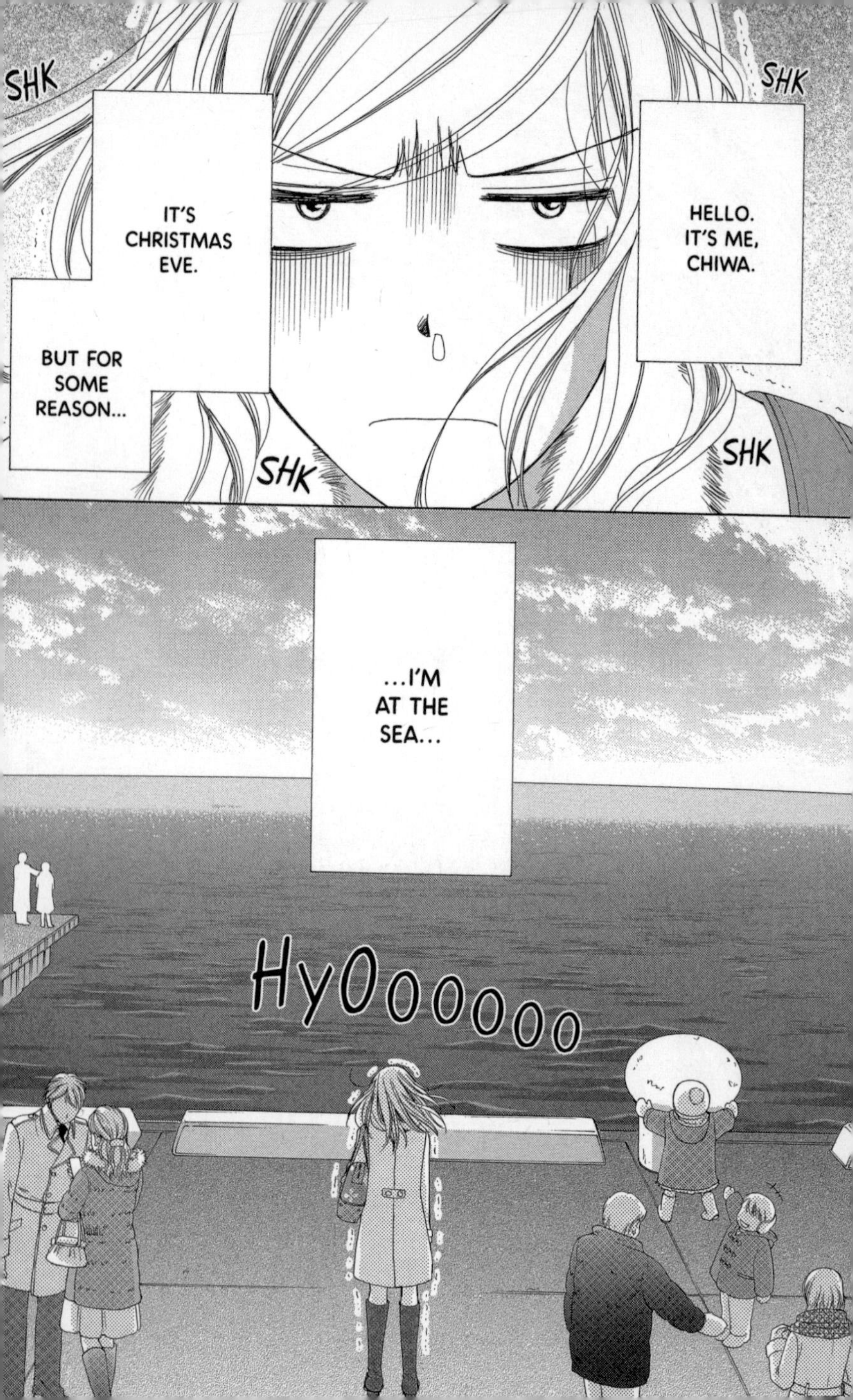
SHK
HELLO. IT'S ME, CHIWA.
IT'S CHRISTMAS EVE.
SHK
BUT FOR SOME REASON...
SHK
SHK
...I'M AT THE SEA...
HyOOOOOOO

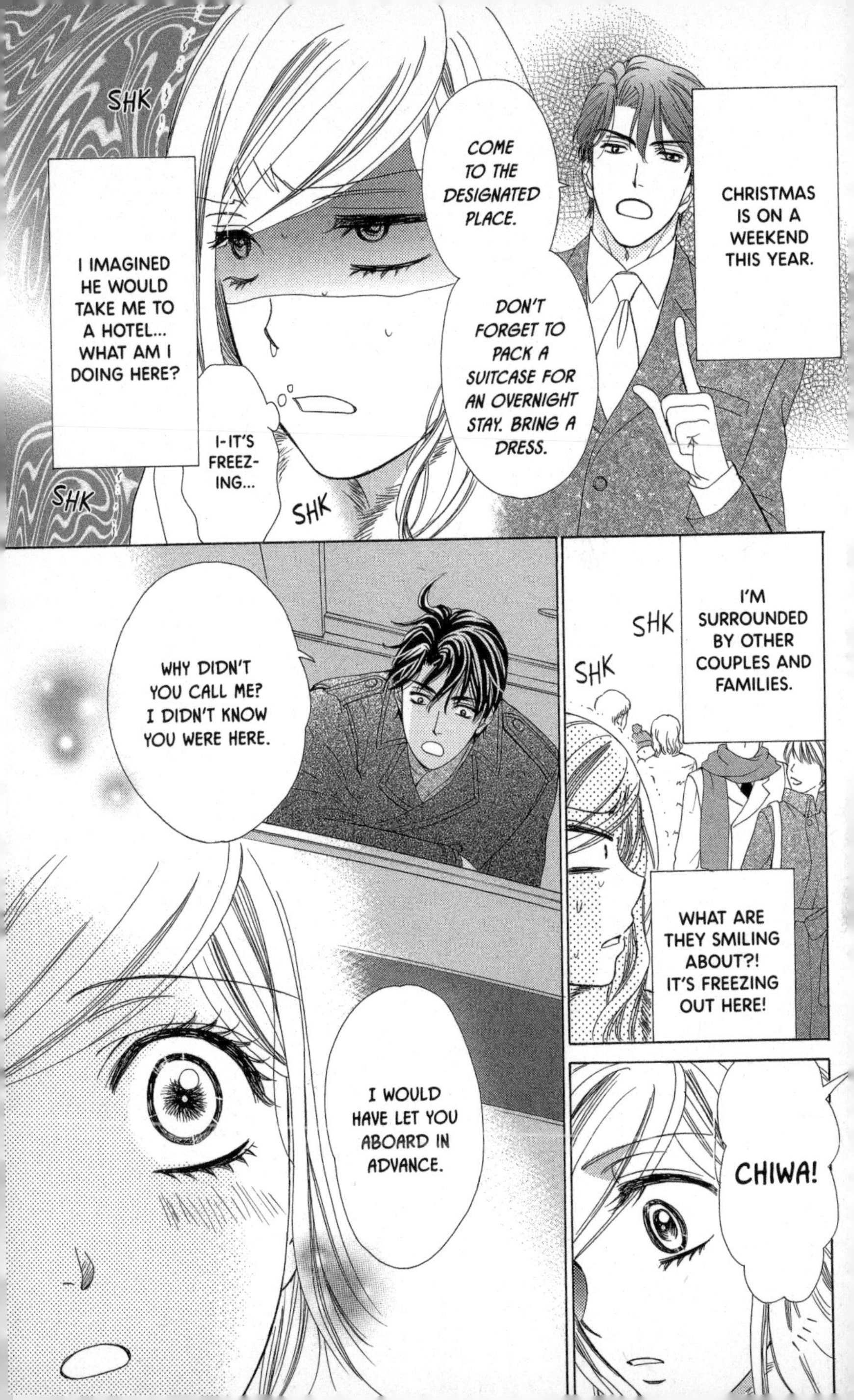
CHRISTMAS IS ON A WEEKEND THIS YEAR.
COME TO THE DESIGNATED PLACE.
DON'T FORGET TO PACK A SUITCASE FOR AN OVERNIGHT STAY. BRING A DRESS.
SHK
I IMAGINED HE WOULD TAKE ME TO A HOTEL... WHAT AM I DOING HERE?
I-IT'S FREEZ-ING...
SHK
SHK
I'M SURROUNDED BY OTHER COUPLES AND FAMILIES.
SHK
SHK
WHAT ARE THEY SMILING ABOUT?! IT'S FREEZING OUT HERE!
CHIWA!
WHY DIDN'T YOU CALL ME? I DIDN'T KNOW YOU WERE HERE.
I WOULD HAVE LET YOU ABOARD IN ADVANCE.

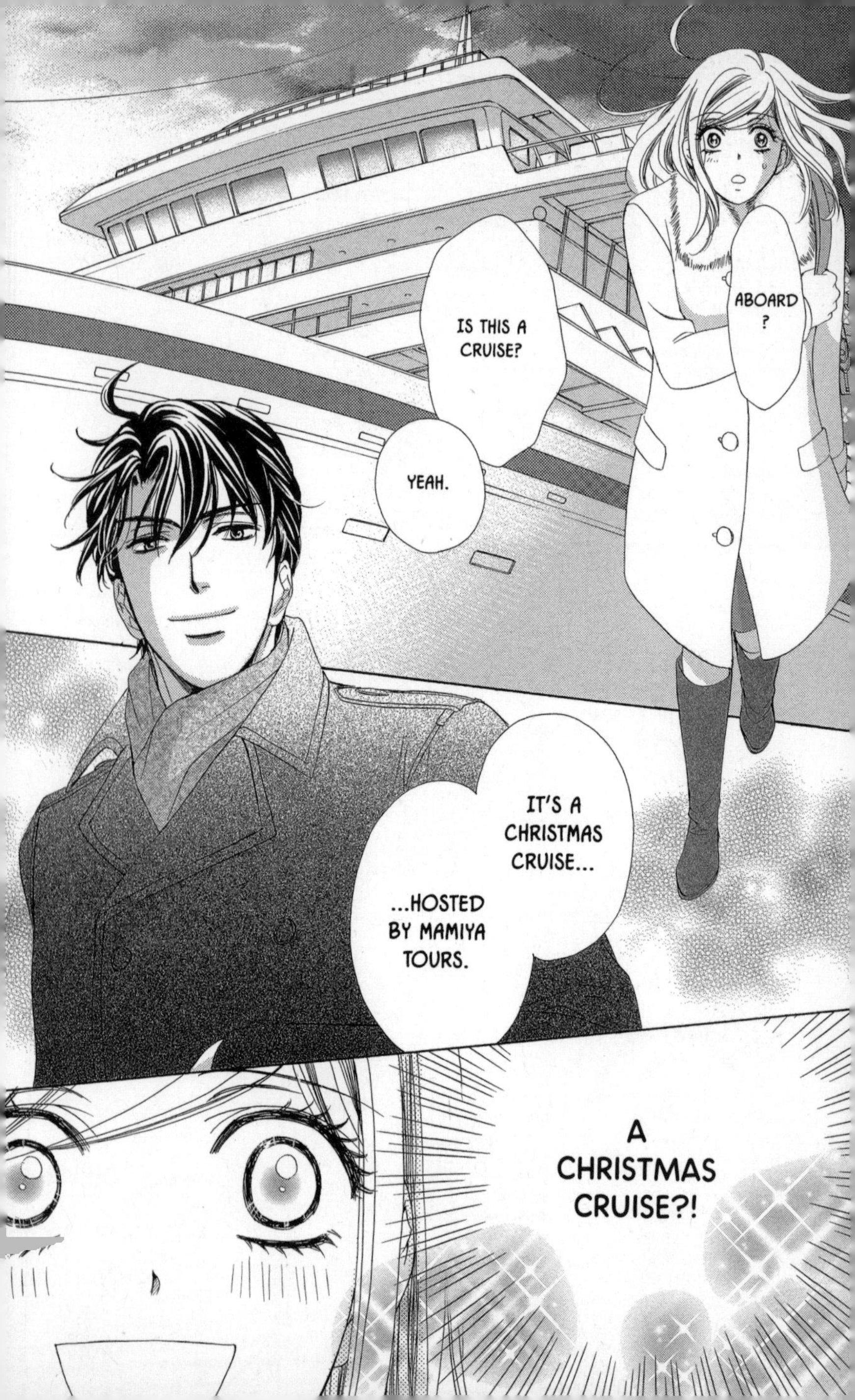
ABOARD?
IS THIS A CRUISE?
YEAH.
IT'S A CHRISTMAS CRUISE...
...HOSTED BY MAMIYA TOURS.
A CHRISTMAS CRUISE?!

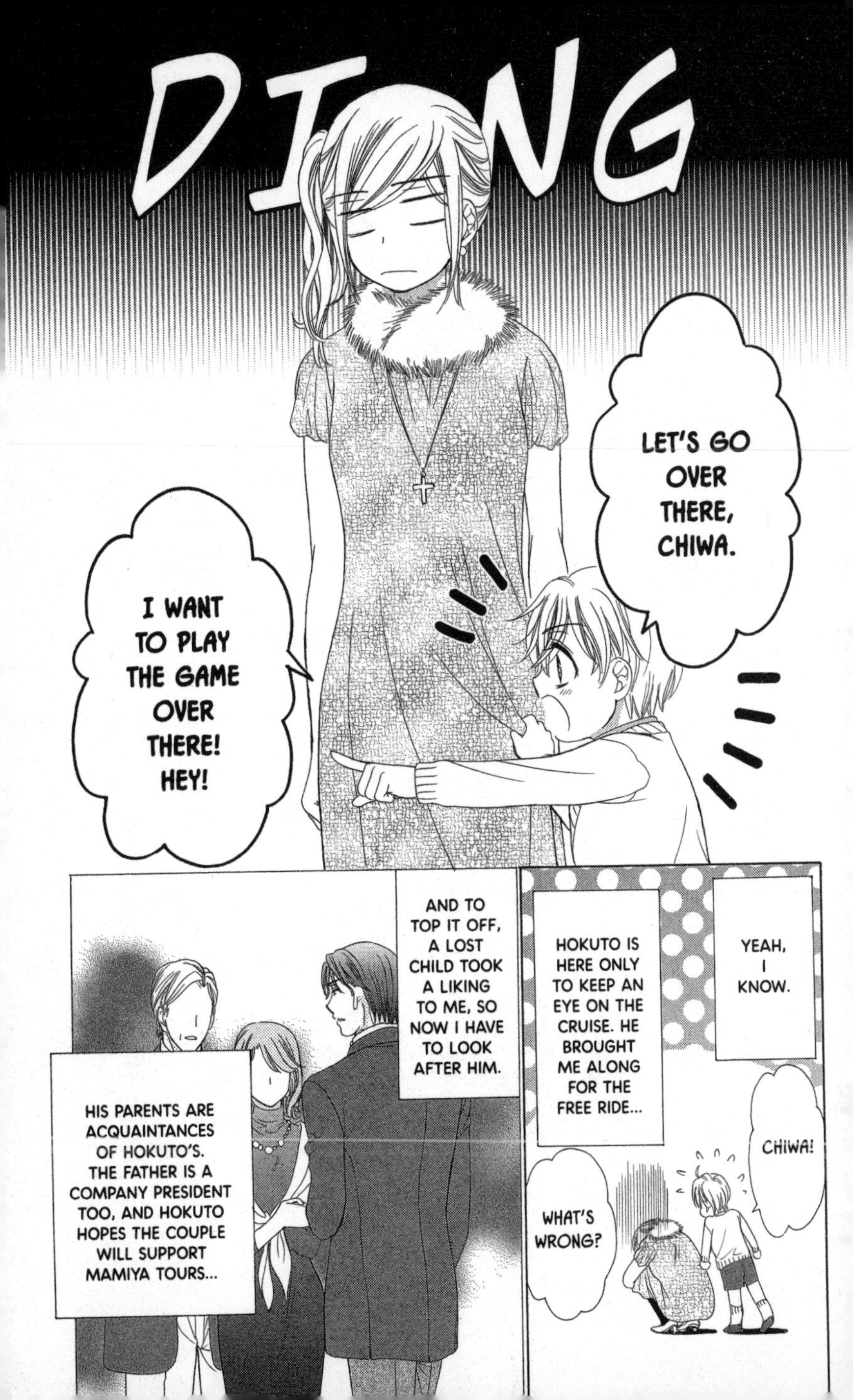
DING
LET'S GO OVER THERE, CHIWA.
I WANT TO PLAY THE GAME OVER THERE! HEY!
YEAH, I KNOW.
HOKUTO IS HERE ONLY TO KEEP AN EYE ON THE CRUISE. HE BROUGHT ME ALONG FOR THE FREE RIDE...
CHIWA!
WHAT'S WRONG?
AND TO TOP IT OFF, A LOST CHILD TOOK A LIKING TO ME, SO NOW I HAVE TO LOOK AFTER HIM.
HIS PARENTS ARE ACQUAINTANCES OF HOKUTO'S. THE FATHER IS A COMPANY PRESIDENT TOO, AND HOKUTO HOPES THE COUPLE WILL SUPPORT MAMIYA TOURS...

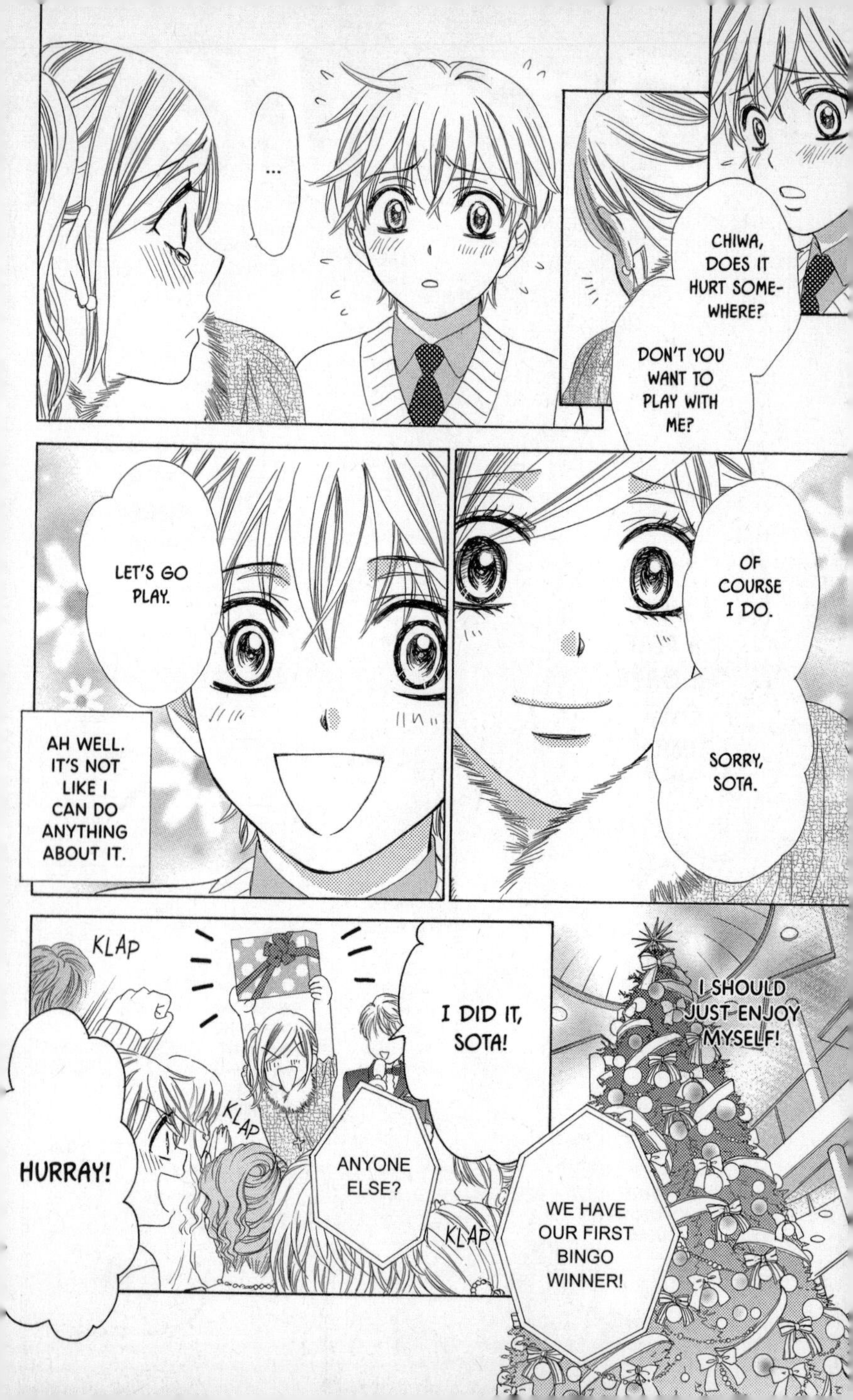
CHIWA, DOES IT HURT SOME-WHERE?
DON'T YOU WANT TO PLAY WITH ME?
...
OF COURSE I DO.
SORRY, SOTA.
LET'S GO PLAY.
AH WELL. IT'S NOT LIKE I CAN DO ANYTHING ABOUT IT.
I SHOULD JUST ENJOY MYSELF!
WE HAVE OUR FIRST BINGO WINNER!
KLAP
ANYONE ELSE?
I DID IT, SOTA!
KLAP
KLAP
HURRAY!

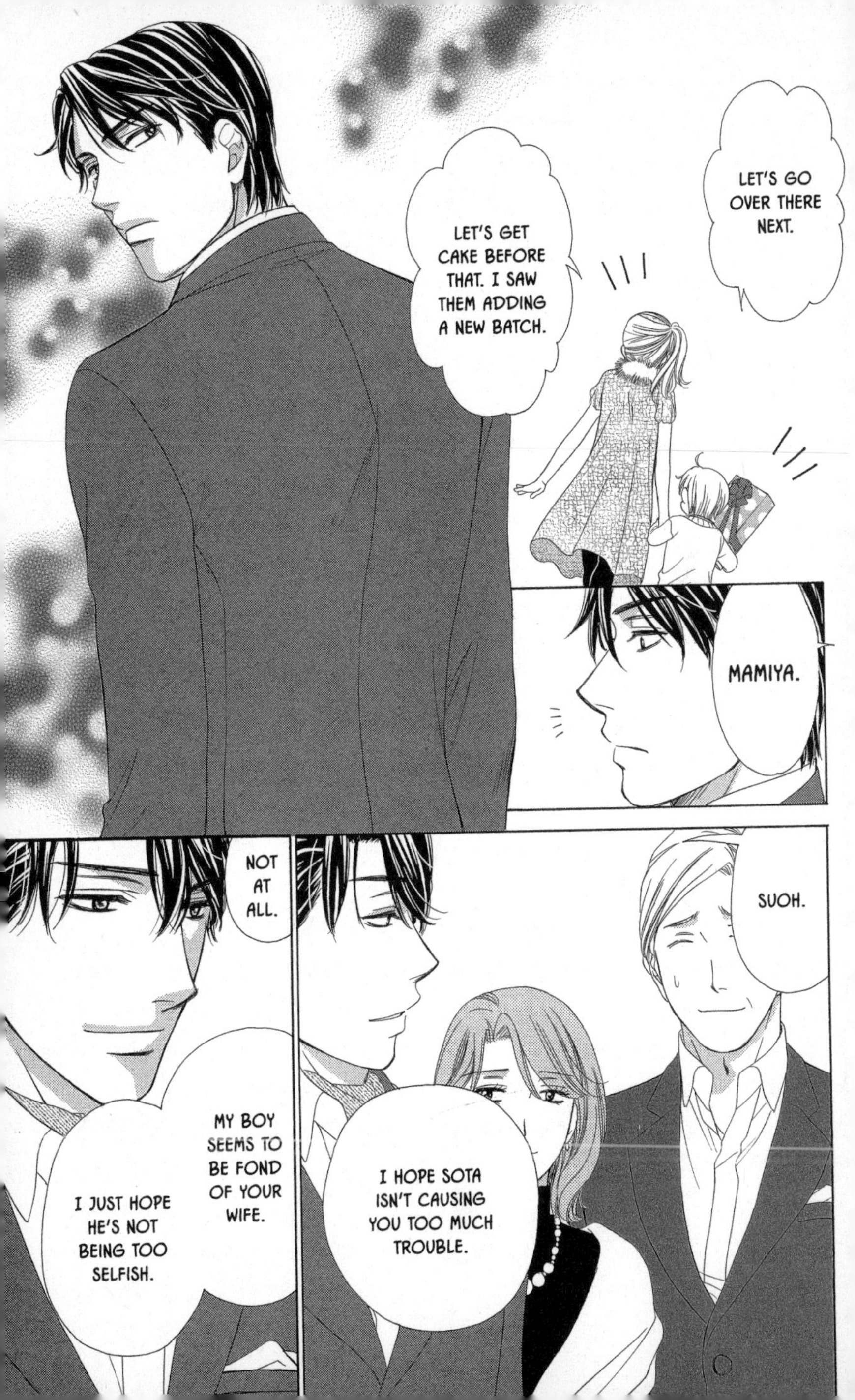
LET'S GO OVER THERE NEXT.
LET'S GET CAKE BEFORE THAT. I SAW THEM ADDING A NEW BATCH.
MAMIYA.
SUOH.
I HOPE SOTA ISN'T CAUSING YOU TOO MUCH TROUBLE.
NOT AT ALL.
MY BOY SEEMS TO BE FOND OF YOUR WIFE.
I JUST HOPE HE'S NOT BEING TOO SELFISH.

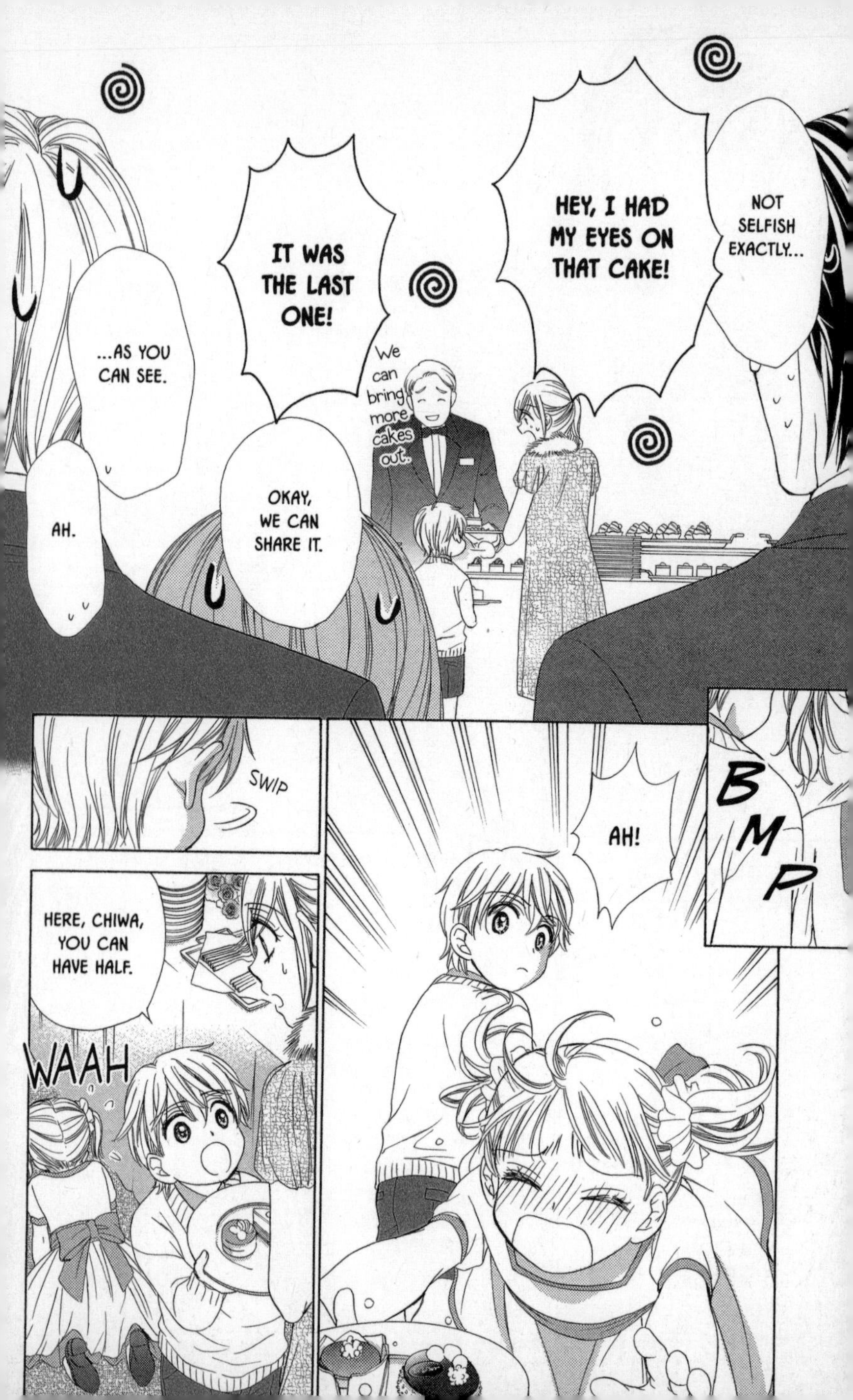
NOT SELFISH EXACTLY...
HEY, I HAD MY EYES ON THAT CAKE!
IT WAS THE LAST ONE!
We can bring more cakes out.
OKAY, WE CAN SHARE IT.
...AS YOU CAN SEE.
AH.
BMP
AH!
SWIP
HERE, CHIWA, YOU CAN HAVE HALF.
WAAH

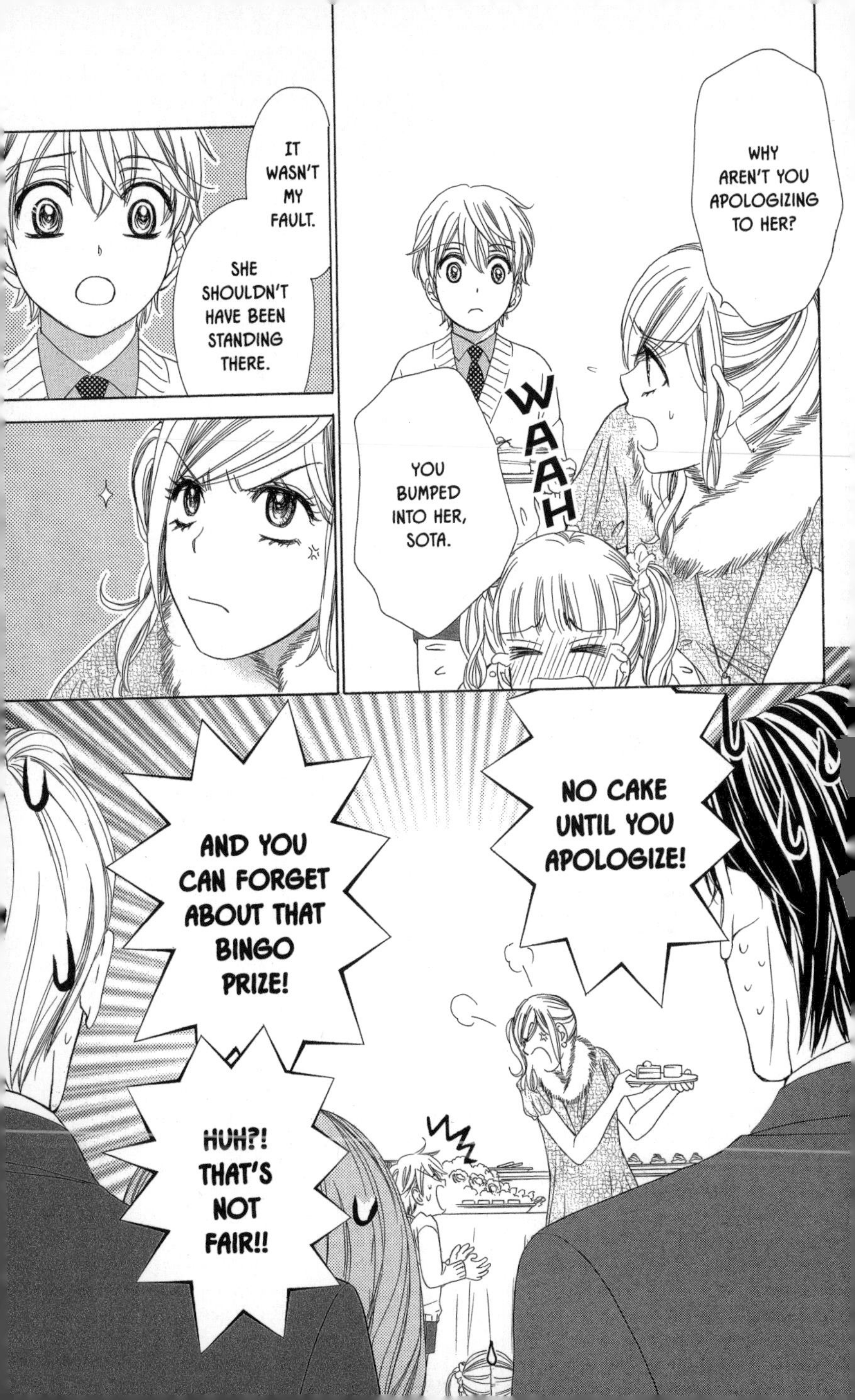
WHY AREN'T YOU APOLOGIZING TO HER?
WAAH
YOU BUMPED INTO HER, SOTA.
IT WASN'T MY FAULT.
SHE SHOULDN'T HAVE BEEN STANDING THERE.
NO CAKE UNTIL YOU APOLOGIZE!
AND YOU CAN FORGET ABOUT THAT BINGO PRIZE!
HUH?! THAT'S NOT FAIR!!

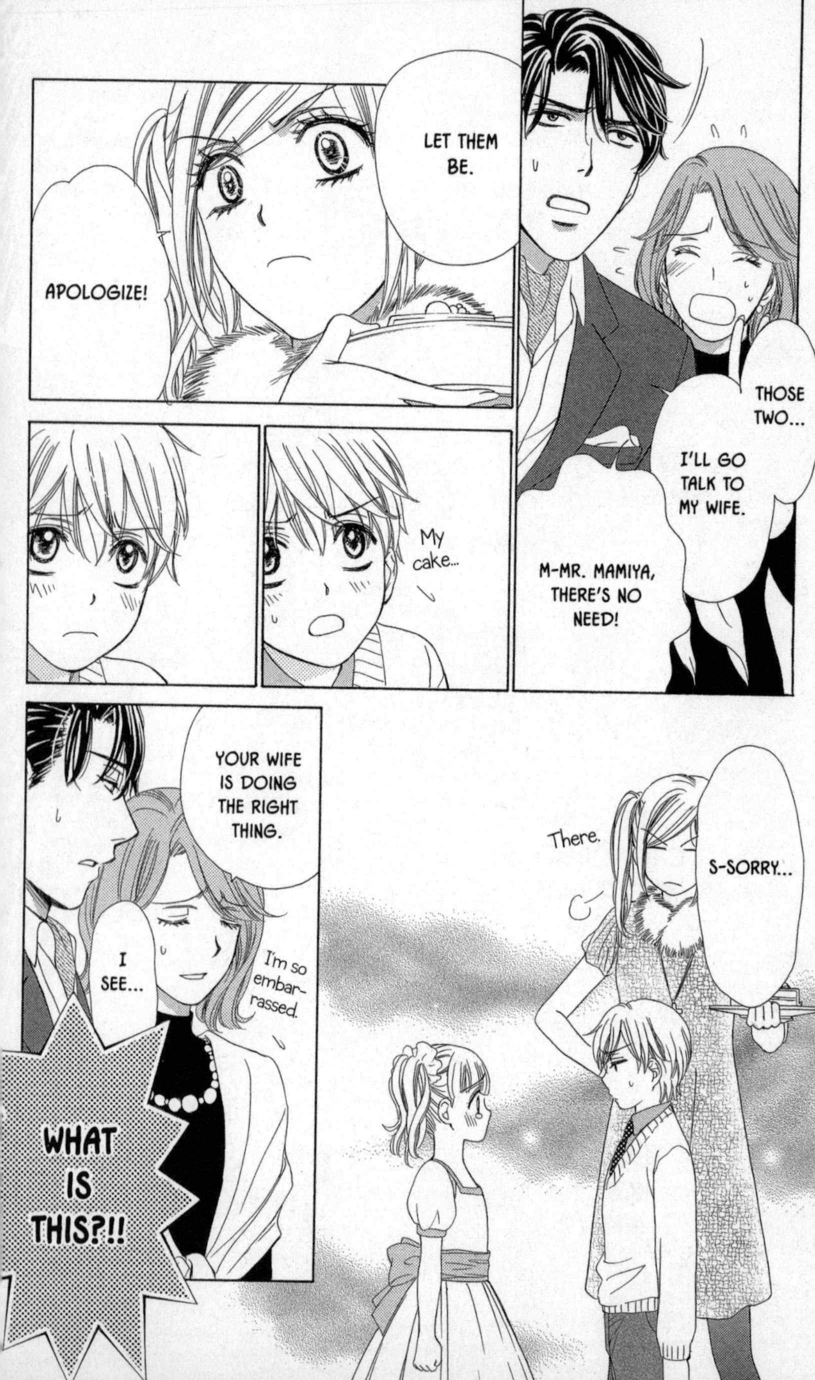

THOSE TWO...
I'LL GO TALK TO MY WIFE.
M-MR. MAMIYA, THERE'S NO NEED!
LET THEM BE.
APOLOGIZE!
My cake...
S-SORRY...
There.
YOUR WIFE IS DOING THE RIGHT THING.
I'm so embarrassed.
I SEE...
WHAT IS THIS?!!

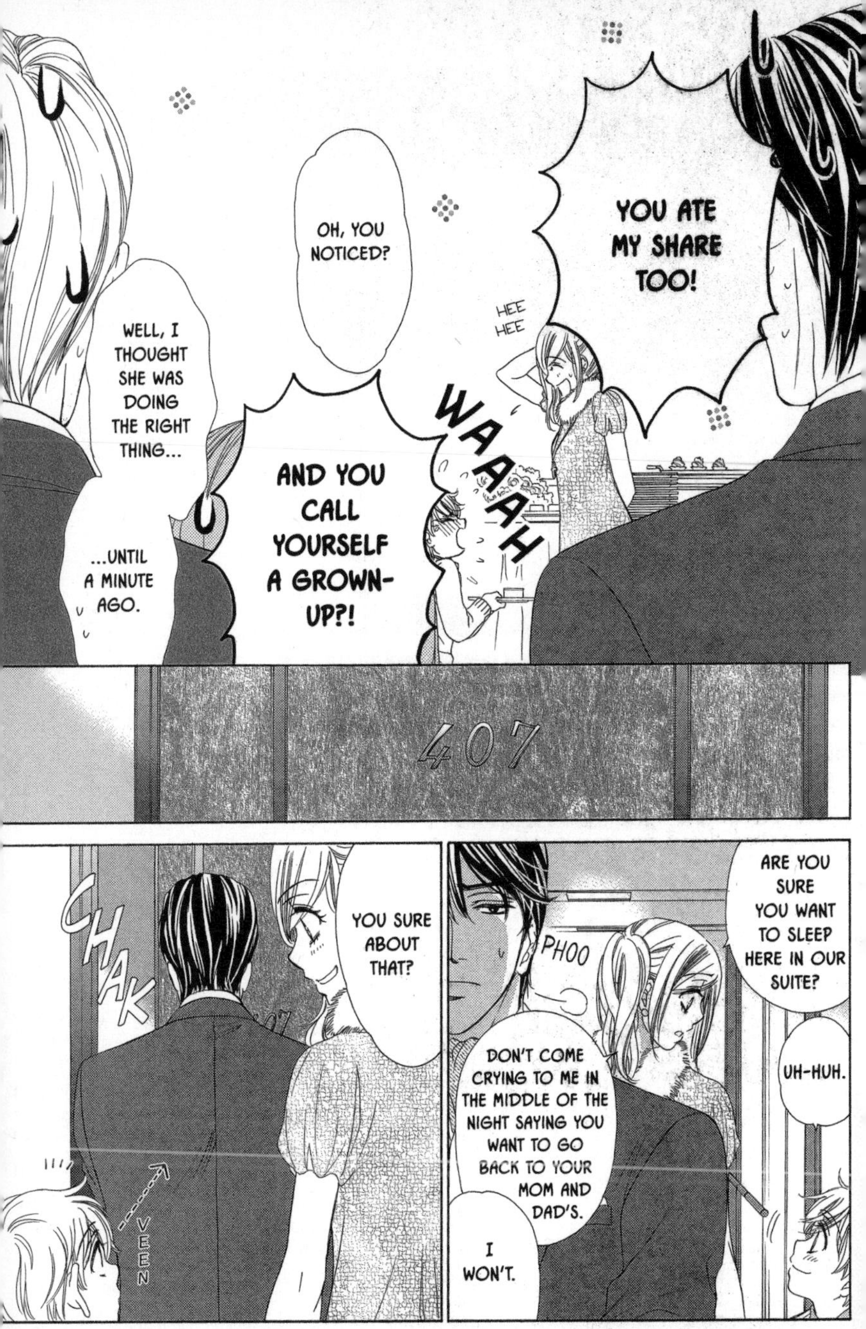
YOU ATE MY SHARE TOO!
HEE HEE
OH, YOU NOTICED?
WAAAAH
AND YOU CALL YOURSELF A GROWN-UP?!
WELL, I THOUGHT SHE WAS DOING THE RIGHT THING...
...UNTIL A MINUTE AGO.
407
ARE YOU SURE YOU WANT TO SLEEP HERE IN OUR SUITE?
PHOO
UH-HUH.
DON'T COME CRYING TO ME IN THE MIDDLE OF THE NIGHT SAYING YOU WANT TO GO BACK TO YOUR MOM AND DAD'S.
I WON'T.
YOU SURE ABOUT THAT?
CHAK
VEEN

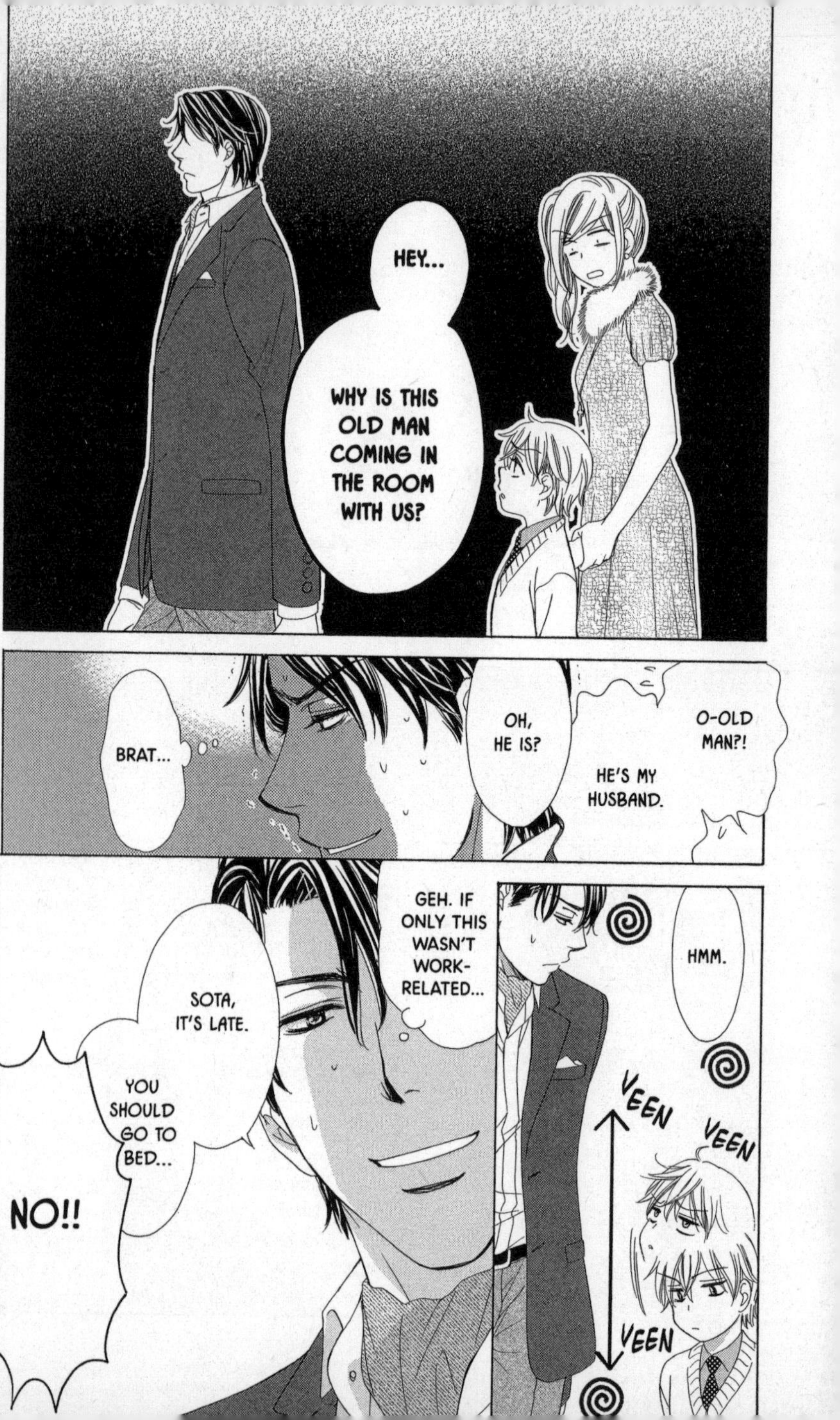
HEY...
WHY IS THIS OLD MAN COMING IN THE ROOM WITH US?
O-OLD MAN?!
HE'S MY HUSBAND.
OH, HE IS?
BRAT...
HMM.
VEEN
VEEN
VEEN
GEH. IF ONLY THIS WASN'T WORK-RELATED...
SOTA, IT'S LATE.
YOU SHOULD GO TO BED...
NO!!

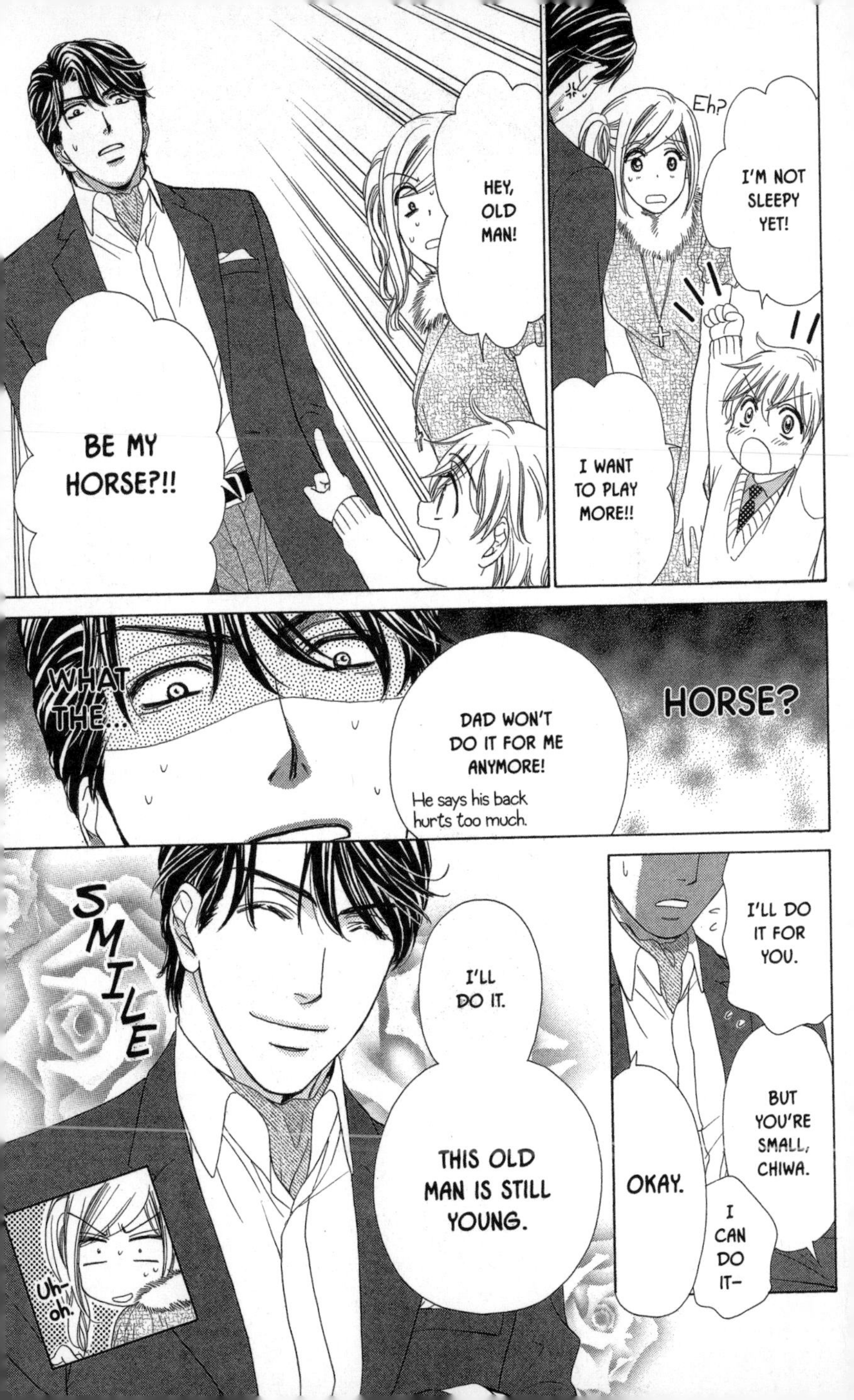

Eh?
I'M NOT SLEEPY YET!
I WANT TO PLAY MORE!!
HEY, OLD MAN!
BE MY HORSE?!!
HORSE?
DAD WON'T DO IT FOR ME ANYMORE!
He says his back hurts too much.
WHAT THE...
I'LL DO IT FOR YOU.
BUT YOU'RE SMALL, CHIWA.
I CAN DO IT—
OKAY.
I'LL DO IT.
THIS OLD MAN IS STILL YOUNG.
SMILE
Uh-oh.

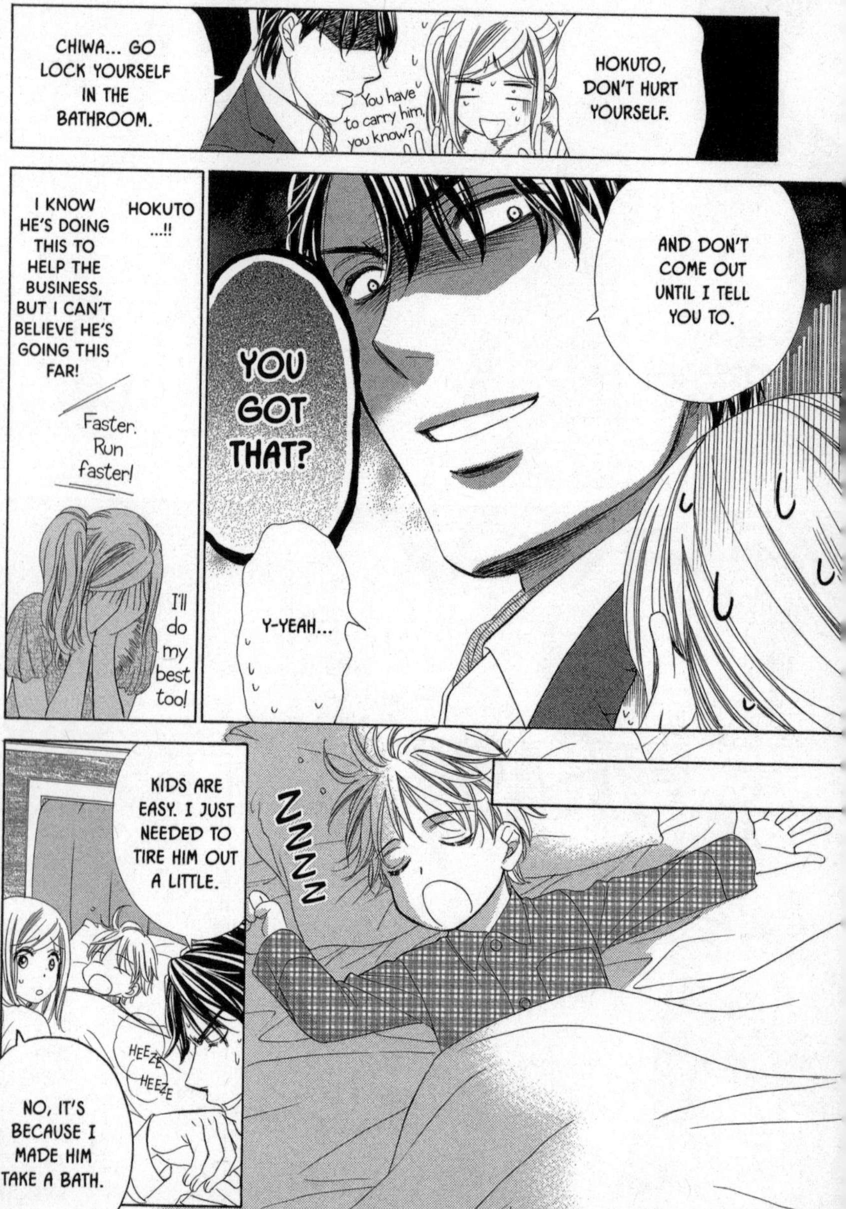
HOKUTO, DON'T HURT YOURSELF.
You have to carry him, you know?
CHIWA... GO LOCK YOURSELF IN THE BATHROOM.
AND DON'T COME OUT UNTIL I TELL YOU TO.
YOU GOT THAT?
Y-YEAH...
HOKUTO ...!!
I KNOW HE'S DOING THIS TO HELP THE BUSINESS, BUT I CAN'T BELIEVE HE'S GOING THIS FAR!
Faster. Run faster!
I'll do my best too!
ZZZZ
KIDS ARE EASY. I JUST NEEDED TO TIRE HIM OUT A LITTLE.
HEEZE
HEEZE
NO, IT'S BECAUSE I MADE HIM TAKE A BATH.

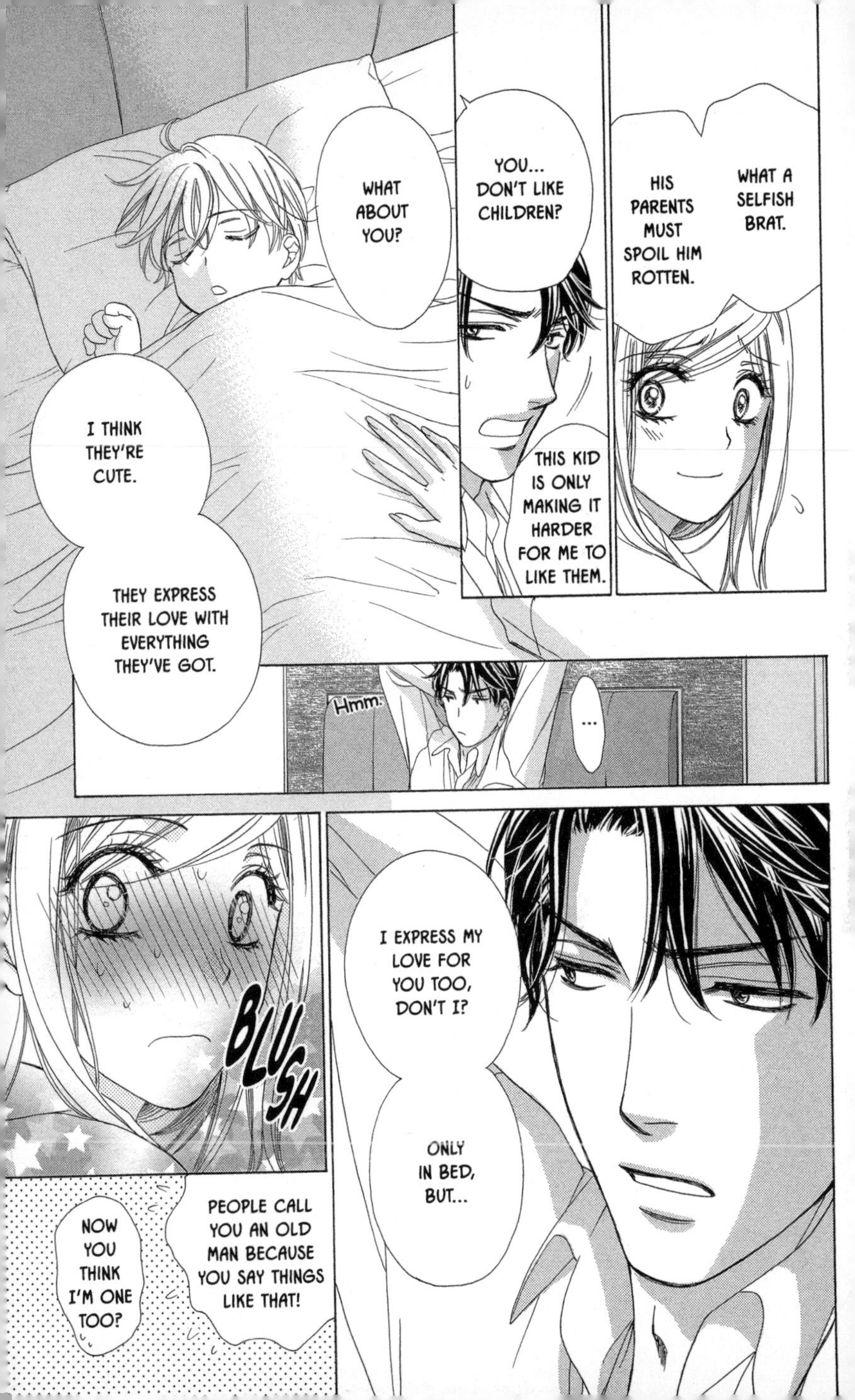
WHAT A SELFISH BRAT.
HIS PARENTS MUST SPOIL HIM ROTTEN.
YOU... DON'T LIKE CHILDREN?
THIS KID IS ONLY MAKING IT HARDER FOR ME TO LIKE THEM.
WHAT ABOUT YOU?
I THINK THEY'RE CUTE.
THEY EXPRESS THEIR LOVE WITH EVERYTHING THEY'VE GOT.
...
Hmm.
I EXPRESS MY LOVE FOR YOU TOO, DON'T I?
ONLY IN BED, BUT...
BLUSH
PEOPLE CALL YOU AN OLD MAN BECAUSE YOU SAY THINGS LIKE THAT!
NOW YOU THINK I'M ONE TOO?

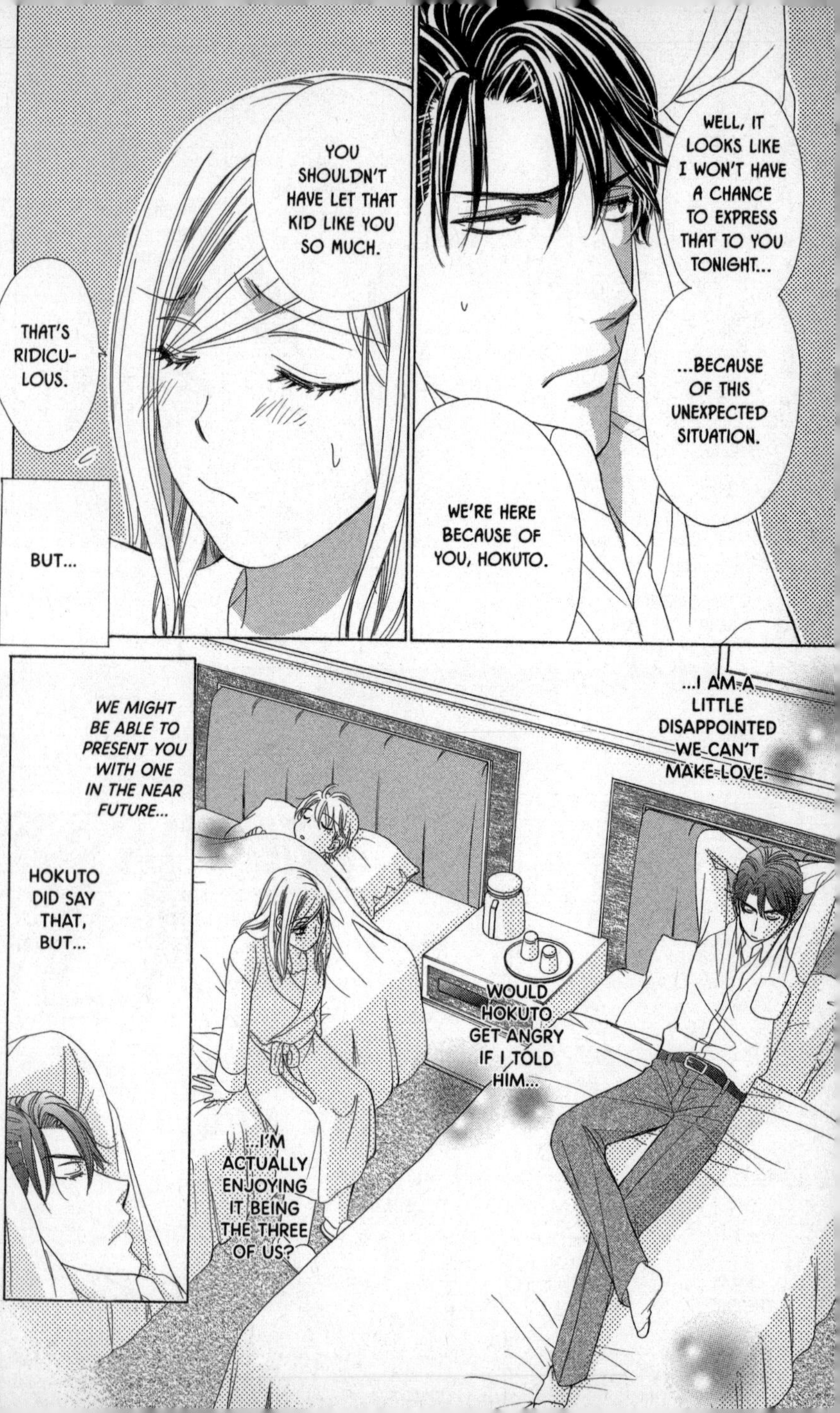
WELL, IT LOOKS LIKE I WON'T HAVE A CHANCE TO EXPRESS THAT TO YOU TONIGHT...
...BECAUSE OF THIS UNEXPECTED SITUATION.
WE'RE HERE BECAUSE OF YOU, HOKUTO.
YOU SHOULDN'T HAVE LET THAT KID LIKE YOU SO MUCH.
THAT'S RIDICULOUS.
BUT...
...I AM A LITTLE DISAPPOINTED WE CAN'T MAKE LOVE.
WE MIGHT BE ABLE TO PRESENT YOU WITH ONE IN THE NEAR FUTURE...
HOKUTO DID SAY THAT, BUT...
WOULD HOKUTO GET ANGRY IF I TOLD HIM...
...I'M ACTUALLY ENJOYING IT BEING THE THREE OF US?

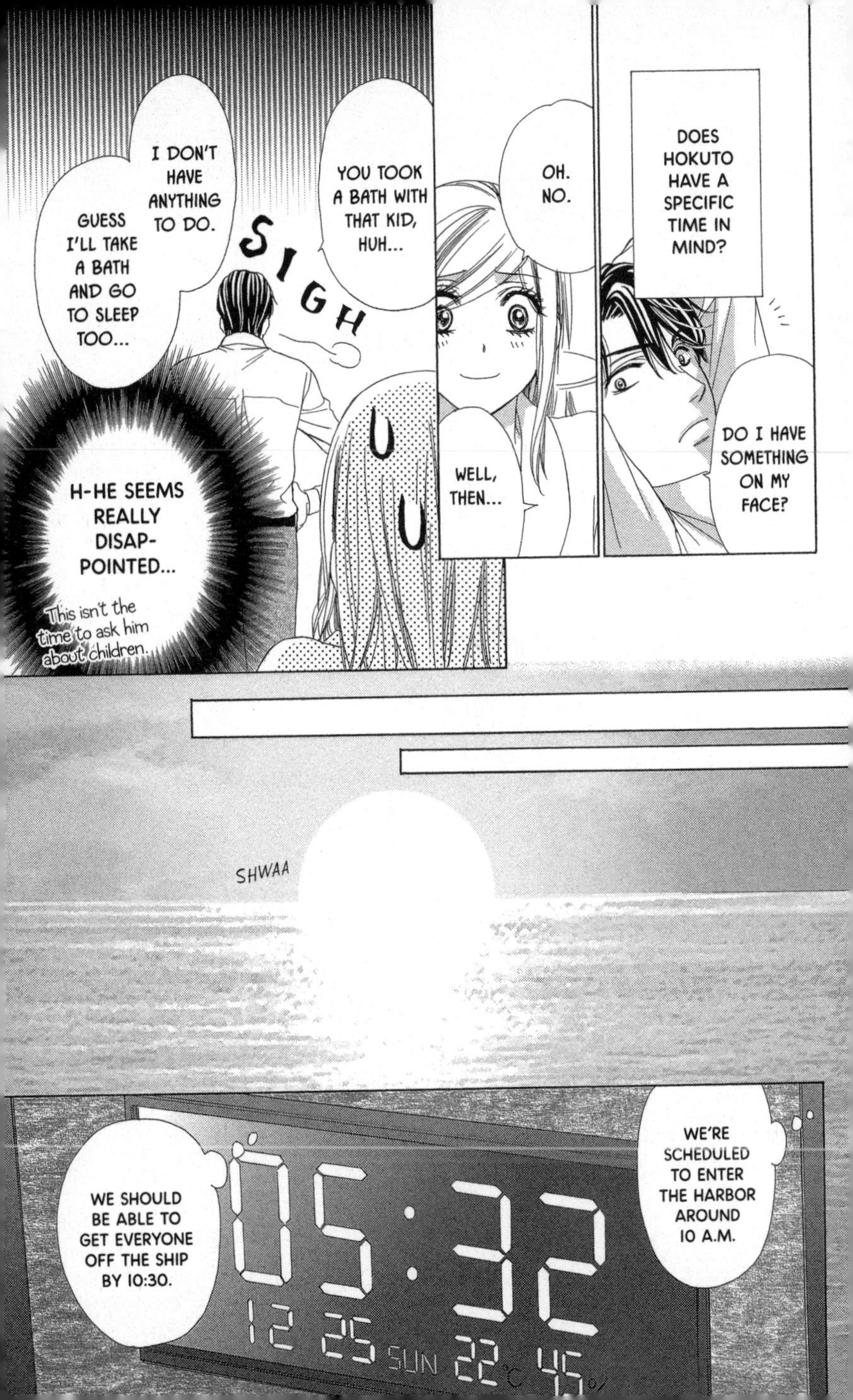
DOES HOKUTO HAVE A SPECIFIC TIME IN MIND?
DO I HAVE SOMETHING ON MY FACE?
OH. NO.
WELL, THEN...
YOU TOOK A BATH WITH THAT KID, HUH...
SIGH
I DON'T HAVE ANYTHING TO DO.
GUESS I'LL TAKE A BATH AND GO TO SLEEP TOO...
H-HE SEEMS REALLY DISAP-POINTED...
This isn't the time to ask him about children.
SHWAA
WE'RE SCHEDULED TO ENTER THE HARBOR AROUND 10 A.M.
05:32
12 25 SUN 22°C 45
WE SHOULD BE ABLE TO GET EVERYONE OFF THE SHIP BY 10:30.

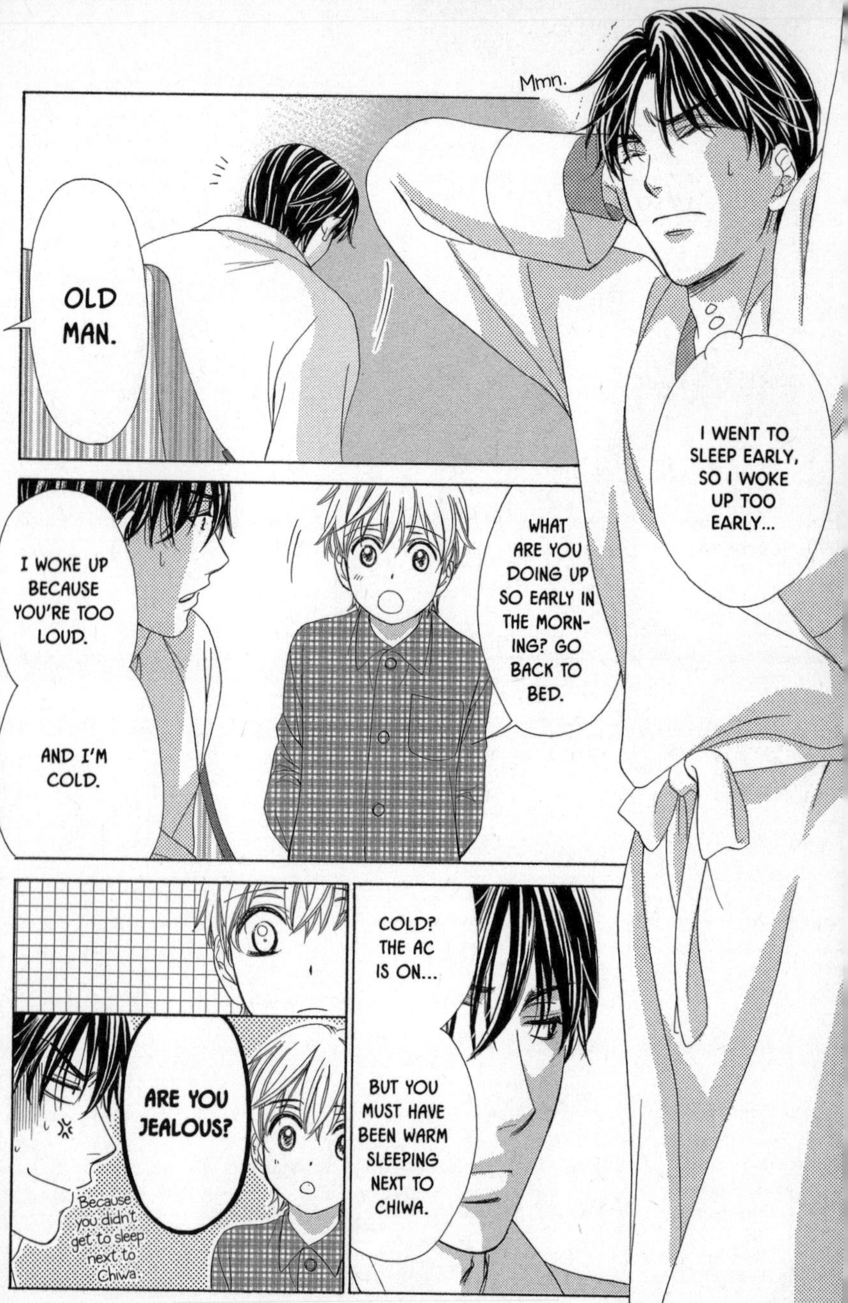
Mmn.
I WENT TO SLEEP EARLY, SO I WOKE UP TOO EARLY...
OLD MAN.
WHAT ARE YOU DOING UP SO EARLY IN THE MORNING? GO BACK TO BED.
I WOKE UP BECAUSE YOU'RE TOO LOUD.
AND I'M COLD.
COLD? THE AC IS ON...
BUT YOU MUST HAVE BEEN WARM SLEEPING NEXT TO CHIWA.
ARE YOU JEALOUS?
Because you didn't get to sleep next to Chiwa.

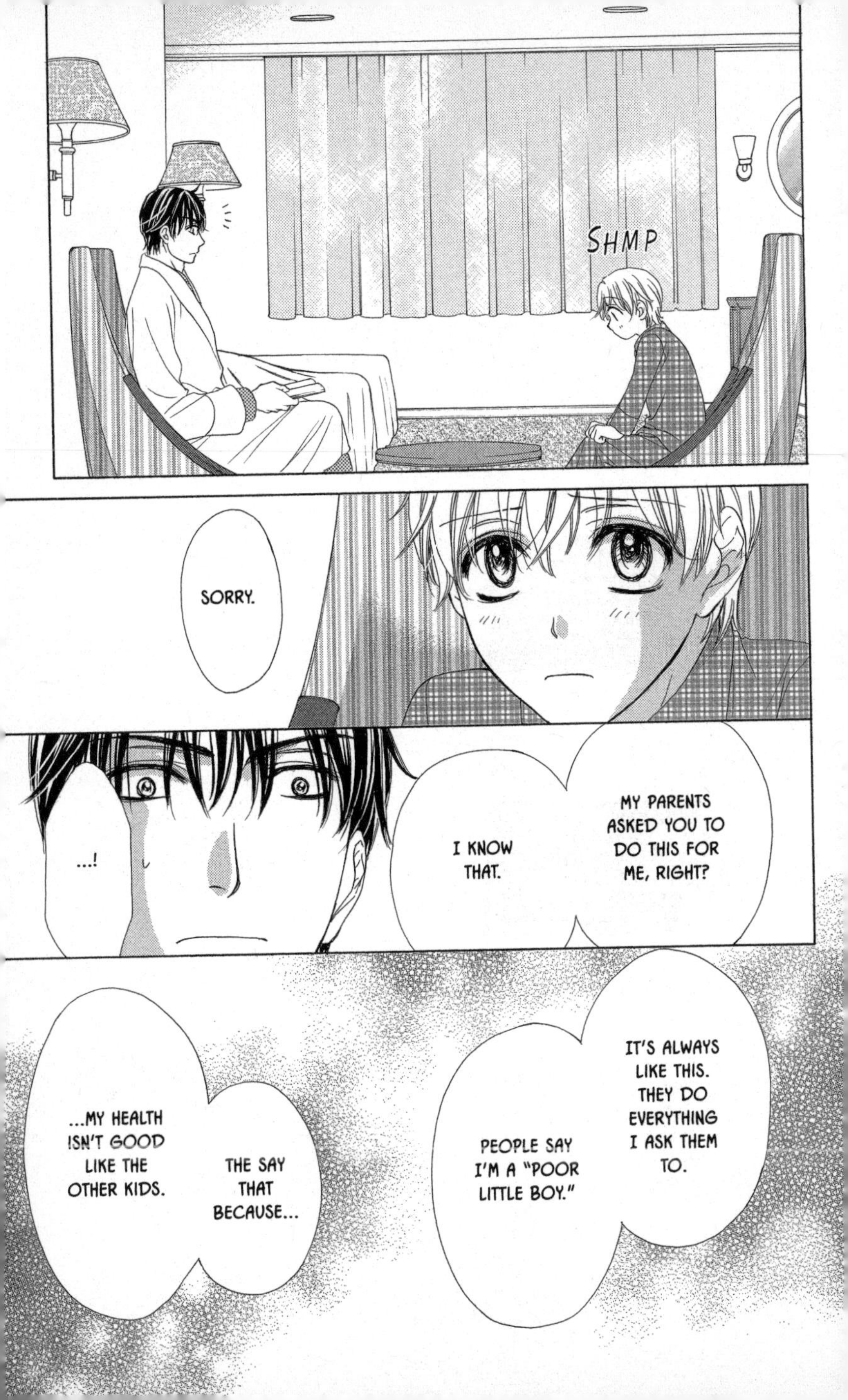
SHMP
SORRY.
MY PARENTS ASKED YOU TO DO THIS FOR ME, RIGHT?
I KNOW THAT.
...!
IT'S ALWAYS LIKE THIS. THEY DO EVERYTHING I ASK THEM TO.
PEOPLE SAY I'M A "POOR LITTLE BOY."
THE SAY THAT BECAUSE...
...MY HEALTH ISN'T GOOD LIKE THE OTHER KIDS.

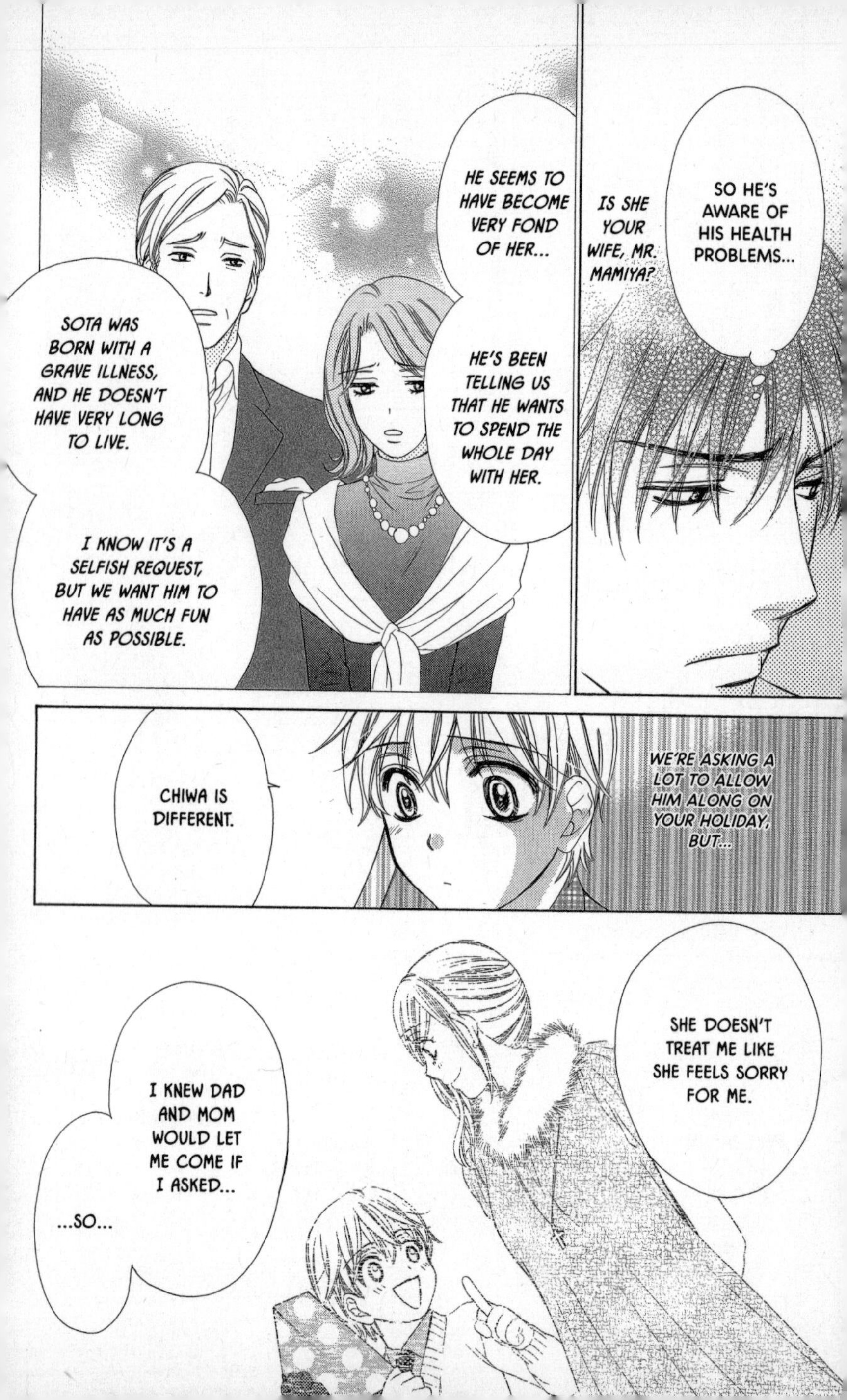
SO HE'S AWARE OF HIS HEALTH PROBLEMS...
IS SHE YOUR WIFE, MR. MAMIYA?
HE SEEMS TO HAVE BECOME VERY FOND OF HER...
HE'S BEEN TELLING US THAT HE WANTS TO SPEND THE WHOLE DAY WITH HER.
SOTA WAS BORN WITH A GRAVE ILLNESS, AND HE DOESN'T HAVE VERY LONG TO LIVE.
I KNOW IT'S A SELFISH REQUEST, BUT WE WANT HIM TO HAVE AS MUCH FUN AS POSSIBLE.
WE'RE ASKING A LOT TO ALLOW HIM ALONG ON YOUR HOLIDAY, BUT...
CHIWA IS DIFFERENT.
SHE DOESN'T TREAT ME LIKE SHE FEELS SORRY FOR ME.
I KNEW DAD AND MOM WOULD LET ME COME IF I ASKED...
...SO...

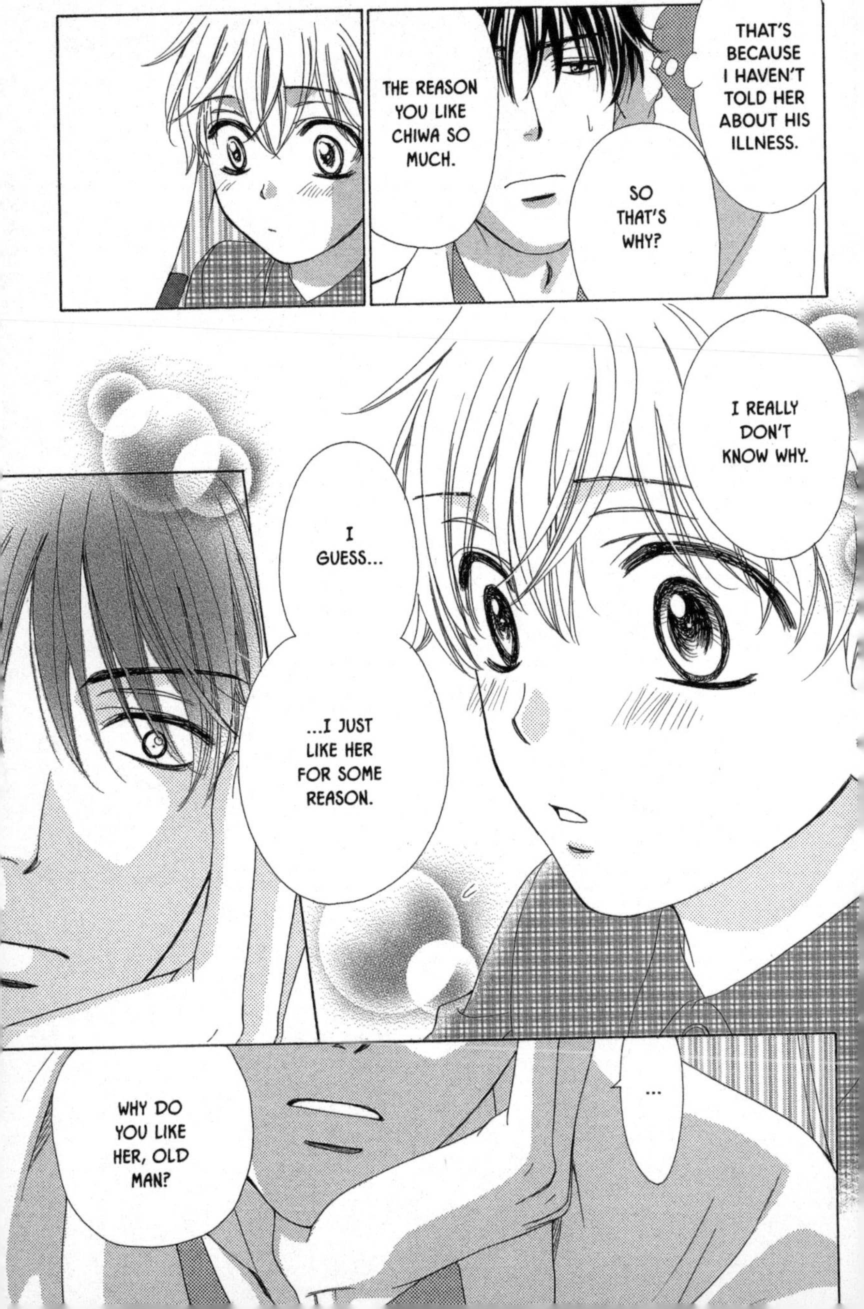
THAT'S BECAUSE I HAVEN'T TOLD HER ABOUT HIS ILLNESS.
SO THAT'S WHY?
THE REASON YOU LIKE CHIWA SO MUCH.
I REALLY DON'T KNOW WHY.
I GUESS...
...I JUST LIKE HER FOR SOME REASON.
...
WHY DO YOU LIKE HER, OLD MAN?

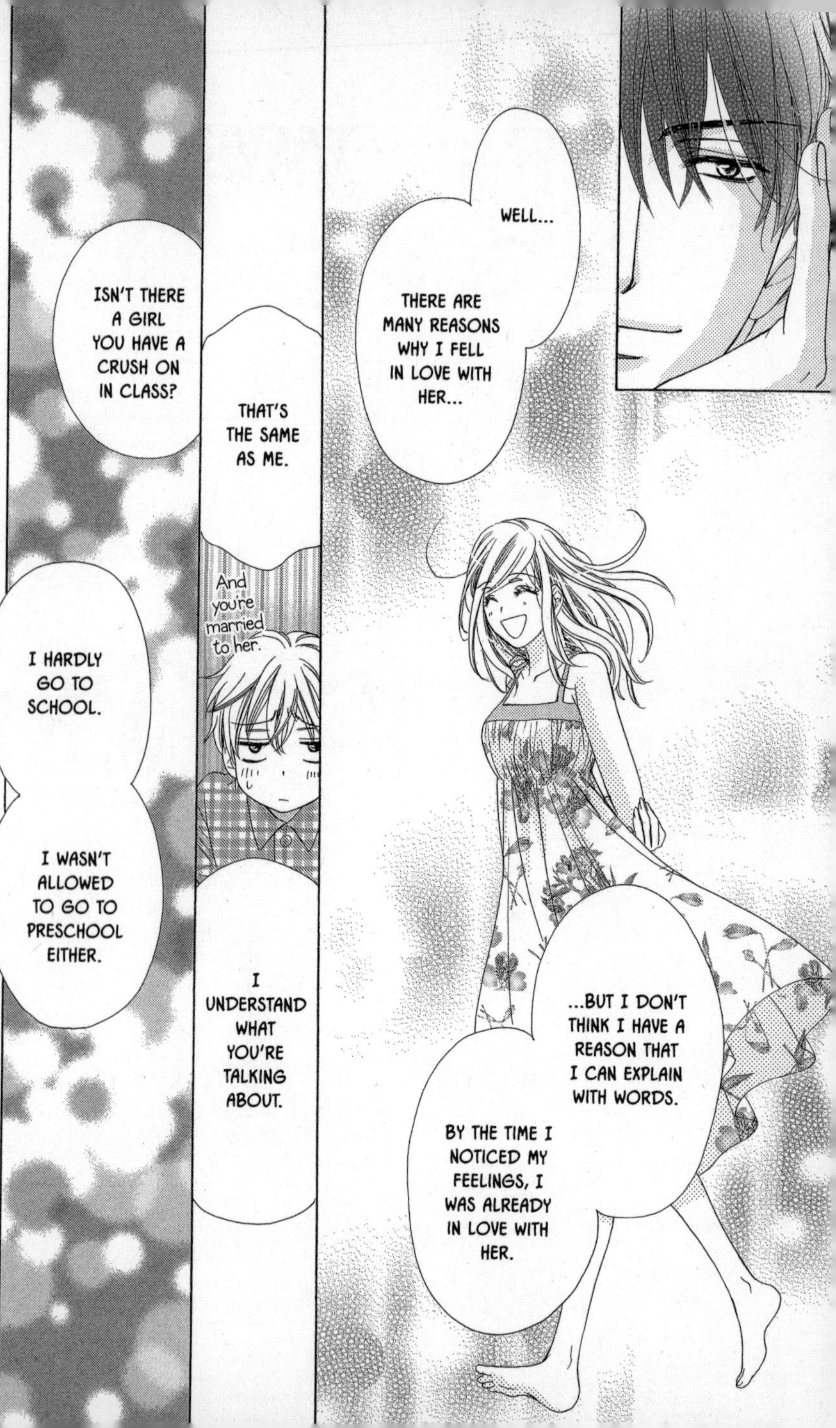
WELL...
THERE ARE MANY REASONS WHY I FELL IN LOVE WITH HER...
...BUT I DON'T THINK I HAVE A REASON THAT I CAN EXPLAIN WITH WORDS.
BY THE TIME I NOTICED MY FEELINGS, I WAS ALREADY IN LOVE WITH HER.
THAT'S THE SAME AS ME.
And you're married to her.
I UNDERSTAND WHAT YOU'RE TALKING ABOUT.
ISN'T THERE A GIRL YOU HAVE A CRUSH ON IN CLASS?
I HARDLY GO TO SCHOOL.
I WASN'T ALLOWED TO GO TO PRESCHOOL EITHER.

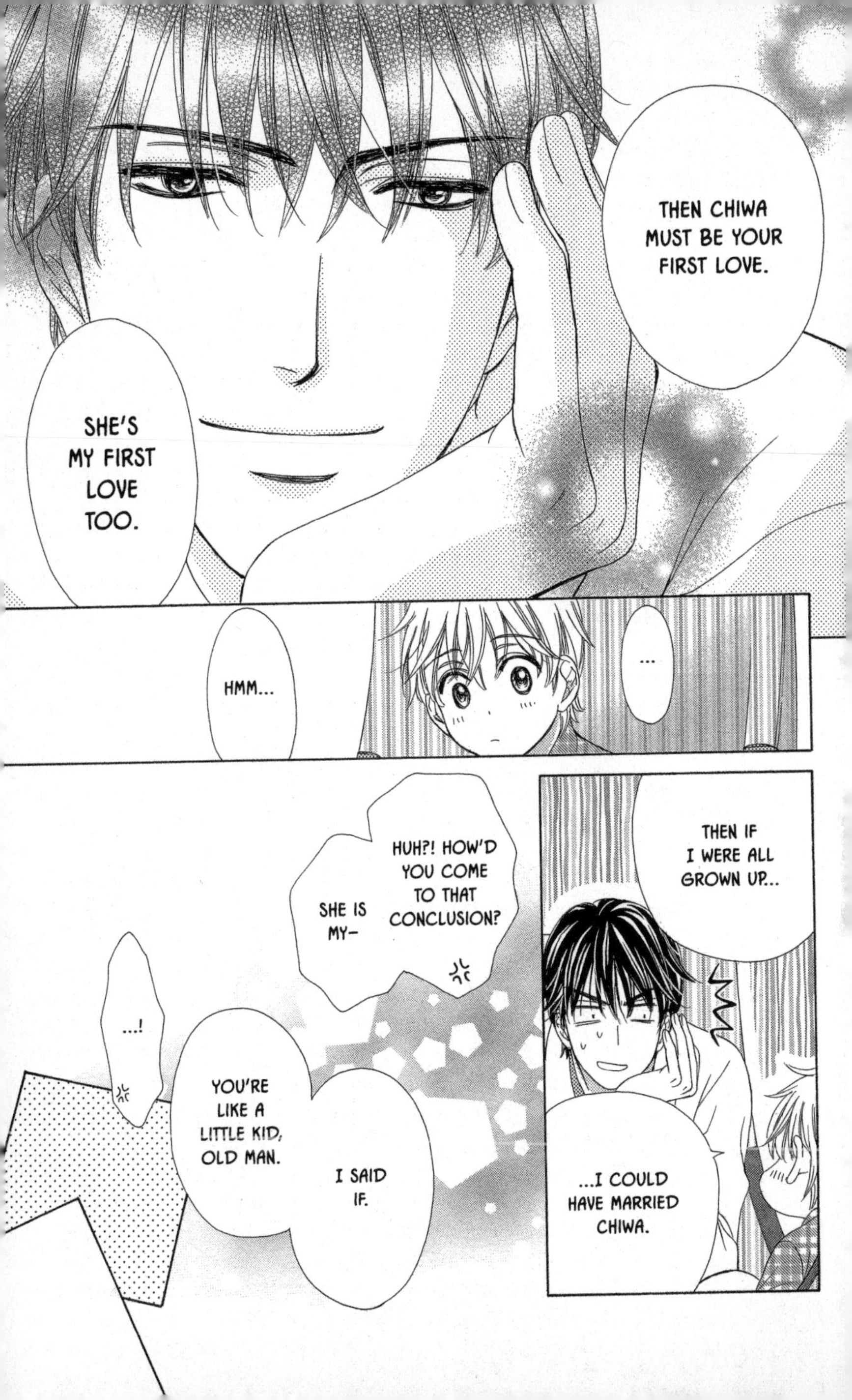
THEN CHIWA MUST BE YOUR FIRST LOVE.
SHE'S MY FIRST LOVE TOO.
...
HMM...
THEN IF I WERE ALL GROWN UP...
...I COULD HAVE MARRIED CHIWA.
HUH?! HOW'D YOU COME TO THAT CONCLUSION?
SHE IS MY—
I SAID IF.
YOU'RE LIKE A LITTLE KID, OLD MAN.
...!

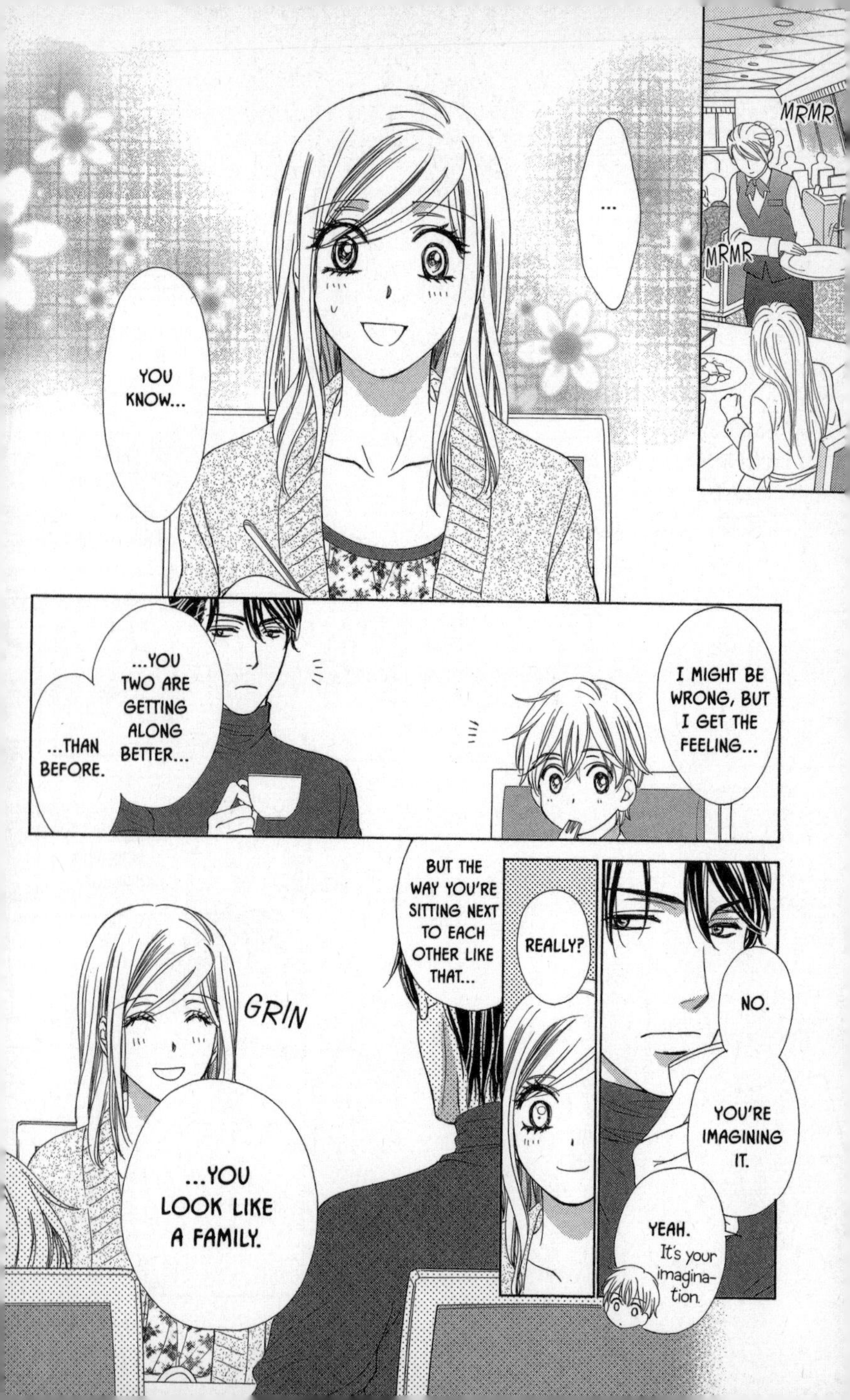
MRMR
MRMR
...
YOU KNOW...
I MIGHT BE WRONG, BUT I GET THE FEELING...
...YOU TWO ARE GETTING ALONG BETTER...
...THAN BEFORE.
NO.
YOU'RE IMAGINING IT.
YEAH.
It's your imagination.
REALLY?
BUT THE WAY YOU'RE SITTING NEXT TO EACH OTHER LIKE THAT...
GRIN
...YOU LOOK LIKE A FAMILY.

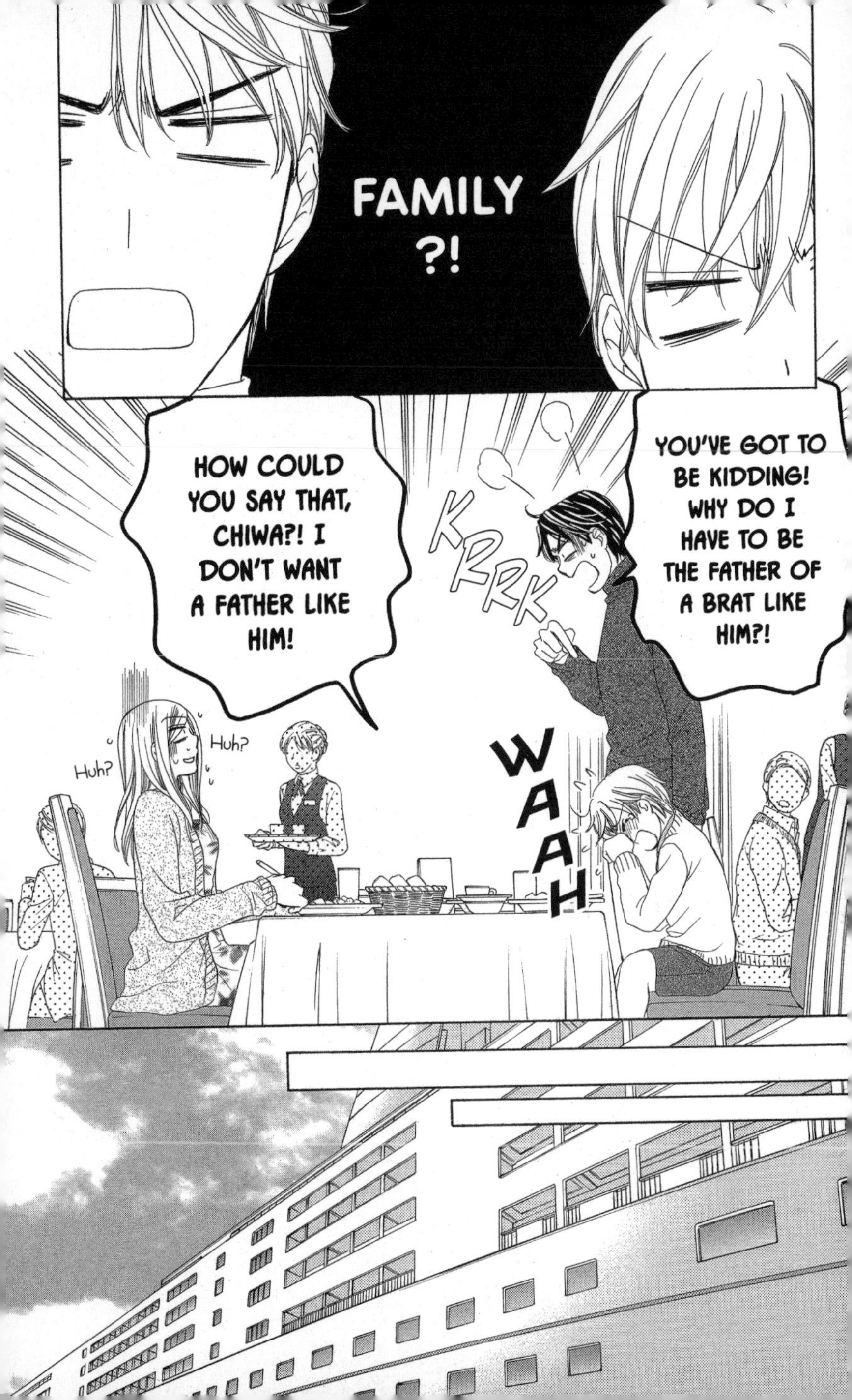
FAMILY ?!
YOU'VE GOT TO BE KIDDING! WHY DO I HAVE TO BE THE FATHER OF A BRAT LIKE HIM?!
KRRK
HOW COULD YOU SAY THAT, CHIWA?! I DON'T WANT A FATHER LIKE HIM!
WAAAH
Huh?
Huh?

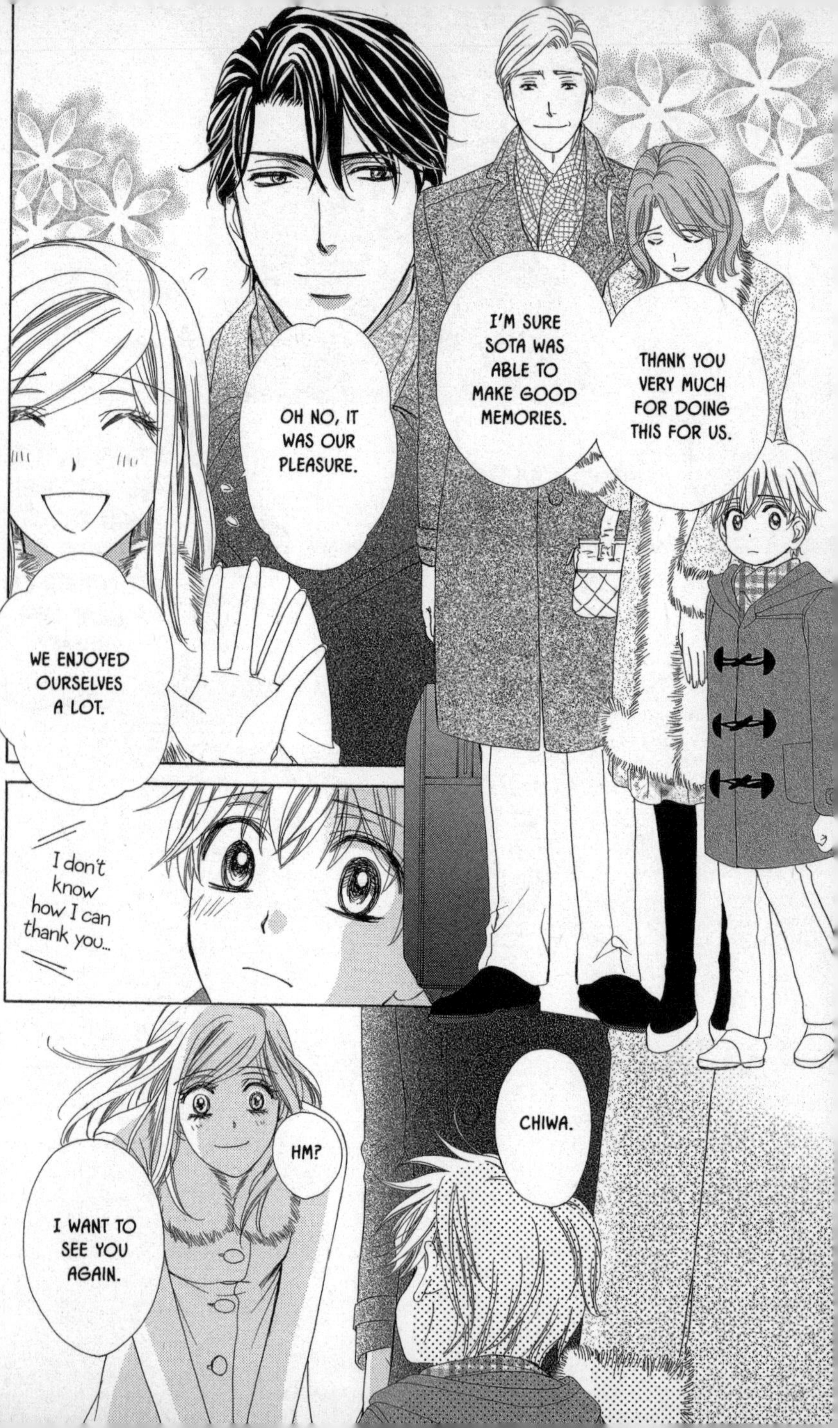
THANK YOU VERY MUCH FOR DOING THIS FOR US.
I'M SURE SOTA WAS ABLE TO MAKE GOOD MEMORIES.
OH NO, IT WAS OUR PLEASURE.
WE ENJOYED OURSELVES A LOT.
I don't know how I can thank you...
CHIWA.
HM?
I WANT TO SEE YOU AGAIN.

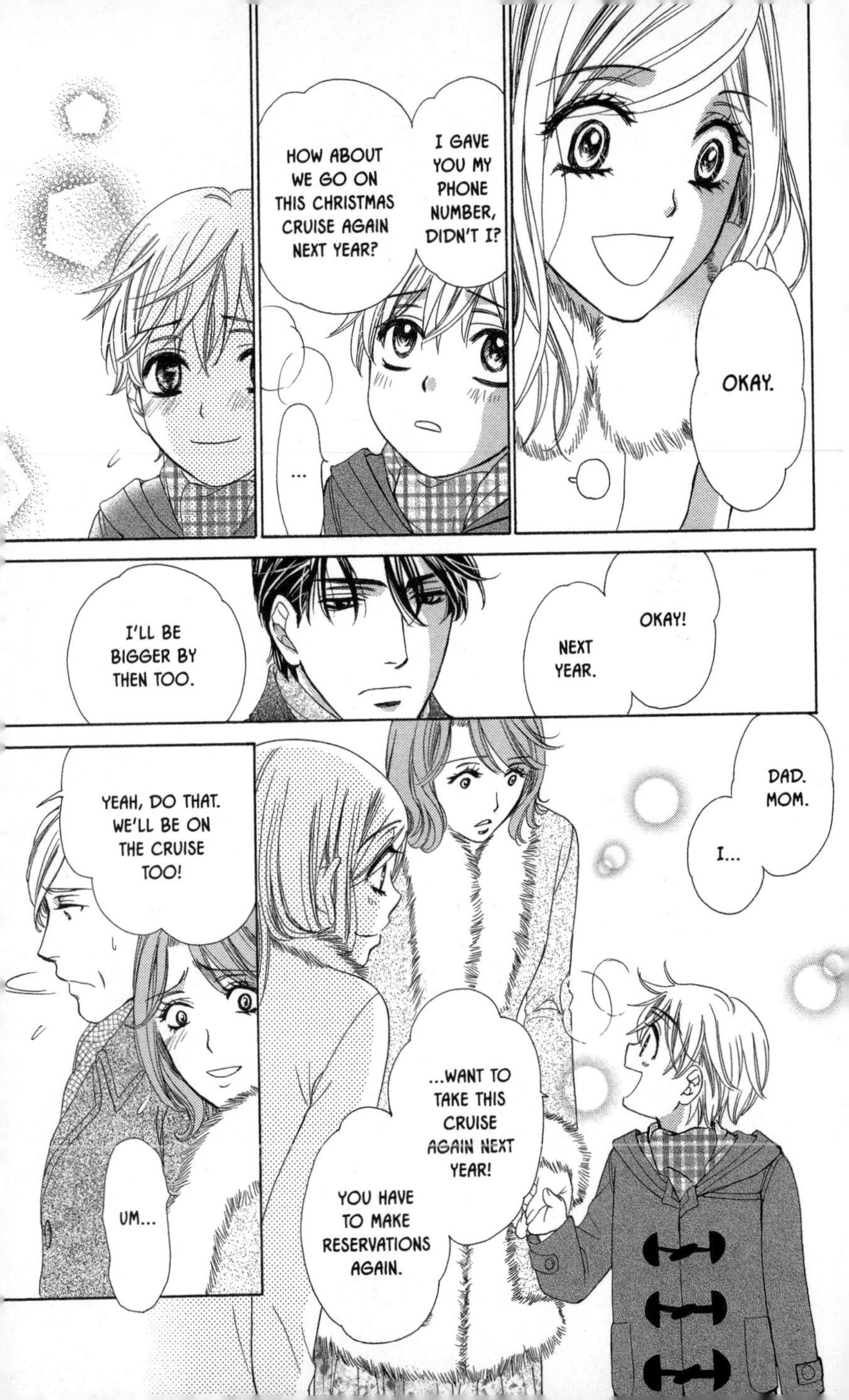
OKAY.
I GAVE YOU MY PHONE NUMBER, DIDN'T I?
HOW ABOUT WE GO ON THIS CHRISTMAS CRUISE AGAIN NEXT YEAR?
...
OKAY!
NEXT YEAR.
I'LL BE BIGGER BY THEN TOO.
DAD. MOM.
I...
...WANT TO TAKE THIS CRUISE AGAIN NEXT YEAR!
YOU HAVE TO MAKE RESERVATIONS AGAIN.
YEAH, DO THAT. WE'LL BE ON THE CRUISE TOO!
UM...

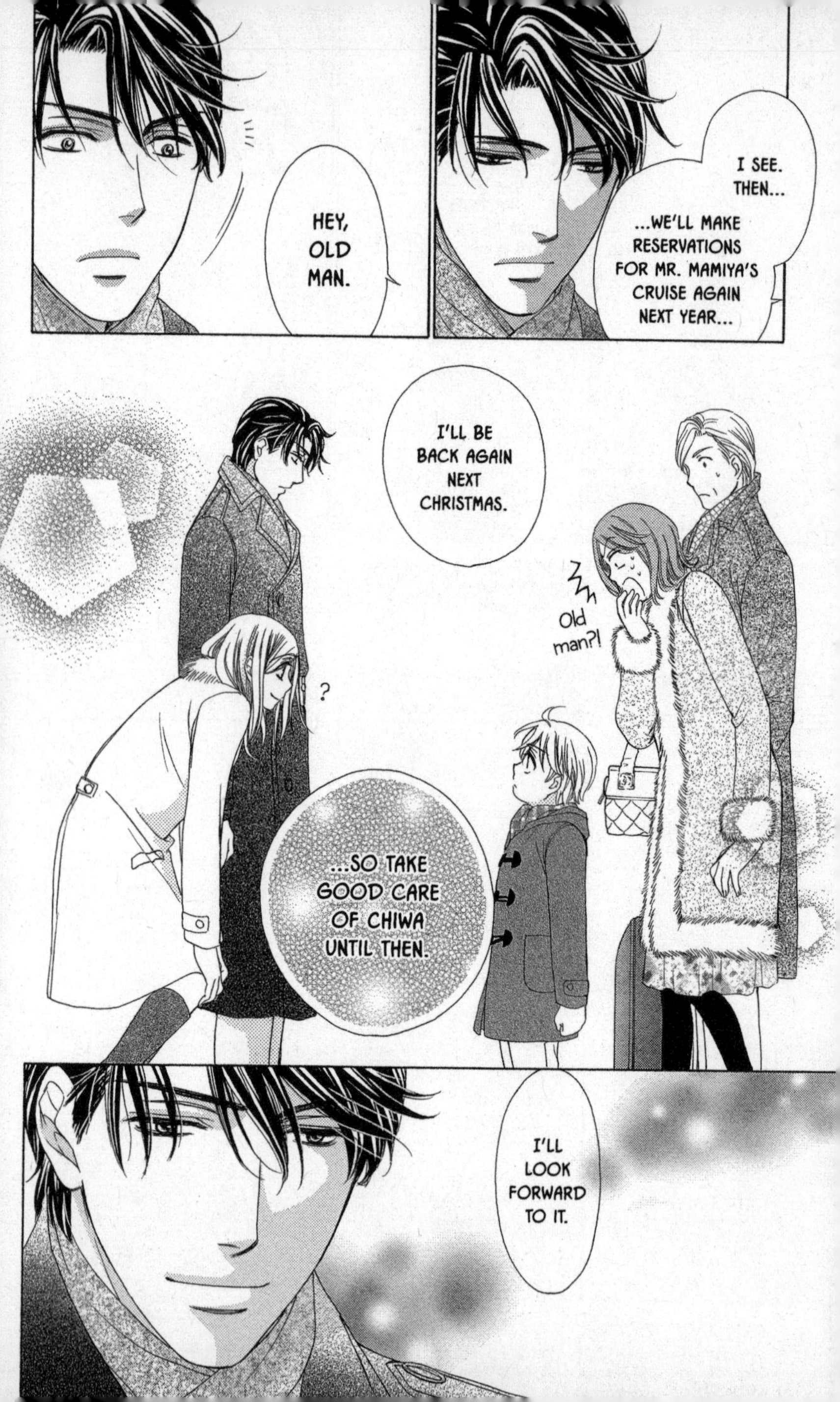
I SEE. THEN...
...WE'LL MAKE RESERVATIONS FOR MR. MAMIYA'S CRUISE AGAIN NEXT YEAR...
HEY, OLD MAN.
I'LL BE BACK AGAIN NEXT CHRISTMAS.
Old man?!
...SO TAKE GOOD CARE OF CHIWA UNTIL THEN.
I'LL LOOK FORWARD TO IT.

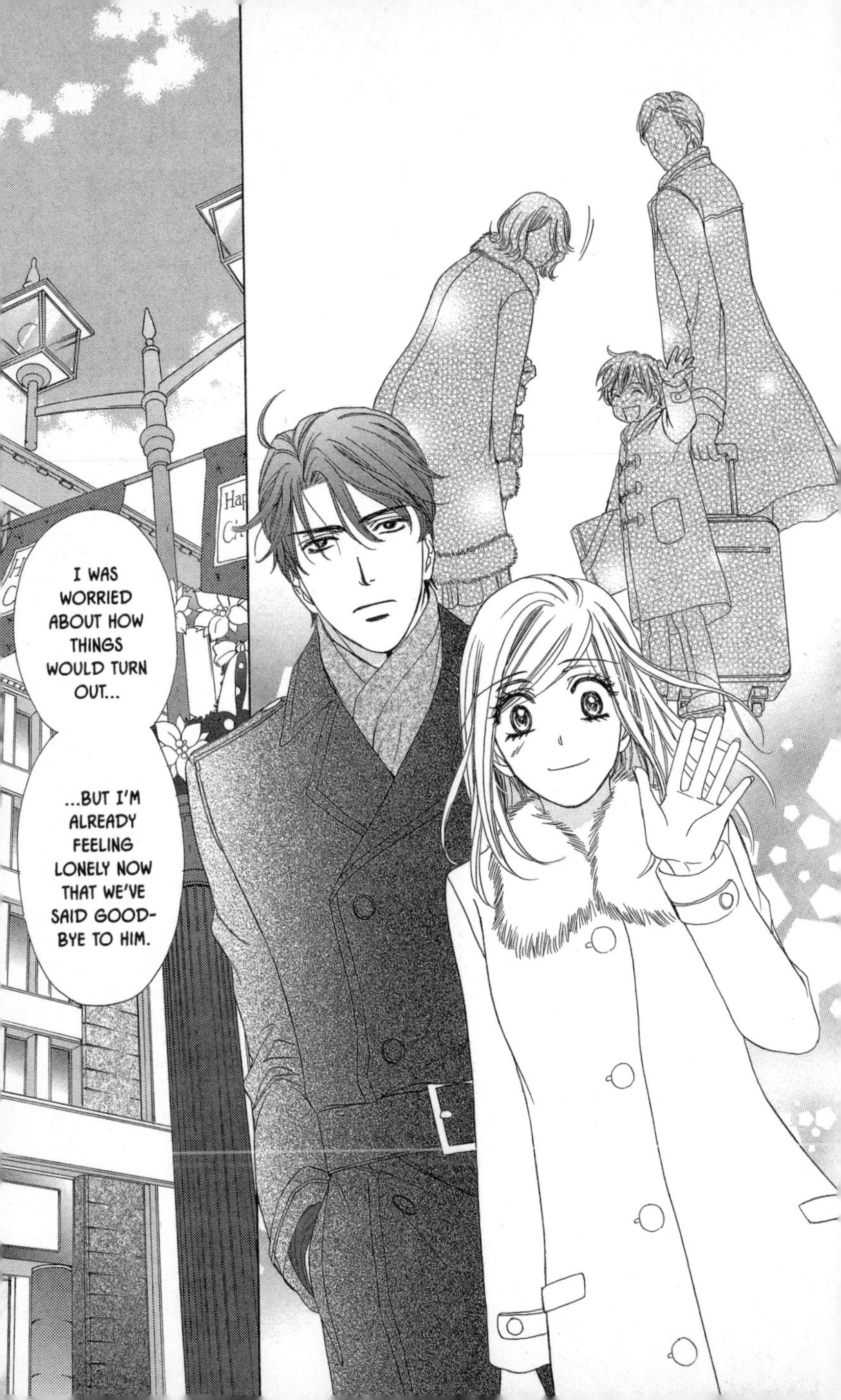
I WAS WORRIED ABOUT HOW THINGS WOULD TURN OUT...
...BUT I'M ALREADY FEELING LONELY NOW THAT WE'VE SAID GOOD-BYE TO HIM.

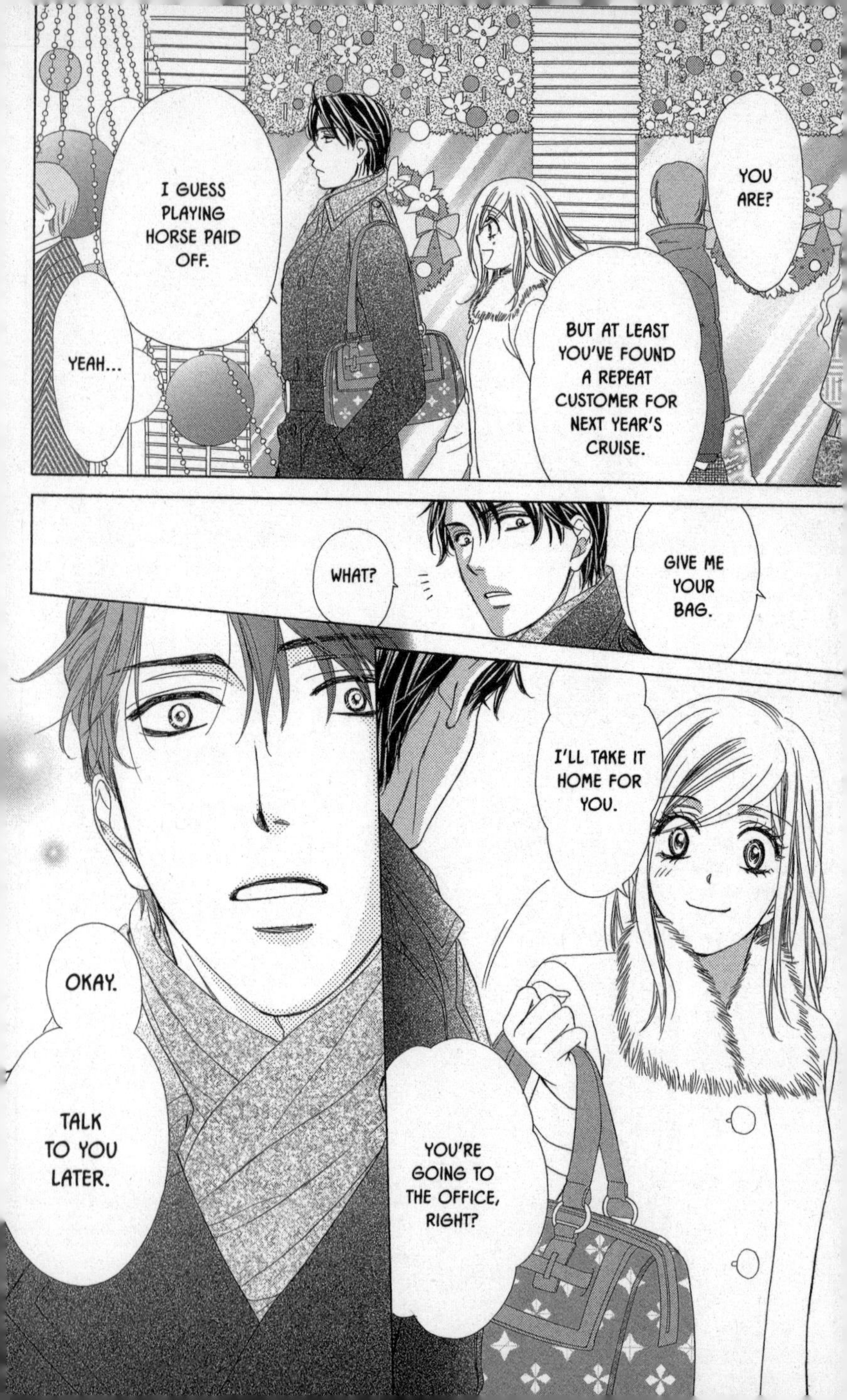
YOU ARE?
BUT AT LEAST YOU'VE FOUND A REPEAT CUSTOMER FOR NEXT YEAR'S CRUISE.
I GUESS PLAYING HORSE PAID OFF.
YEAH...
GIVE ME YOUR BAG.
WHAT?
I'LL TAKE IT HOME FOR YOU.
YOU'RE GOING TO THE OFFICE, RIGHT?
OKAY.
TALK TO YOU LATER.

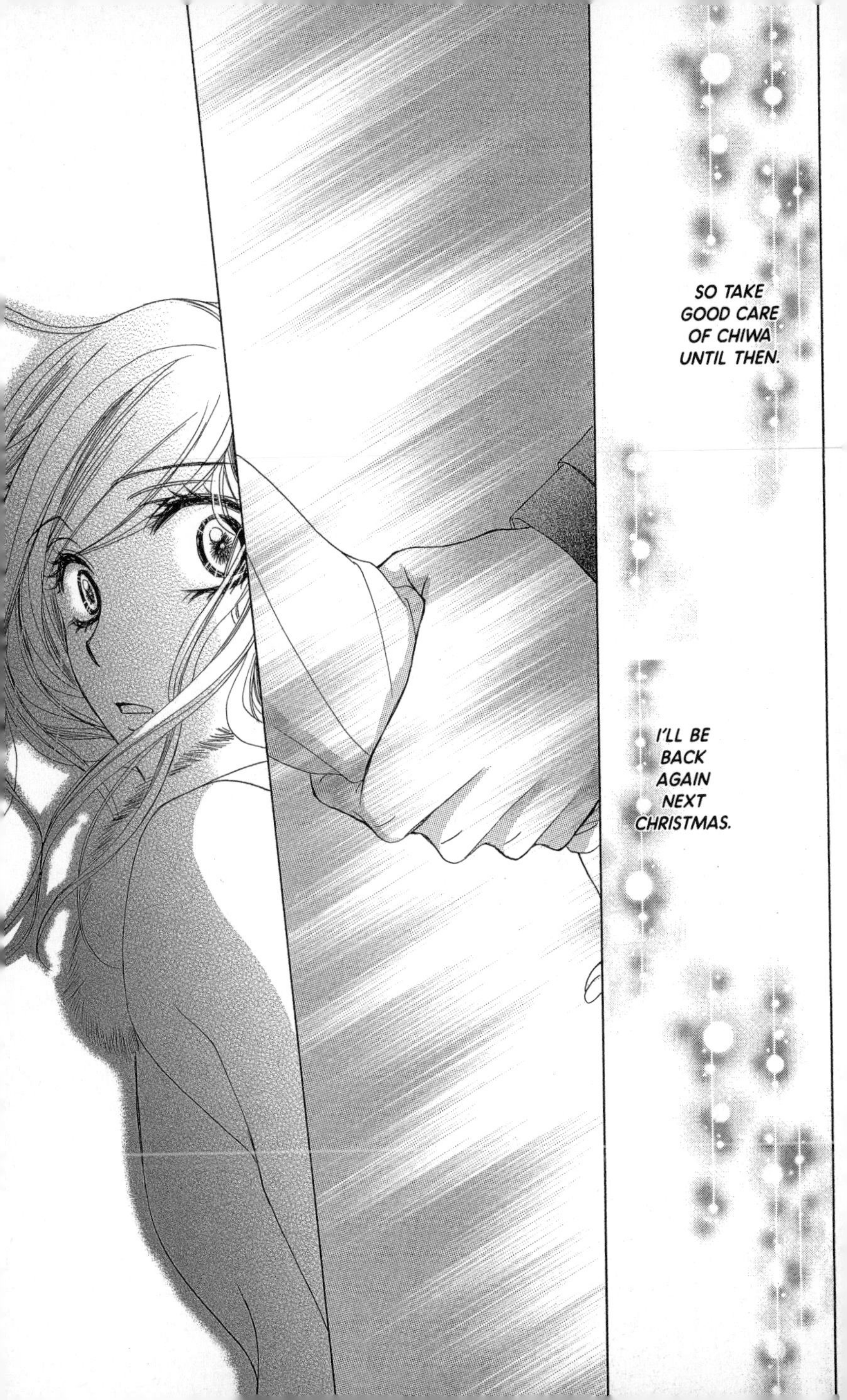
SO TAKE GOOD CARE OF CHIWA UNTIL THEN.
I'LL BE BACK AGAIN NEXT CHRISTMAS.

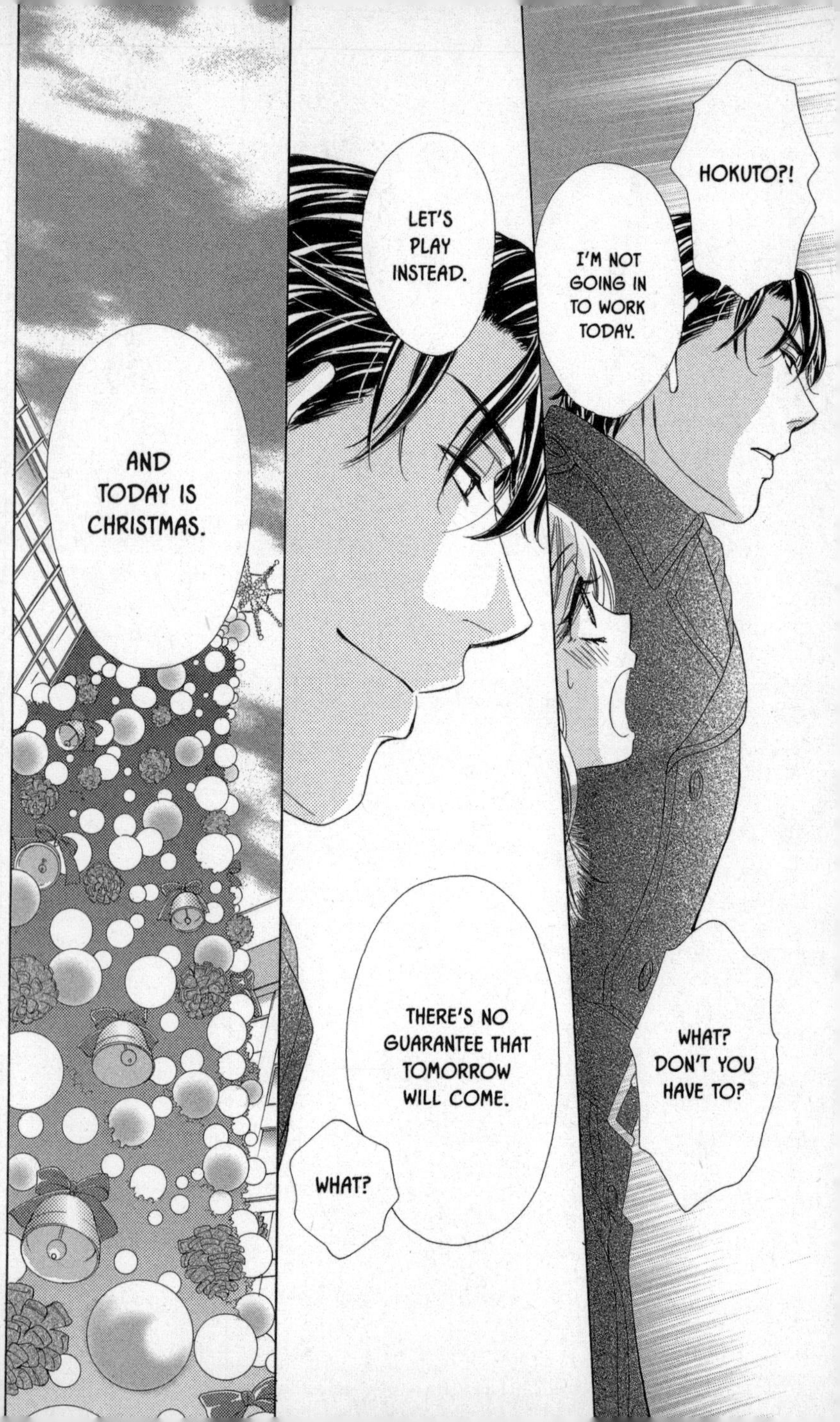
HOKUTO?!
I'M NOT GOING IN TO WORK TODAY.
WHAT? DON'T YOU HAVE TO?
LET'S PLAY INSTEAD.
THERE'S NO GUARANTEE THAT TOMORROW WILL COME.
WHAT?
AND TODAY IS CHRISTMAS.

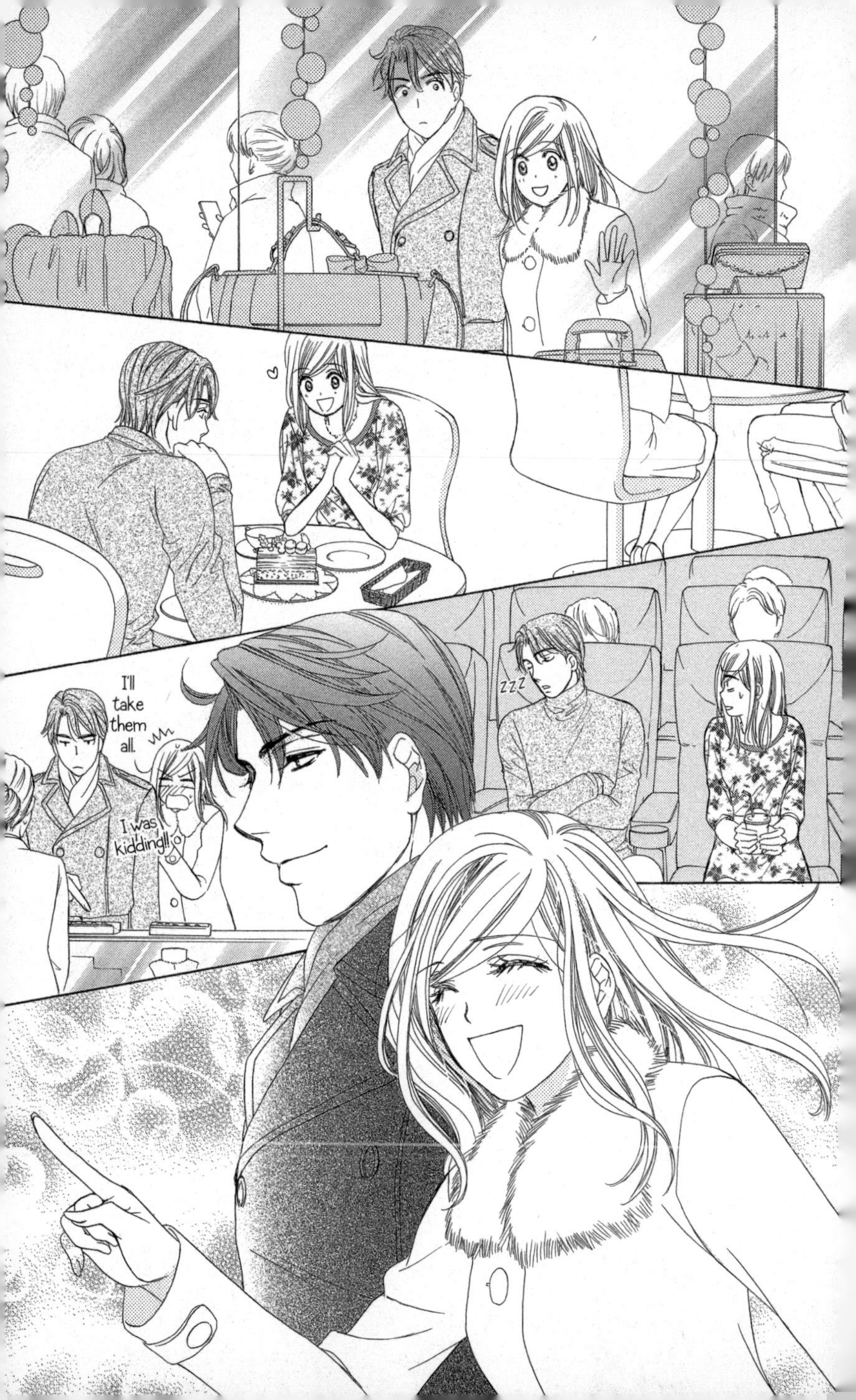
zzz
I'll take them all.
I was kidding!!

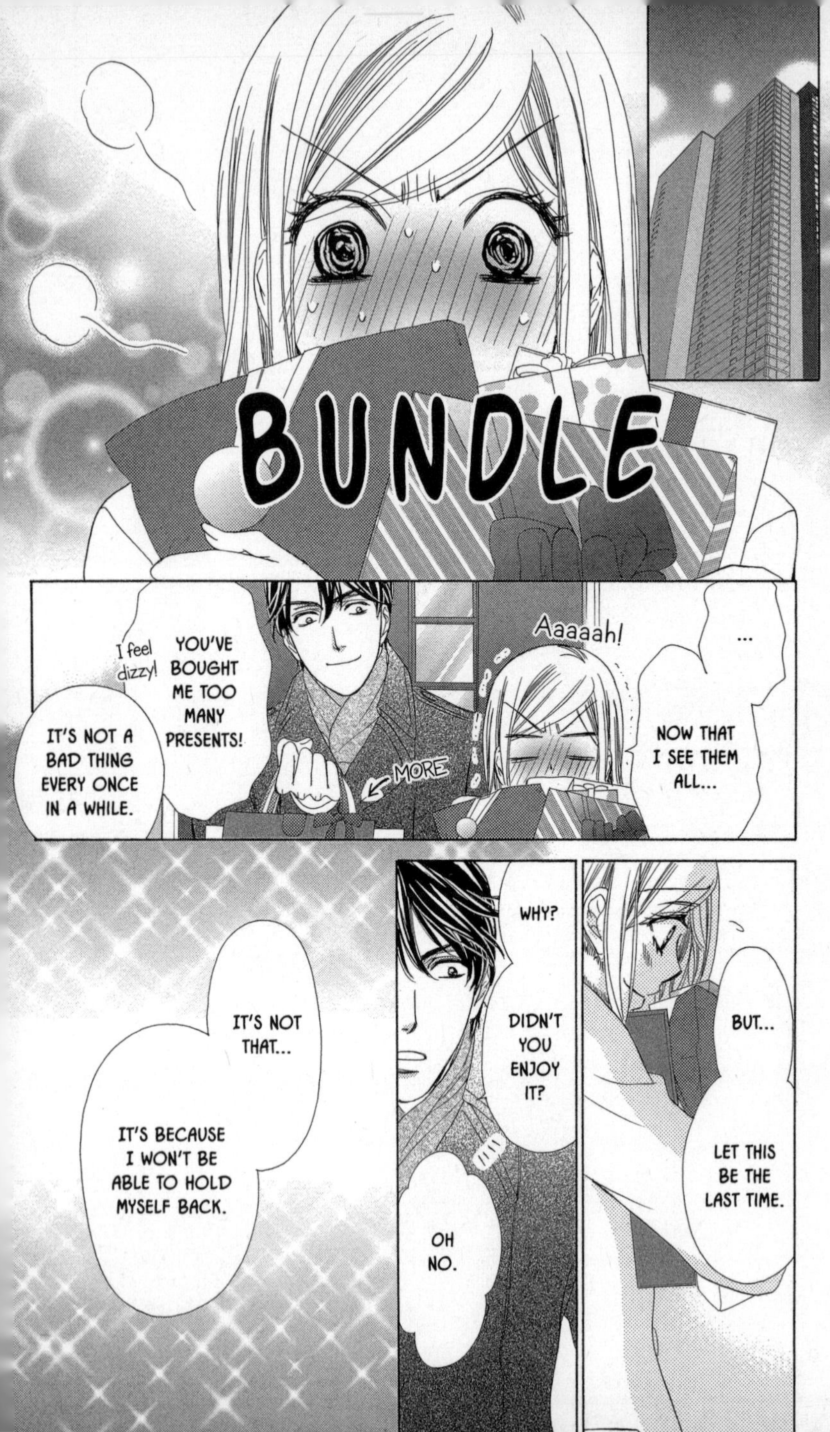
BUNDLE
...
Aaaaah!
NOW THAT I SEE THEM ALL...
YOU'VE BOUGHT ME TOO MANY PRESENTS!
I feel dizzy!
MORE
IT'S NOT A BAD THING EVERY ONCE IN A WHILE.
BUT...
LET THIS BE THE LAST TIME.
WHY?
DIDN'T YOU ENJOY IT?
OH NO.
IT'S NOT THAT...
IT'S BECAUSE I WON'T BE ABLE TO HOLD MYSELF BACK.

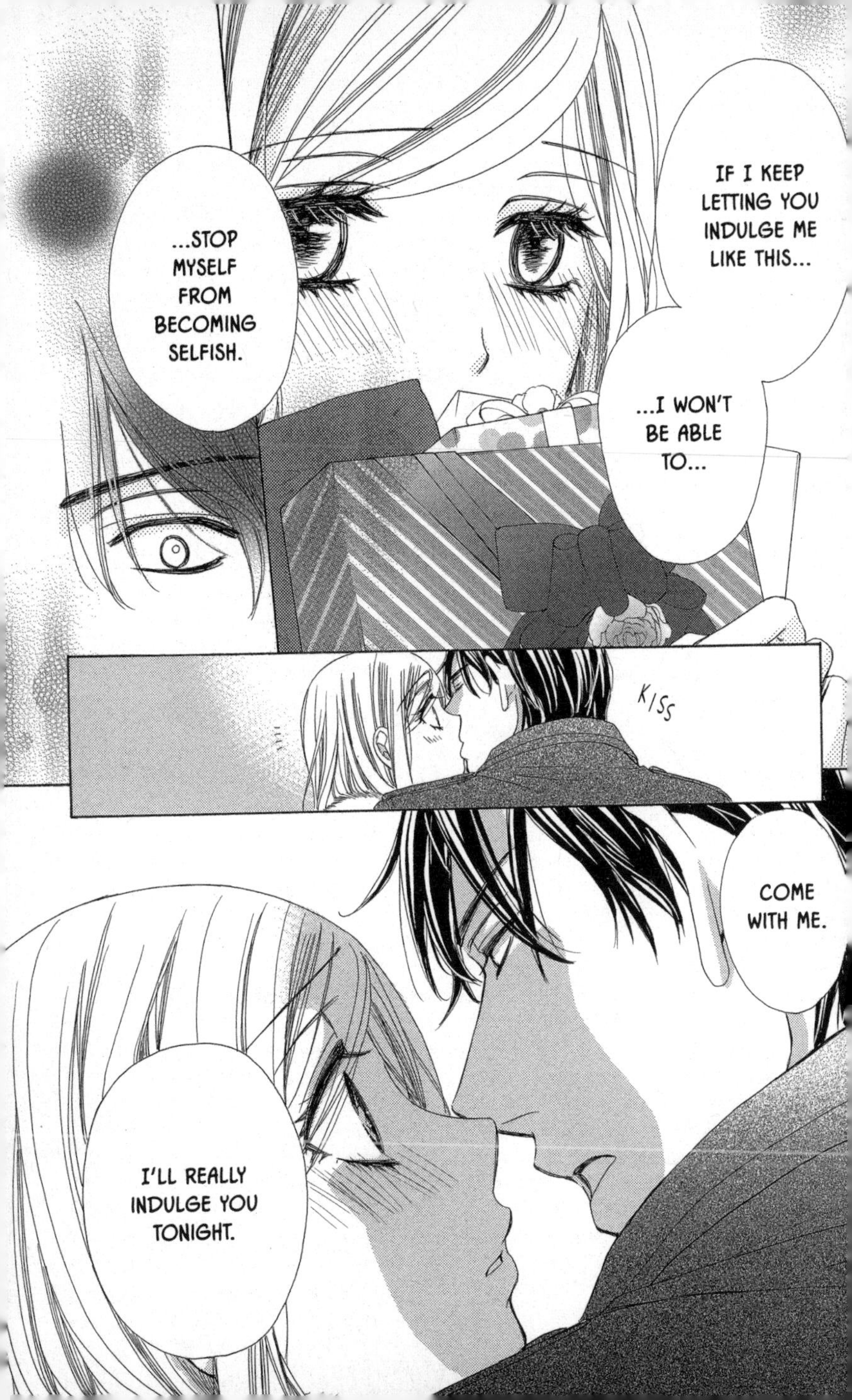
IF I KEEP LETTING YOU INDULGE ME LIKE THIS...
...I WON'T BE ABLE TO...
...STOP MYSELF FROM BECOMING SELFISH.
KISS
COME WITH ME.
I'LL REALLY INDULGE YOU TONIGHT.

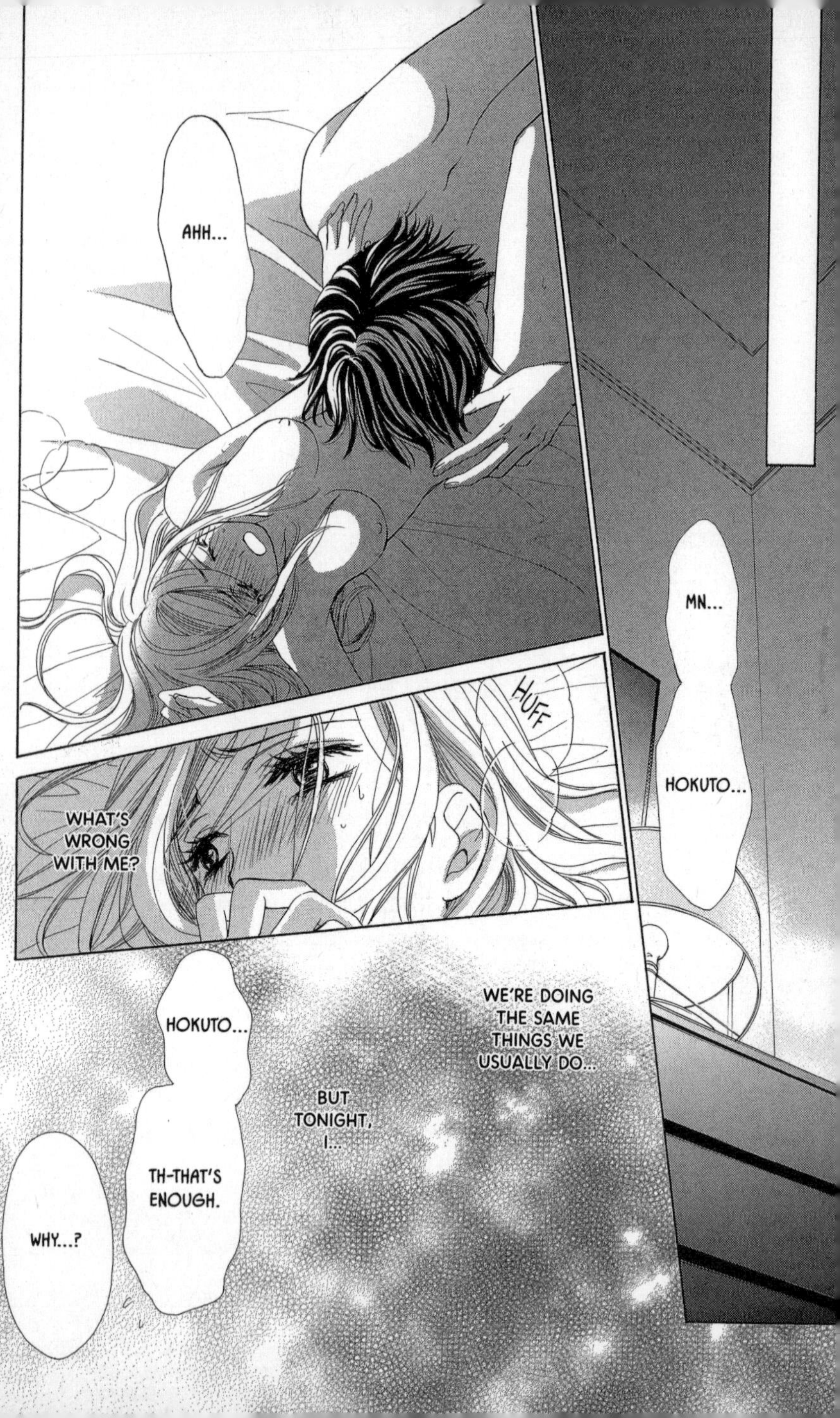
MN...
HOKUTO...
AHH...
HUFF
WHAT'S WRONG WITH ME?
WE'RE DOING THE SAME THINGS WE USUALLY DO...
BUT TONIGHT, I...
HOKUTO...
TH-THAT'S ENOUGH.
WHY...?

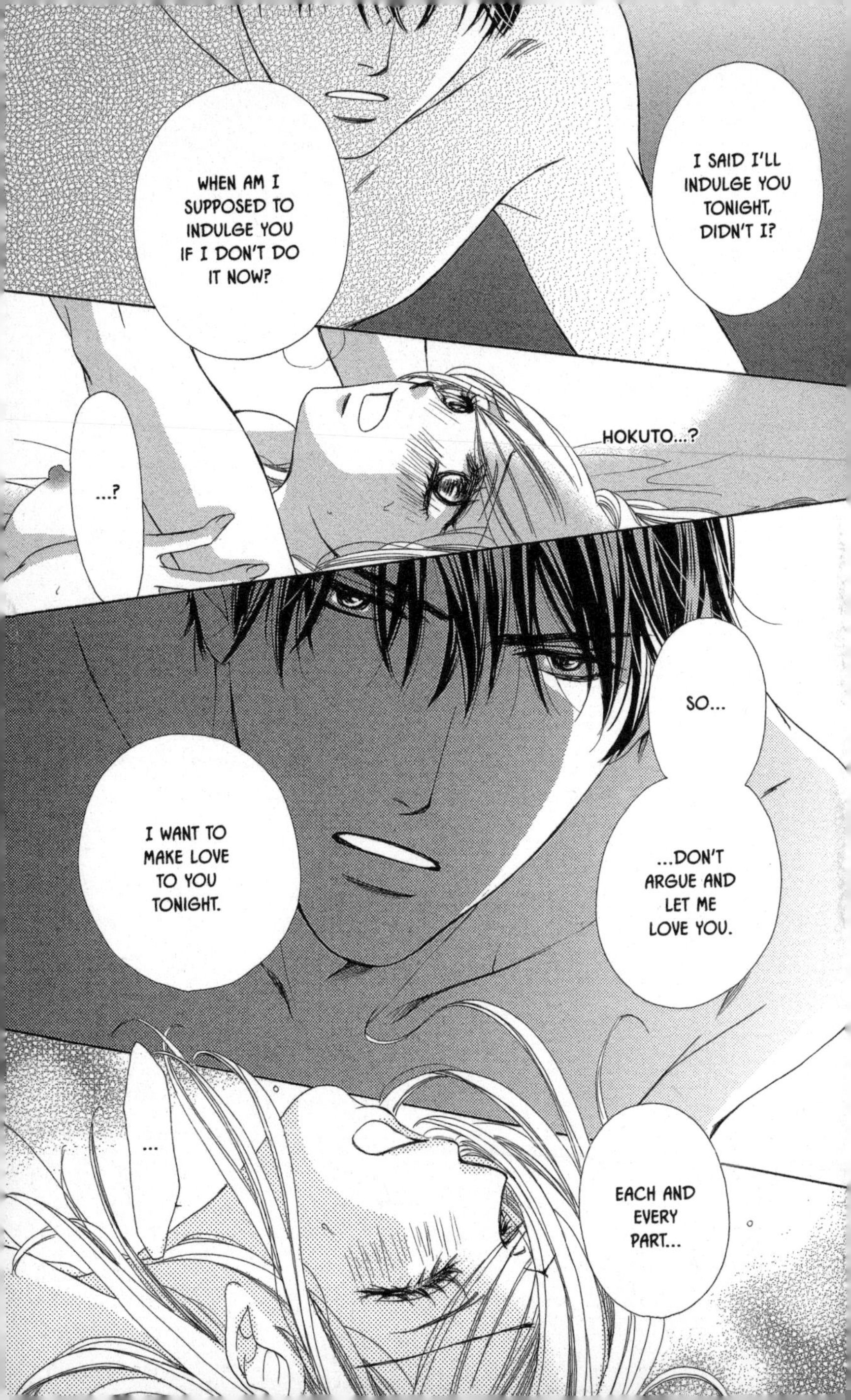
I SAID I'LL INDULGE YOU TONIGHT, DIDN'T I?
WHEN AM I SUPPOSED TO INDULGE YOU IF I DON'T DO IT NOW?
HOKUTO...?
...?
SO...
...DON'T ARGUE AND LET ME LOVE YOU.
I WANT TO MAKE LOVE TO YOU TONIGHT.
EACH AND EVERY PART...
...

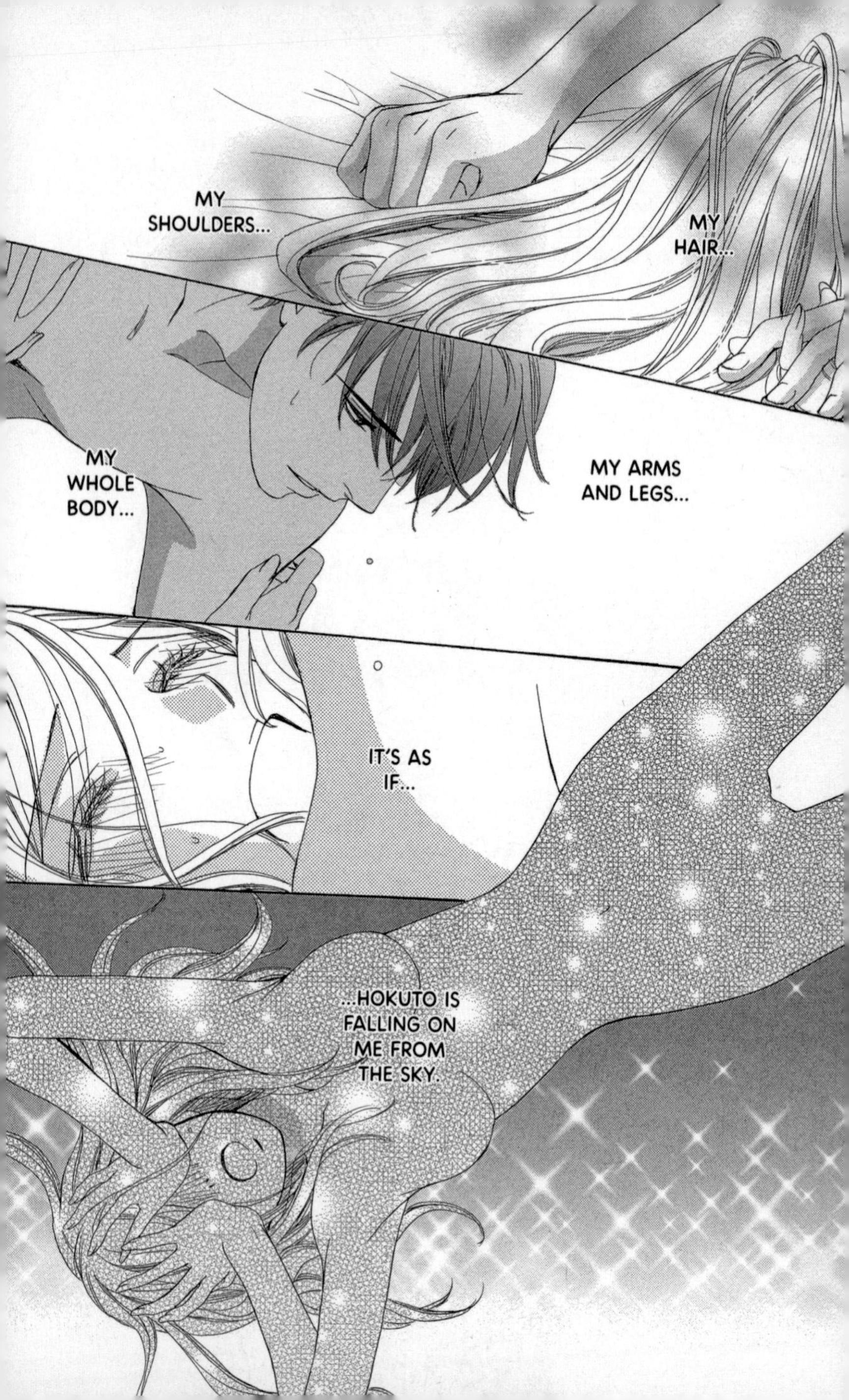
MY HAIR...
MY SHOULDERS...
MY ARMS AND LEGS...
MY WHOLE BODY...
IT'S AS IF...
...HOKUTO IS FALLING ON ME FROM THE SKY.

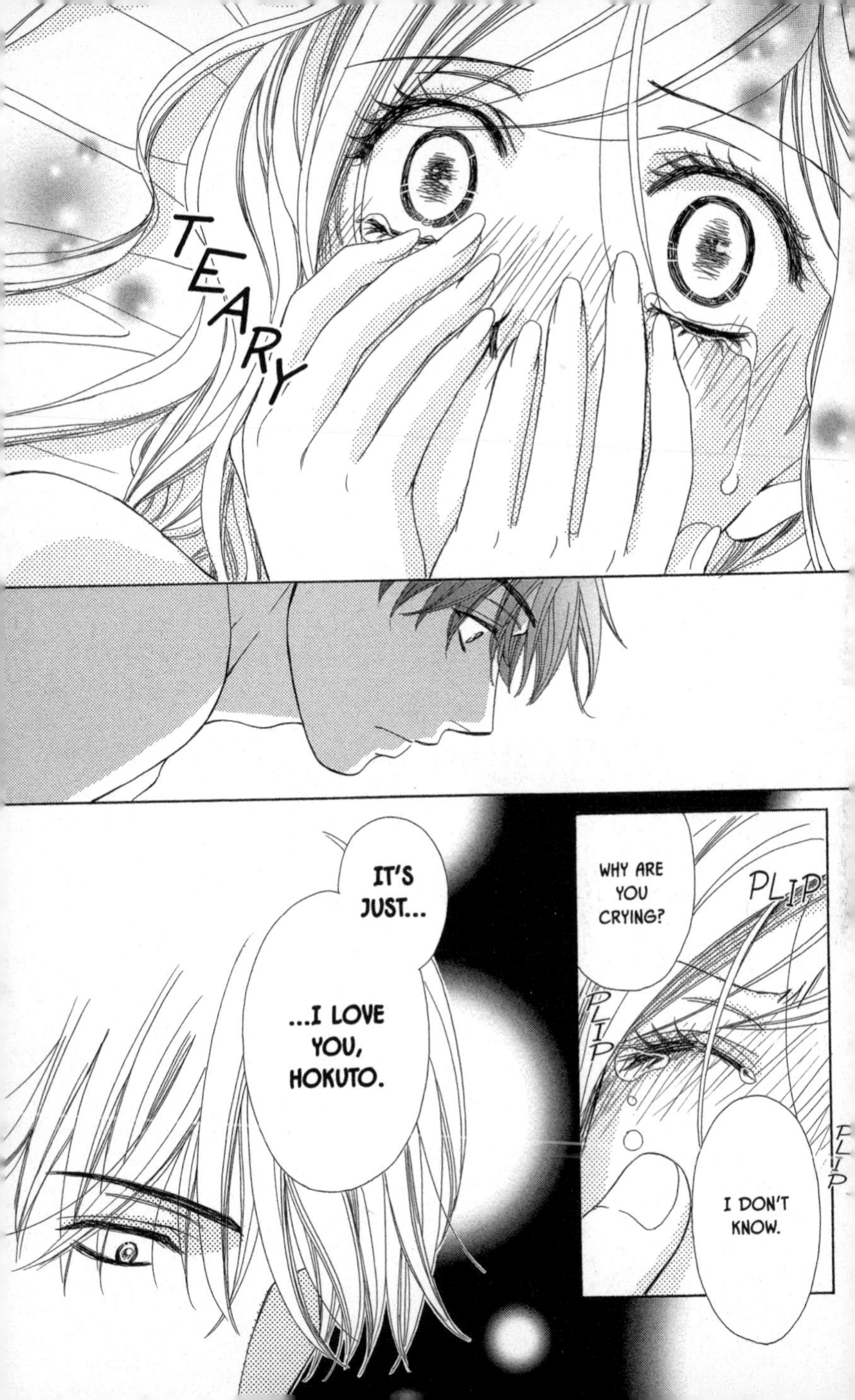
TEARY
WHY ARE YOU CRYING?
PLIP
PLIP
PLIP
I DON'T KNOW.
IT'S JUST...
...I LOVE YOU, HOKUTO.

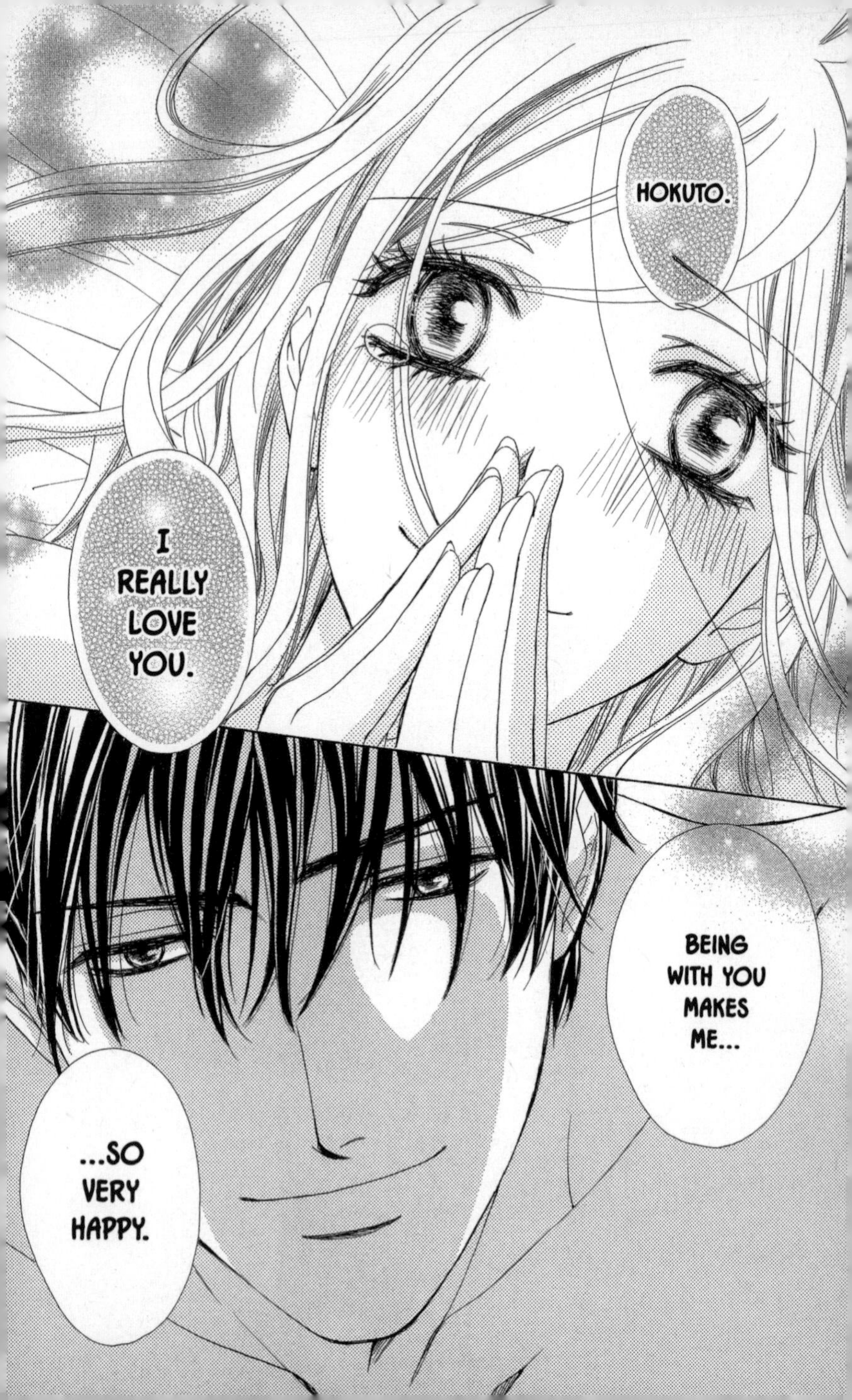

HOKUTO.
I REALLY LOVE YOU.
BEING WITH YOU MAKES ME...
...SO VERY HAPPY.

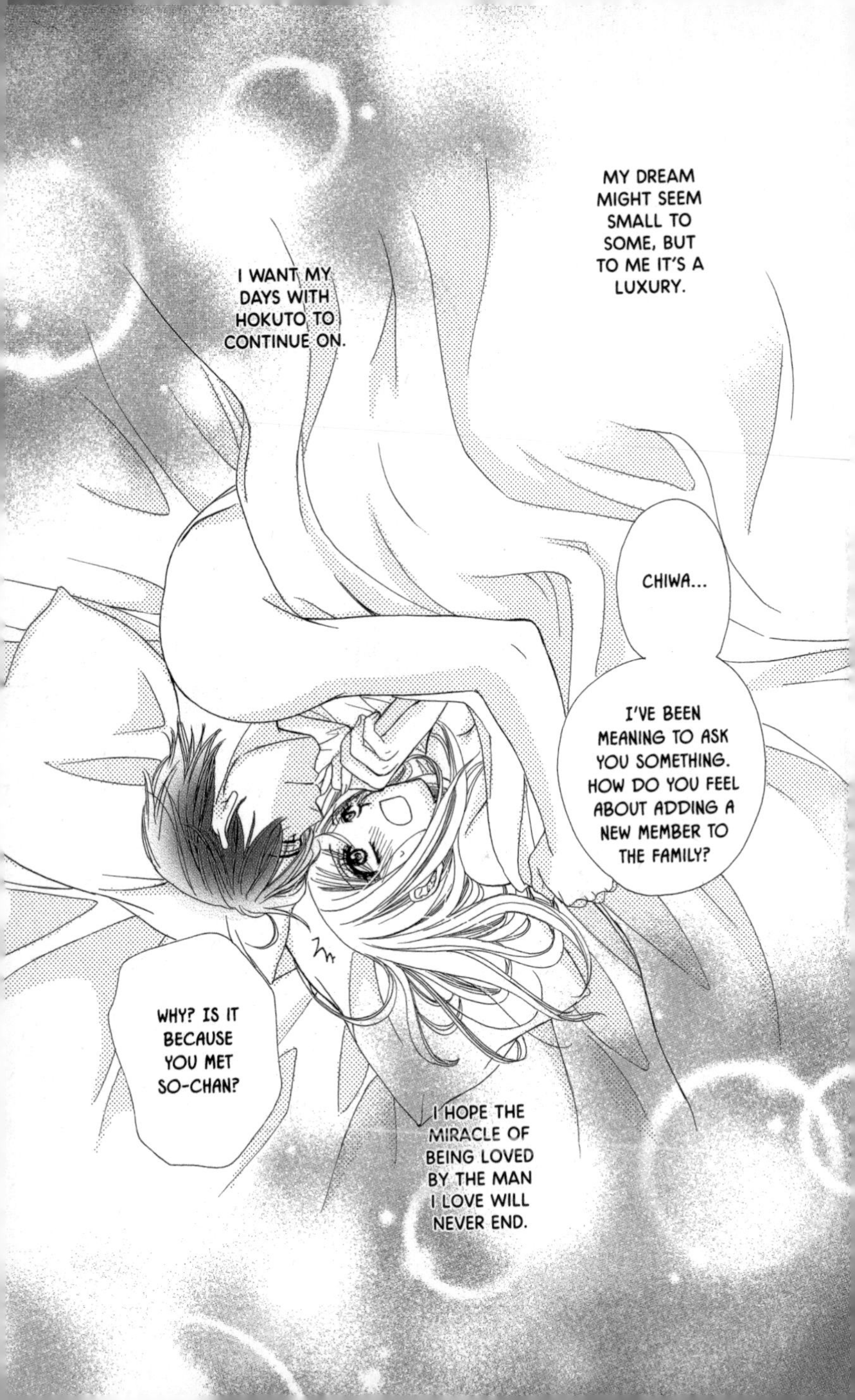
MY DREAM MIGHT SEEM SMALL TO SOME, BUT TO ME IT'S A LUXURY.
I WANT MY DAYS WITH HOKUTO TO CONTINUE ON.
CHIWA...
I'VE BEEN MEANING TO ASK YOU SOMETHING. HOW DO YOU FEEL ABOUT ADDING A NEW MEMBER TO THE FAMILY?
WHY? IS IT BECAUSE YOU MET SO-CHAN?
I HOPE THE MIRACLE OF BEING LOVED BY THE MAN I LOVE WILL NEVER END.

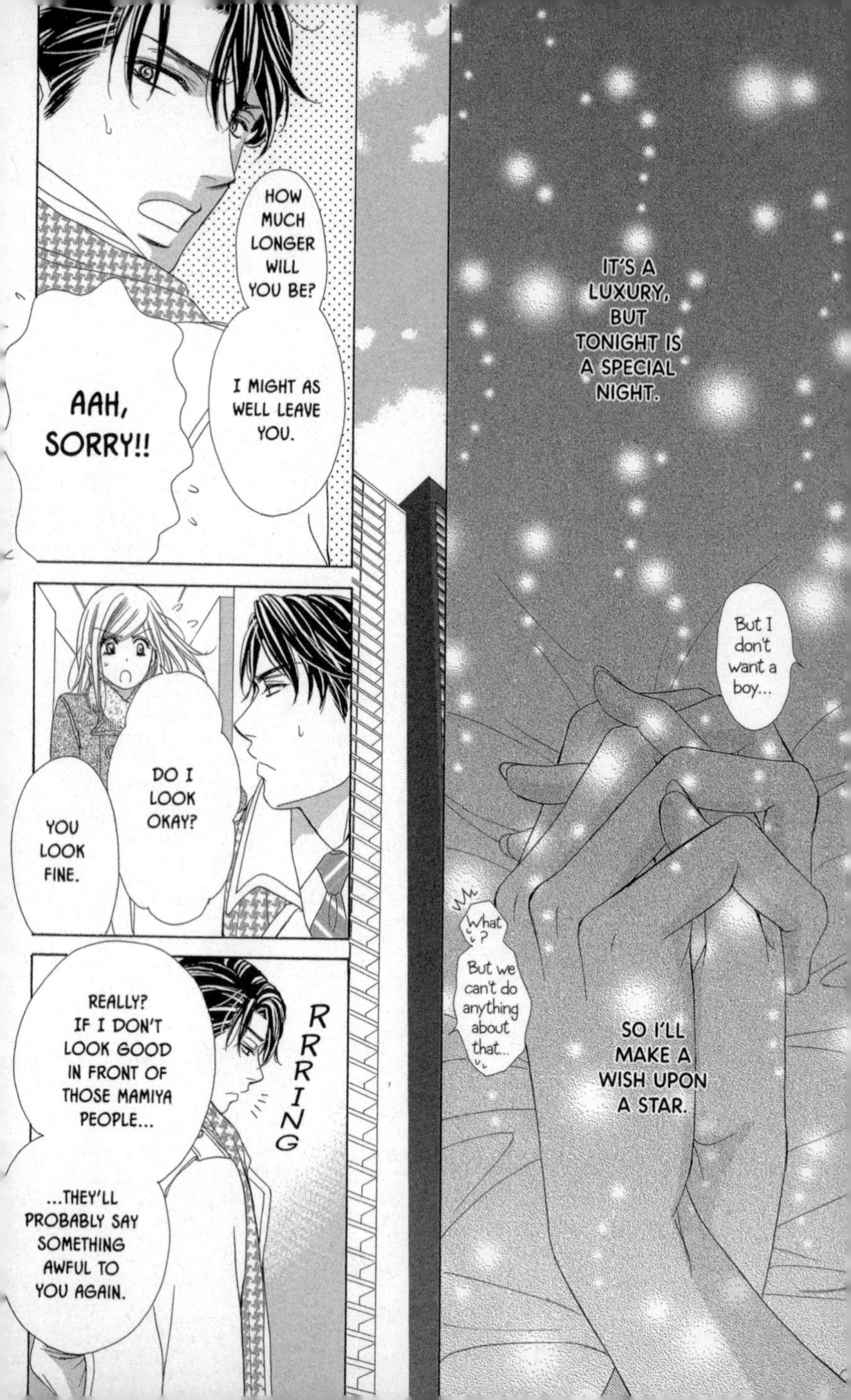
IT'S A LUXURY, BUT TONIGHT IS A SPECIAL NIGHT.
But I don't want a boy...
What? But we can't do anything about that...
SO I'LL MAKE A WISH UPON A STAR.
HOW MUCH LONGER WILL YOU BE?
I MIGHT AS WELL LEAVE YOU.
AAH, SORRY!!
DO I LOOK OKAY?
YOU LOOK FINE.
REALLY? IF I DON'T LOOK GOOD IN FRONT OF THOSE MAMIYA PEOPLE...
RRRING
...THEY'LL PROBABLY SAY SOMETHING AWFUL TO YOU AGAIN.

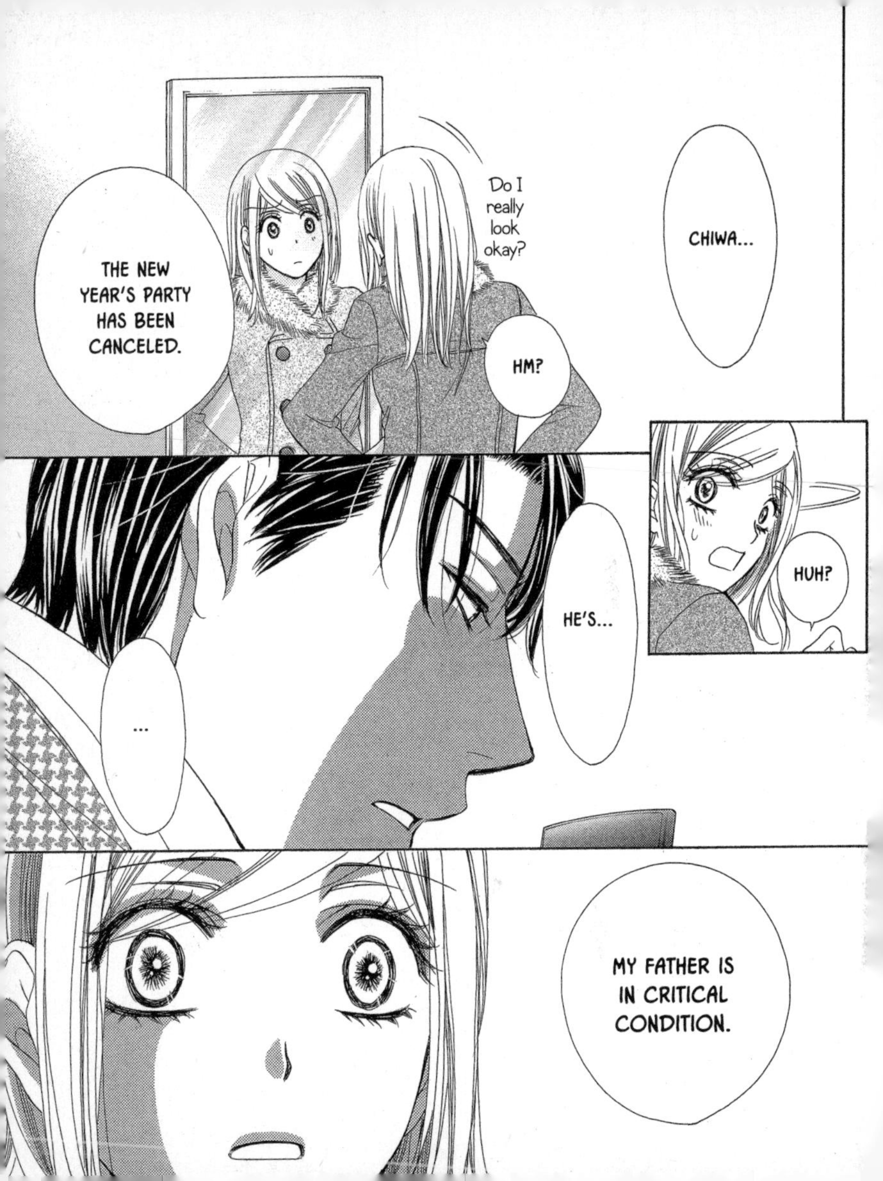
CHIWA...
Do I really look okay?
HM?
THE NEW YEAR'S PARTY HAS BEEN CANCELED.
HUH?
HE'S...
...
MY FATHER IS IN CRITICAL CONDITION.

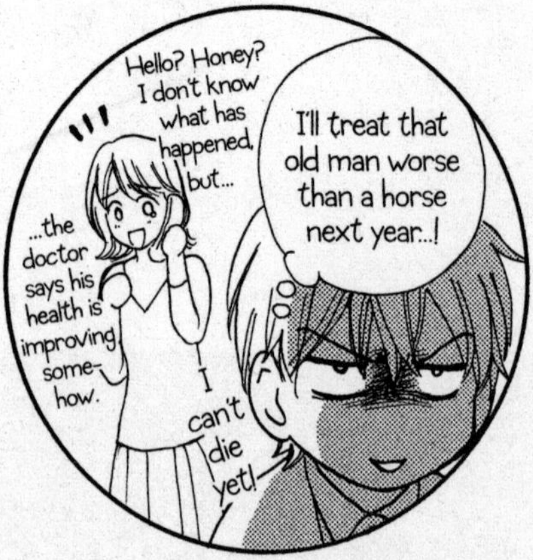
Hello? Honey? I don't know what has happened, but...
...the doctor says his health is improving some-how.
I'll treat that old man worse than a horse next year...!
I can't die yet!

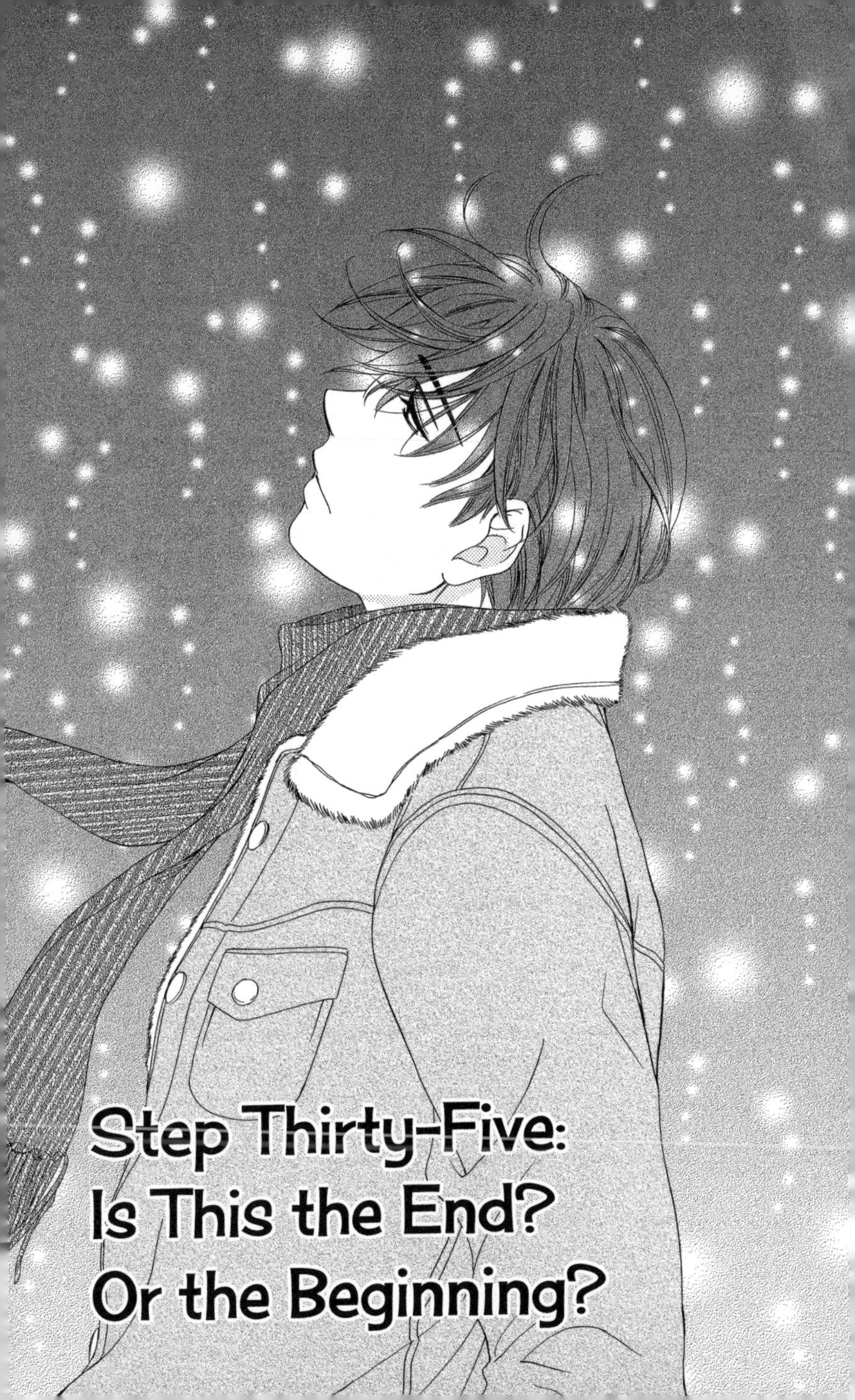

Step Thirty-Five: Is This the End? Or the Beginning?

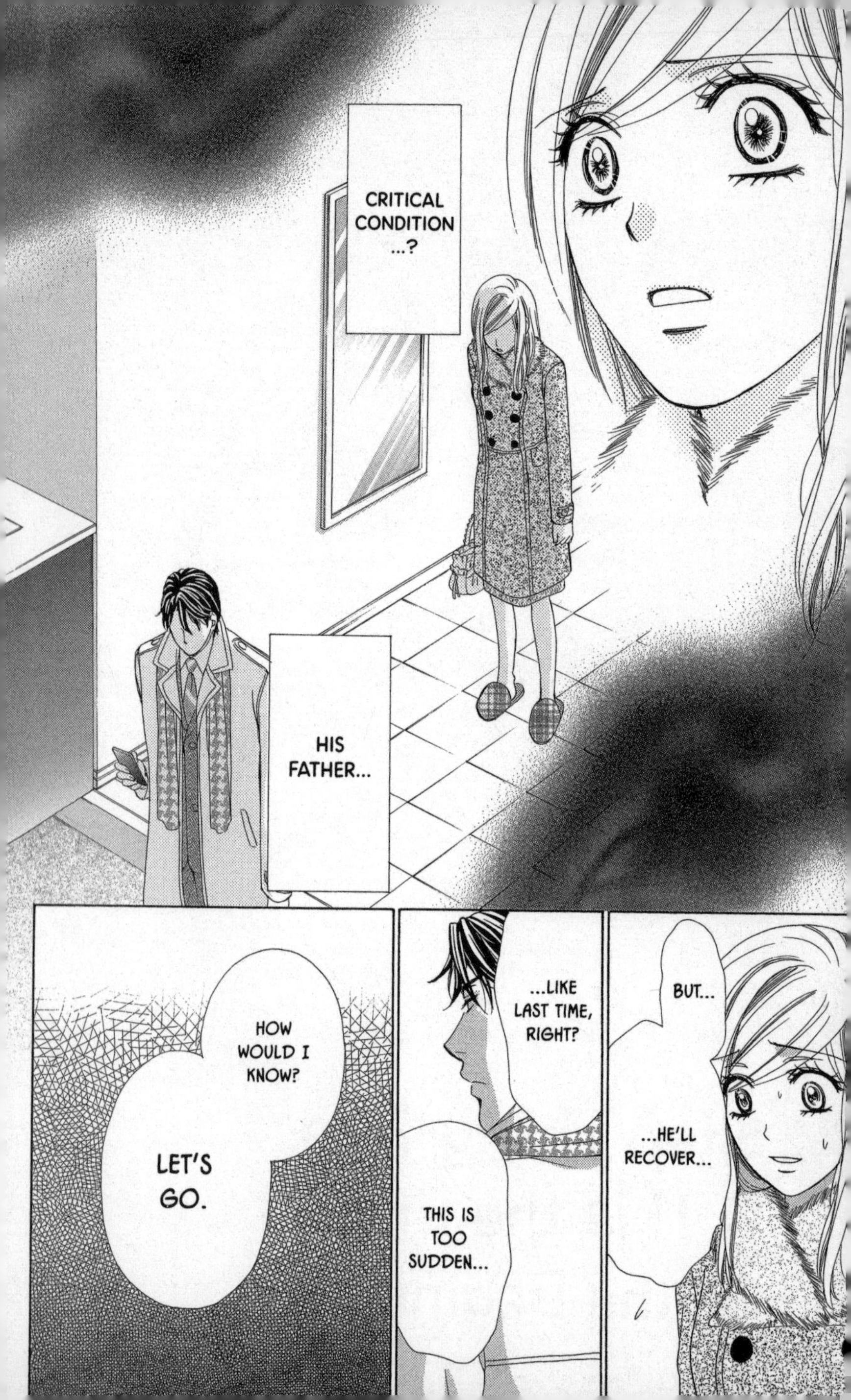
CRITICAL CONDITION ...?
HIS FATHER...
BUT...
...HE'LL RECOVER...
...LIKE LAST TIME, RIGHT?
THIS IS TOO SUDDEN...
HOW WOULD I KNOW?
LET'S GO.

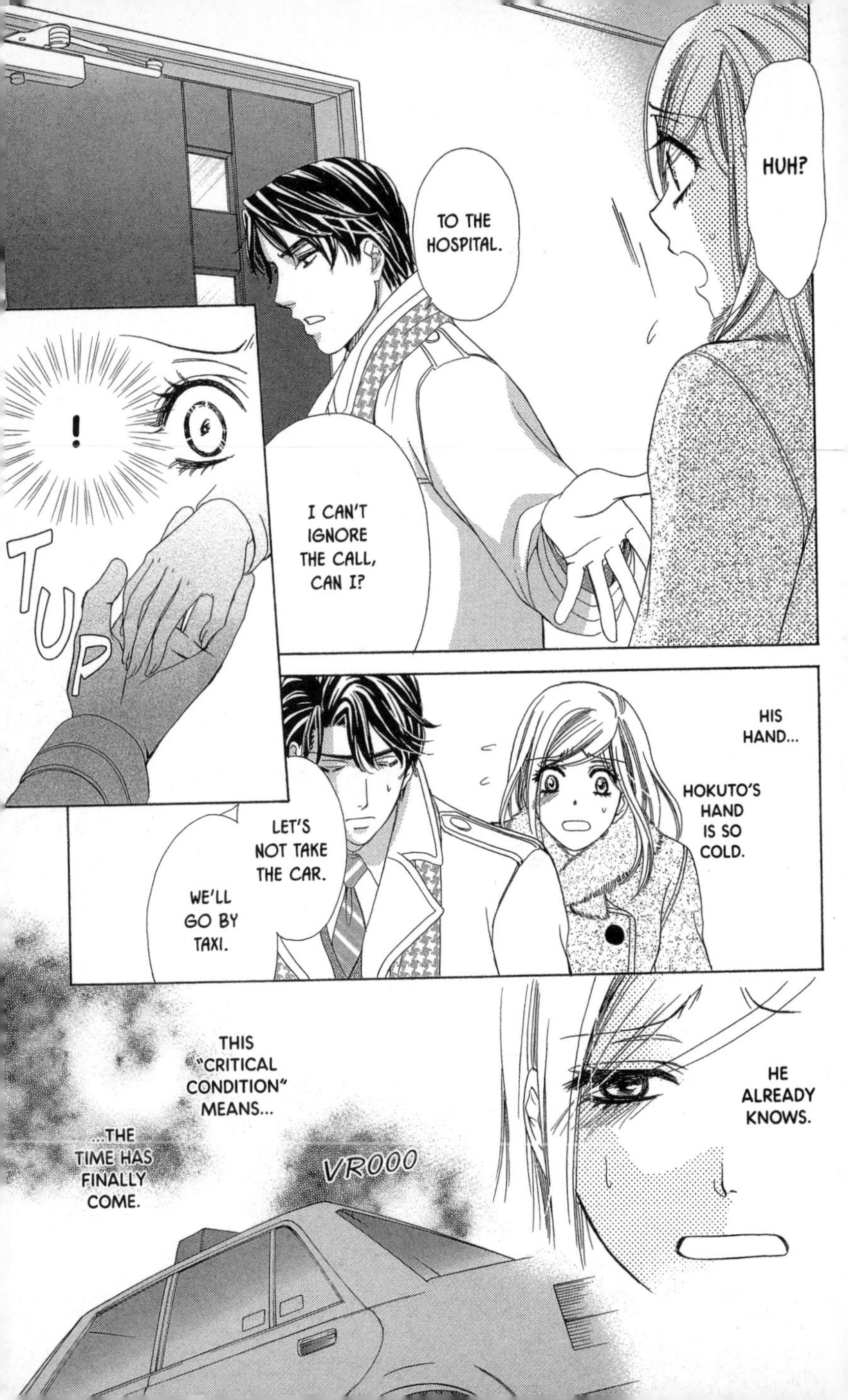
HUH?
TO THE HOSPITAL.
I CAN'T IGNORE THE CALL, CAN I?
!
TUP
HIS HAND...
HOKUTO'S HAND IS SO COLD.
LET'S NOT TAKE THE CAR.
WE'LL GO BY TAXI.
HE ALREADY KNOWS.
THIS "CRITICAL CONDITION" MEANS...
...THE TIME HAS FINALLY COME.
VROOO

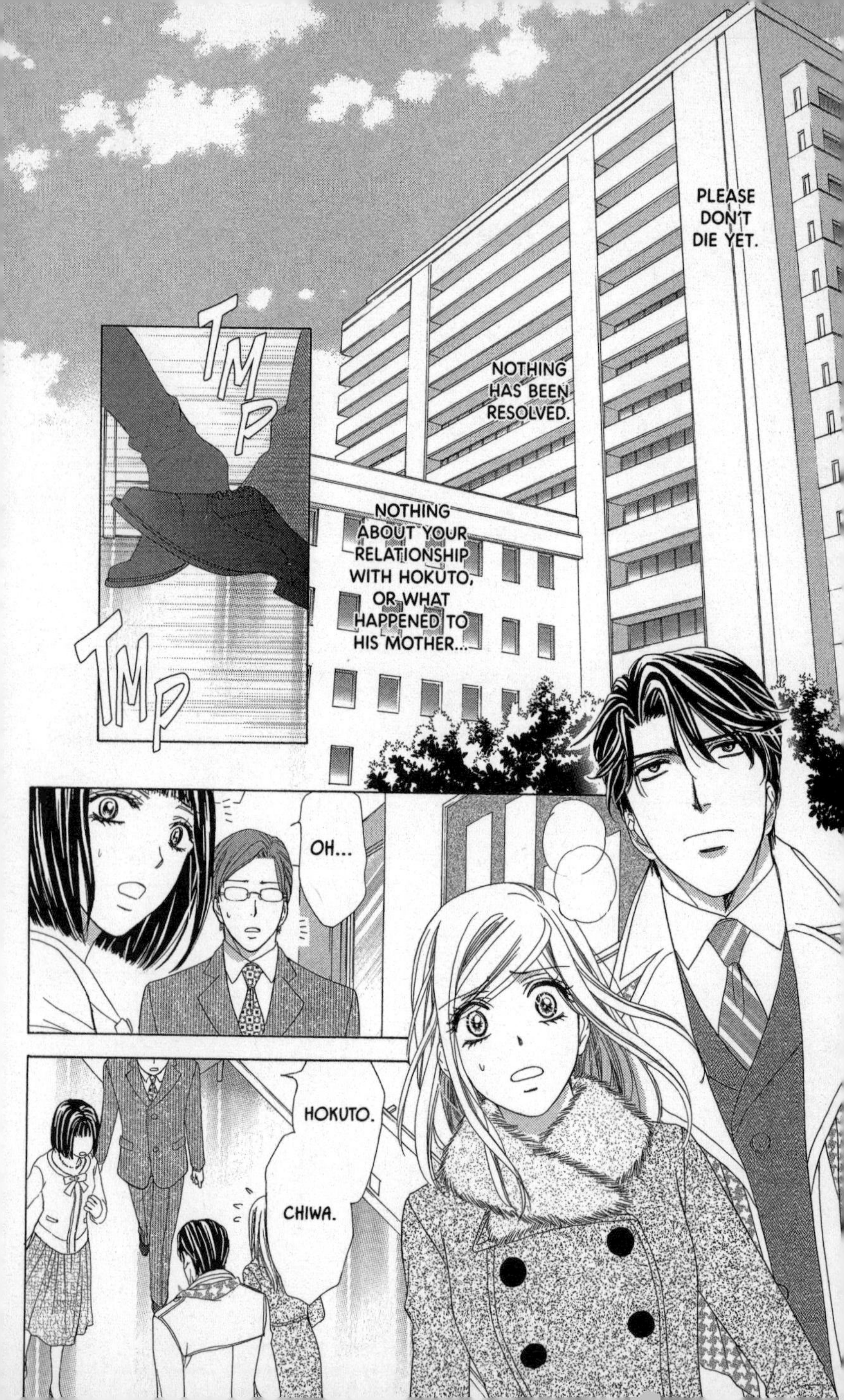
PLEASE DON'T DIE YET.
NOTHING HAS BEEN RESOLVED.
NOTHING ABOUT YOUR RELATIONSHIP WITH HOKUTO, OR WHAT HAPPENED TO HIS MOTHER...
TMP
TMP
OH...
HOKUTO.
CHIWA.

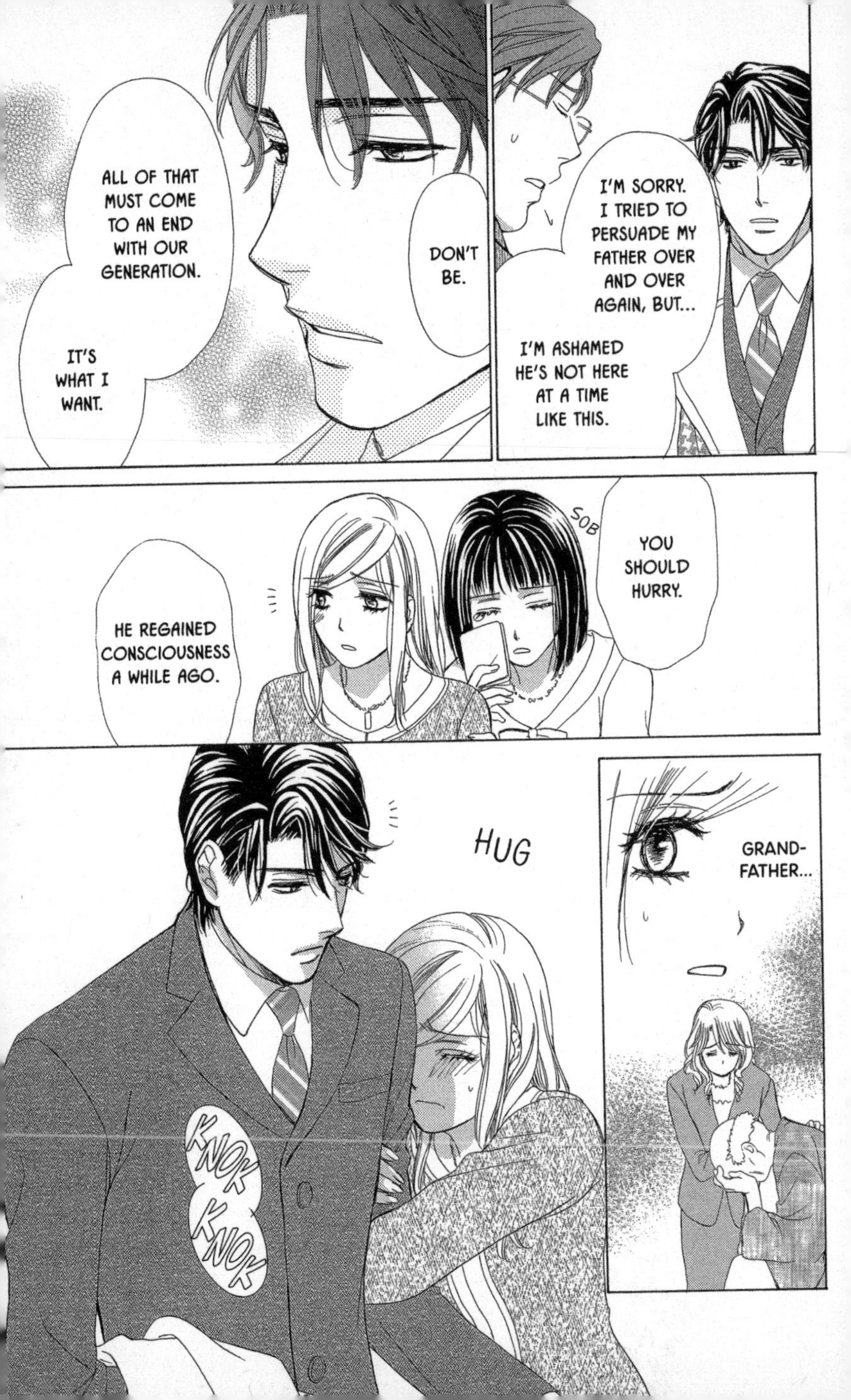
I'M SORRY. I TRIED TO PERSUADE MY FATHER OVER AND OVER AGAIN, BUT...
I'M ASHAMED HE'S NOT HERE AT A TIME LIKE THIS.
DON'T BE.
ALL OF THAT MUST COME TO AN END WITH OUR GENERATION.
IT'S WHAT I WANT.
SOB
YOU SHOULD HURRY.
HE REGAINED CONSCIOUSNESS A WHILE AGO.
GRAND-FATHER...
HUG
KNOK KNOK

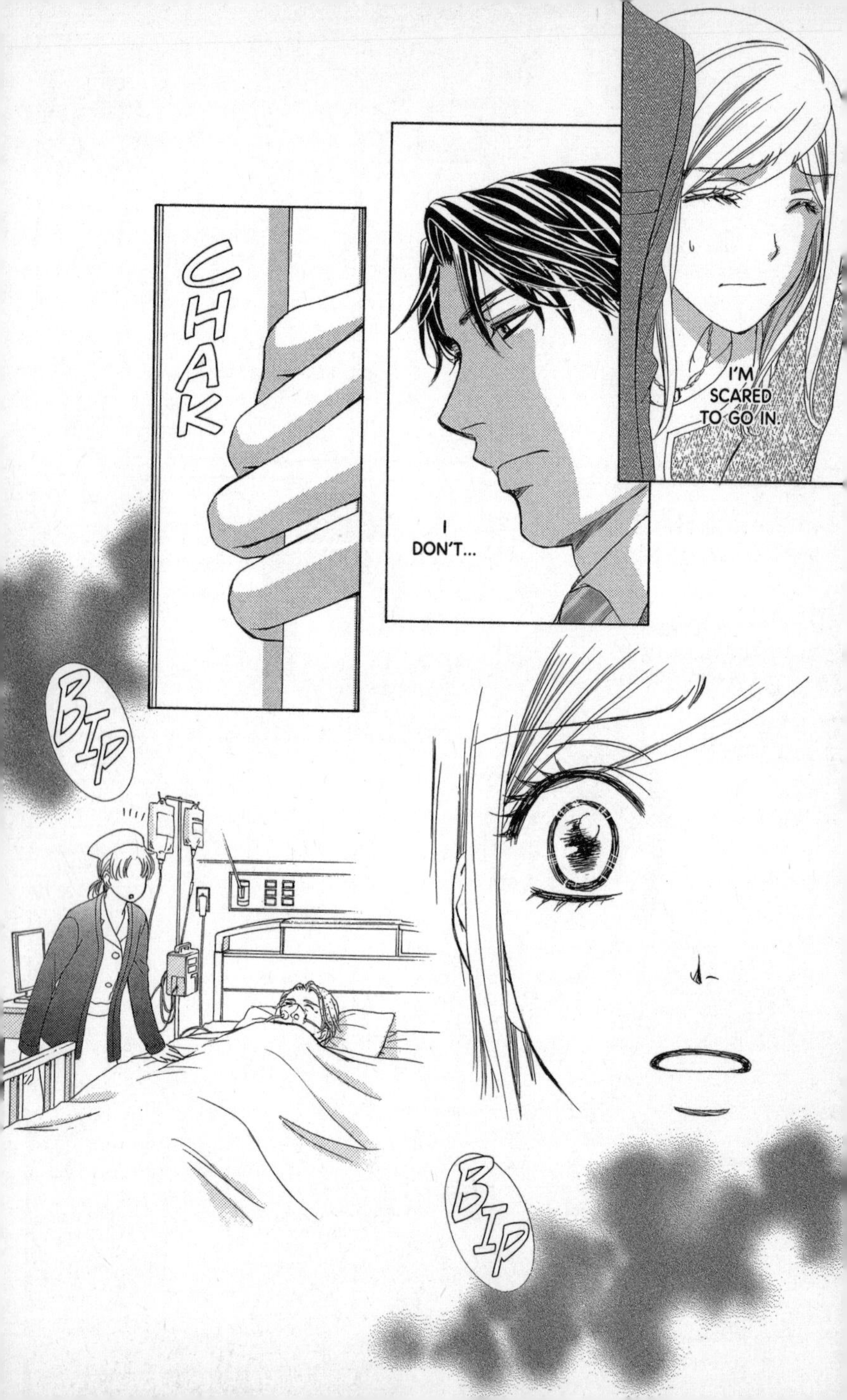
I'M SCARED TO GO IN.
I DON'T...
CHAK
BIP
BIP

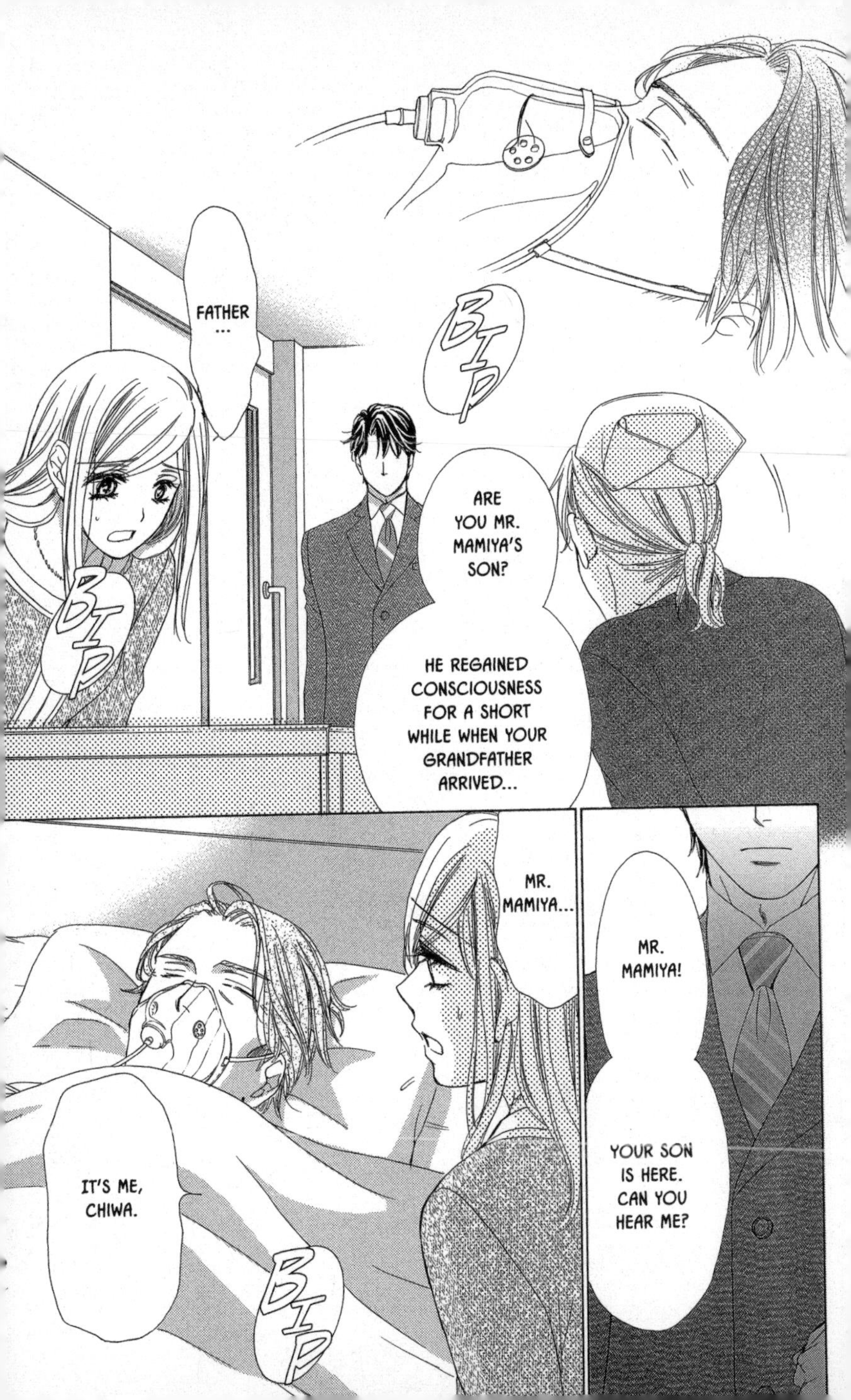
BIP
FATHER...
BIP
ARE YOU MR. MAMIYA'S SON?
HE REGAINED CONSCIOUSNESS FOR A SHORT WHILE WHEN YOUR GRANDFATHER ARRIVED...
MR. MAMIYA!
YOUR SON IS HERE. CAN YOU HEAR ME?
MR. MAMIYA...
IT'S ME, CHIWA.
BIP

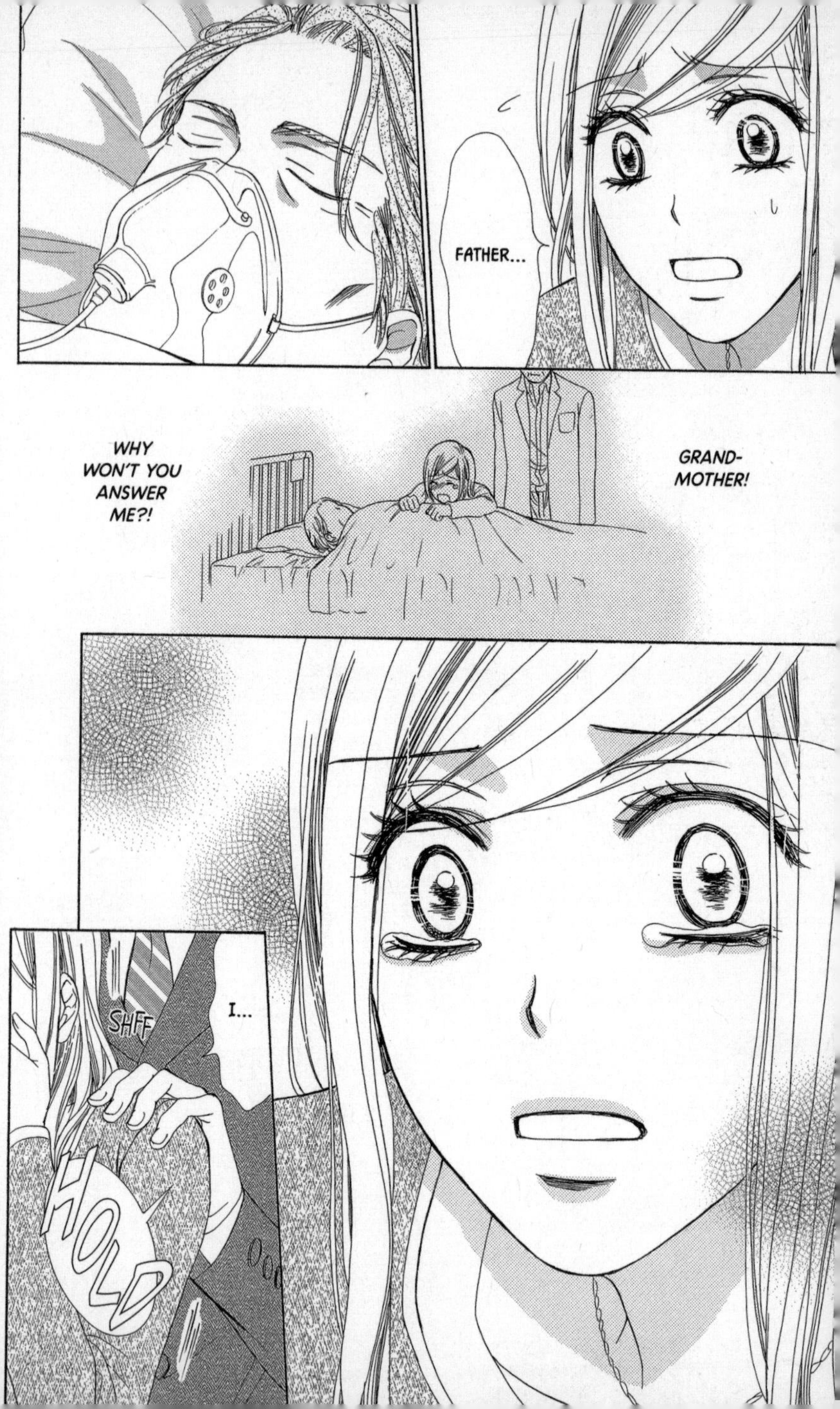
FATHER...
GRAND-MOTHER!
WHY WON'T YOU ANSWER ME?!
I...
SHFF
HOLD

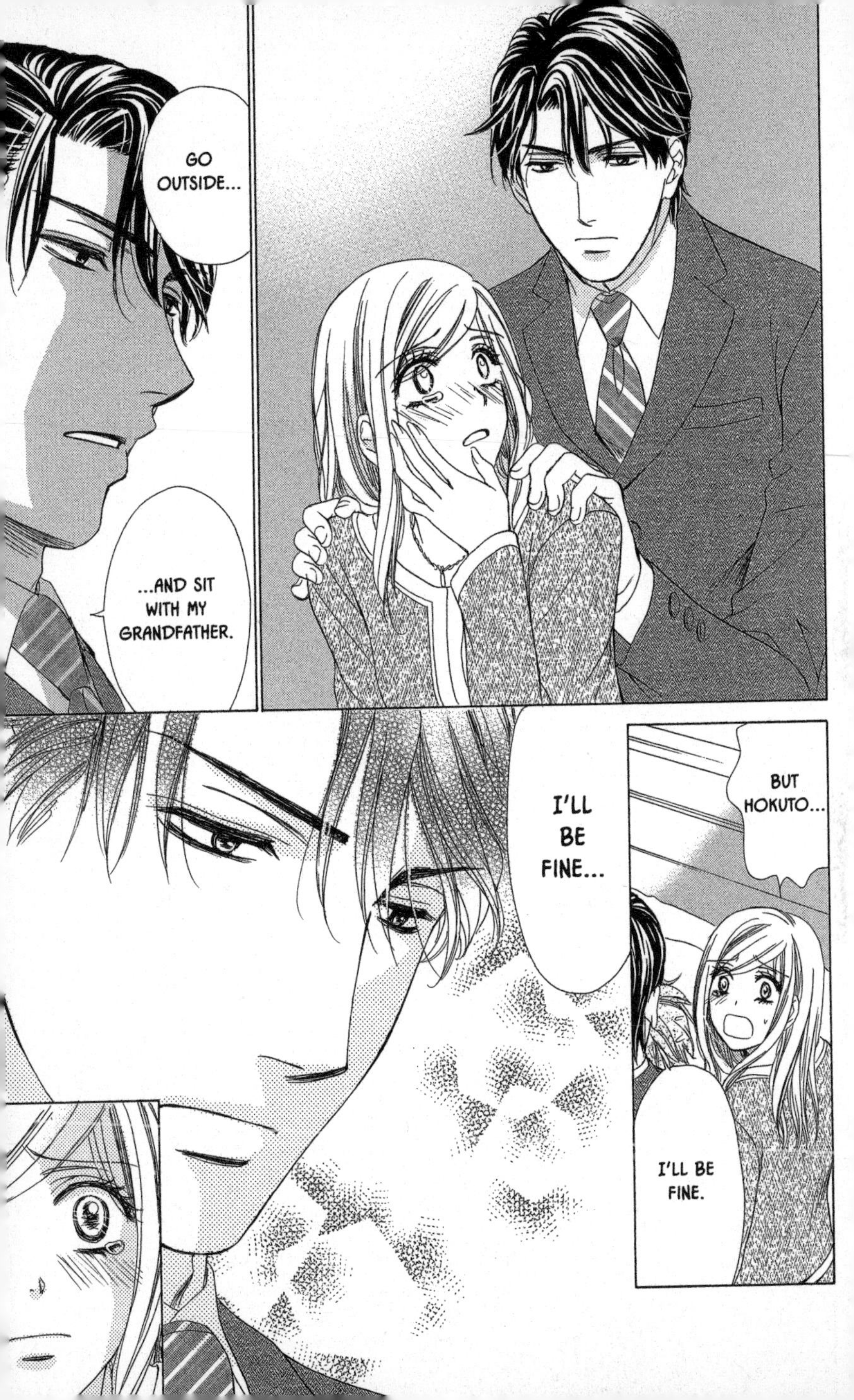
GO OUTSIDE...
...AND SIT WITH MY GRANDFATHER.
BUT HOKUTO...
I'LL BE FINE.
I'LL BE FINE...

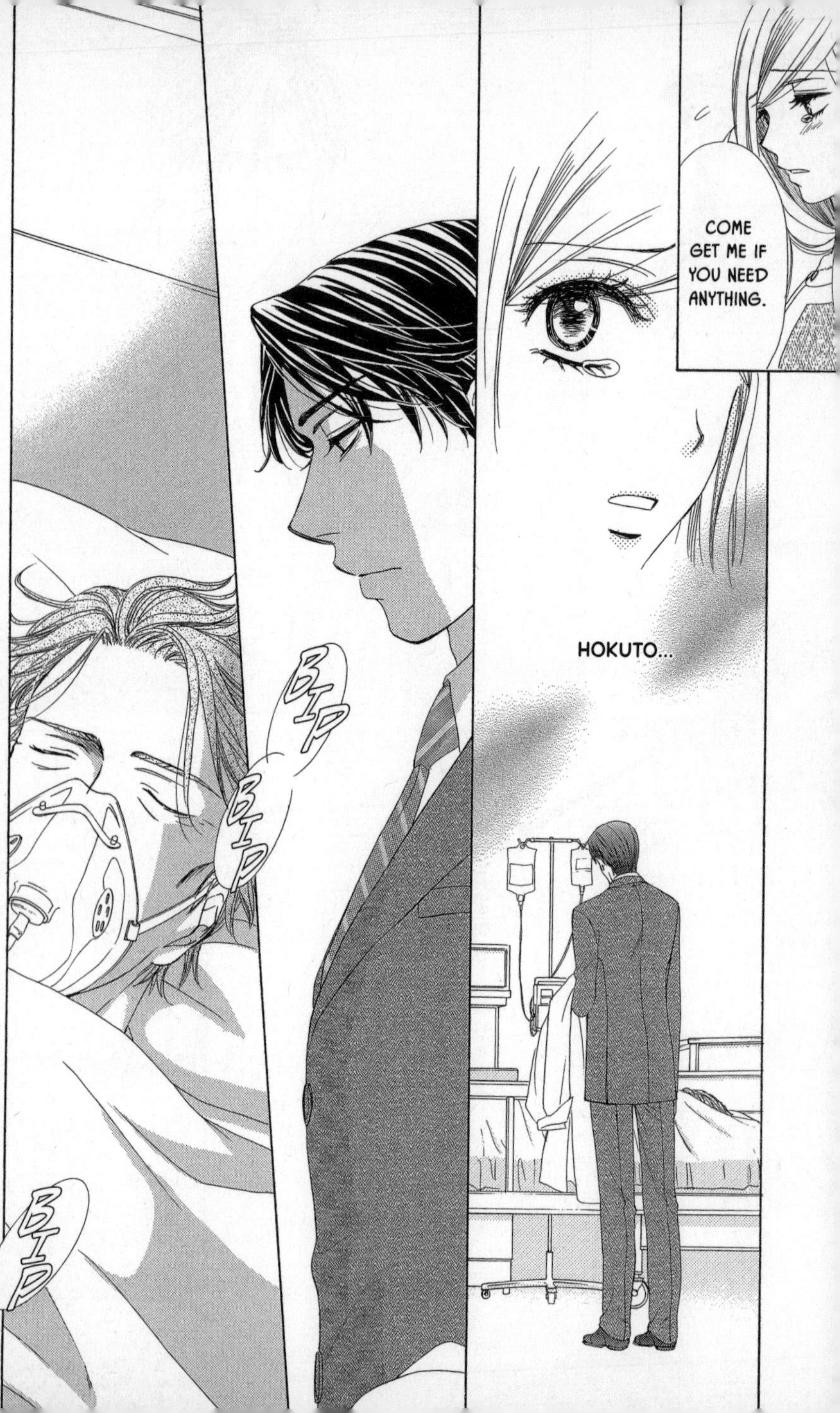
COME GET ME IF YOU NEED ANYTHING.
HOKUTO...
BIP
BIP
BIP

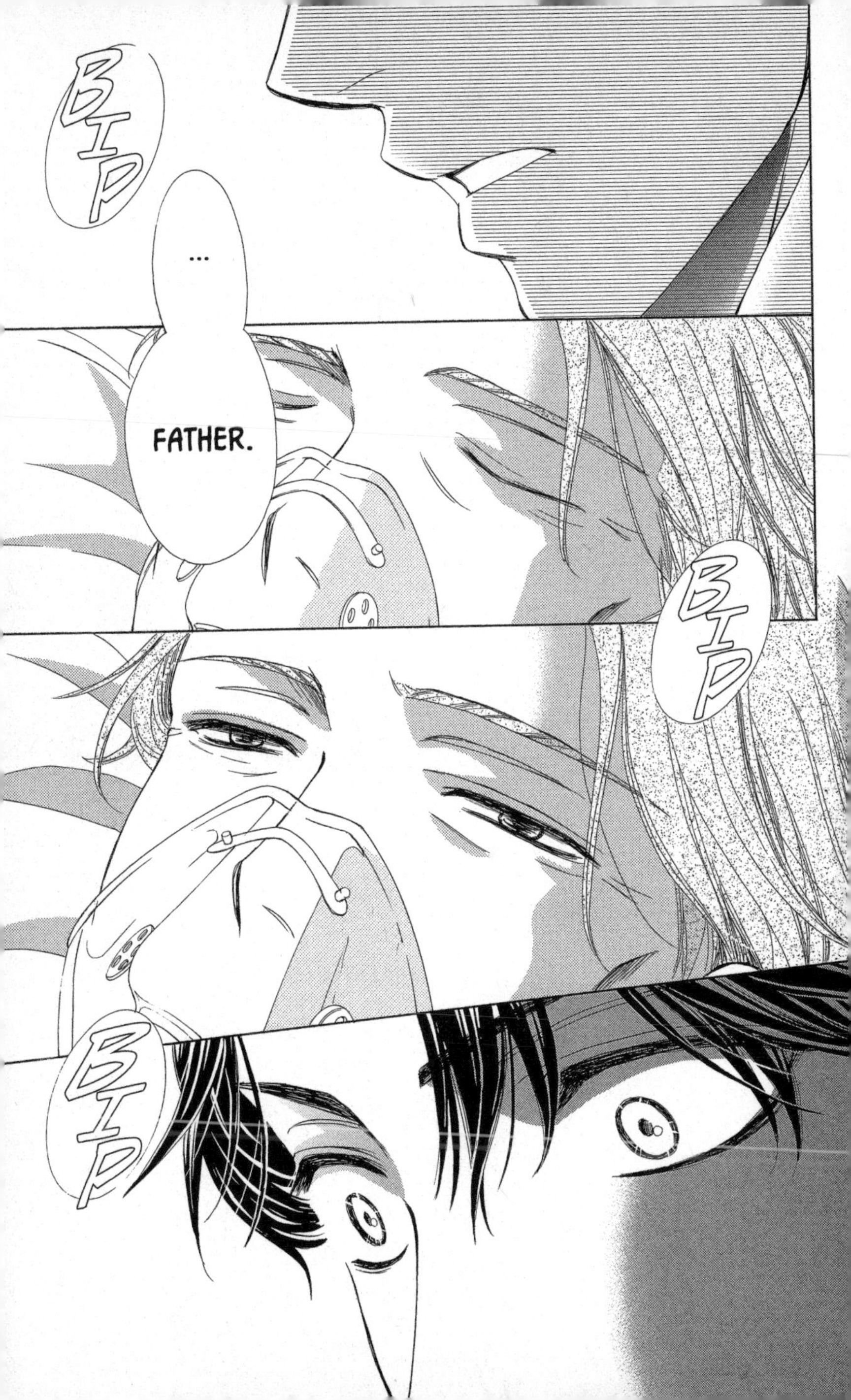
BIP
...
FATHER.
BIP
BIP

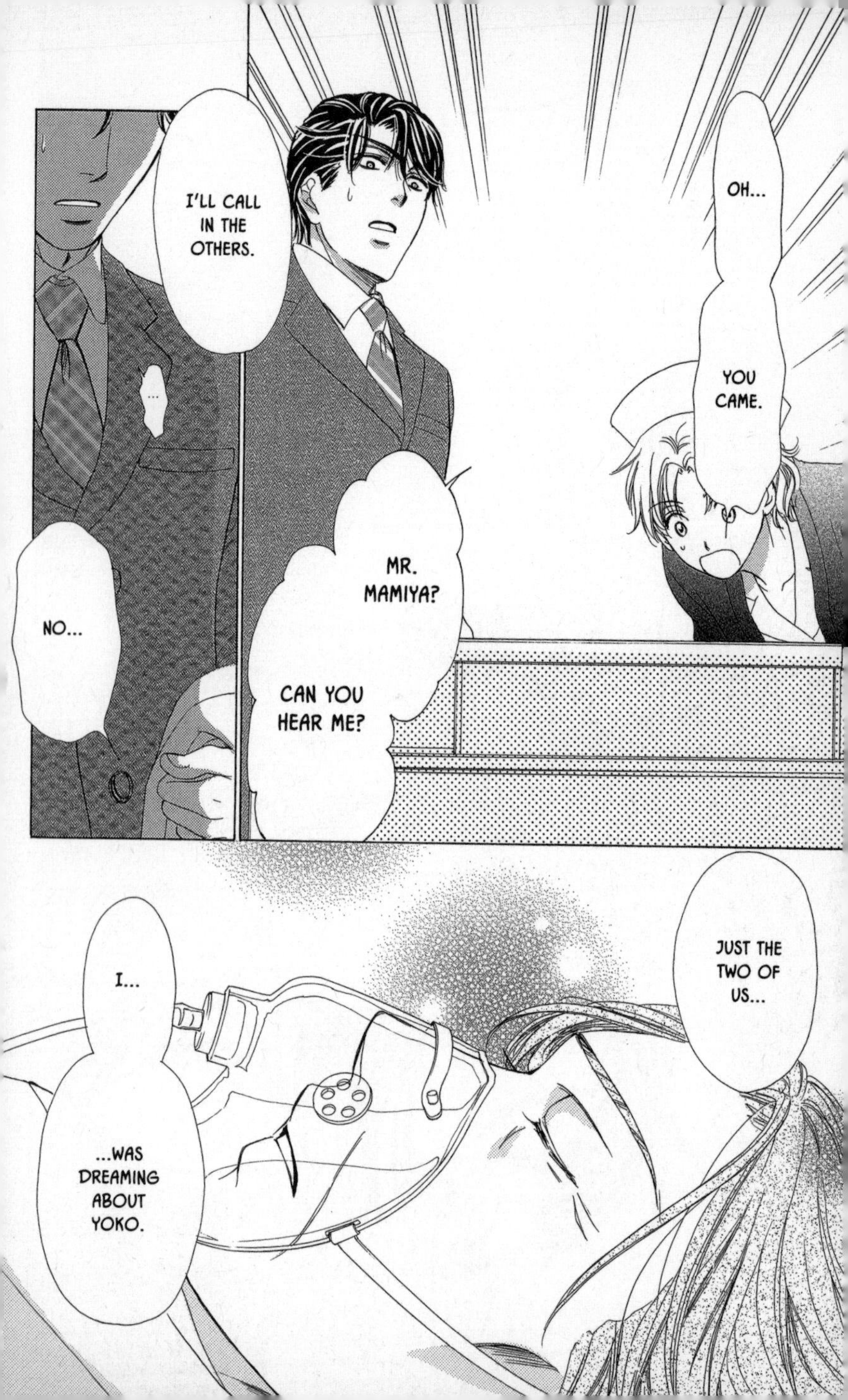
OH...
YOU CAME.
MR. MAMIYA?
CAN YOU HEAR ME?
I'LL CALL IN THE OTHERS.
...
NO...
JUST THE TWO OF US...
I...
...WAS DREAMING ABOUT YOKO.

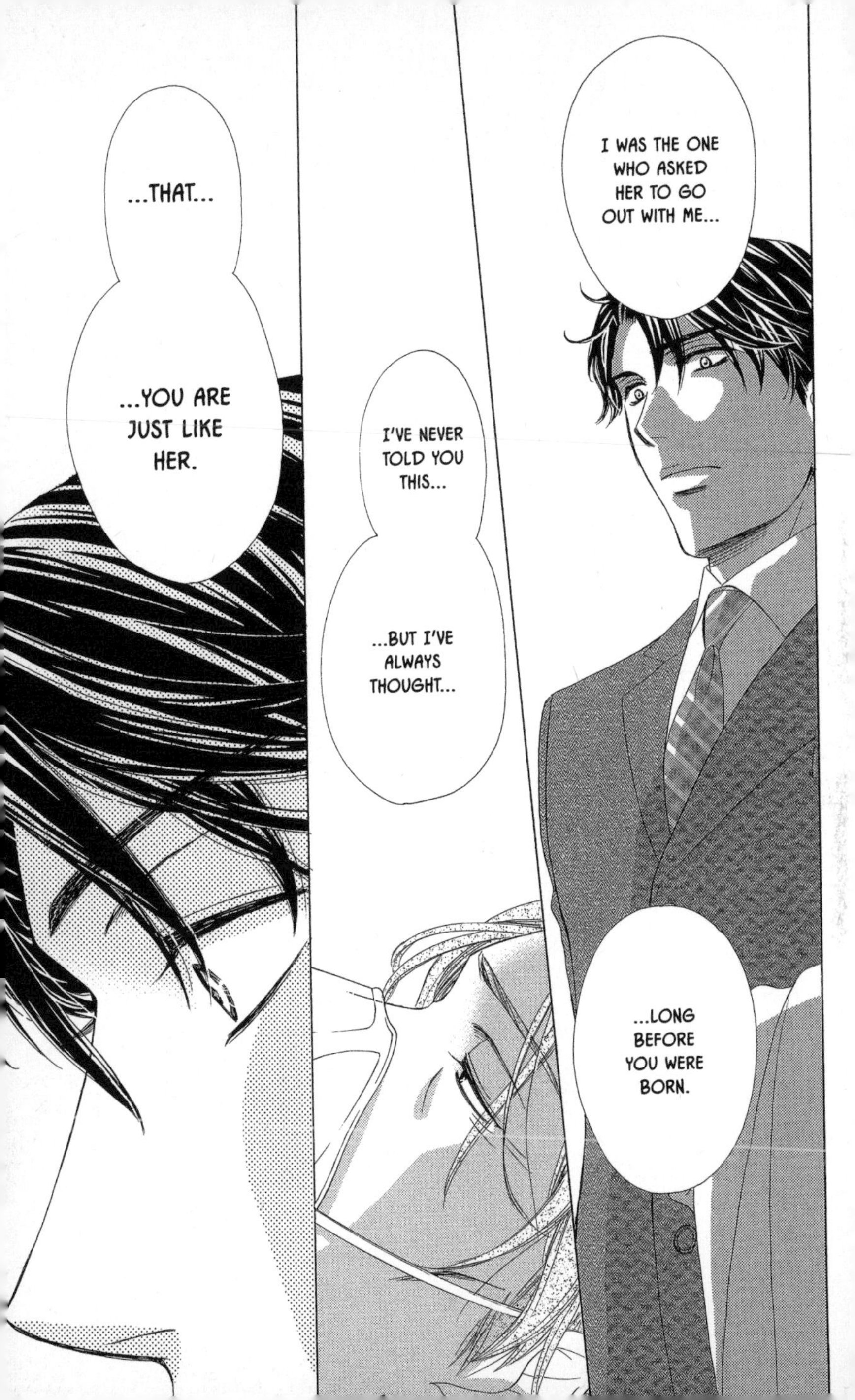
I WAS THE ONE WHO ASKED HER TO GO OUT WITH ME...
...LONG BEFORE YOU WERE BORN.
I'VE NEVER TOLD YOU THIS...
...BUT I'VE ALWAYS THOUGHT...
...THAT...
...YOU ARE JUST LIKE HER.

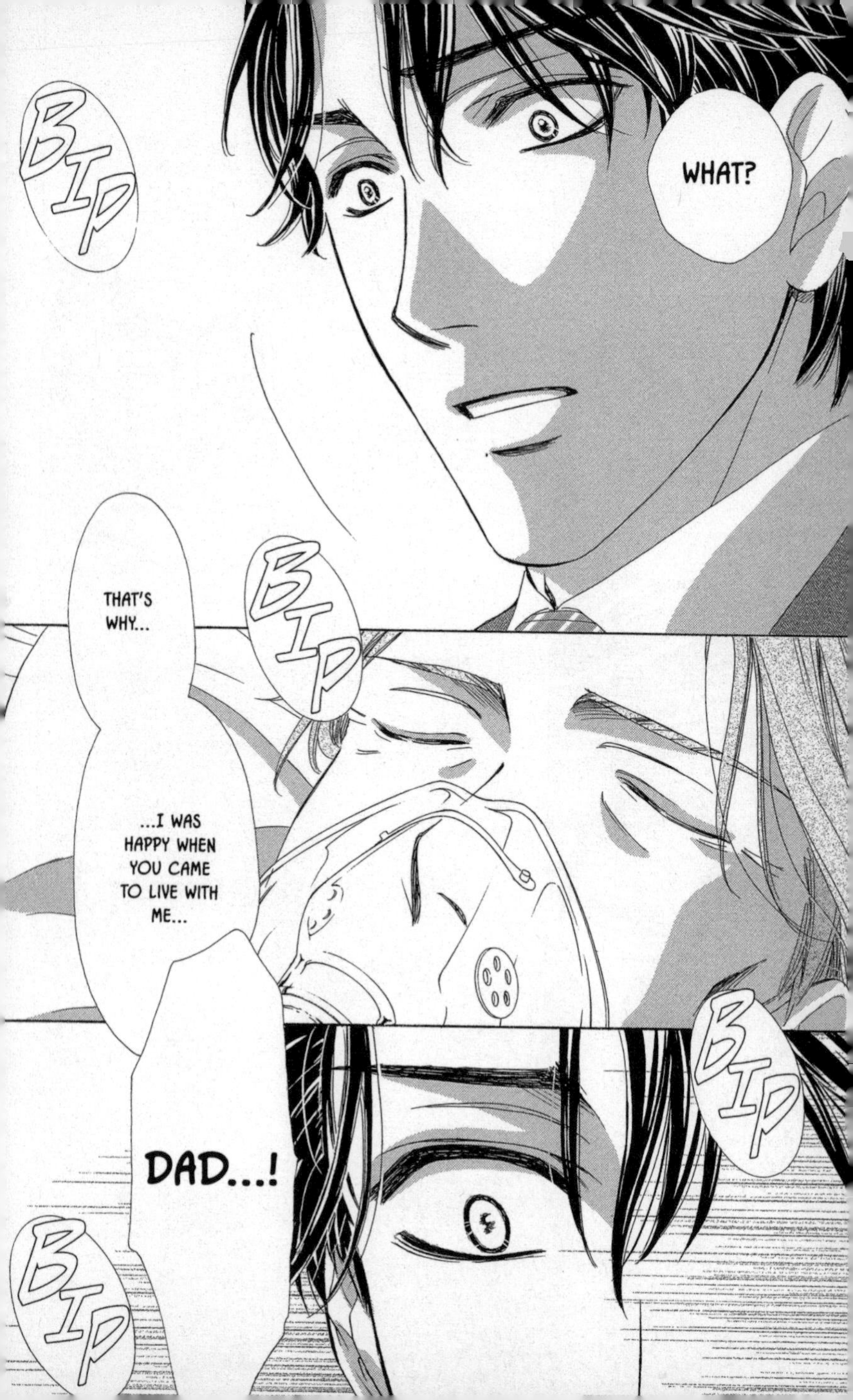
WHAT?
BIP
BIP
THAT'S WHY...
...I WAS HAPPY WHEN YOU CAME TO LIVE WITH ME...
BIP
DAD...!
BIP

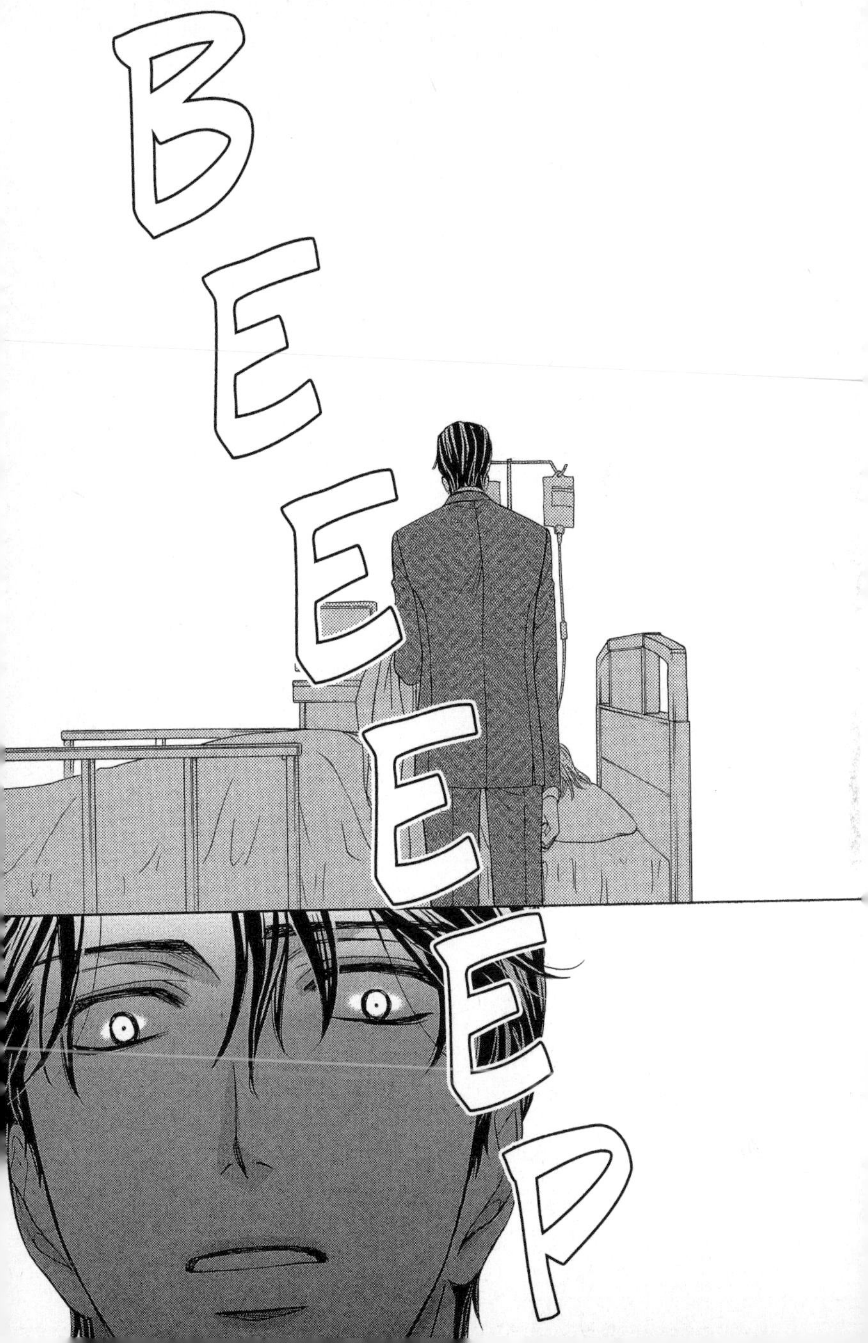
BEEEEP

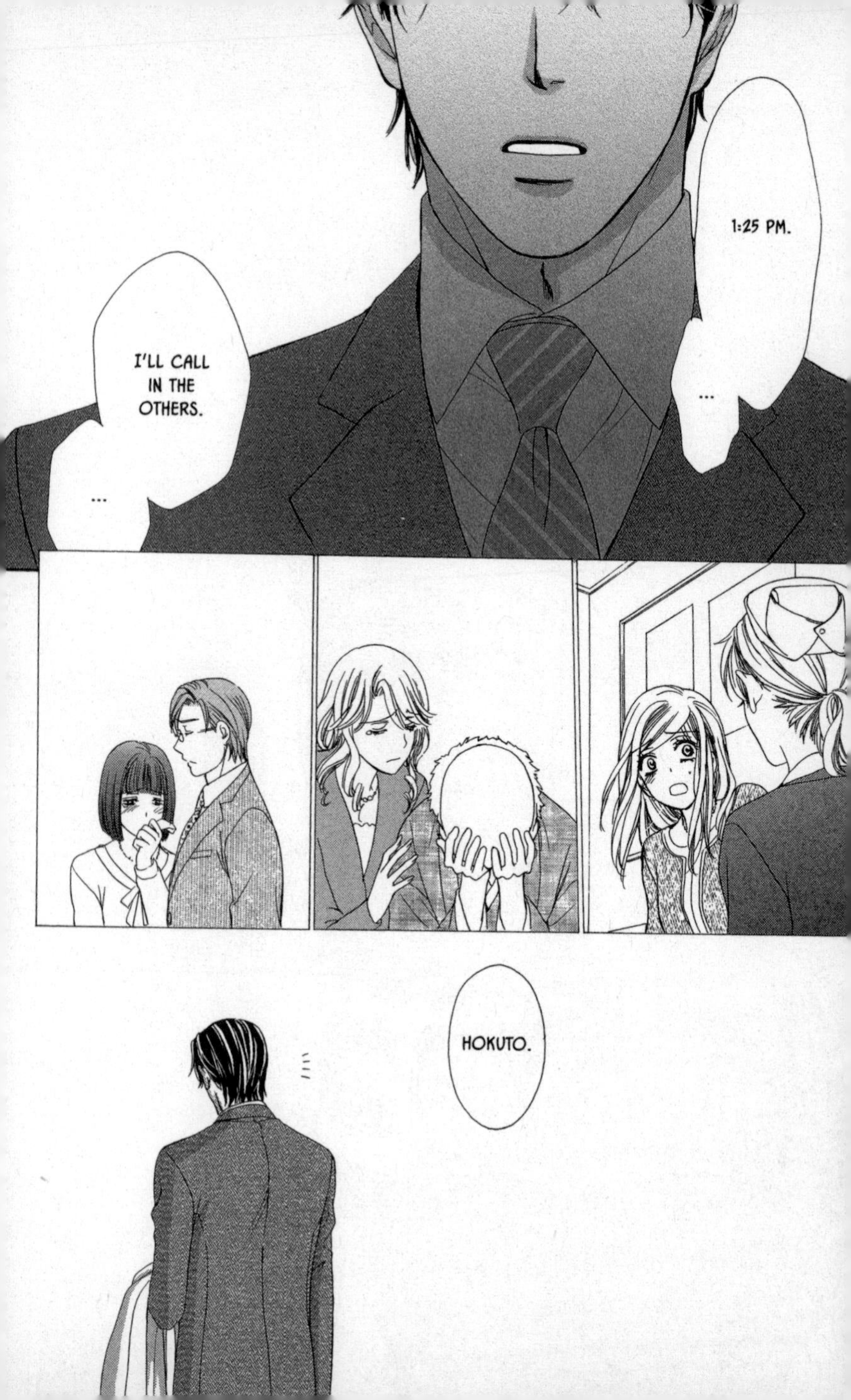
1:25 PM.
...
I'LL CALL IN THE OTHERS.
...
HOKUTO.

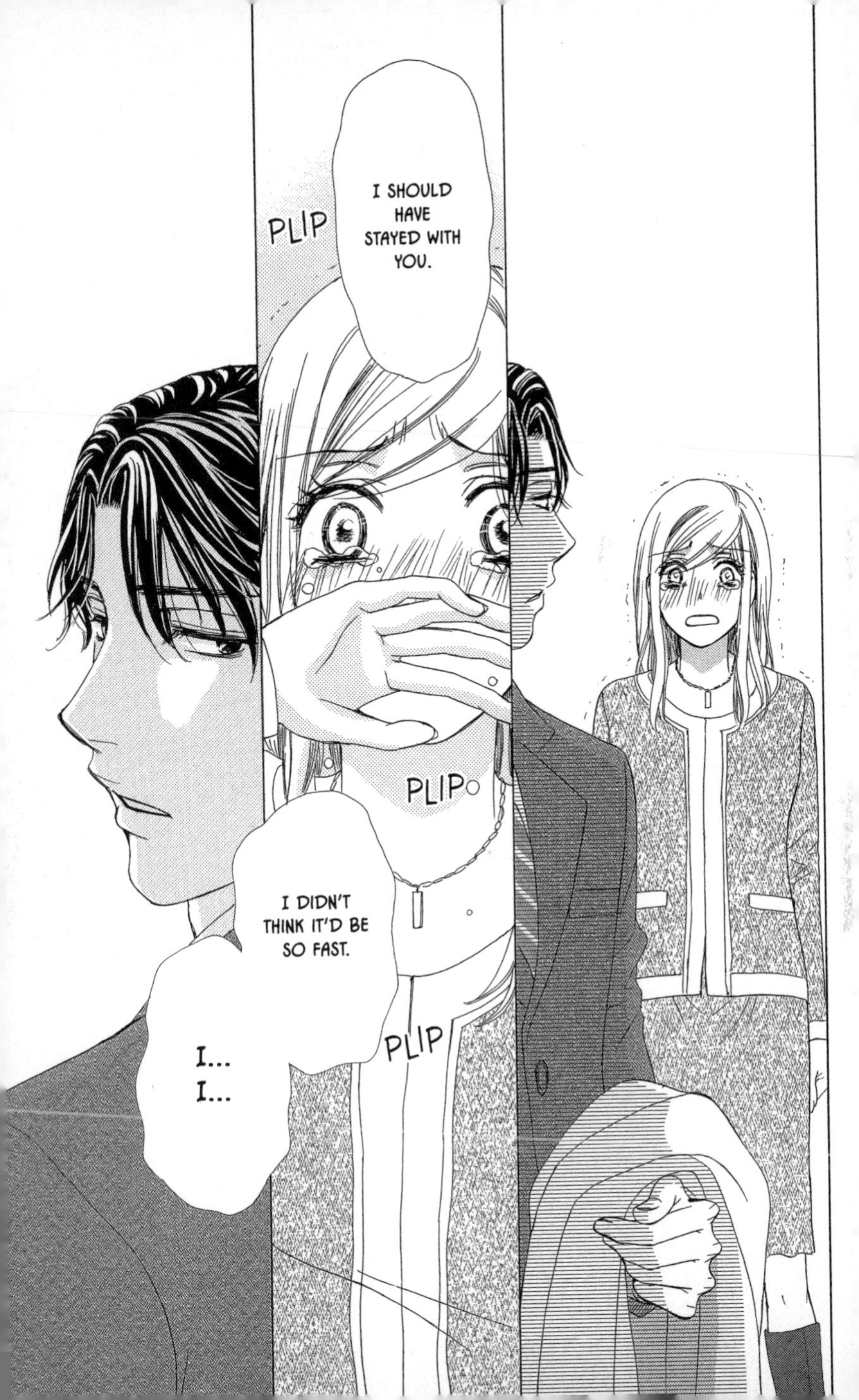
I SHOULD HAVE STAYED WITH YOU.
PLIP
PLIP
I DIDN'T THINK IT'D BE SO FAST.
PLIP
I... I...

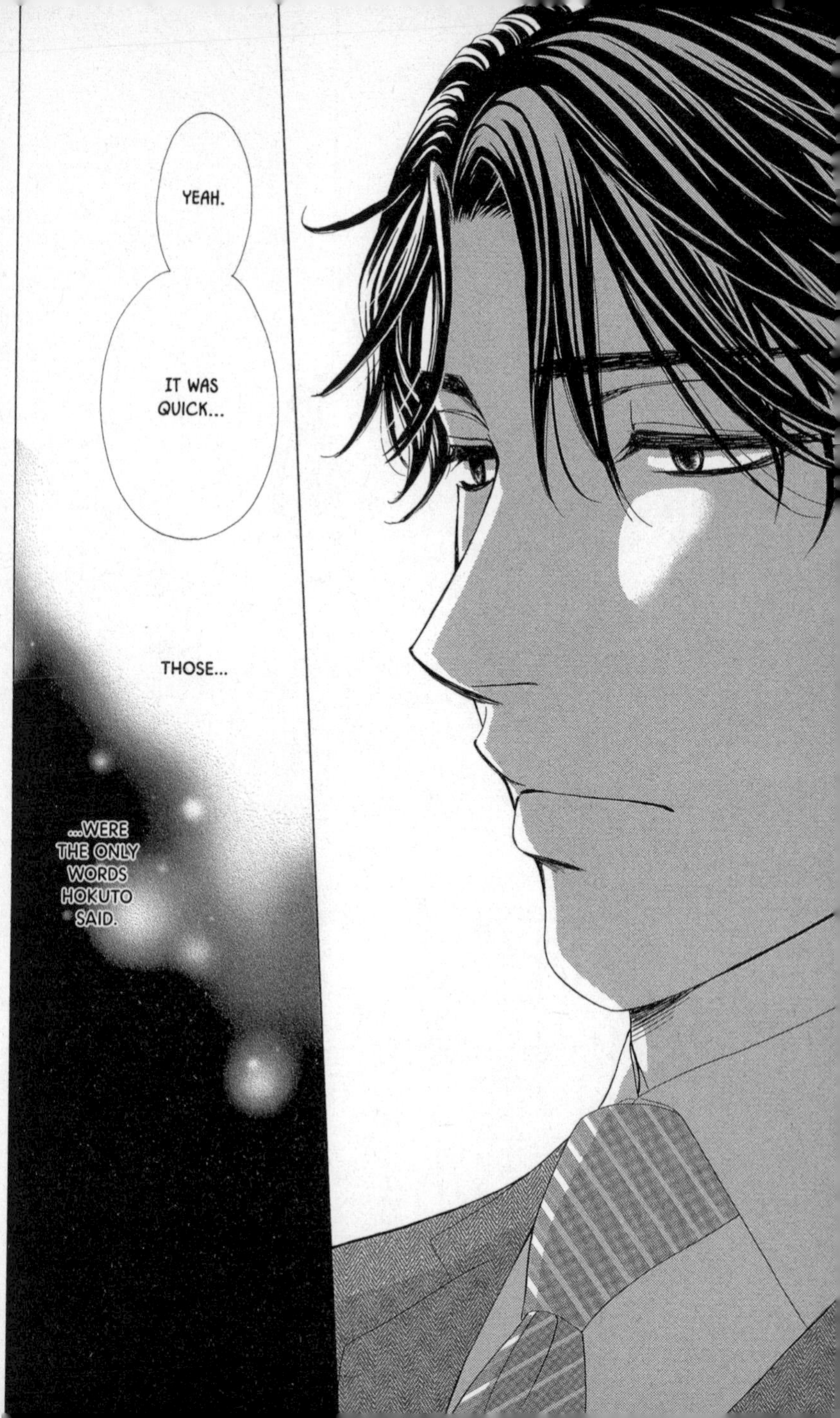
YEAH.
IT WAS QUICK...
THOSE...
...WERE THE ONLY WORDS HOKUTO SAID.

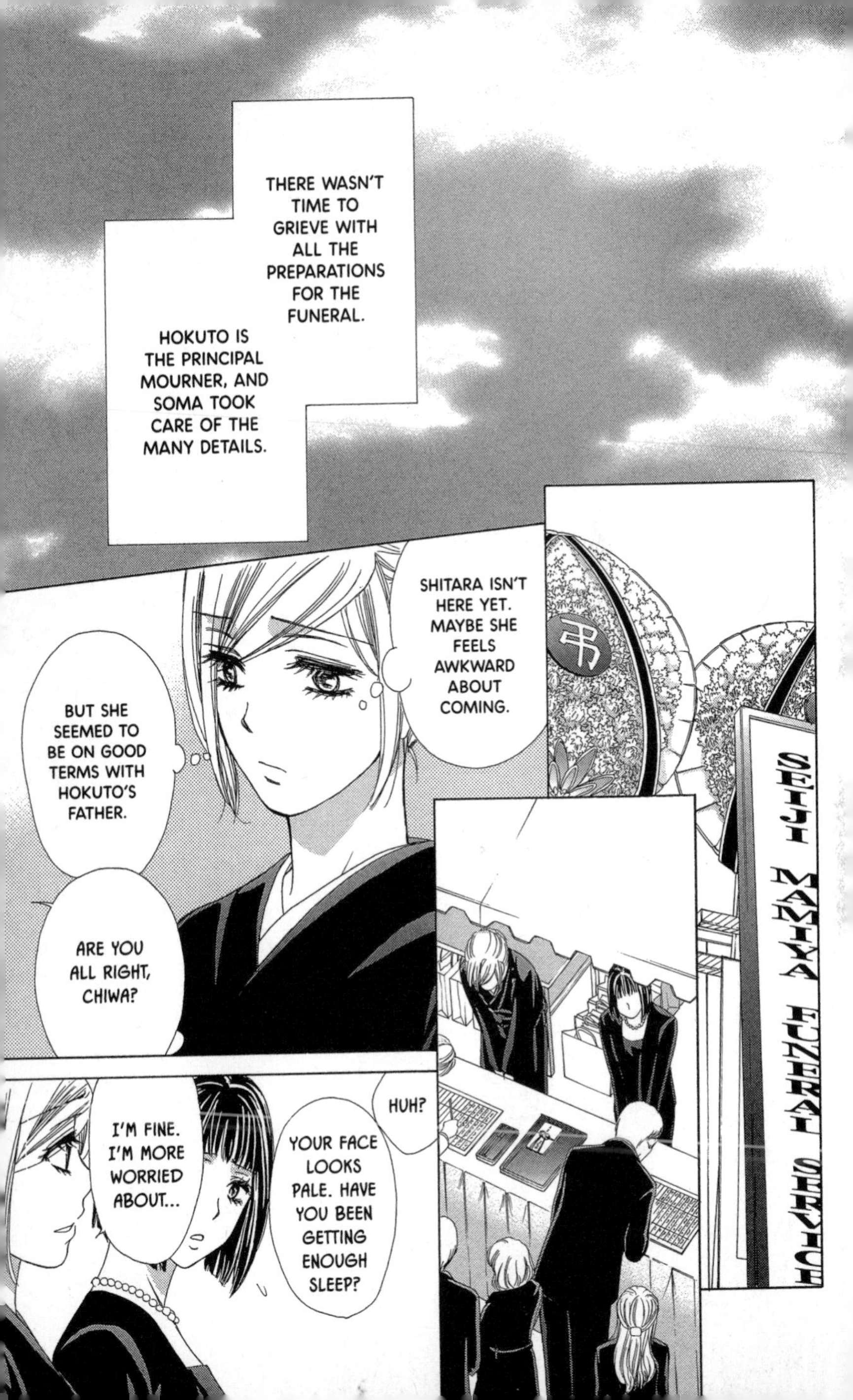
THERE WASN'T TIME TO GRIEVE WITH ALL THE PREPARATIONS FOR THE FUNERAL.
HOKUTO IS THE PRINCIPAL MOURNER, AND SOMA TOOK CARE OF THE MANY DETAILS.
SEIJI MAMIYA FUNERAL SERVICE
SHITARA ISN'T HERE YET. MAYBE SHE FEELS AWKWARD ABOUT COMING.
BUT SHE SEEMED TO BE ON GOOD TERMS WITH HOKUTO'S FATHER.
ARE YOU ALL RIGHT, CHIWA?
HUH?
YOUR FACE LOOKS PALE. HAVE YOU BEEN GETTING ENOUGH SLEEP?
I'M FINE. I'M MORE WORRIED ABOUT...

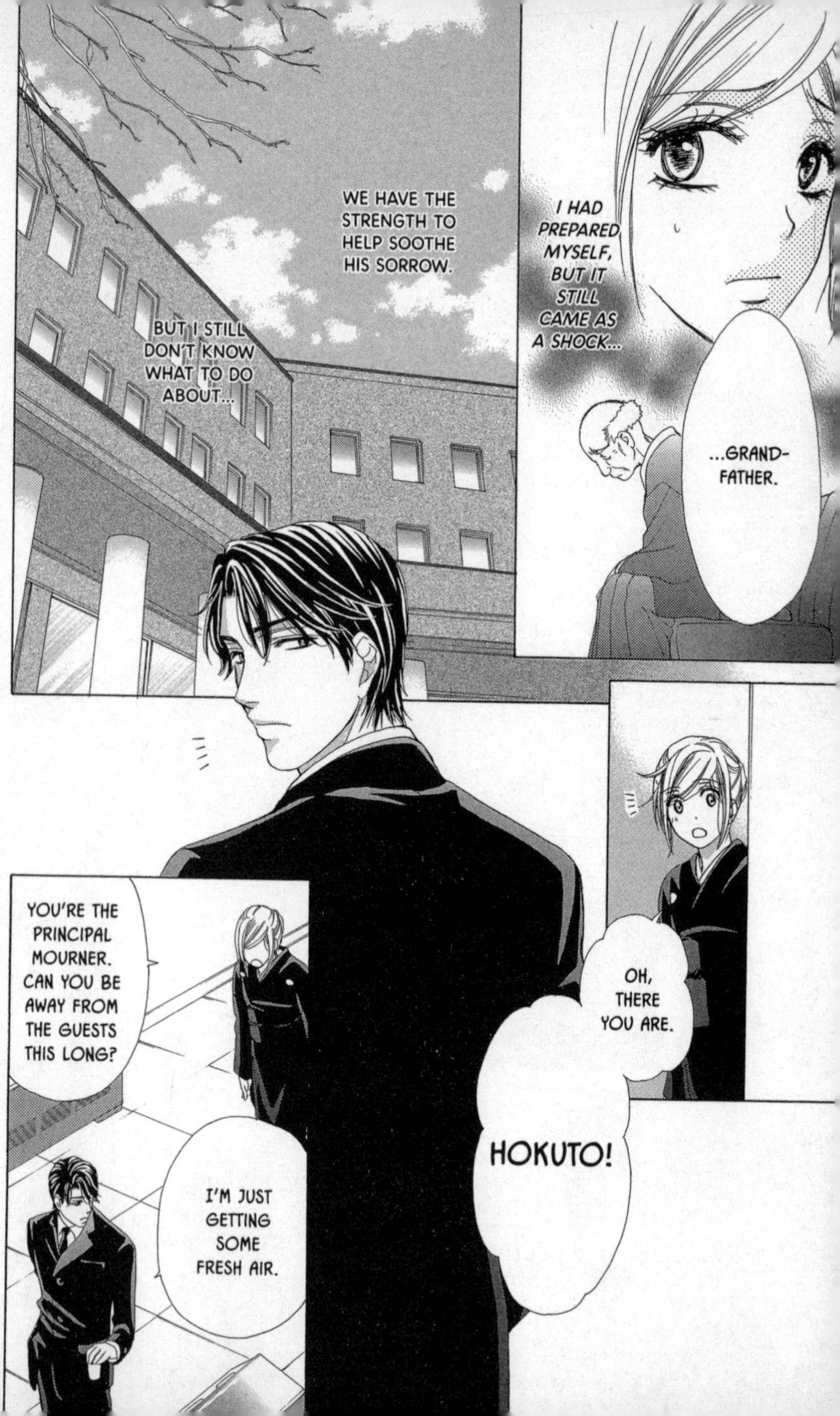
I HAD PREPARED MYSELF, BUT IT STILL CAME AS A SHOCK...
...GRAND-FATHER.
WE HAVE THE STRENGTH TO HELP SOOTHE HIS SORROW.
BUT I STILL DON'T KNOW WHAT TO DO ABOUT...
OH, THERE YOU ARE.
HOKUTO!
YOU'RE THE PRINCIPAL MOURNER. CAN YOU BE AWAY FROM THE GUESTS THIS LONG?
I'M JUST GETTING SOME FRESH AIR.

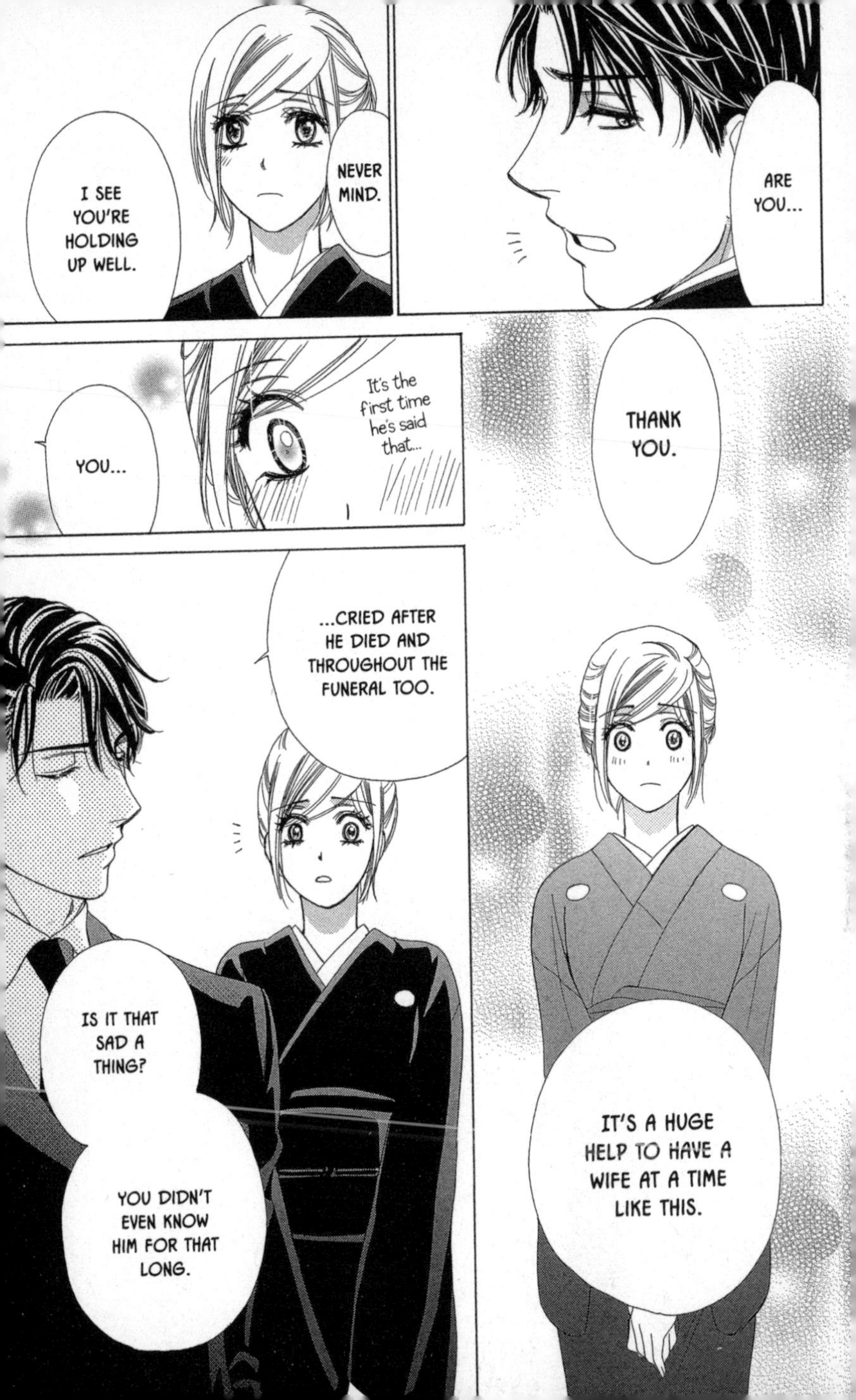
ARE YOU...
NEVER MIND.
I SEE YOU'RE HOLDING UP WELL.
THANK YOU.
IT'S A HUGE HELP TO HAVE A WIFE AT A TIME LIKE THIS.
It's the first time he's said that...
YOU...
...CRIED AFTER HE DIED AND THROUGHOUT THE FUNERAL TOO.
IS IT THAT SAD A THING?
YOU DIDN'T EVEN KNOW HIM FOR THAT LONG.

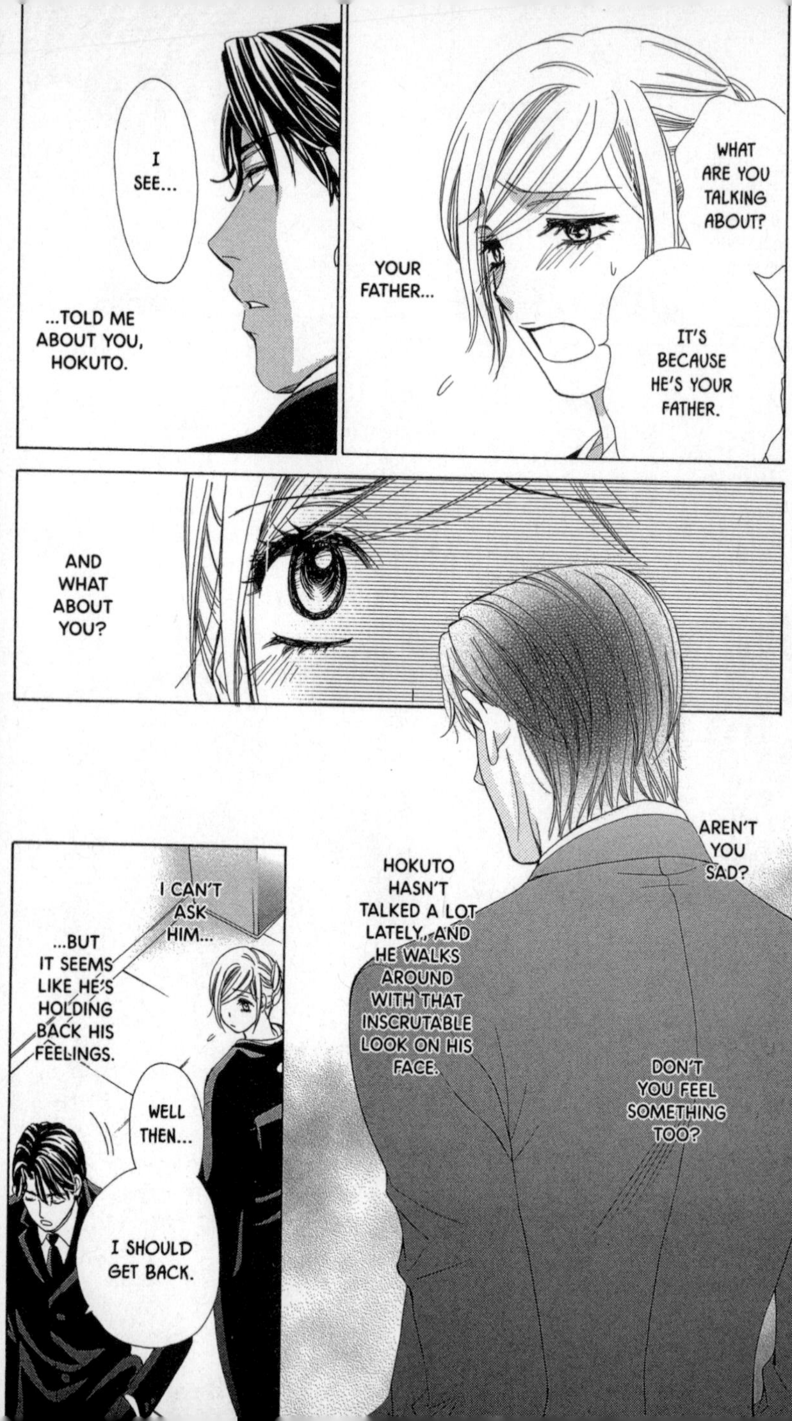
WHAT ARE YOU TALKING ABOUT?
YOUR FATHER...
IT'S BECAUSE HE'S YOUR FATHER.
I SEE...
...TOLD ME ABOUT YOU, HOKUTO.
AND WHAT ABOUT YOU?
AREN'T YOU SAD?
HOKUTO HASN'T TALKED A LOT LATELY, AND HE WALKS AROUND WITH THAT INSCRUTABLE LOOK ON HIS FACE.
DON'T YOU FEEL SOMETHING TOO?
I CAN'T ASK HIM...
...BUT IT SEEMS LIKE HE'S HOLDING BACK HIS FEELINGS.
WELL THEN...
I SHOULD GET BACK.

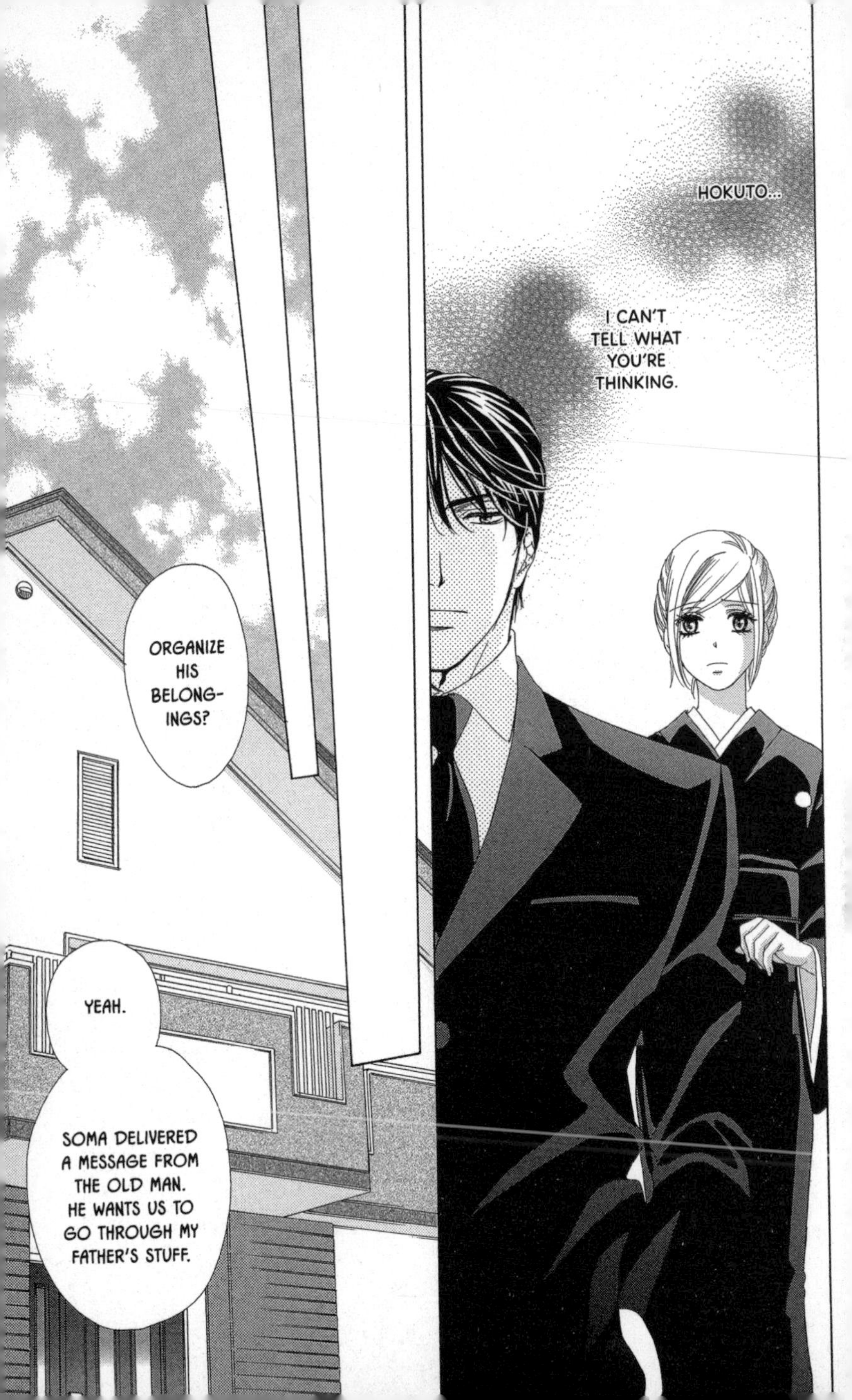
HOKUTO...
I CAN'T TELL WHAT YOU'RE THINKING.
ORGANIZE HIS BELONG-INGS?
YEAH.
SOMA DELIVERED A MESSAGE FROM THE OLD MAN. HE WANTS US TO GO THROUGH MY FATHER'S STUFF.

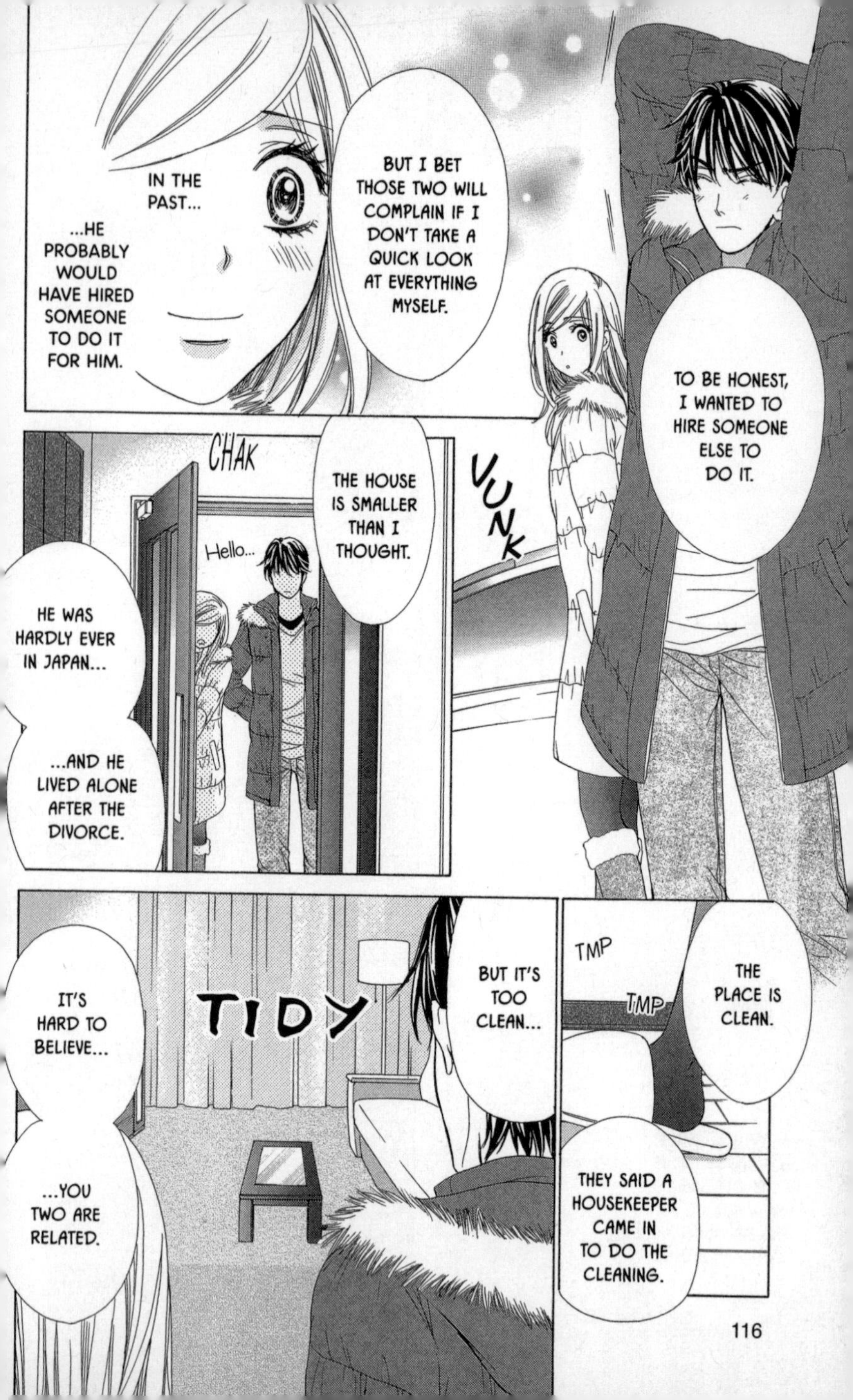
TO BE HONEST, I WANTED TO HIRE SOMEONE ELSE TO DO IT.
VUNK
BUT I BET THOSE TWO WILL COMPLAIN IF I DON'T TAKE A QUICK LOOK AT EVERYTHING MYSELF.
IN THE PAST...
...HE PROBABLY WOULD HAVE HIRED SOMEONE TO DO IT FOR HIM.
CHAK
THE HOUSE IS SMALLER THAN I THOUGHT.
Hello...
HE WAS HARDLY EVER IN JAPAN...
...AND HE LIVED ALONE AFTER THE DIVORCE.
THE PLACE IS CLEAN.
TMP
TMP
THEY SAID A HOUSEKEEPER CAME IN TO DO THE CLEANING.
BUT IT'S TOO CLEAN...
TIDY
IT'S HARD TO BELIEVE...
...YOU TWO ARE RELATED.

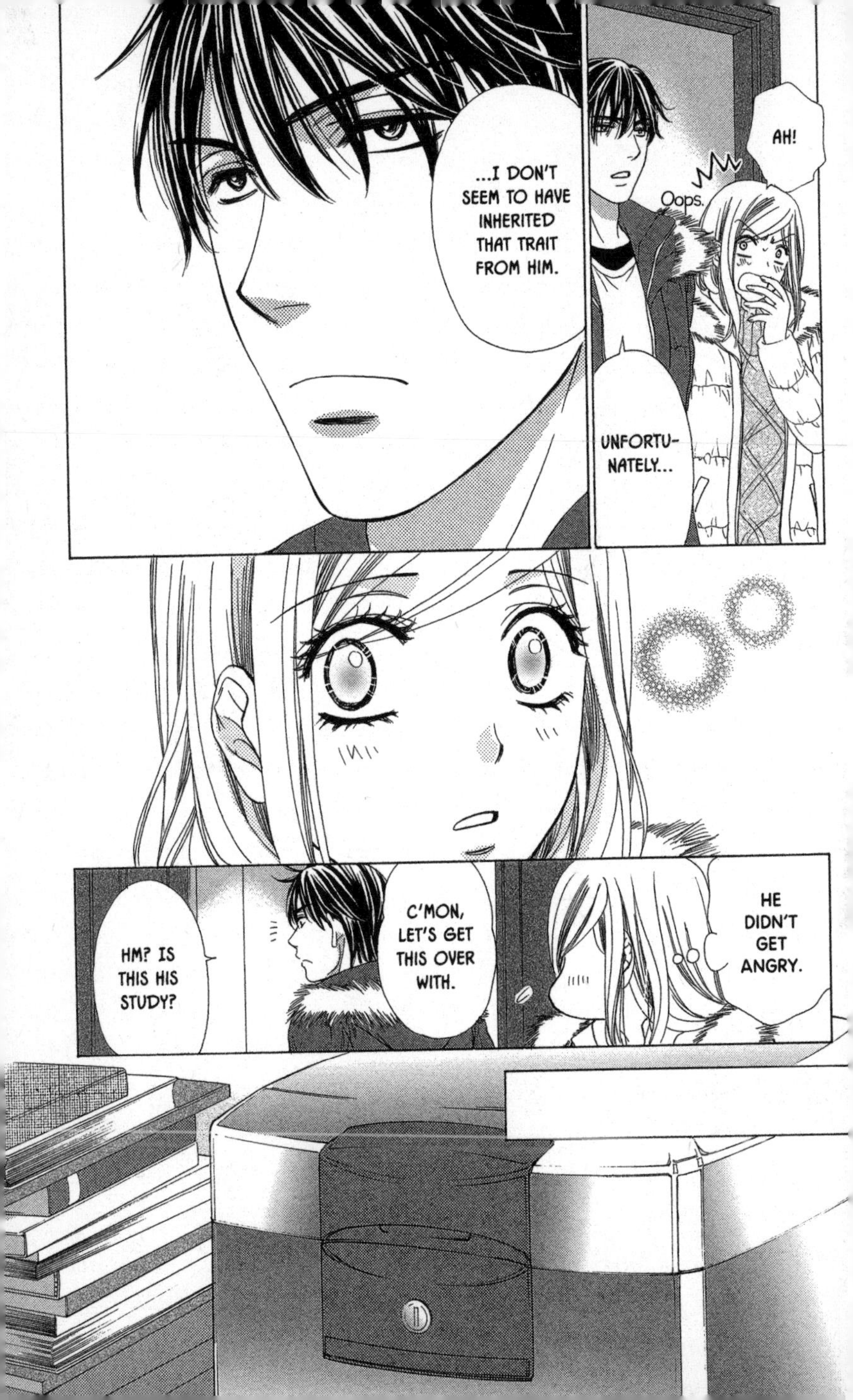
AH!
Oops.
UNFORTU-NATELY...
...I DON'T SEEM TO HAVE INHERITED THAT TRAIT FROM HIM.
HE DIDN'T GET ANGRY.
C'MON, LET'S GET THIS OVER WITH.
HM? IS THIS HIS STUDY?

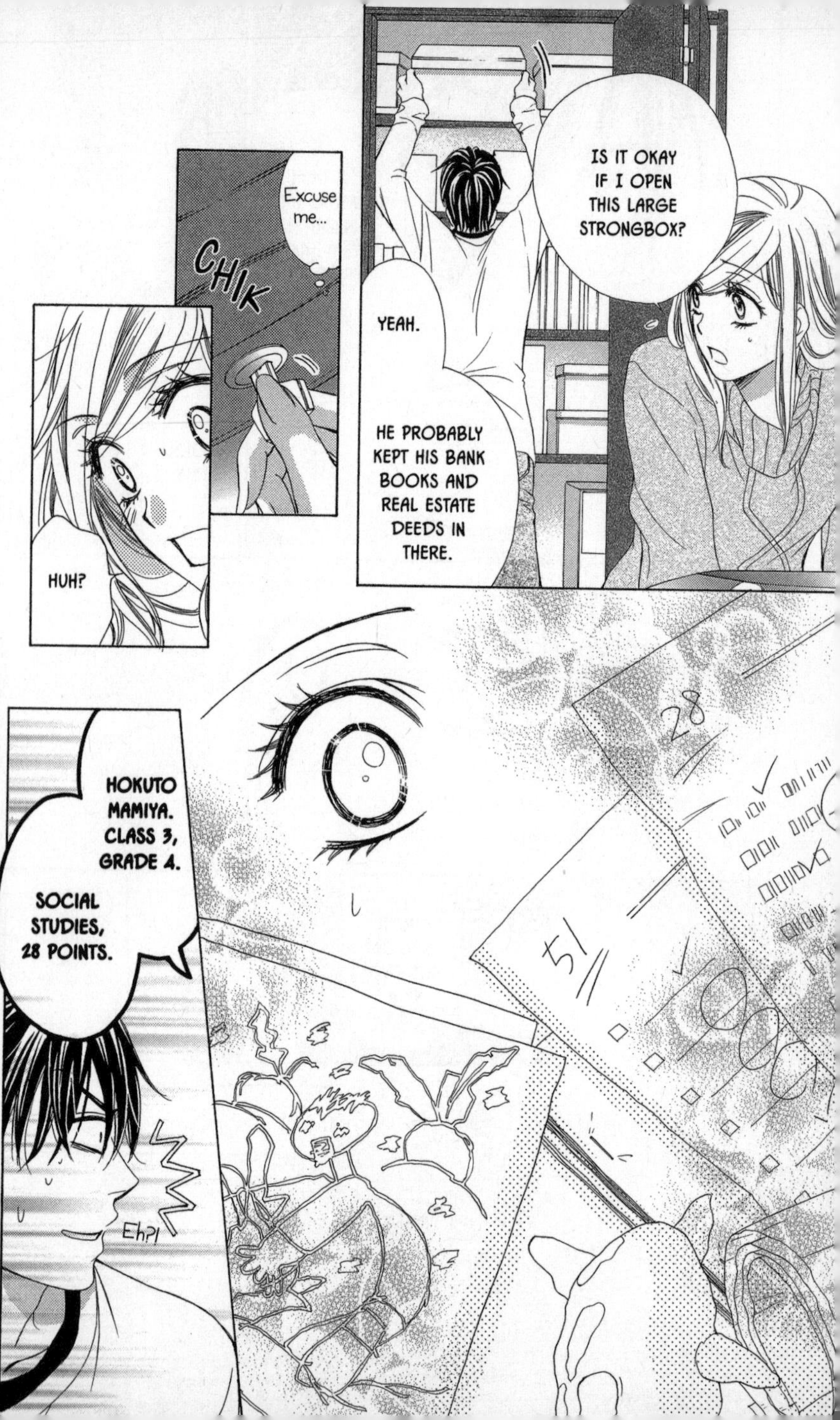
IS IT OKAY IF I OPEN THIS LARGE STRONGBOX?
YEAH.
HE PROBABLY KEPT HIS BANK BOOKS AND REAL ESTATE DEEDS IN THERE.
Excuse me...
CHIK
HUH?
28
51
HOKUTO MAMIYA. CLASS 3, GRADE 4.
SOCIAL STUDIES, 28 POINTS.
Eh?!

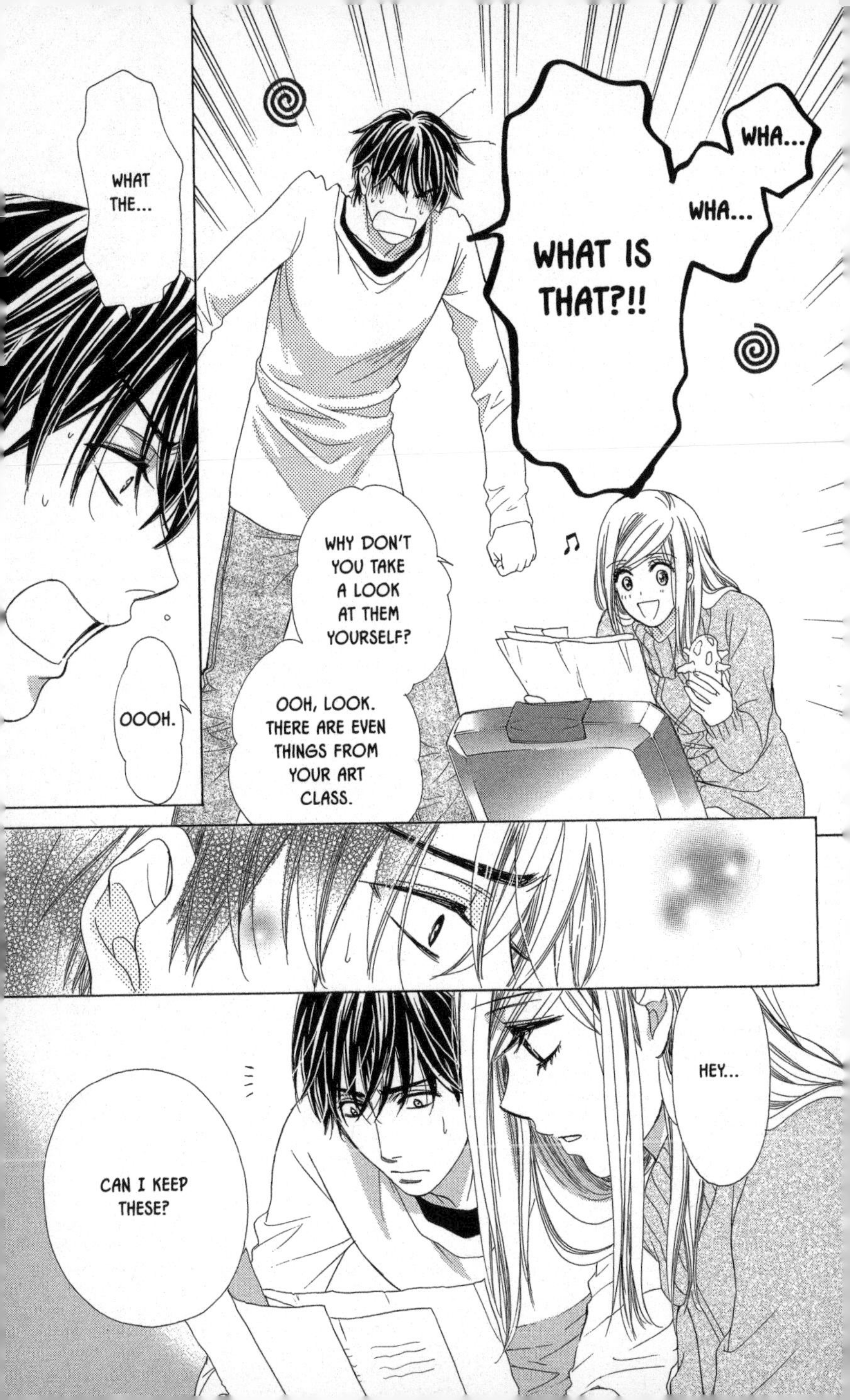
WHA...
WHA...
WHAT IS THAT?!!
WHY DON'T YOU TAKE A LOOK AT THEM YOURSELF?
OOH, LOOK. THERE ARE EVEN THINGS FROM YOUR ART CLASS.
WHAT THE...
OOOH.
HEY...
CAN I KEEP THESE?

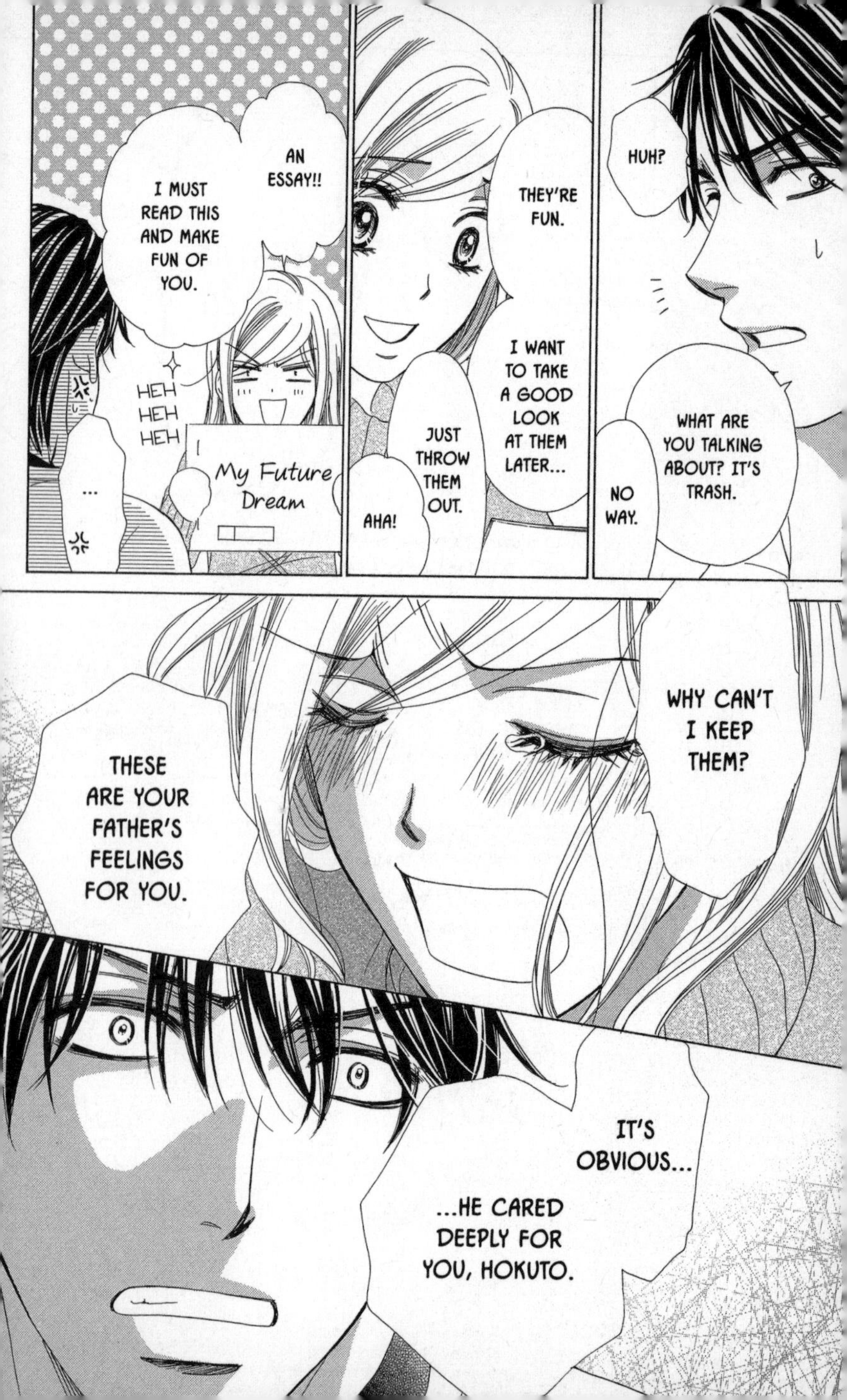
HUH?
WHAT ARE YOU TALKING ABOUT? IT'S TRASH.
NO WAY.
THEY'RE FUN.
I WANT TO TAKE A GOOD LOOK AT THEM LATER...
JUST THROW THEM OUT.
AHA!
AN ESSAY!!
I MUST READ THIS AND MAKE FUN OF YOU.
HEH HEH HEH
My Future Dream
...
WHY CAN'T I KEEP THEM?
THESE ARE YOUR FATHER'S FEELINGS FOR YOU.
IT'S OBVIOUS...
...HE CARED DEEPLY FOR YOU, HOKUTO.

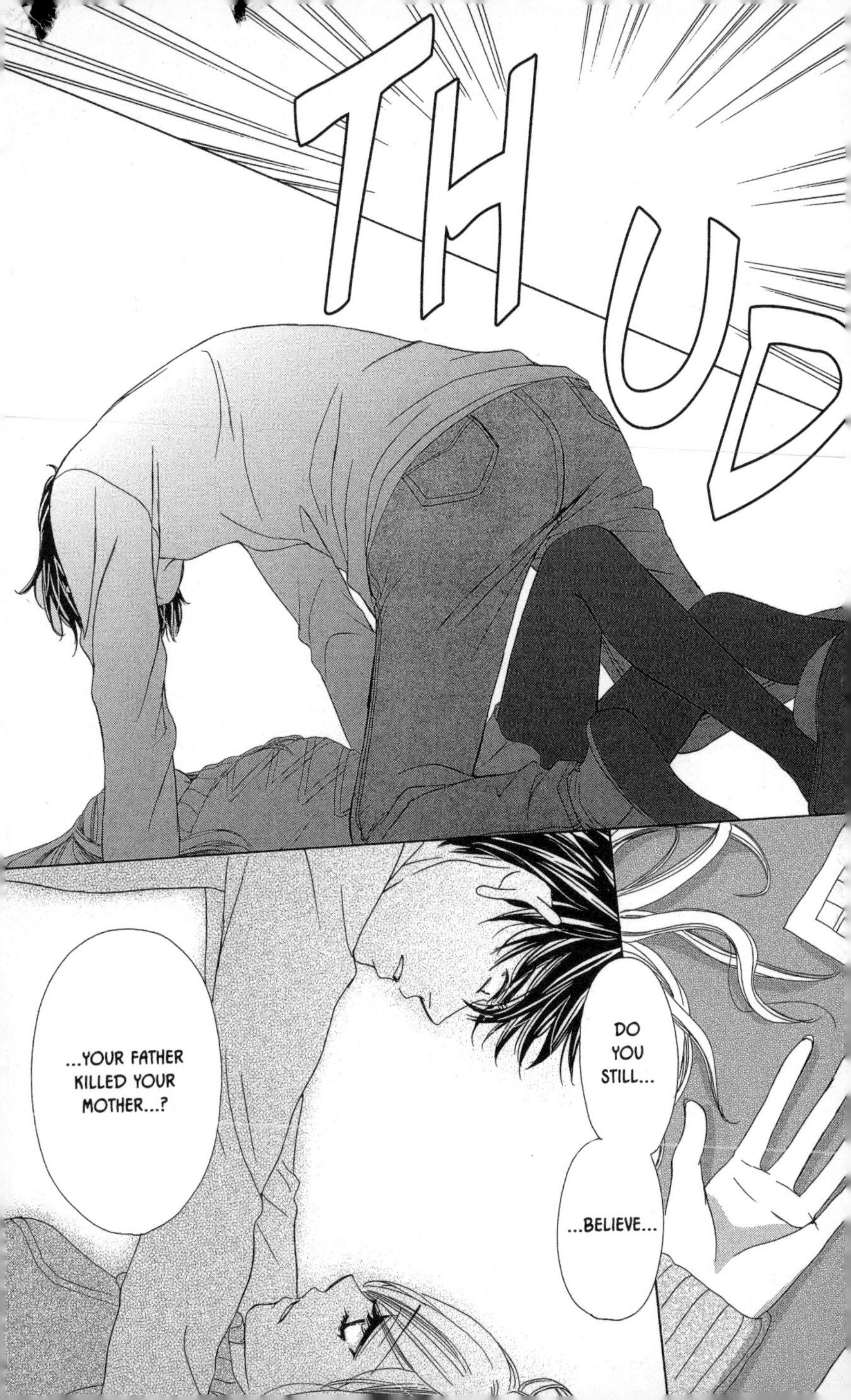
THUD
DO YOU STILL...
...BELIEVE...
...YOUR FATHER KILLED YOUR MOTHER...?

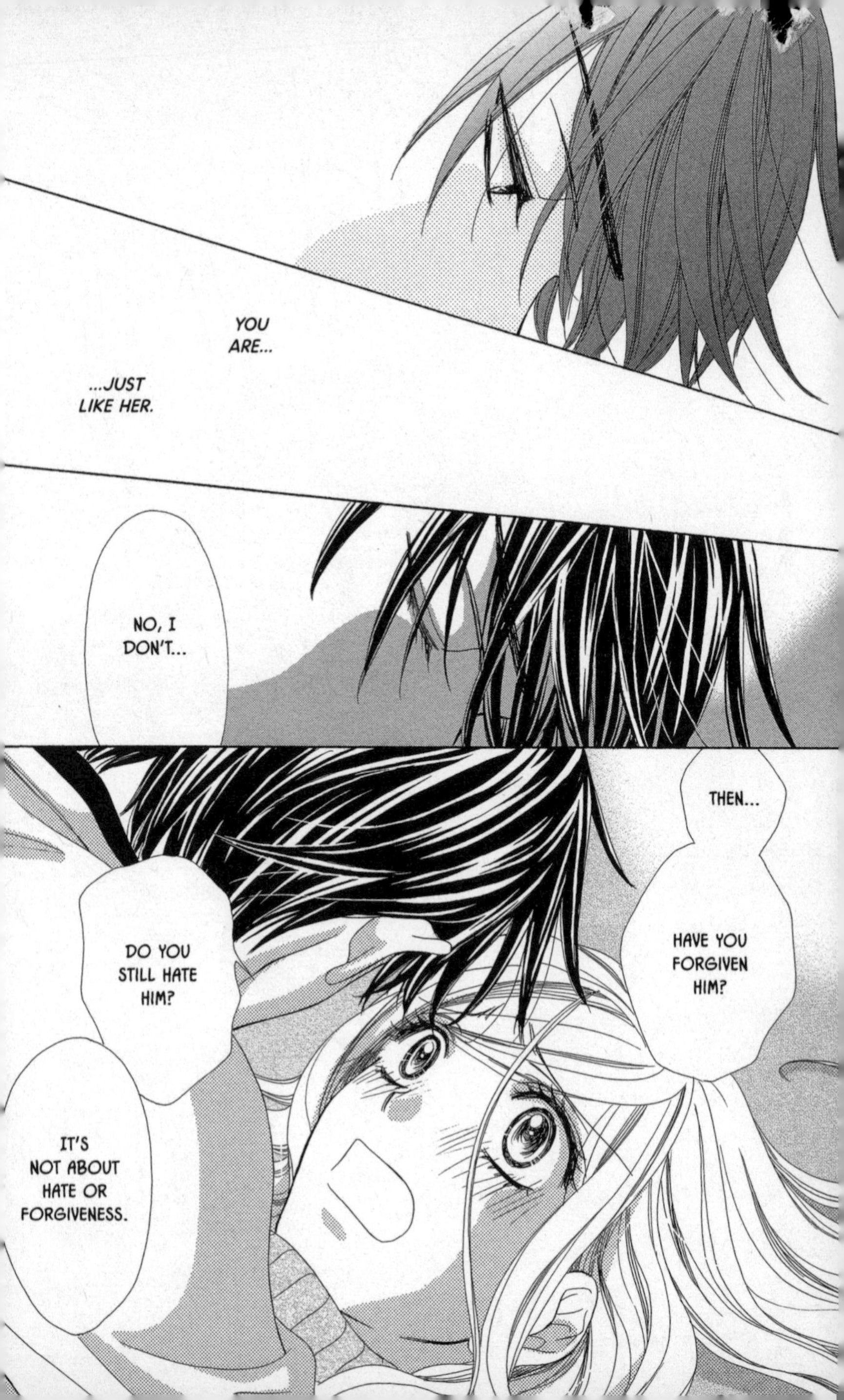
YOU ARE...
...JUST LIKE HER.
NO, I DON'T...
THEN...
HAVE YOU FORGIVEN HIM?
DO YOU STILL HATE HIM?
IT'S NOT ABOUT HATE OR FORGIVENESS.

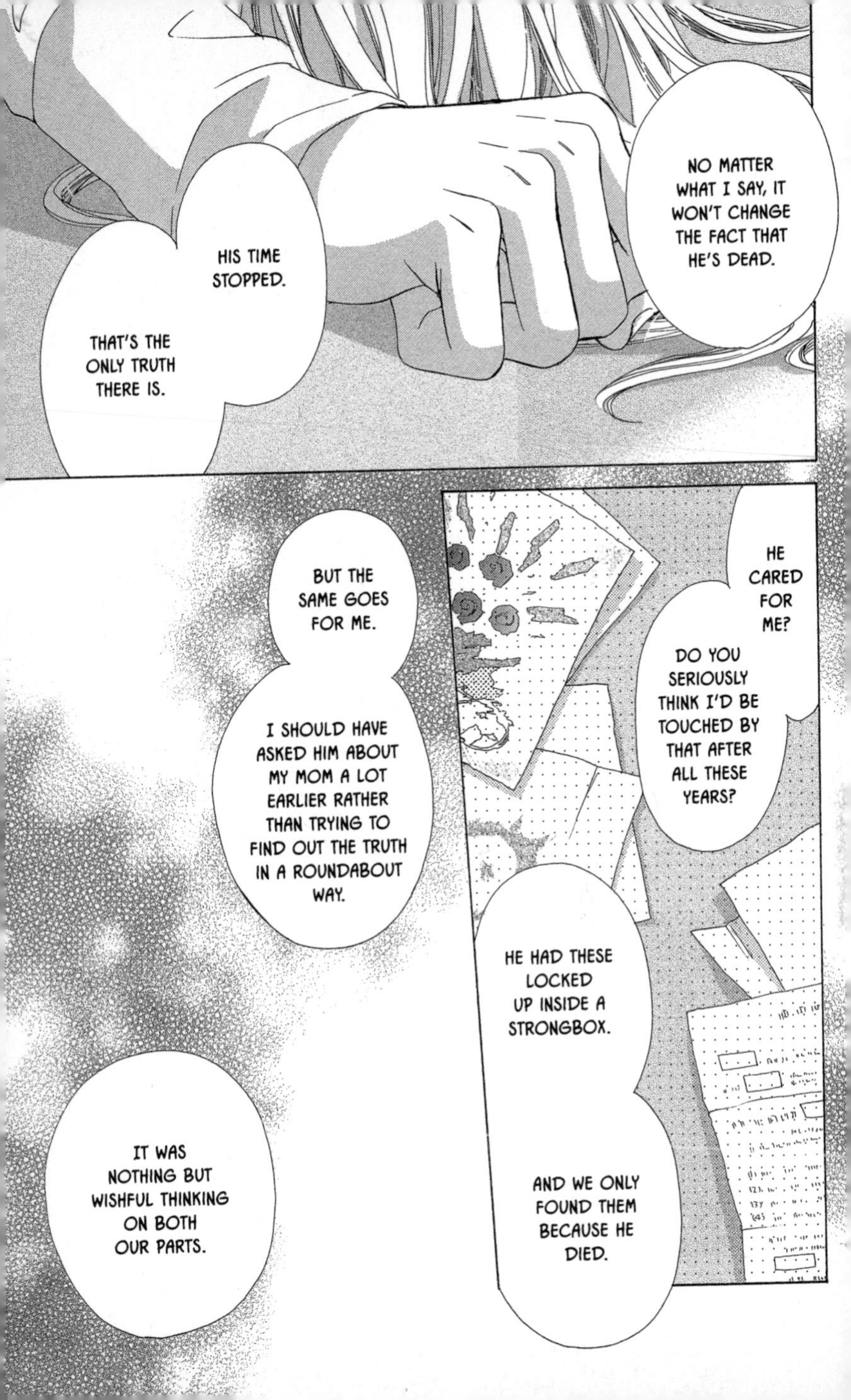
NO MATTER WHAT I SAY, IT WON'T CHANGE THE FACT THAT HE'S DEAD.
HIS TIME STOPPED.
THAT'S THE ONLY TRUTH THERE IS.
HE CARED FOR ME?
DO YOU SERIOUSLY THINK I'D BE TOUCHED BY THAT AFTER ALL THESE YEARS?
HE HAD THESE LOCKED UP INSIDE A STRONGBOX.
AND WE ONLY FOUND THEM BECAUSE HE DIED.
BUT THE SAME GOES FOR ME.
I SHOULD HAVE ASKED HIM ABOUT MY MOM A LOT EARLIER RATHER THAN TRYING TO FIND OUT THE TRUTH IN A ROUNDABOUT WAY.
IT WAS NOTHING BUT WISHFUL THINKING ON BOTH OUR PARTS.

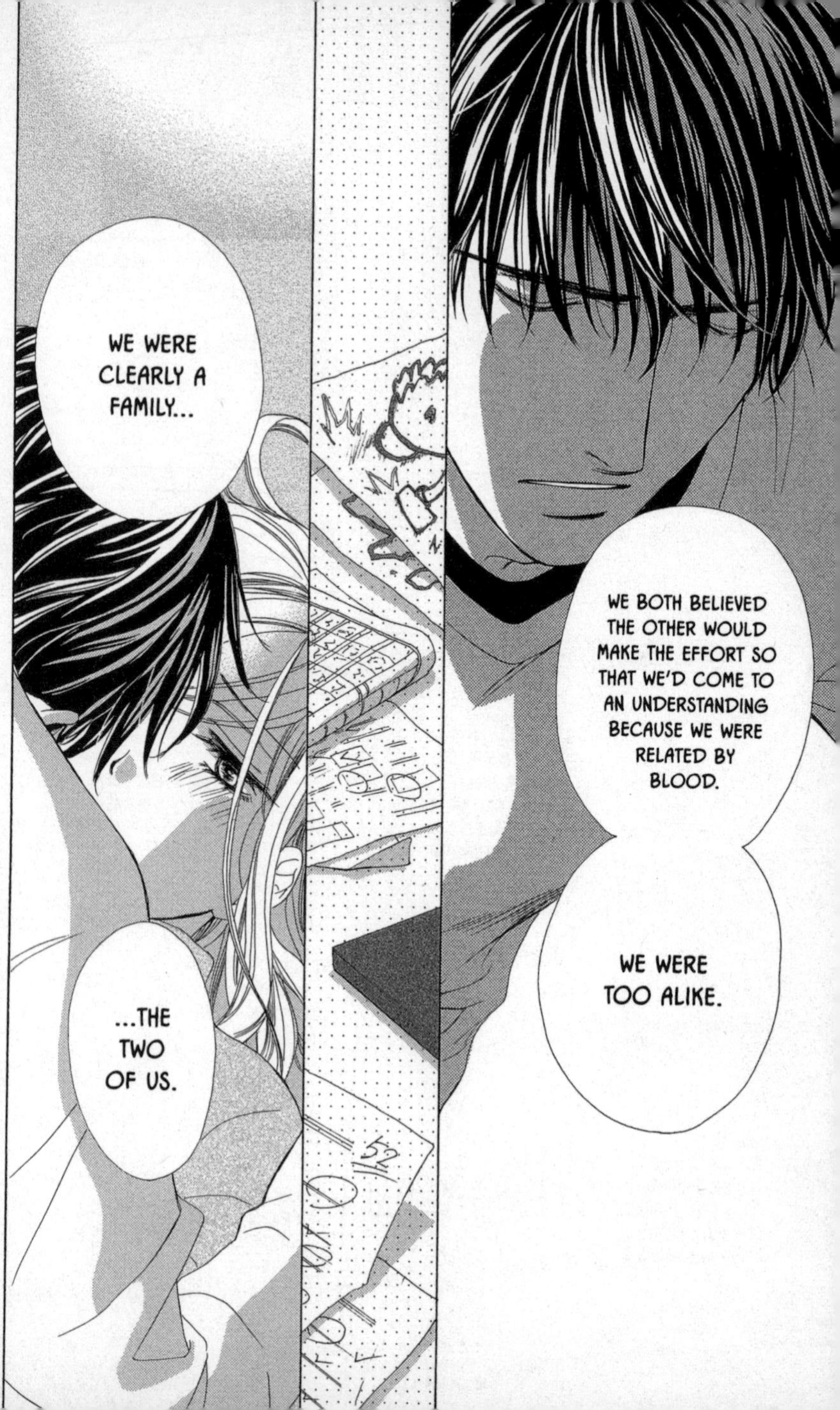
WE BOTH BELIEVED THE OTHER WOULD MAKE THE EFFORT SO THAT WE'D COME TO AN UNDERSTANDING BECAUSE WE WERE RELATED BY BLOOD.
WE WERE TOO ALIKE.
WE WERE CLEARLY A FAMILY...
...THE TWO OF US.

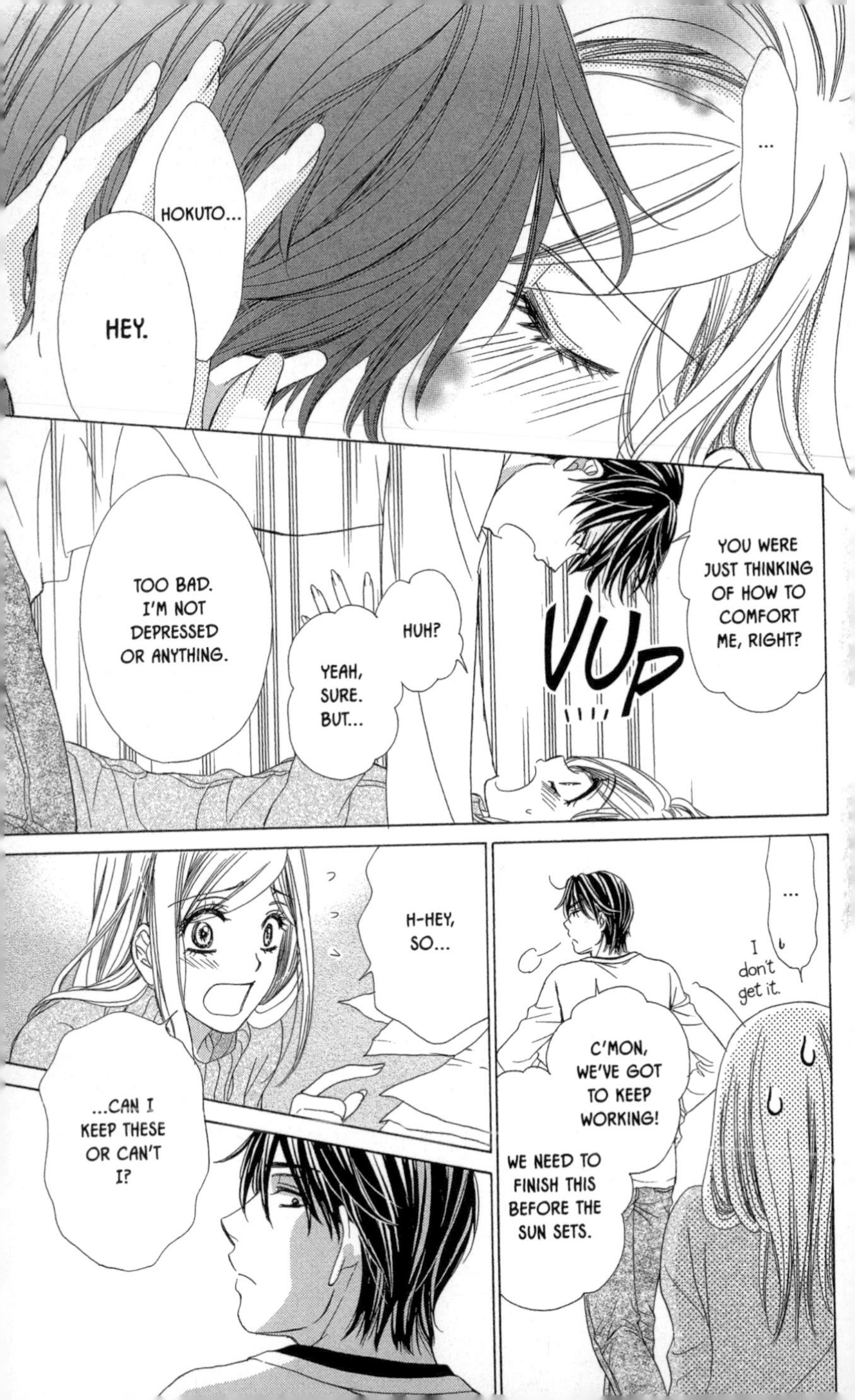
...
HOKUTO...
HEY.
YOU WERE JUST THINKING OF HOW TO COMFORT ME, RIGHT?
VUP
HUH?
YEAH, SURE. BUT...
TOO BAD. I'M NOT DEPRESSED OR ANYTHING.
...
I don't get it.
C'MON, WE'VE GOT TO KEEP WORKING!
WE NEED TO FINISH THIS BEFORE THE SUN SETS.
H-HEY, SO...
...CAN I KEEP THESE OR CAN'T I?

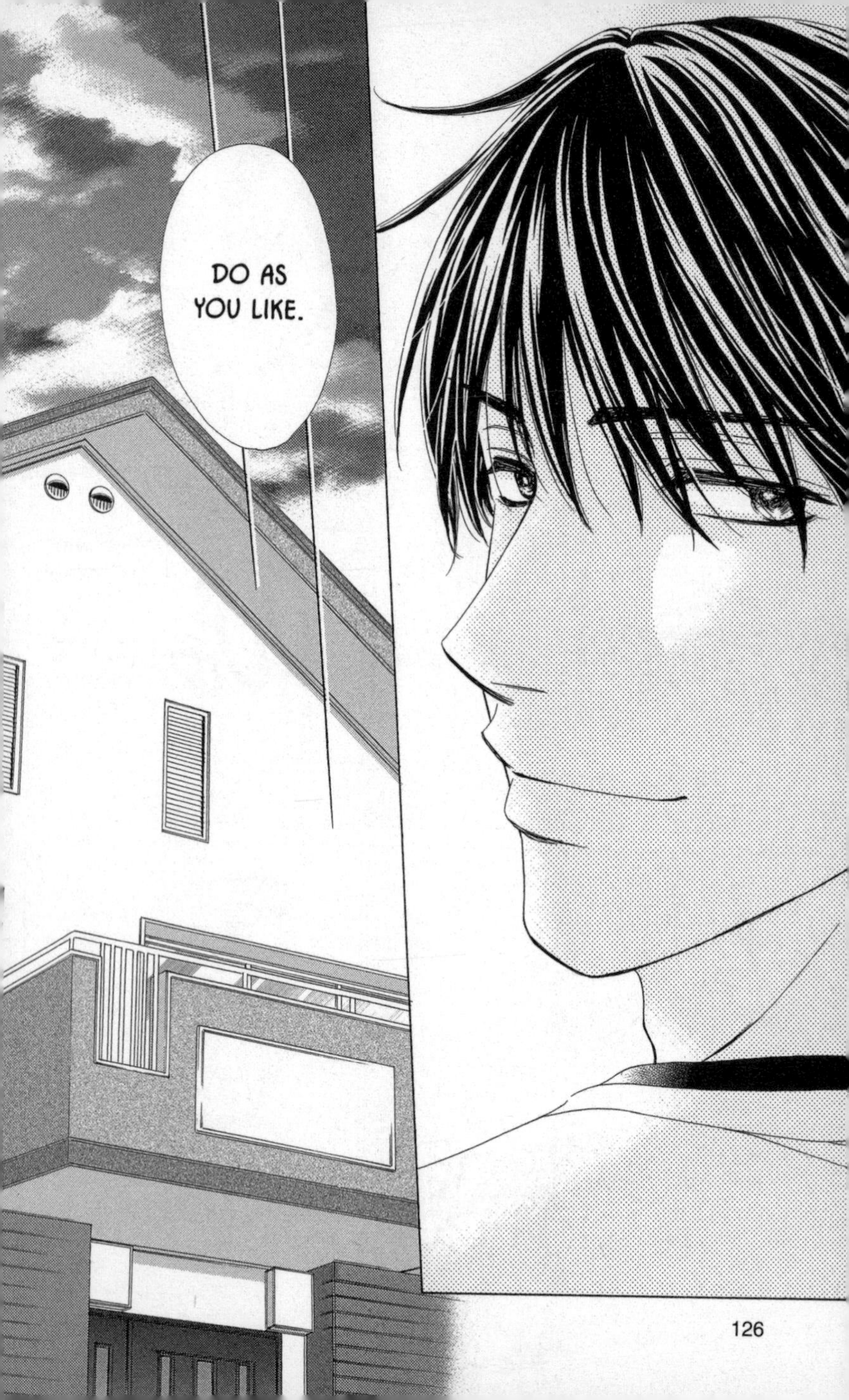
DO AS YOU LIKE.

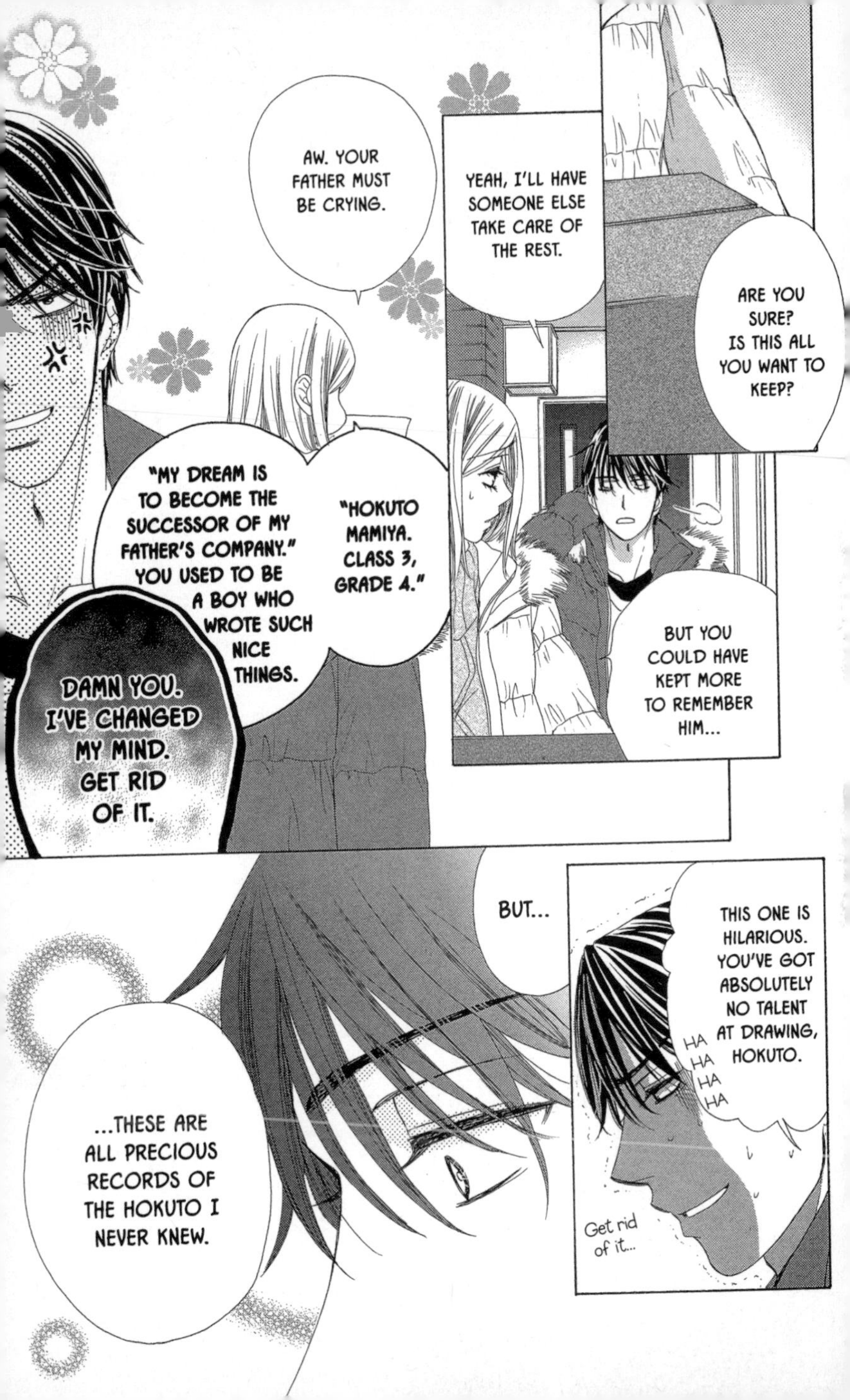
ARE YOU SURE? IS THIS ALL YOU WANT TO KEEP?
YEAH, I'LL HAVE SOMEONE ELSE TAKE CARE OF THE REST.
BUT YOU COULD HAVE KEPT MORE TO REMEMBER HIM...
AW. YOUR FATHER MUST BE CRYING.
"HOKUTO MAMIYA. CLASS 3, GRADE 4."
"MY DREAM IS TO BECOME THE SUCCESSOR OF MY FATHER'S COMPANY." YOU USED TO BE A BOY WHO WROTE SUCH NICE THINGS.
DAMN YOU. I'VE CHANGED MY MIND. GET RID OF IT.
THIS ONE IS HILARIOUS. YOU'VE GOT ABSOLUTELY NO TALENT AT DRAWING, HOKUTO.
HA HA HA HA
Get rid of it...
BUT...
...THESE ARE ALL PRECIOUS RECORDS OF THE HOKUTO I NEVER KNEW.

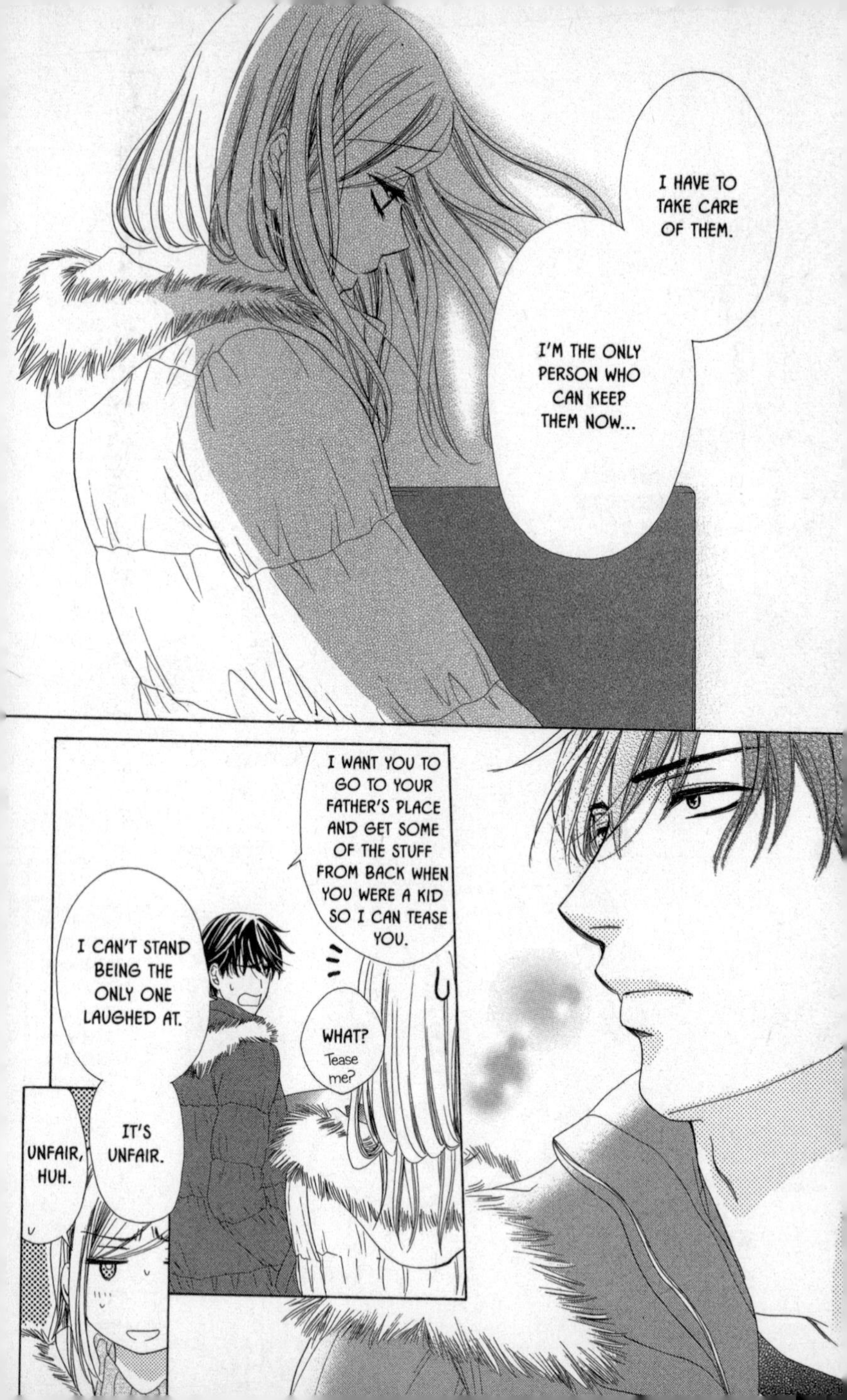
I HAVE TO TAKE CARE OF THEM.
I'M THE ONLY PERSON WHO CAN KEEP THEM NOW...
I WANT YOU TO GO TO YOUR FATHER'S PLACE AND GET SOME OF THE STUFF FROM BACK WHEN YOU WERE A KID SO I CAN TEASE YOU.
WHAT? Tease me?
I CAN'T STAND BEING THE ONLY ONE LAUGHED AT.
IT'S UNFAIR.
UNFAIR, HUH.

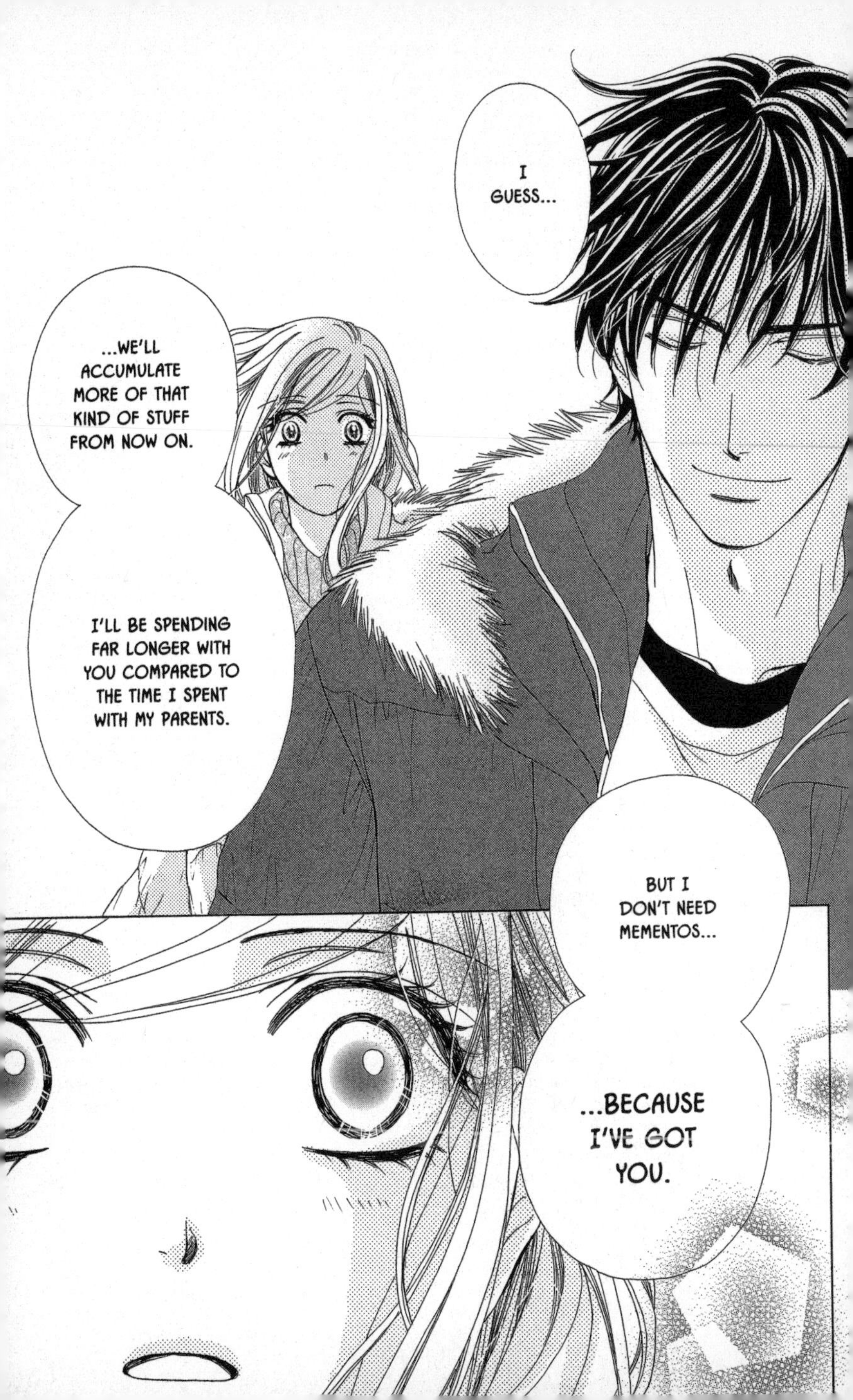
I GUESS...
...WE'LL ACCUMULATE MORE OF THAT KIND OF STUFF FROM NOW ON.
I'LL BE SPENDING FAR LONGER WITH YOU COMPARED TO THE TIME I SPENT WITH MY PARENTS.
BUT I DON'T NEED MEMENTOS...
...BECAUSE I'VE GOT YOU.

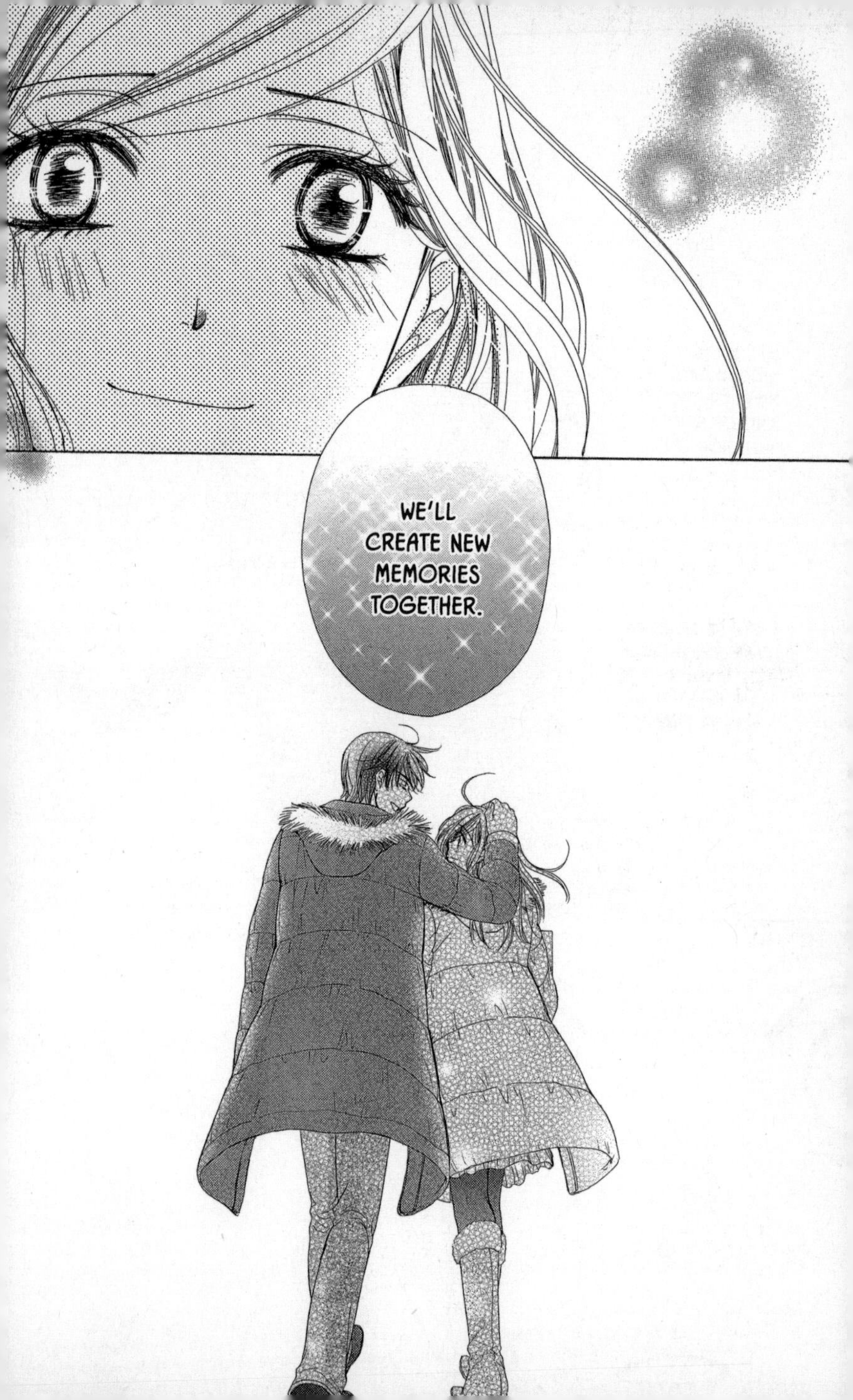
WE'LL CREATE NEW MEMORIES TOGETHER.

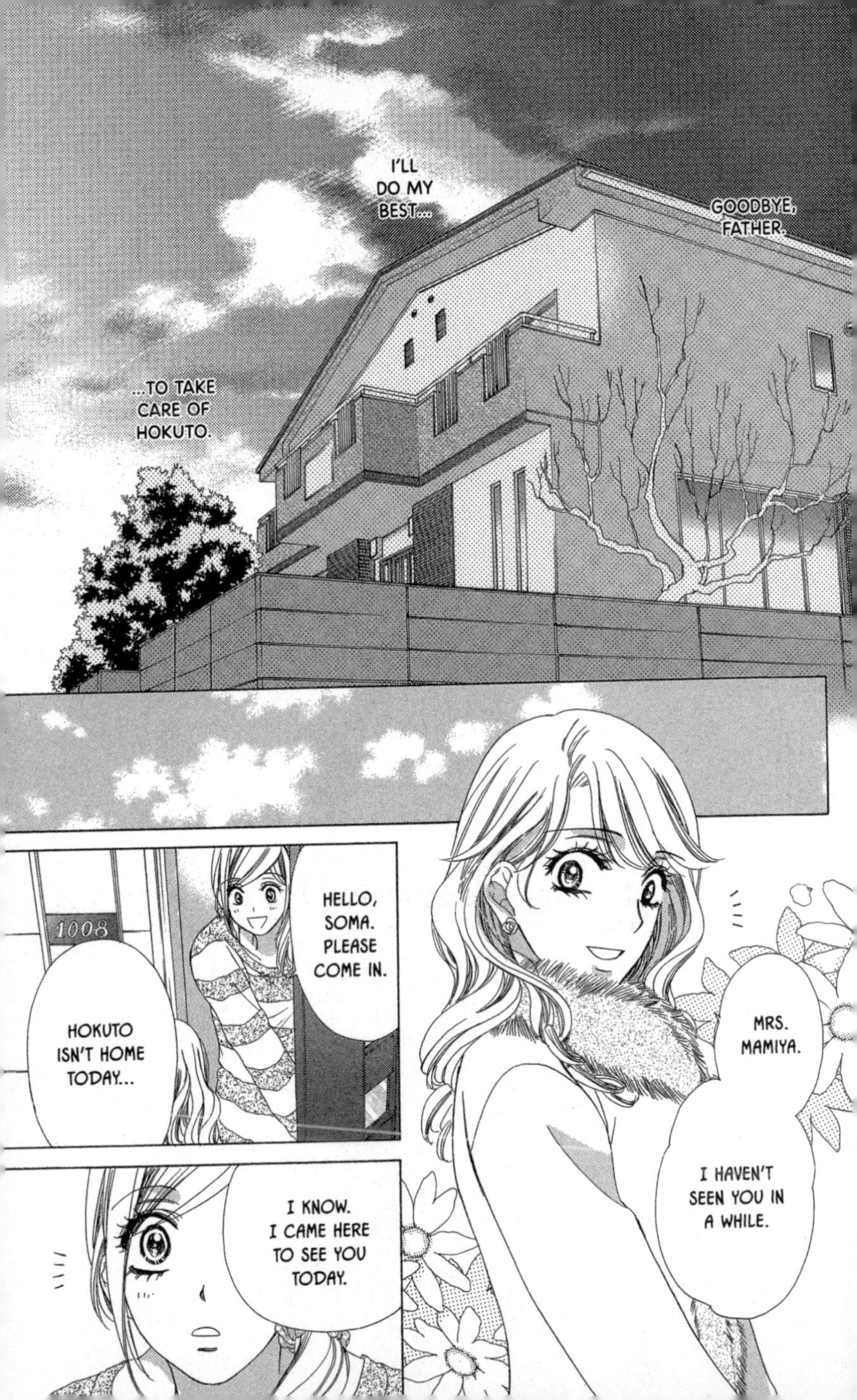
GOODBYE, FATHER.
I'LL DO MY BEST...
...TO TAKE CARE OF HOKUTO.
MRS. MAMIYA.
I HAVEN'T SEEN YOU IN A WHILE.
HELLO, SOMA. PLEASE COME IN.
1008
HOKUTO ISN'T HOME TODAY...
I KNOW. I CAME HERE TO SEE YOU TODAY.

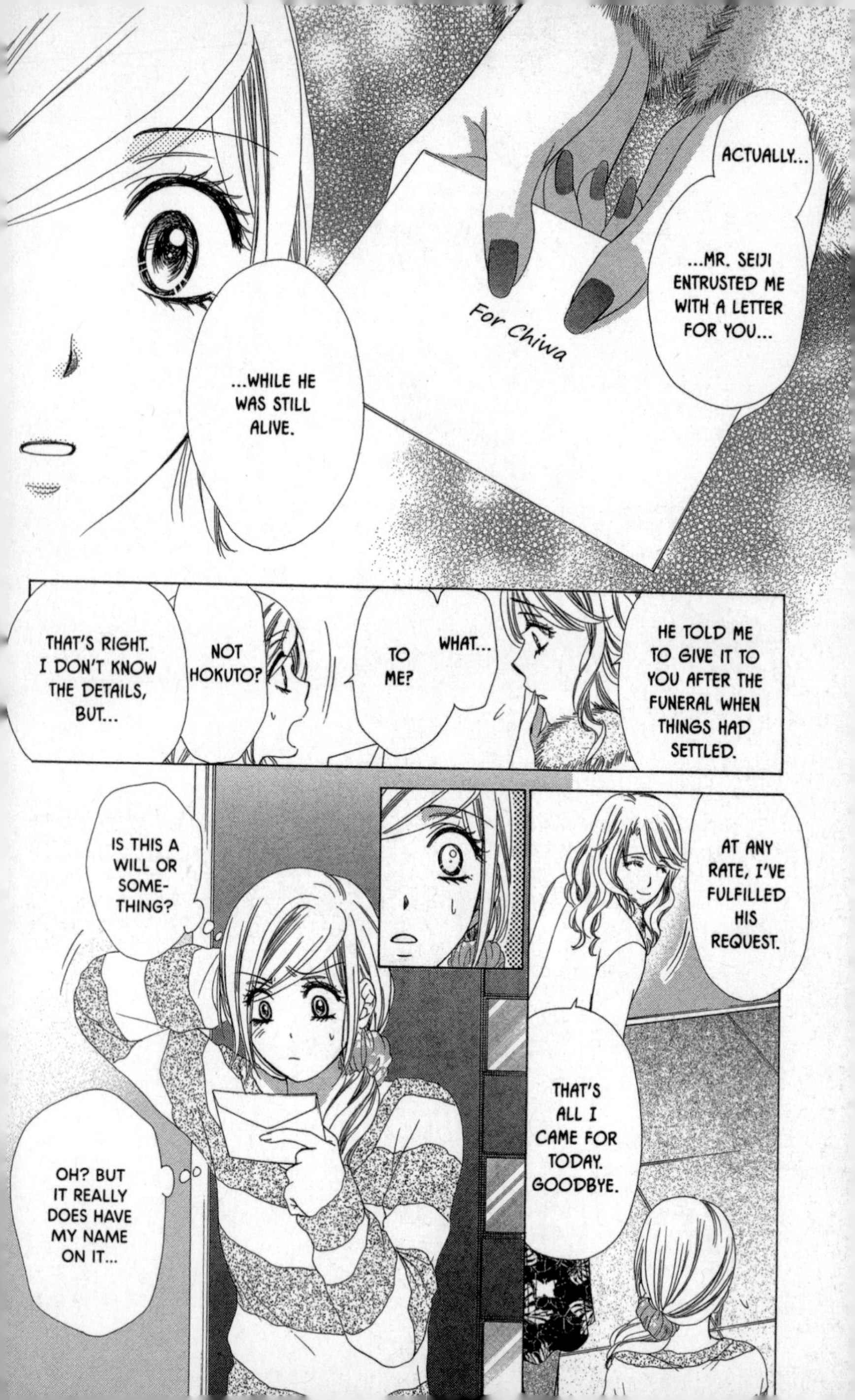
ACTUALLY...
...MR. SEIJI ENTRUSTED ME WITH A LETTER FOR YOU...
For Chiwa
...WHILE HE WAS STILL ALIVE.
HE TOLD ME TO GIVE IT TO YOU AFTER THE FUNERAL WHEN THINGS HAD SETTLED.
WHAT...
TO ME?
NOT HOKUTO?
THAT'S RIGHT. I DON'T KNOW THE DETAILS, BUT...
AT ANY RATE, I'VE FULFILLED HIS REQUEST.
THAT'S ALL I CAME FOR TODAY. GOODBYE.
IS THIS A WILL OR SOME-THING?
OH? BUT IT REALLY DOES HAVE MY NAME ON IT...

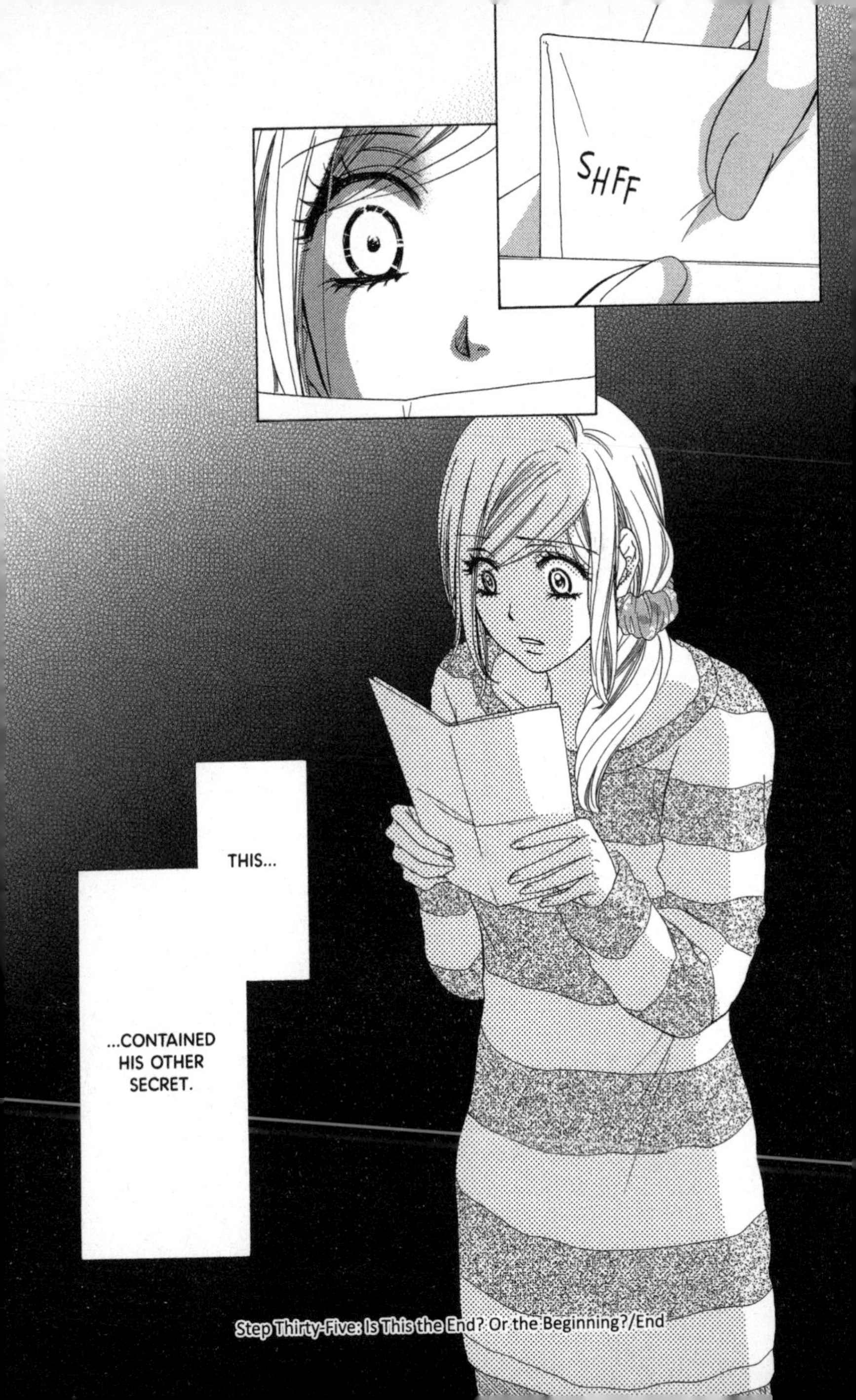
SHFF
THIS...
...CONTAINED HIS OTHER SECRET.
Step Thirty-Five: Is This the End? Or the Beginning?/End

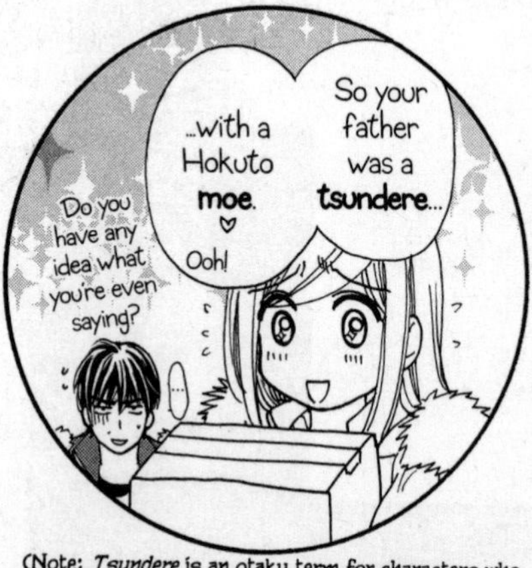
So your father was a tsundere...
...with a Hokuto moe. ♡
Ooh!
Do you have any idea what you're even saying?
...

(Note: *Tsundere* is an otaku term for characters who are cold at first but become loving once they open up. *Moe* describes a type of adoration for certain anime or manga characters.)

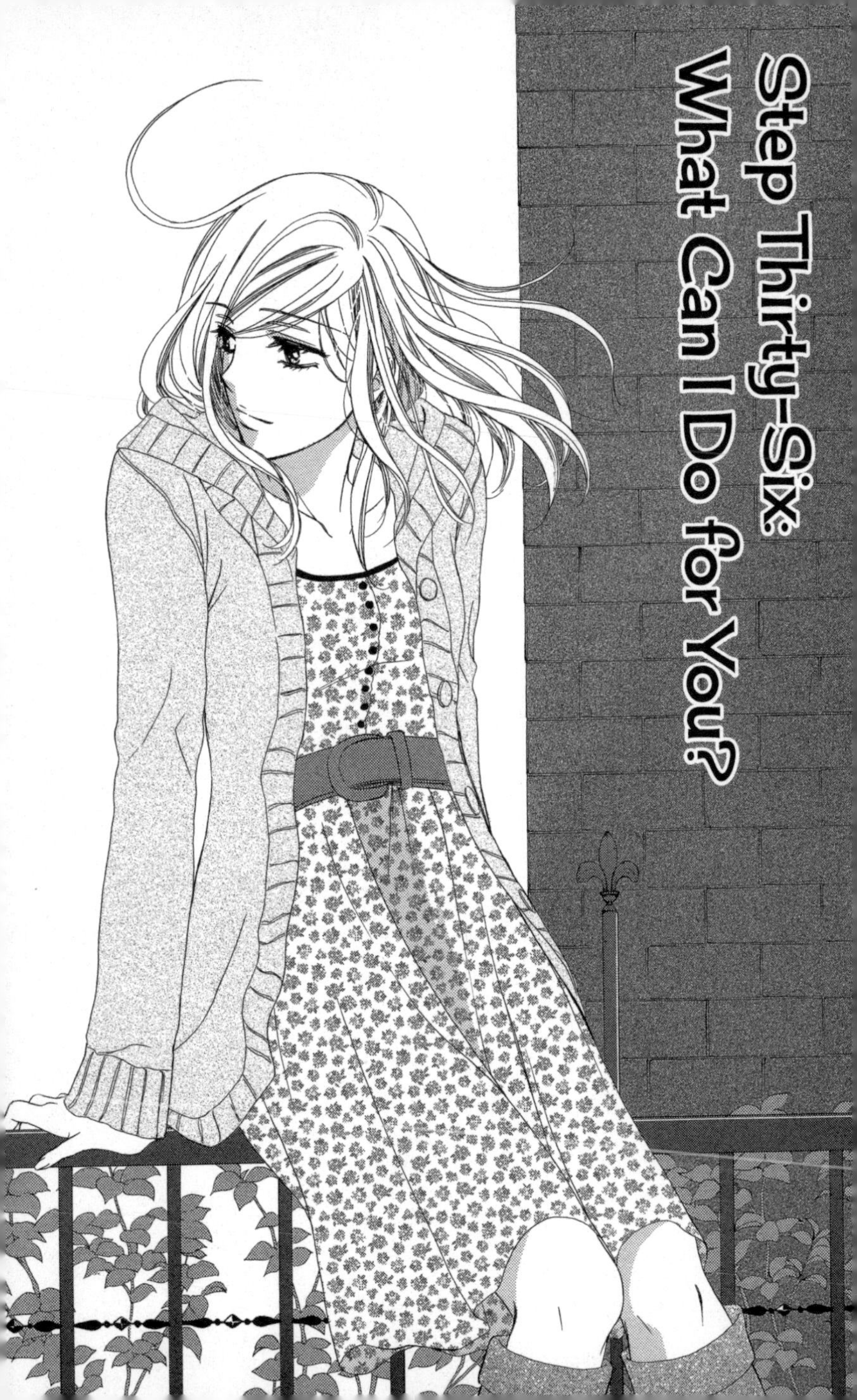
Step Thirty-Six:
What Can I Do for You?

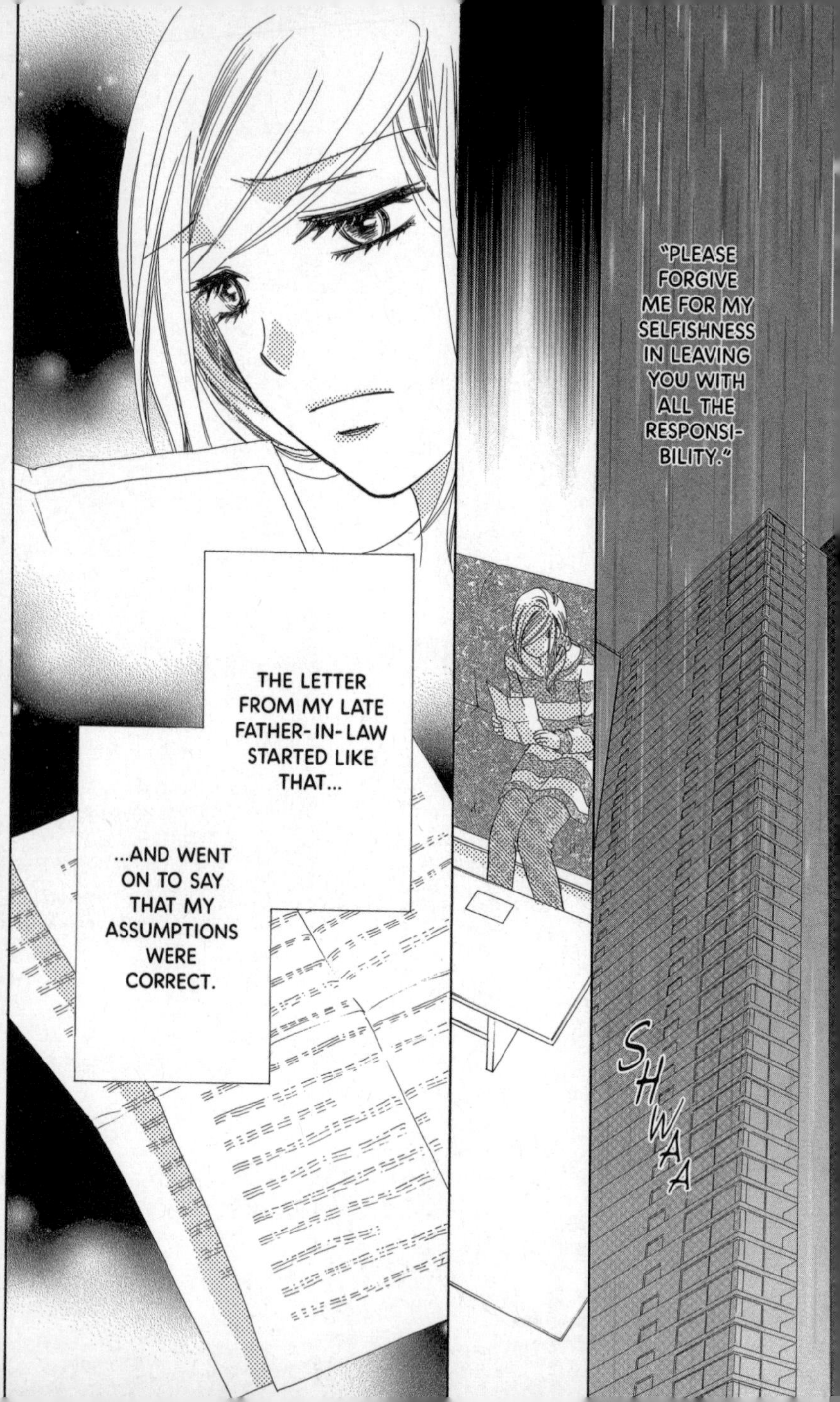
"PLEASE FORGIVE ME FOR MY SELFISHNESS IN LEAVING YOU WITH ALL THE RESPONSI-BILITY."
SHWAA
THE LETTER FROM MY LATE FATHER-IN-LAW STARTED LIKE THAT...
...AND WENT ON TO SAY THAT MY ASSUMPTIONS WERE CORRECT.

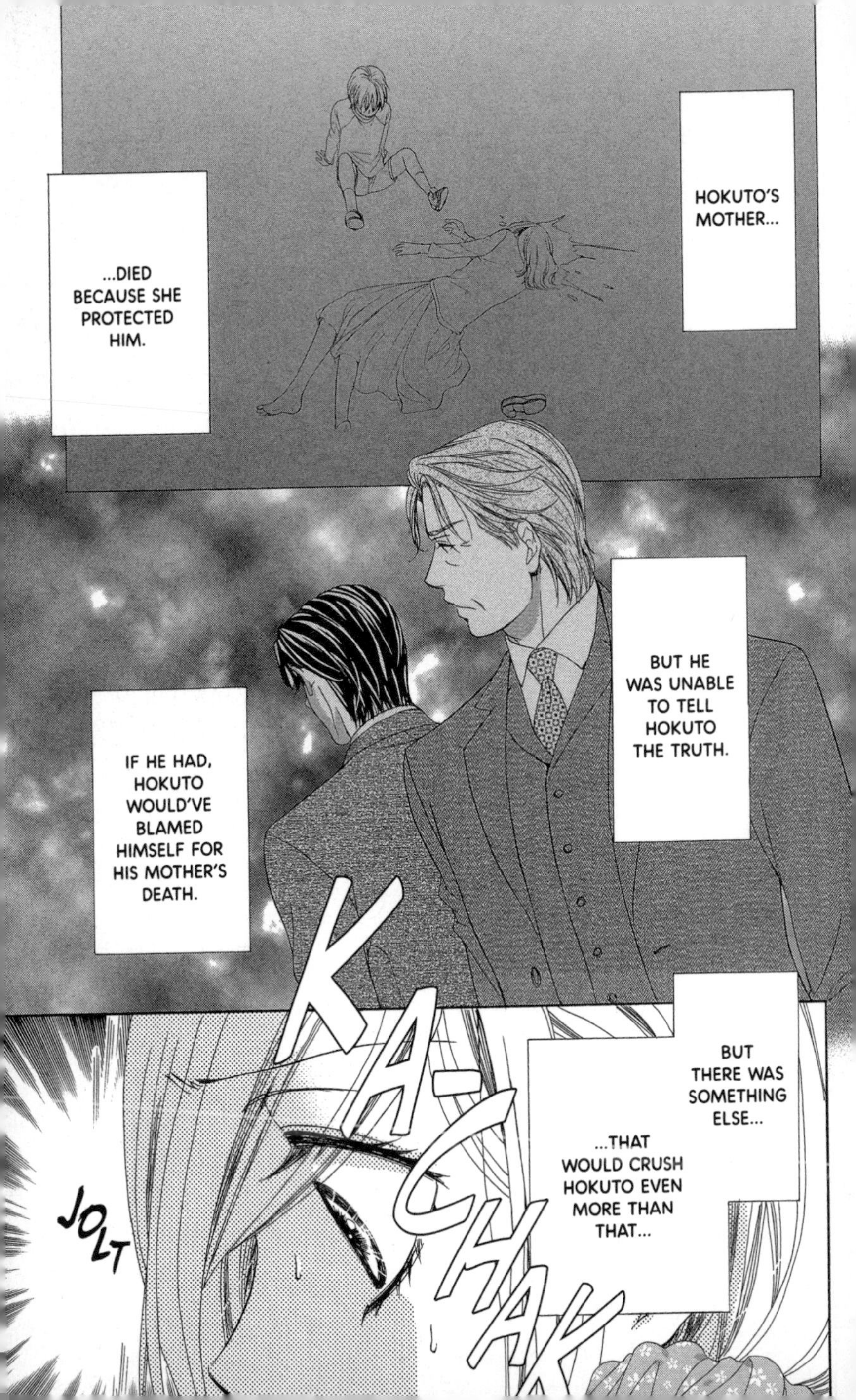
HOKUTO'S MOTHER...
...DIED BECAUSE SHE PROTECTED HIM.
BUT HE WAS UNABLE TO TELL HOKUTO THE TRUTH.
IF HE HAD, HOKUTO WOULD'VE BLAMED HIMSELF FOR HIS MOTHER'S DEATH.
BUT THERE WAS SOMETHING ELSE...
...THAT WOULD CRUSH HOKUTO EVEN MORE THAN THAT...
KA-CHAK
JOLT

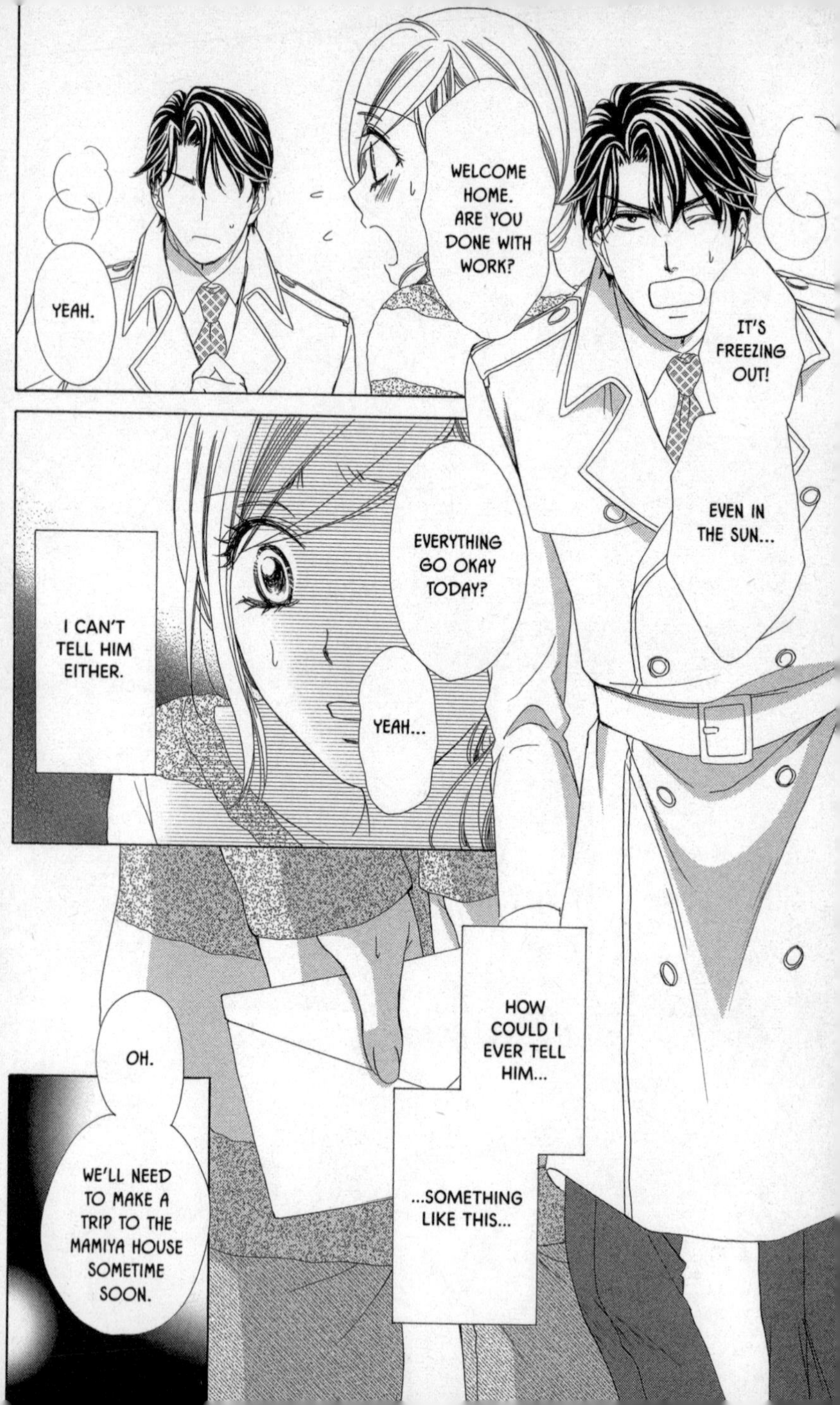
IT'S FREEZING OUT!
EVEN IN THE SUN...
WELCOME HOME. ARE YOU DONE WITH WORK?
YEAH.
EVERYTHING GO OKAY TODAY?
YEAH...
I CAN'T TELL HIM EITHER.
HOW COULD I EVER TELL HIM...
...SOMETHING LIKE THIS...
OH.
WE'LL NEED TO MAKE A TRIP TO THE MAMIYA HOUSE SOMETIME SOON.

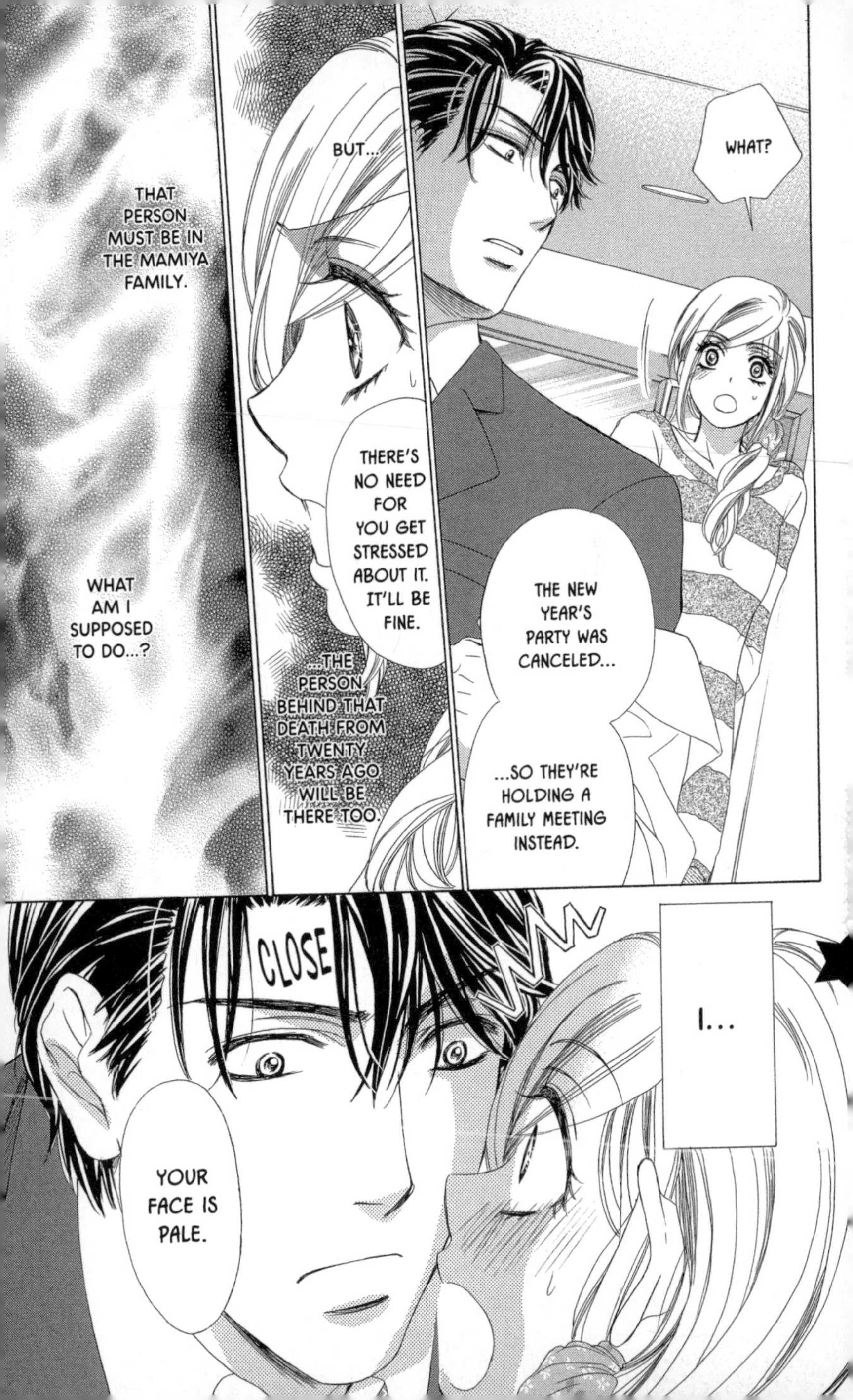
WHAT?
THE NEW YEAR'S PARTY WAS CANCELED...
...SO THEY'RE HOLDING A FAMILY MEETING INSTEAD.
BUT...
THERE'S NO NEED FOR YOU GET STRESSED ABOUT IT. IT'LL BE FINE.
...THE PERSON BEHIND THAT DEATH FROM TWENTY YEARS AGO WILL BE THERE TOO.
THAT PERSON MUST BE IN THE MAMIYA FAMILY.
WHAT AM I SUPPOSED TO DO...?
I...
CLOSE
YOUR FACE IS PALE.

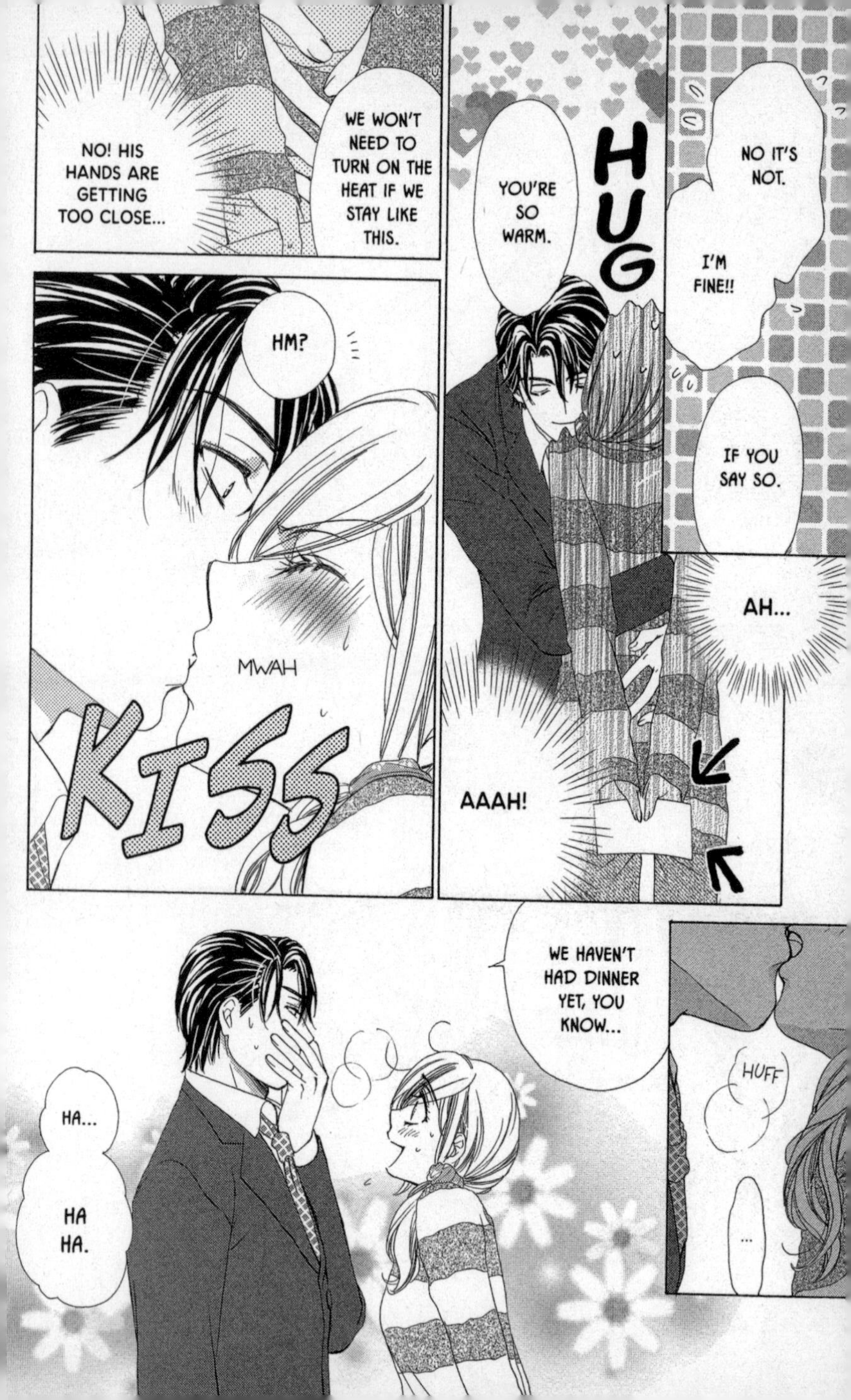
NO IT'S NOT.
I'M FINE!!
IF YOU SAY SO.
AH...
YOU'RE SO WARM.
HUG
AAAH!
WE WON'T NEED TO TURN ON THE HEAT IF WE STAY LIKE THIS.
NO! HIS HANDS ARE GETTING TOO CLOSE...
HM?
MWAH
KISS
HUFF
...
WE HAVEN'T HAD DINNER YET, YOU KNOW...
HA...
HA HA.

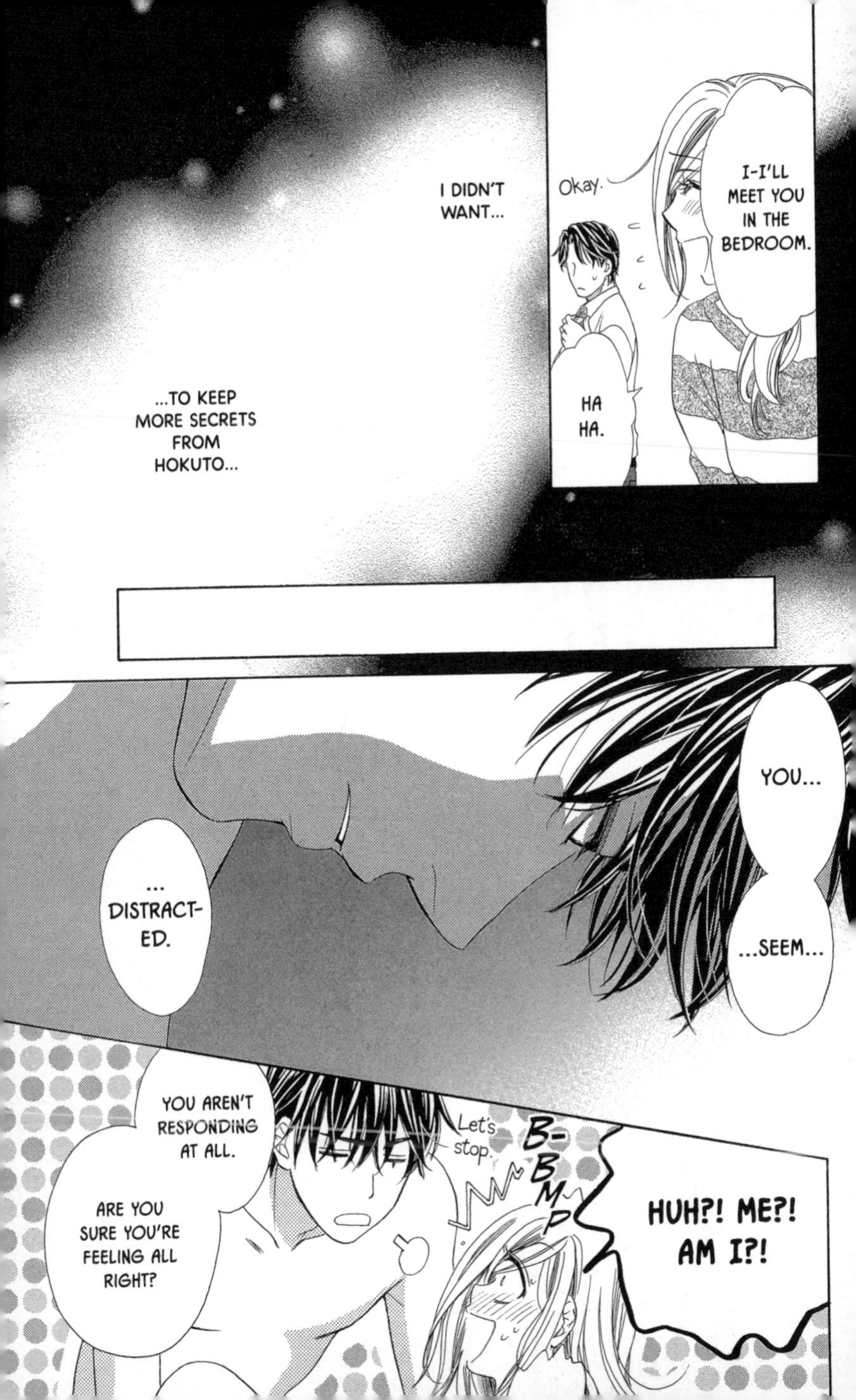
I-I'LL MEET YOU IN THE BEDROOM.
Okay.
HA HA.
I DIDN'T WANT...
...TO KEEP MORE SECRETS FROM HOKUTO...
YOU...
...SEEM...
... DISTRACT-ED.
HUH?! ME?! AM I?!
B-BMP
Let's stop.
YOU AREN'T RESPONDING AT ALL.
ARE YOU SURE YOU'RE FEELING ALL RIGHT?

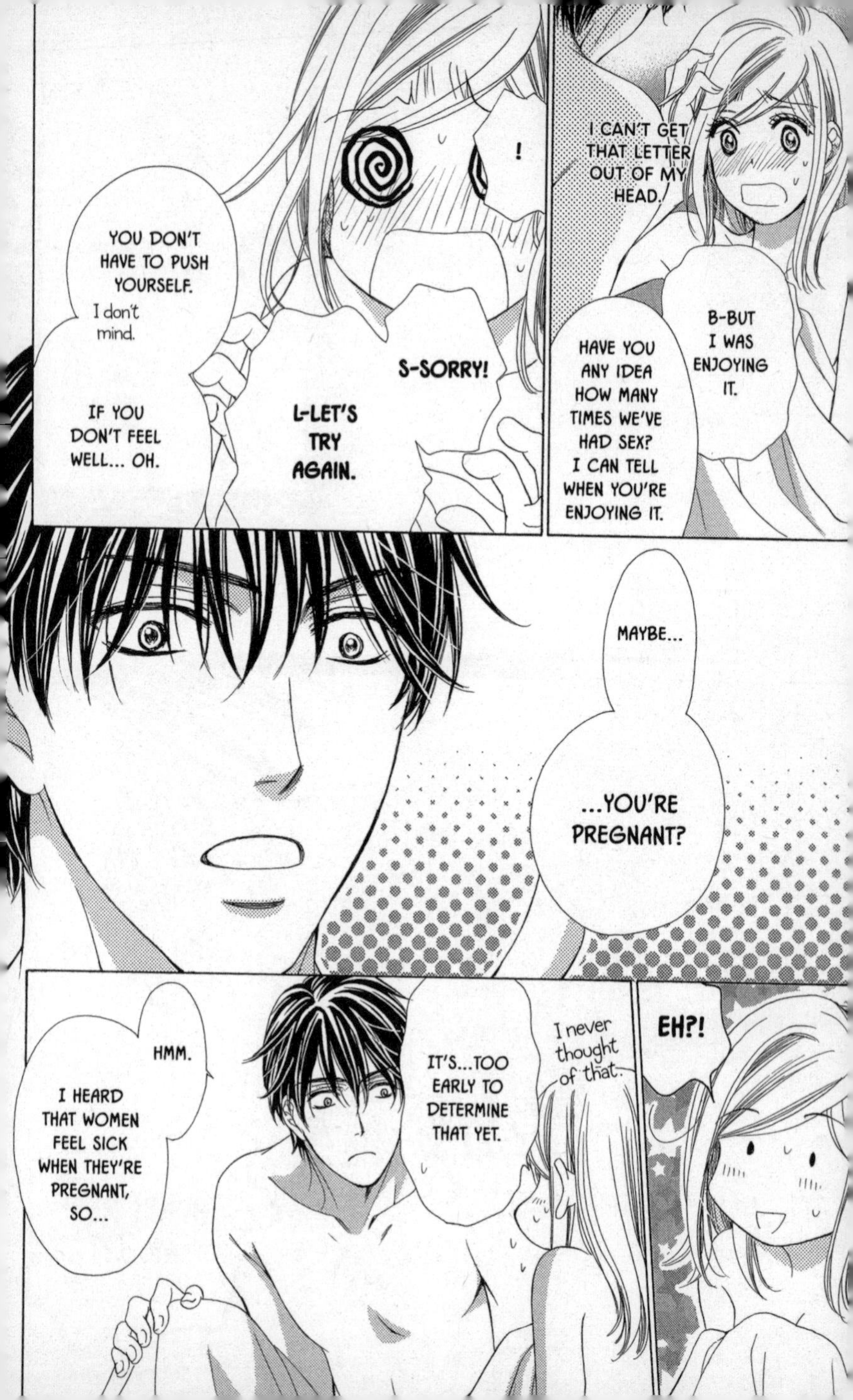
I CAN'T GET THAT LETTER OUT OF MY HEAD.
B-BUT I WAS ENJOYING IT.
HAVE YOU ANY IDEA HOW MANY TIMES WE'VE HAD SEX? I CAN TELL WHEN YOU'RE ENJOYING IT.
!
S-SORRY!
L-LET'S TRY AGAIN.
YOU DON'T HAVE TO PUSH YOURSELF.
I don't mind.
IF YOU DON'T FEEL WELL... OH.
MAYBE...
...YOU'RE PREGNANT?
EH?!
I never thought of that.
IT'S...TOO EARLY TO DETERMINE THAT YET.
HMM.
I HEARD THAT WOMEN FEEL SICK WHEN THEY'RE PREGNANT, SO...

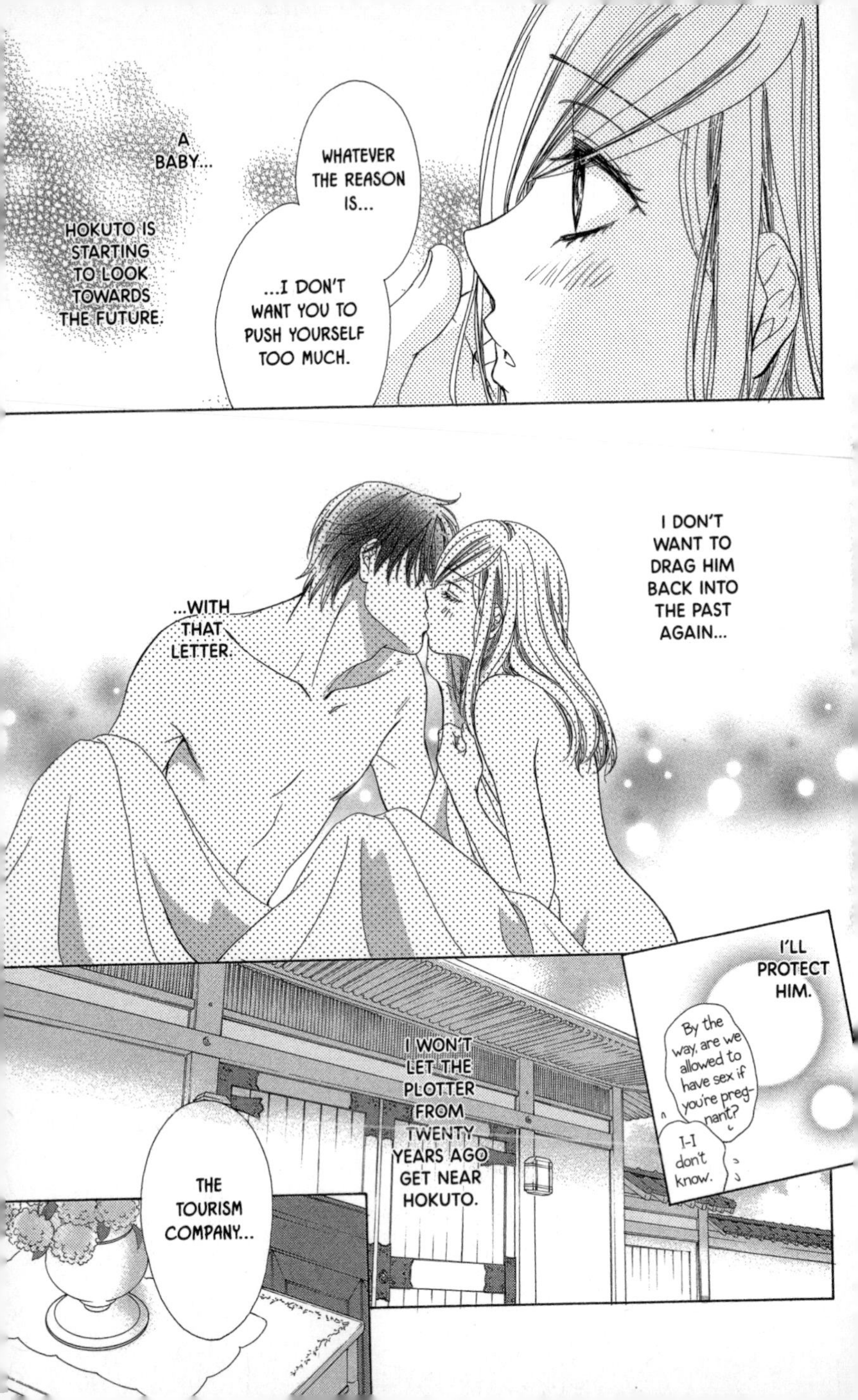
WHATEVER THE REASON IS...
...I DON'T WANT YOU TO PUSH YOURSELF TOO MUCH.
A BABY...
HOKUTO IS STARTING TO LOOK TOWARDS THE FUTURE.
I DON'T WANT TO DRAG HIM BACK INTO THE PAST AGAIN...
...WITH THAT LETTER.
I'LL PROTECT HIM.
By the way, are we allowed to have sex if you're preg-nant?
I-I don't know.
I WON'T LET THE PLOTTER FROM TWENTY YEARS AGO GET NEAR HOKUTO.
THE TOURISM COMPANY...

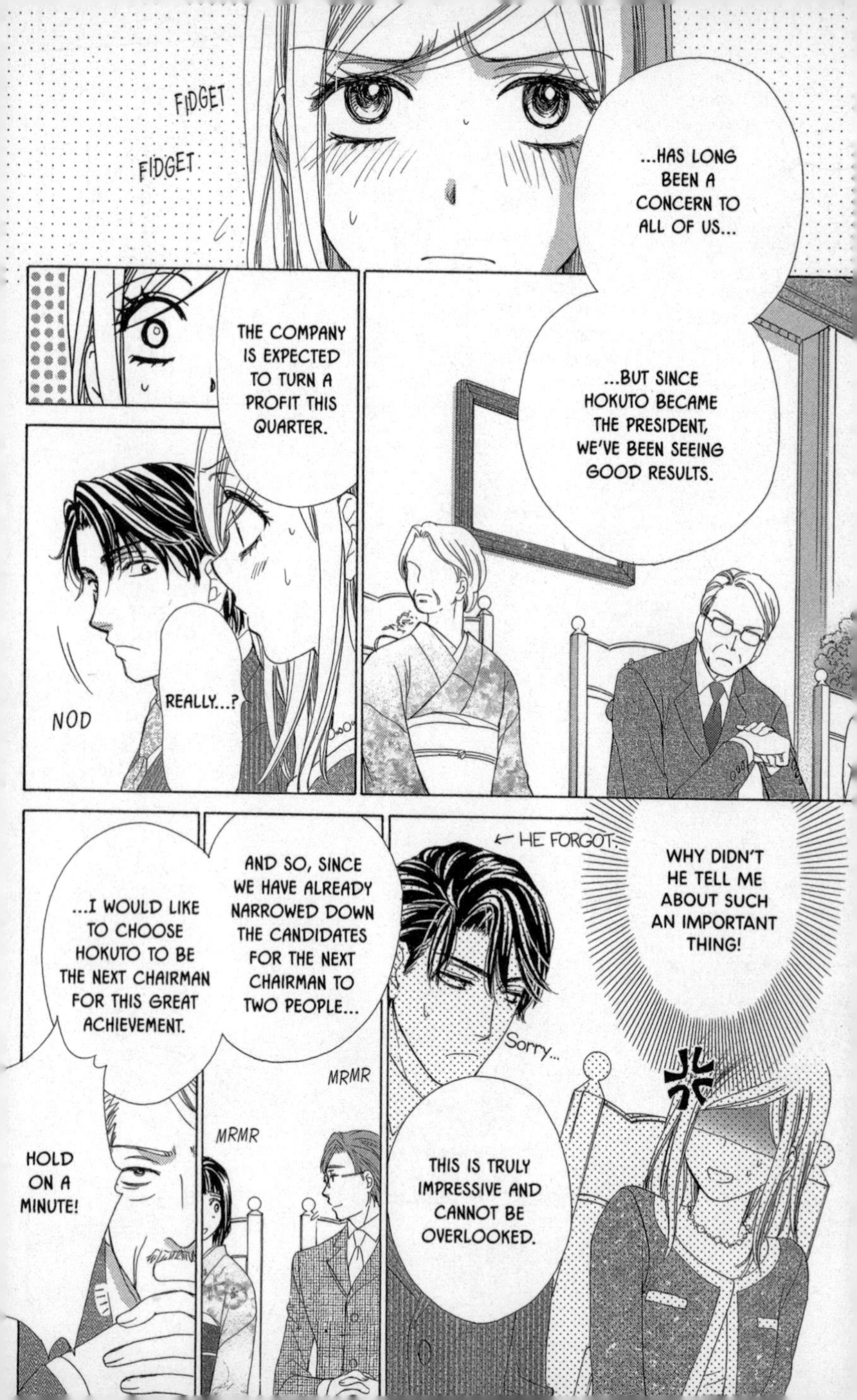
...HAS LONG BEEN A CONCERN TO ALL OF US...
FIDGET
FIDGET
...BUT SINCE HOKUTO BECAME THE PRESIDENT, WE'VE BEEN SEEING GOOD RESULTS.
THE COMPANY IS EXPECTED TO TURN A PROFIT THIS QUARTER.
REALLY...?
NOD
WHY DIDN'T HE TELL ME ABOUT SUCH AN IMPORTANT THING!
← HE FORGOT.
Sorry...
THIS IS TRULY IMPRESSIVE AND CANNOT BE OVERLOOKED.
AND SO, SINCE WE HAVE ALREADY NARROWED DOWN THE CANDIDATES FOR THE NEXT CHAIRMAN TO TWO PEOPLE...
MRMR
MRMR
...I WOULD LIKE TO CHOOSE HOKUTO TO BE THE NEXT CHAIRMAN FOR THIS GREAT ACHIEVEMENT.
HOLD ON A MINUTE!

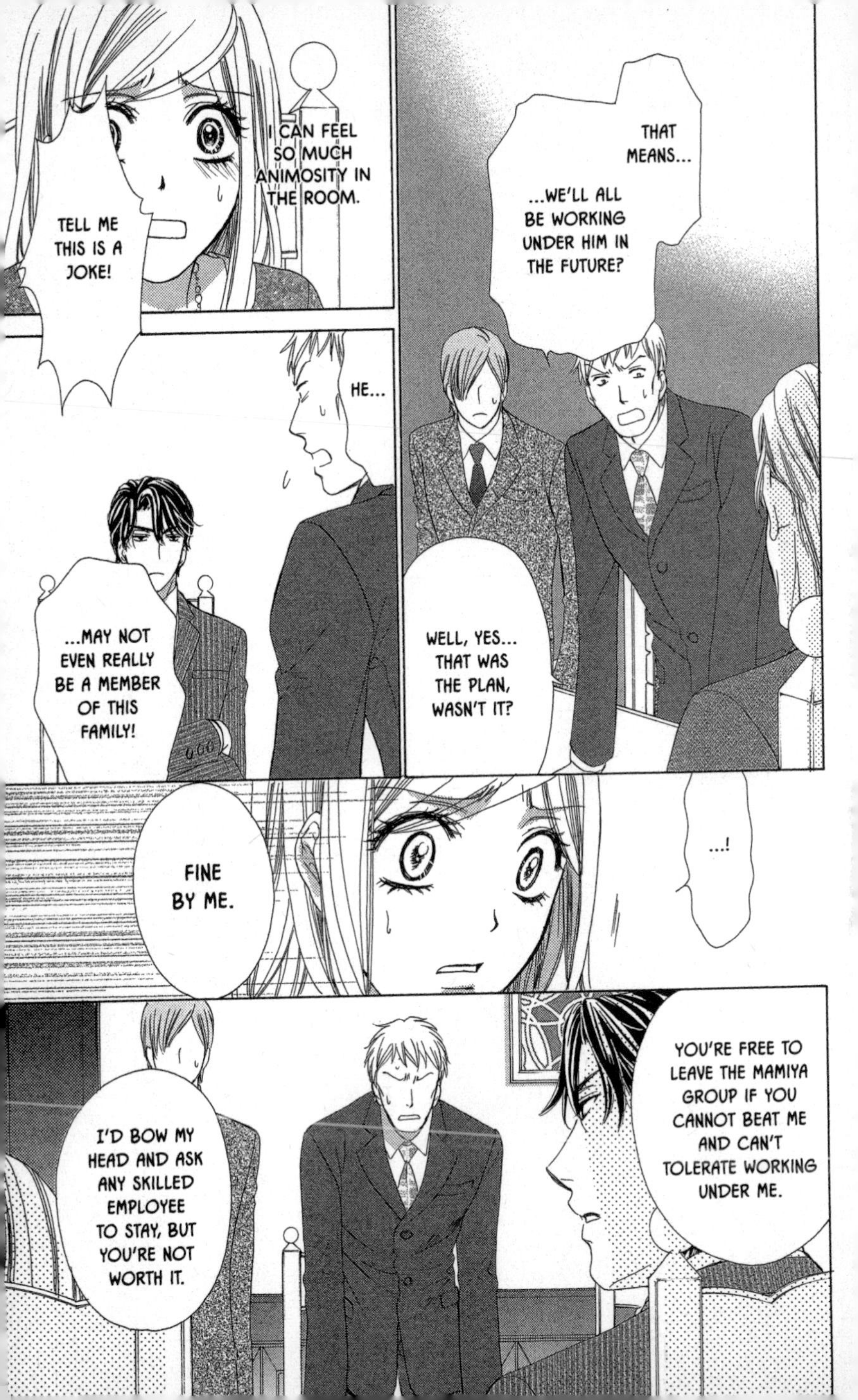
THAT MEANS...
...WE'LL ALL BE WORKING UNDER HIM IN THE FUTURE?
WELL, YES... THAT WAS THE PLAN, WASN'T IT?
I CAN FEEL SO MUCH ANIMOSITY IN THE ROOM.
TELL ME THIS IS A JOKE!
HE...
...MAY NOT EVEN REALLY BE A MEMBER OF THIS FAMILY!
...!
FINE BY ME.
YOU'RE FREE TO LEAVE THE MAMIYA GROUP IF YOU CANNOT BEAT ME AND CAN'T TOLERATE WORKING UNDER ME.
I'D BOW MY HEAD AND ASK ANY SKILLED EMPLOYEE TO STAY, BUT YOU'RE NOT WORTH IT.

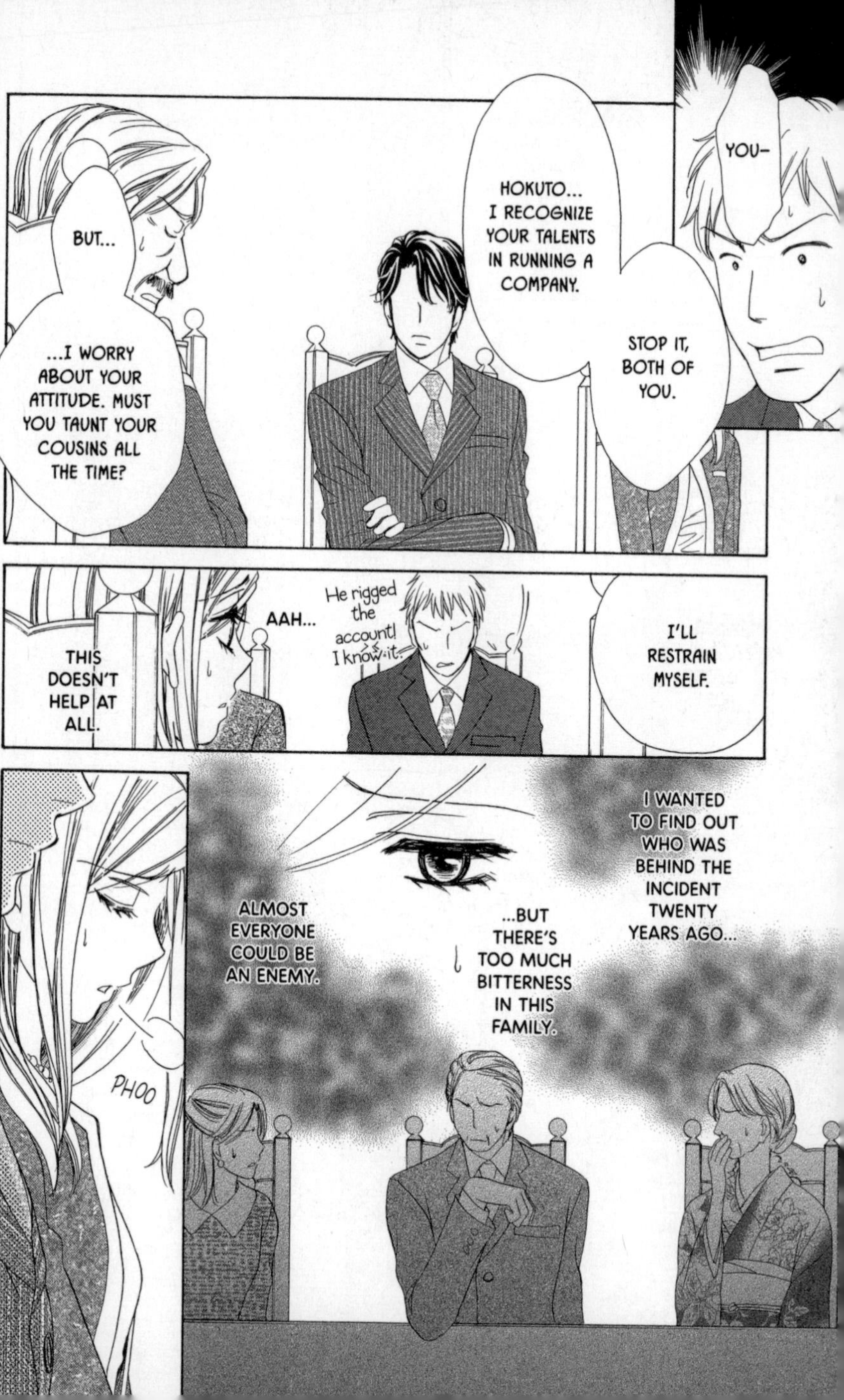
YOU–
HOKUTO... I RECOGNIZE YOUR TALENTS IN RUNNING A COMPANY.
STOP IT, BOTH OF YOU.
BUT...
...I WORRY ABOUT YOUR ATTITUDE. MUST YOU TAUNT YOUR COUSINS ALL THE TIME?
I'LL RESTRAIN MYSELF.
He rigged the account! I know it.
AAH...
THIS DOESN'T HELP AT ALL.
I WANTED TO FIND OUT WHO WAS BEHIND THE INCIDENT TWENTY YEARS AGO...
...BUT THERE'S TOO MUCH BITTERNESS IN THIS FAMILY.
ALMOST EVERYONE COULD BE AN ENEMY.
PHOO

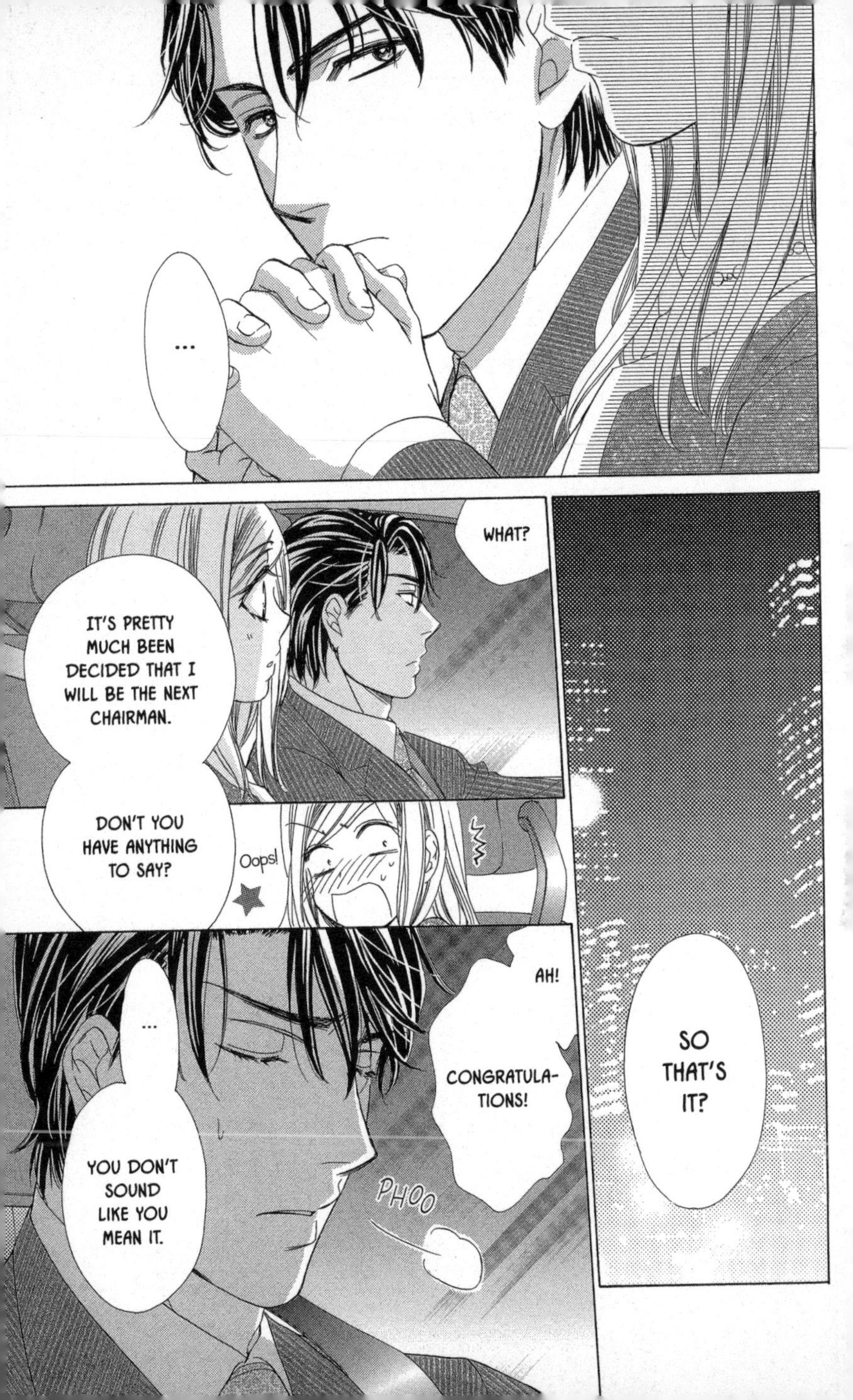
...
SO THAT'S IT?
WHAT?
IT'S PRETTY MUCH BEEN DECIDED THAT I WILL BE THE NEXT CHAIRMAN.
DON'T YOU HAVE ANYTHING TO SAY?
Oops!
AH!
CONGRATULA-TIONS!
PHOO
...
YOU DON'T SOUND LIKE YOU MEAN IT.

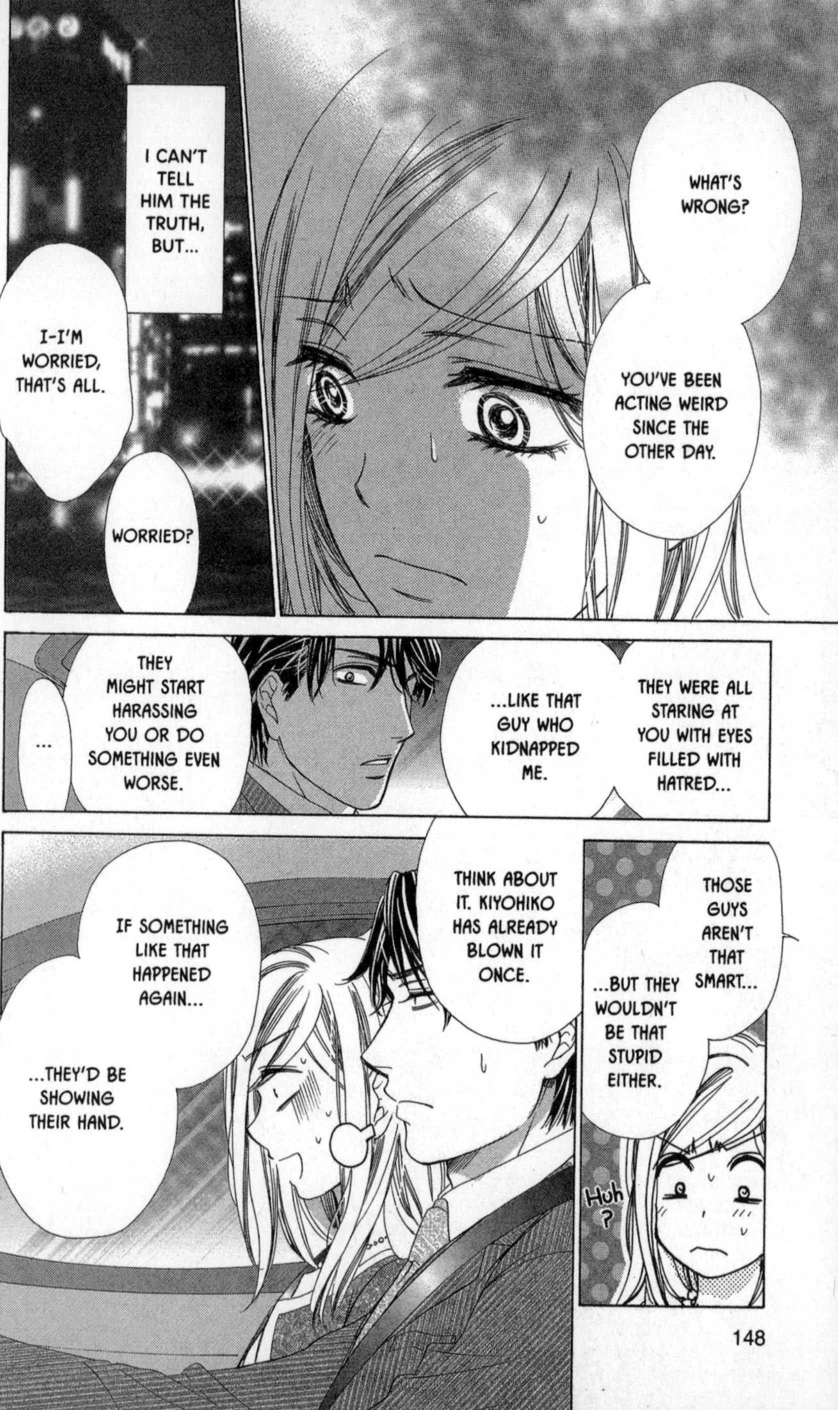
WHAT'S WRONG?
YOU'VE BEEN ACTING WEIRD SINCE THE OTHER DAY.
I CAN'T TELL HIM THE TRUTH, BUT...
I-I'M WORRIED, THAT'S ALL.
WORRIED?
THEY WERE ALL STARING AT YOU WITH EYES FILLED WITH HATRED...
...LIKE THAT GUY WHO KIDNAPPED ME.
THEY MIGHT START HARASSING YOU OR DO SOMETHING EVEN WORSE.
...
THOSE GUYS AREN'T THAT SMART...
...BUT THEY WOULDN'T BE THAT STUPID EITHER.
Huh?
THINK ABOUT IT. KIYOHIKO HAS ALREADY BLOWN IT ONCE.
IF SOMETHING LIKE THAT HAPPENED AGAIN...
...THEY'D BE SHOWING THEIR HAND.

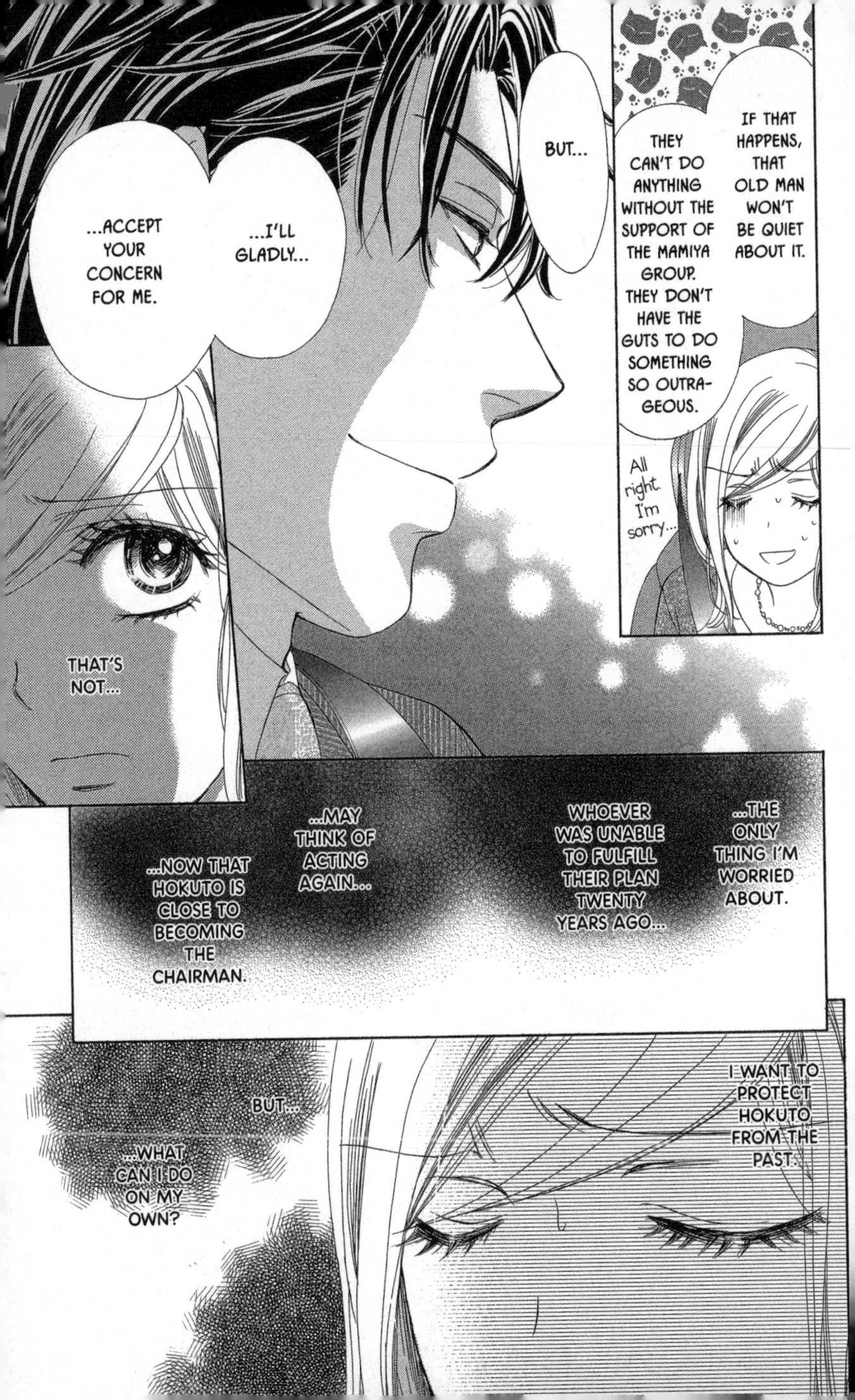
IF THAT HAPPENS, THAT OLD MAN WON'T BE QUIET ABOUT IT.
THEY CAN'T DO ANYTHING WITHOUT THE SUPPORT OF THE MAMIYA GROUP. THEY DON'T HAVE THE GUTS TO DO SOMETHING SO OUTRA-GEOUS.
All right. I'm sorry...
BUT...
...I'LL GLADLY...
...ACCEPT YOUR CONCERN FOR ME.
THAT'S NOT...
...THE ONLY THING I'M WORRIED ABOUT.
WHOEVER WAS UNABLE TO FULFILL THEIR PLAN TWENTY YEARS AGO...
...MAY THINK OF ACTING AGAIN...
...NOW THAT HOKUTO IS CLOSE TO BECOMING THE CHAIRMAN.
I WANT TO PROTECT HOKUTO FROM THE PAST.
BUT...
...WHAT CAN I DO ON MY OWN?

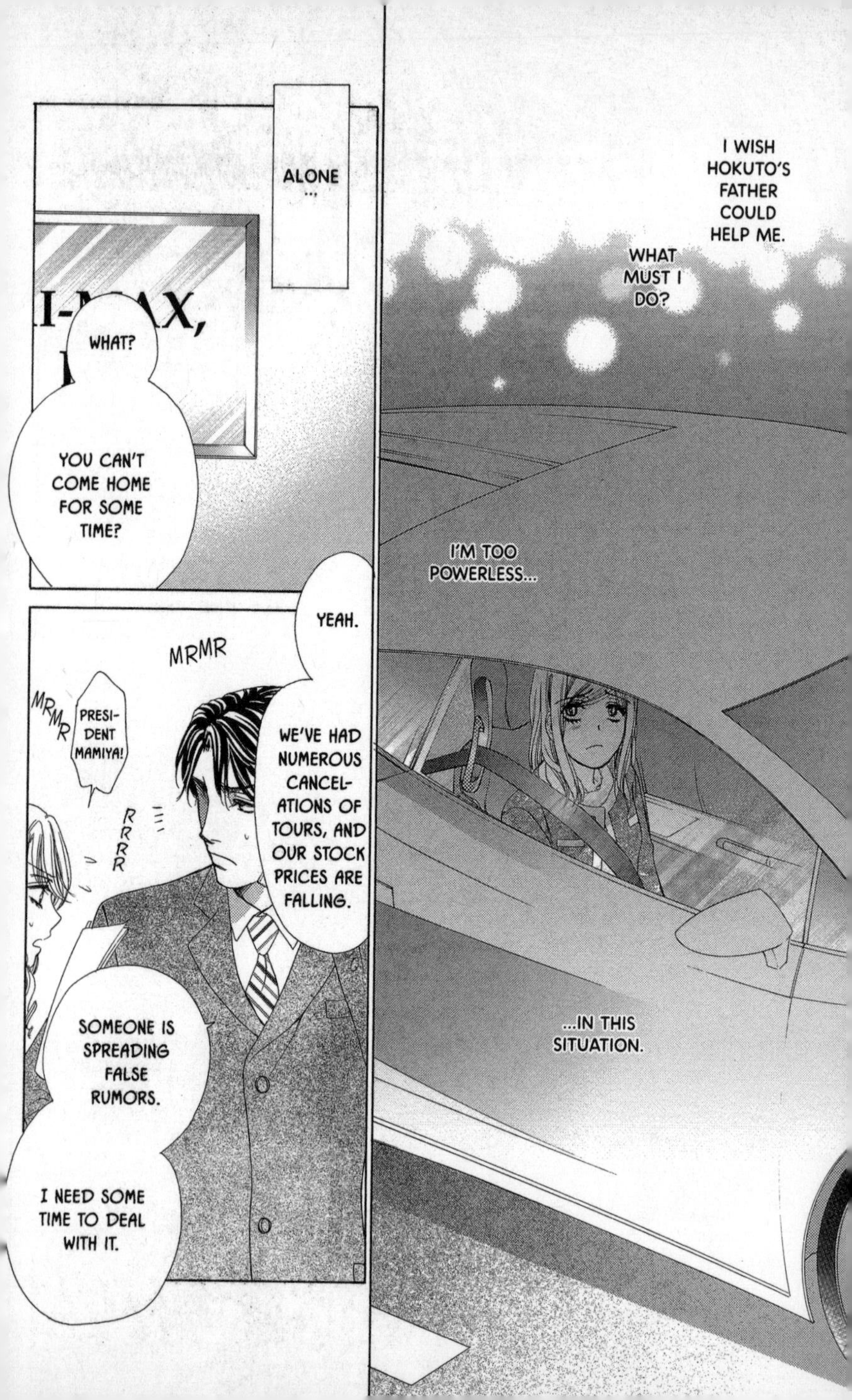
I WISH HOKUTO'S FATHER COULD HELP ME.
WHAT MUST I DO?
I'M TOO POWERLESS...
...IN THIS SITUATION.
ALONE ...
WHAT?
YOU CAN'T COME HOME FOR SOME TIME?
YEAH.
WE'VE HAD NUMEROUS CANCEL-ATIONS OF TOURS, AND OUR STOCK PRICES ARE FALLING.
MRMR
MRMR
PRESI-DENT MAMIYA!
RRRR
SOMEONE IS SPREADING FALSE RUMORS.
I NEED SOME TIME TO DEAL WITH IT.

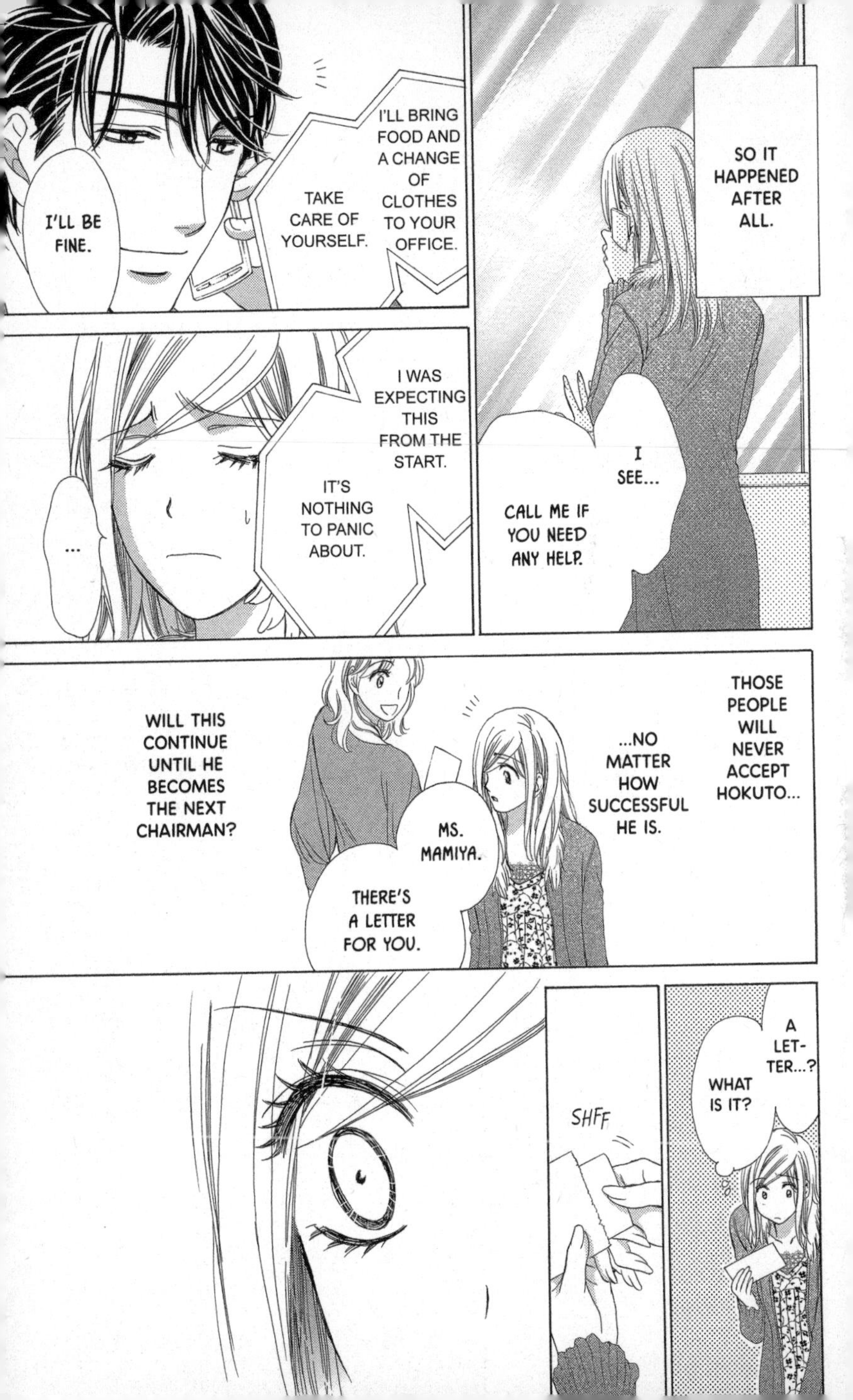
SO IT HAPPENED AFTER ALL.
I SEE...
CALL ME IF YOU NEED ANY HELP.
I'LL BRING FOOD AND A CHANGE OF CLOTHES TO YOUR OFFICE.
TAKE CARE OF YOURSELF.
I'LL BE FINE.
I WAS EXPECTING THIS FROM THE START.
IT'S NOTHING TO PANIC ABOUT.
...
THOSE PEOPLE WILL NEVER ACCEPT HOKUTO...
...NO MATTER HOW SUCCESSFUL HE IS.
MS. MAMIYA.
THERE'S A LETTER FOR YOU.
WILL THIS CONTINUE UNTIL HE BECOMES THE NEXT CHAIRMAN?
A LET-TER...?
WHAT IS IT?
SHFF

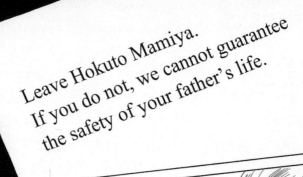

Leave Hokuto Mamiya.
If you do not, we cannot guarantee
the safety of your father's life.

HUH?

WHAT'S UP, MAMIYA?

!!

HEY!

B-BMP

WHAT IS IT?!

VISH

DASH

KRRK

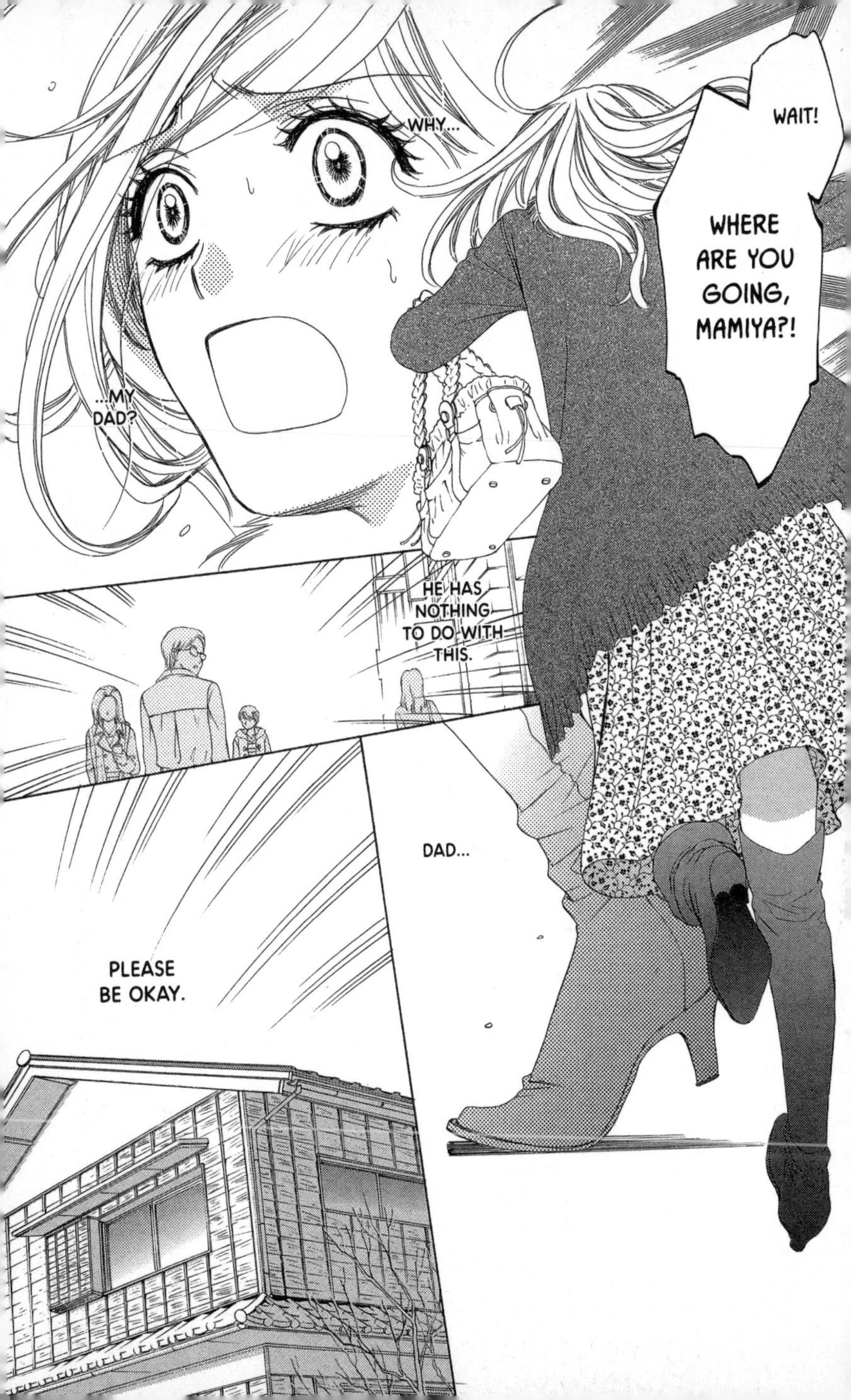
WAIT!
WHERE ARE YOU GOING, MAMIYA?!
WHY...
...MY DAD?
HE HAS NOTHING TO DO WITH THIS.
DAD...
PLEASE BE OKAY.

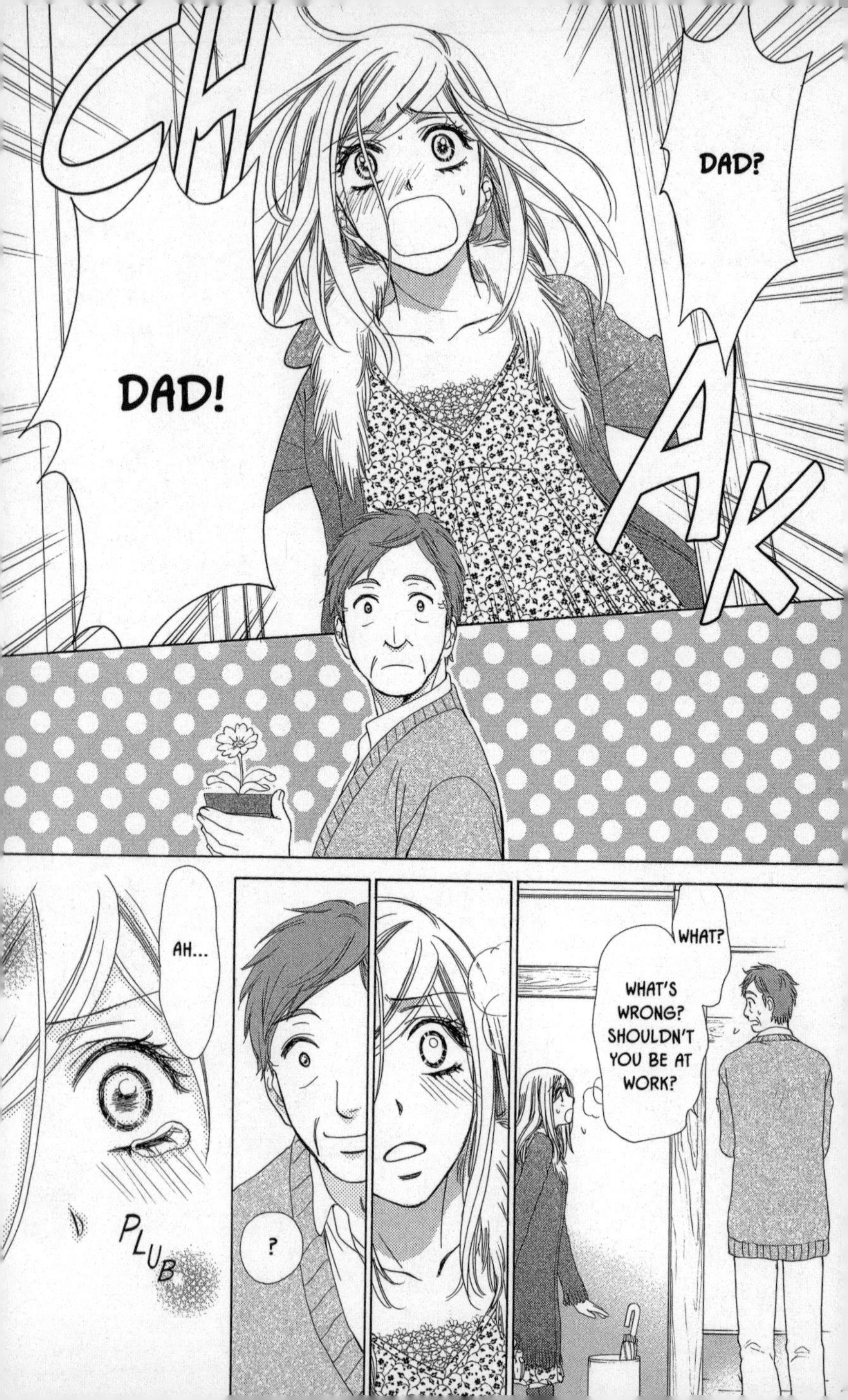
DAD?
CH
AK
DAD!
WHAT?
WHAT'S WRONG? SHOULDN'T YOU BE AT WORK?
?
AH...
PLUB

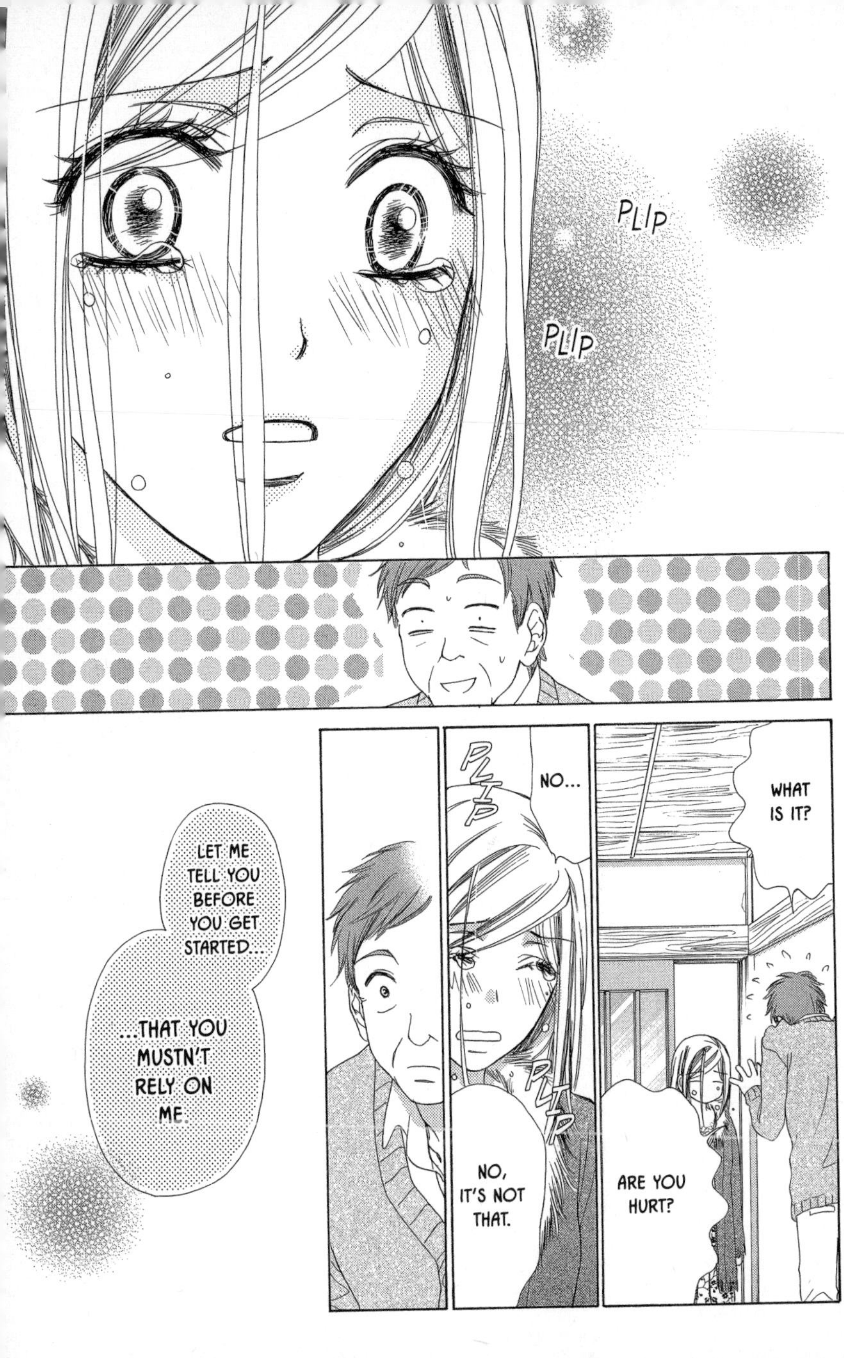
PLIP
PLIP
WHAT IS IT?
ARE YOU HURT?
NO...
PLIP
NO, IT'S NOT THAT.
PLIP
LET ME TELL YOU BEFORE YOU GET STARTED...
...THAT YOU MUSTN'T RELY ON ME.

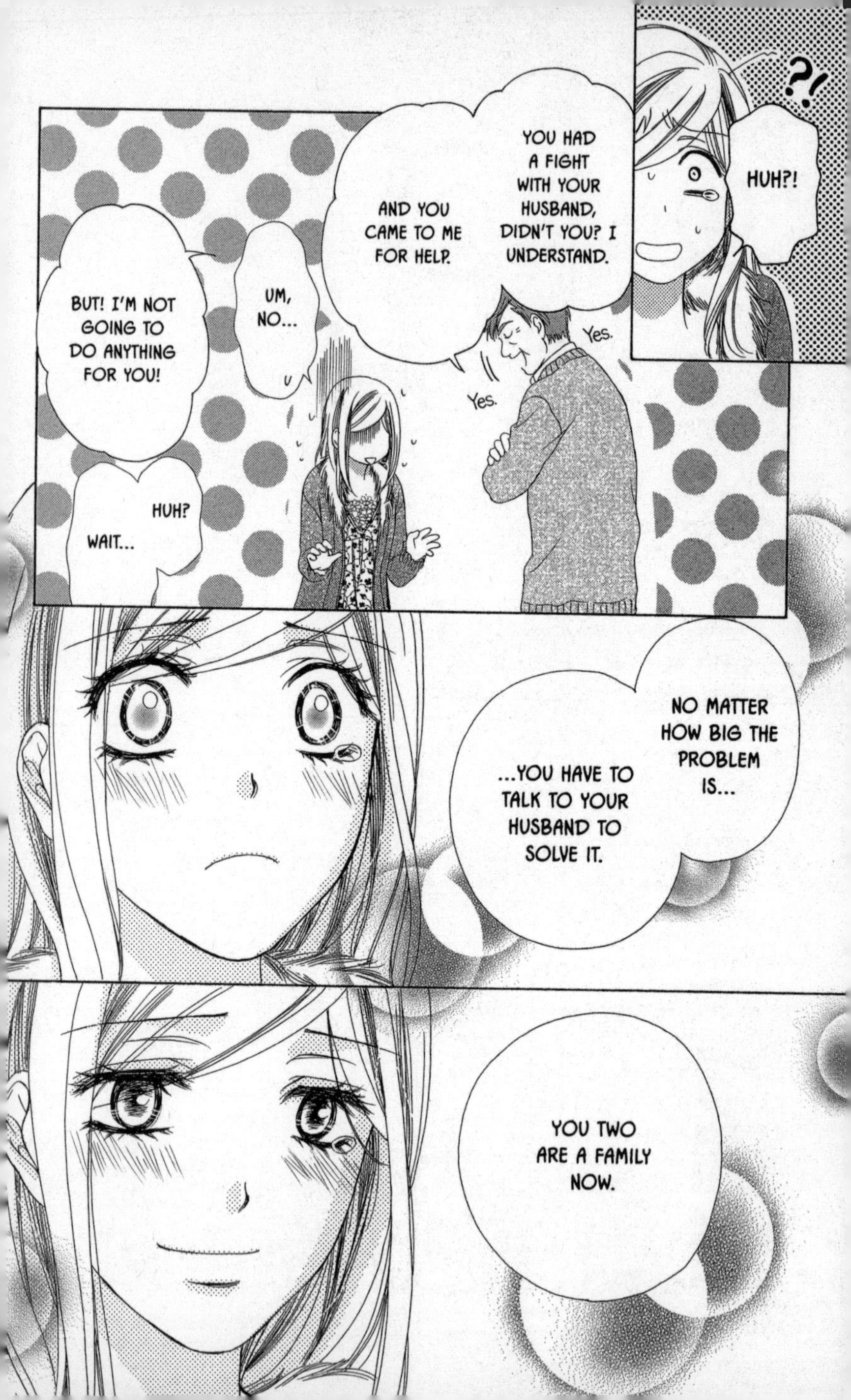
?!
HUH?!
YOU HAD A FIGHT WITH YOUR HUSBAND, DIDN'T YOU? I UNDERSTAND.
AND YOU CAME TO ME FOR HELP.
Yes.
Yes.
UM, NO...
BUT! I'M NOT GOING TO DO ANYTHING FOR YOU!
HUH? WAIT...
NO MATTER HOW BIG THE PROBLEM IS...
...YOU HAVE TO TALK TO YOUR HUSBAND TO SOLVE IT.
YOU TWO ARE A FAMILY NOW.

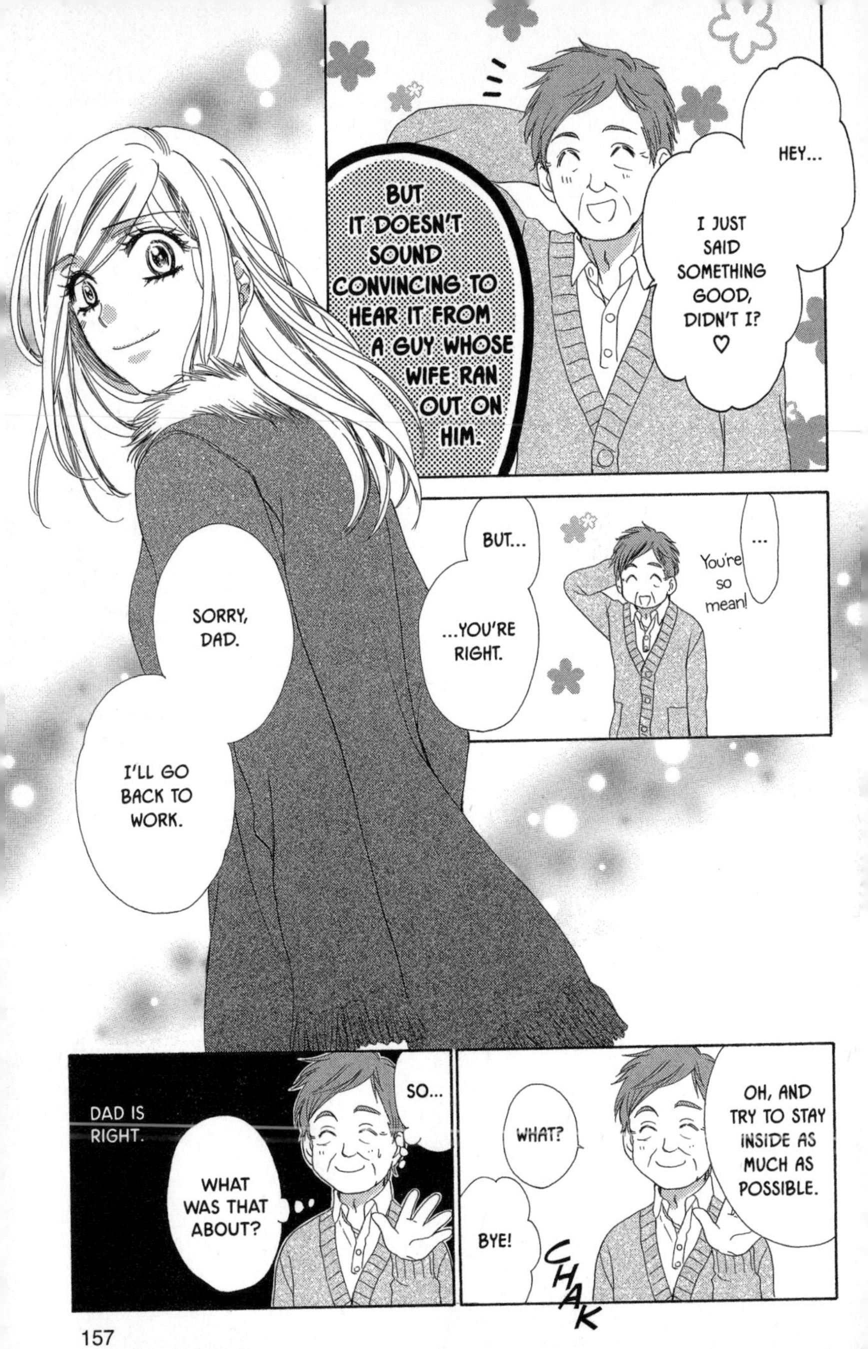
HEY...
I JUST SAID SOMETHING GOOD, DIDN'T I? ♡
BUT IT DOESN'T SOUND CONVINCING TO HEAR IT FROM A GUY WHOSE WIFE RAN OUT ON HIM.
...
You're so mean!
BUT...
...YOU'RE RIGHT.
SORRY, DAD.
I'LL GO BACK TO WORK.
OH, AND TRY TO STAY INSIDE AS MUCH AS POSSIBLE.
WHAT?
BYE!
CHAK
SO...
DAD IS RIGHT.
WHAT WAS THAT ABOUT?

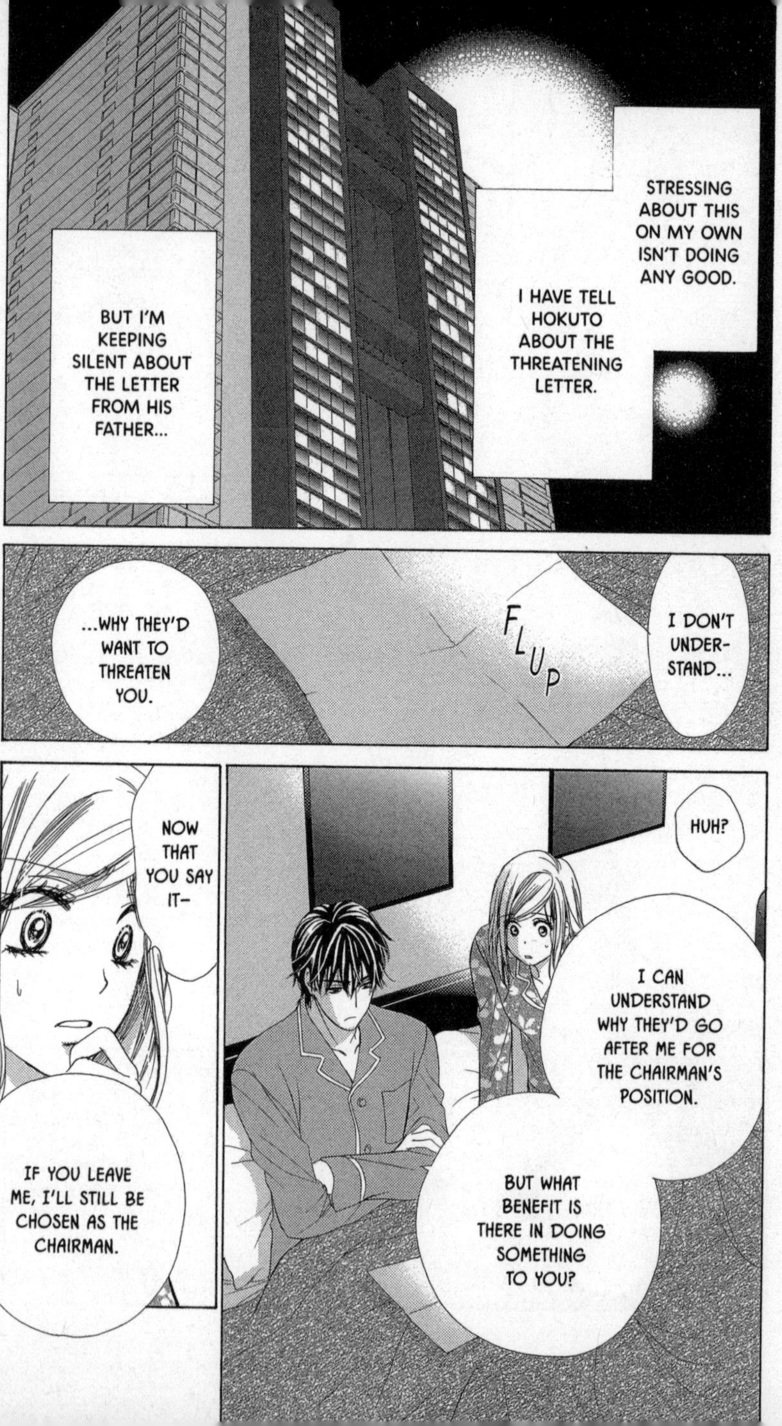
STRESSING ABOUT THIS ON MY OWN ISN'T DOING ANY GOOD.
I HAVE TELL HOKUTO ABOUT THE THREATENING LETTER.
BUT I'M KEEPING SILENT ABOUT THE LETTER FROM HIS FATHER...
I DON'T UNDER-STAND...
FLUP
...WHY THEY'D WANT TO THREATEN YOU.
HUH?
I CAN UNDERSTAND WHY THEY'D GO AFTER ME FOR THE CHAIRMAN'S POSITION.
BUT WHAT BENEFIT IS THERE IN DOING SOMETHING TO YOU?
NOW THAT YOU SAY IT-
IF YOU LEAVE ME, I'LL STILL BE CHOSEN AS THE CHAIRMAN.

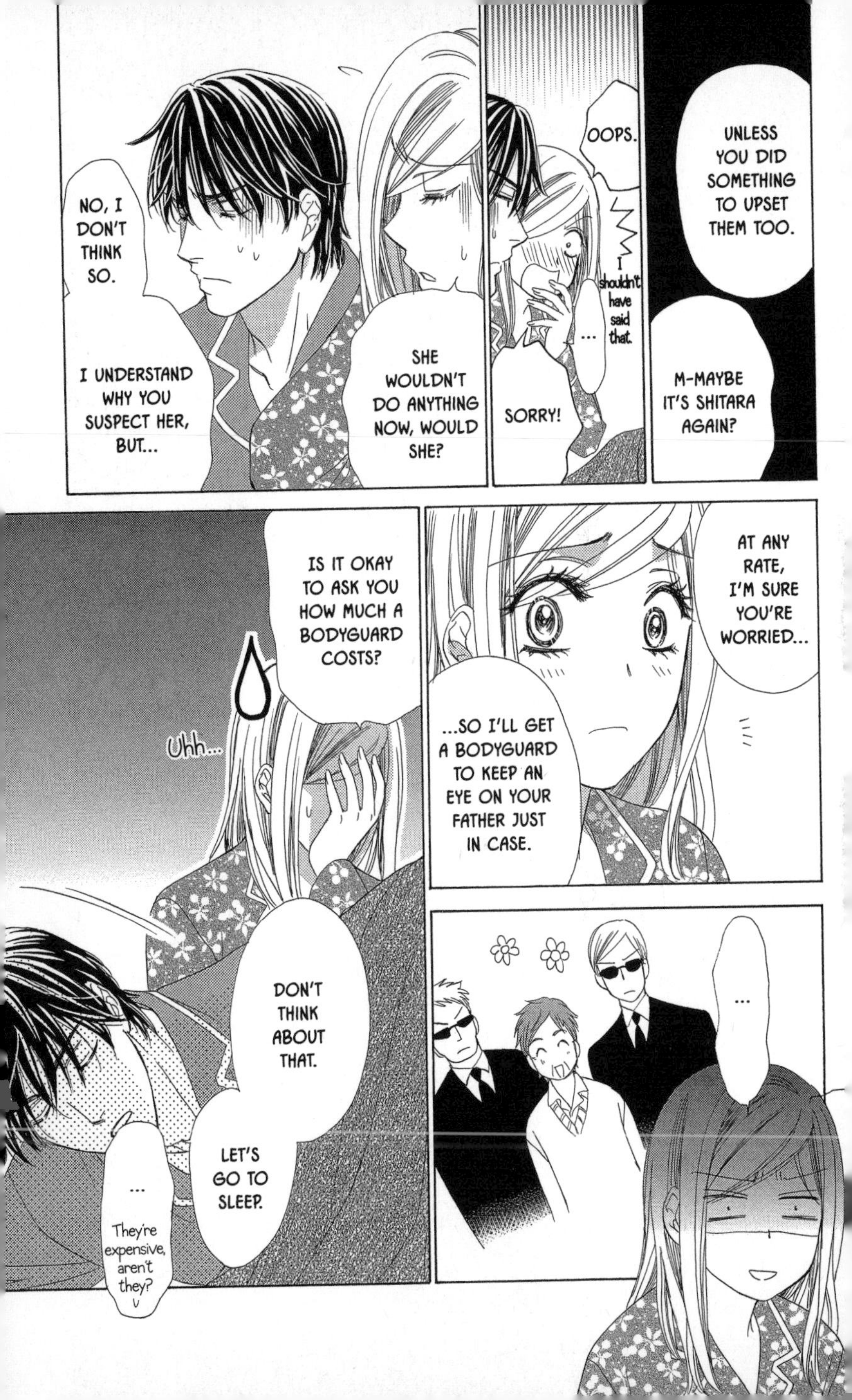
UNLESS YOU DID SOMETHING TO UPSET THEM TOO.
M-MAYBE IT'S SHITARA AGAIN?
OOPS.
I shouldn't have said that.
...
SORRY!
SHE WOULDN'T DO ANYTHING NOW, WOULD SHE?
NO, I DON'T THINK SO.
I UNDERSTAND WHY YOU SUSPECT HER, BUT...
AT ANY RATE, I'M SURE YOU'RE WORRIED...
...SO I'LL GET A BODYGUARD TO KEEP AN EYE ON YOUR FATHER JUST IN CASE.
...
IS IT OKAY TO ASK YOU HOW MUCH A BODYGUARD COSTS?
Uhh...
DON'T THINK ABOUT THAT.
LET'S GO TO SLEEP.
...
They're expensive, aren't they?

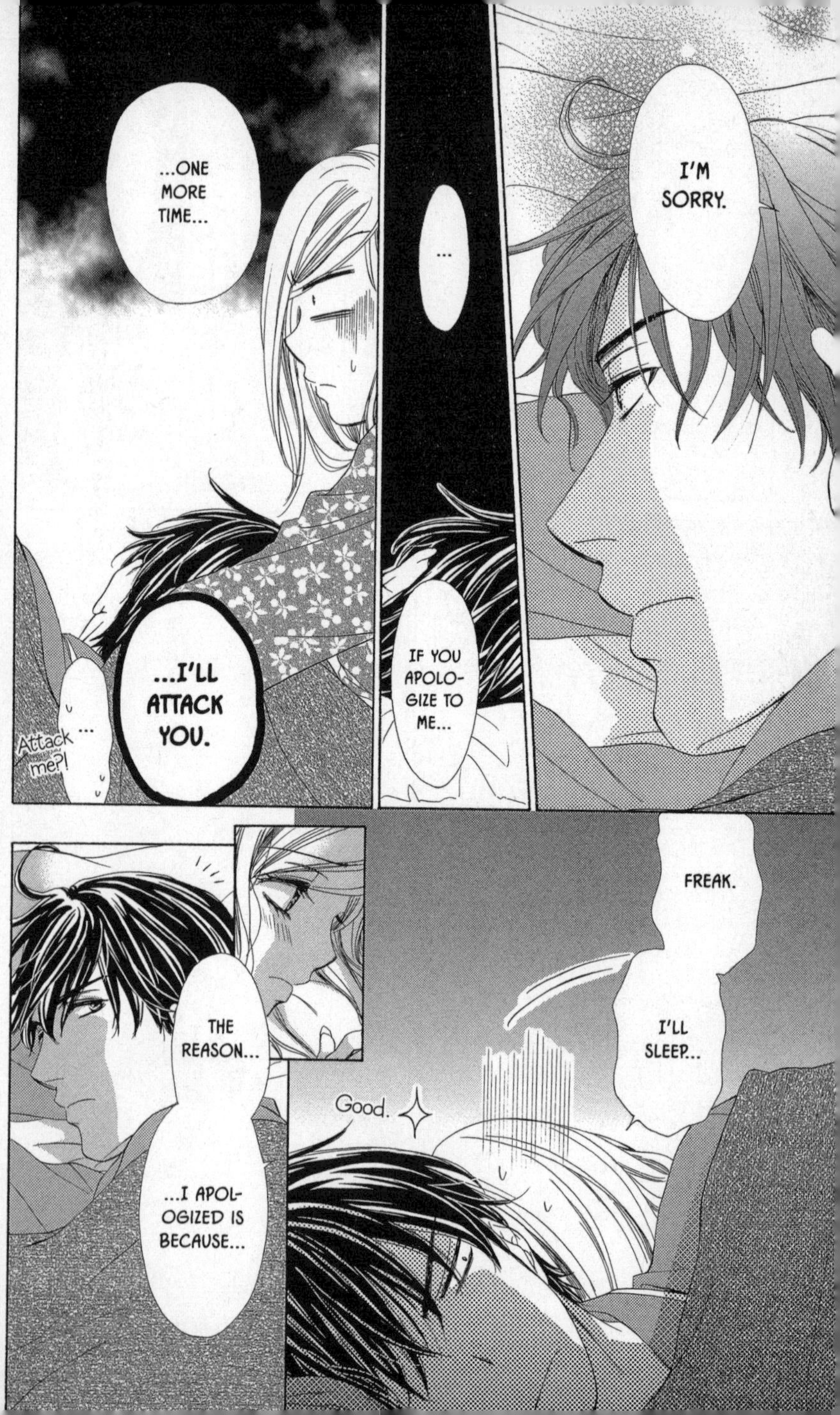
I'M SORRY.
...
IF YOU APOLOGIZE TO ME...
...ONE MORE TIME...
...I'LL ATTACK YOU.
...
Attack me?!
FREAK.
I'LL SLEEP...
Good.
THE REASON...
...I APOLOGIZED IS BECAUSE...

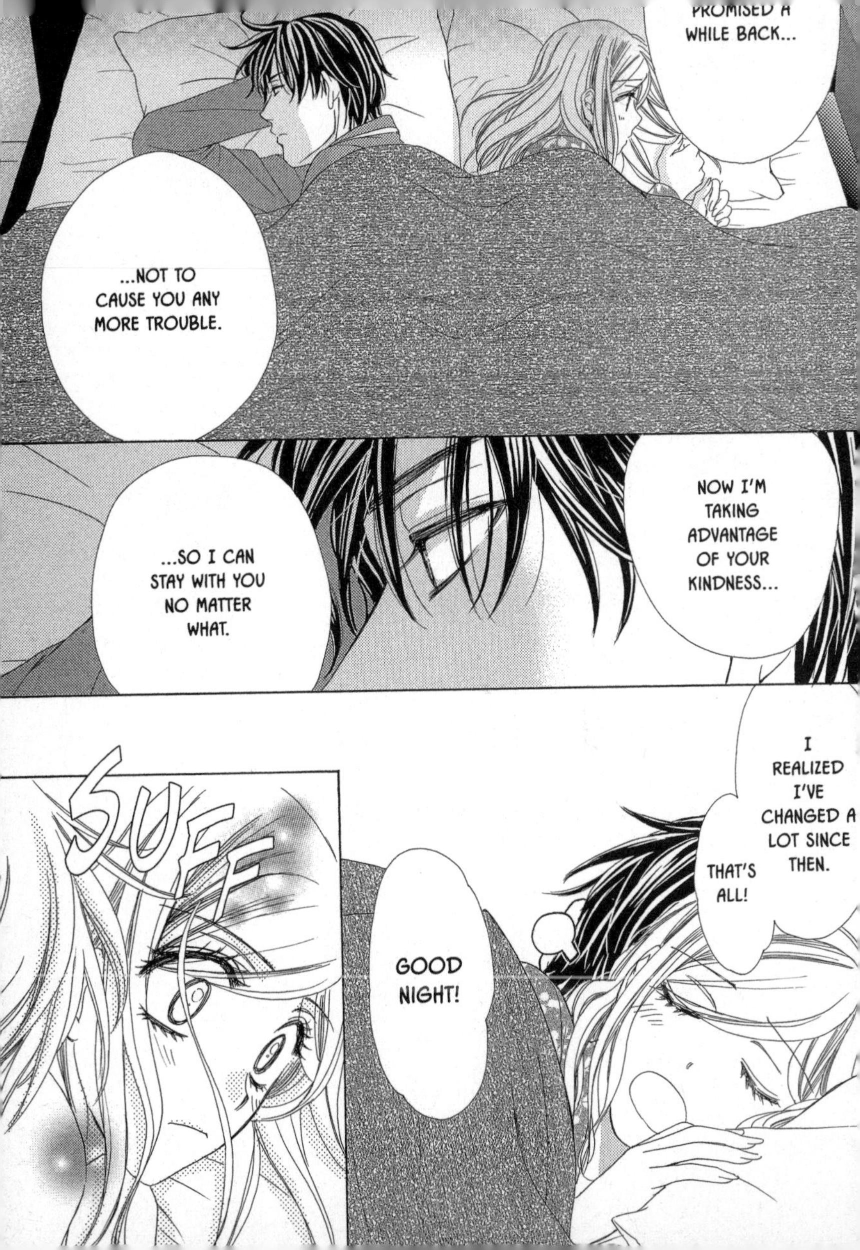
PROMISED A WHILE BACK...
...NOT TO CAUSE YOU ANY MORE TROUBLE.
NOW I'M TAKING ADVANTAGE OF YOUR KINDNESS...
...SO I CAN STAY WITH YOU NO MATTER WHAT.
I REALIZED I'VE CHANGED A LOT SINCE THEN.
THAT'S ALL!
GOOD NIGHT!
SUFF

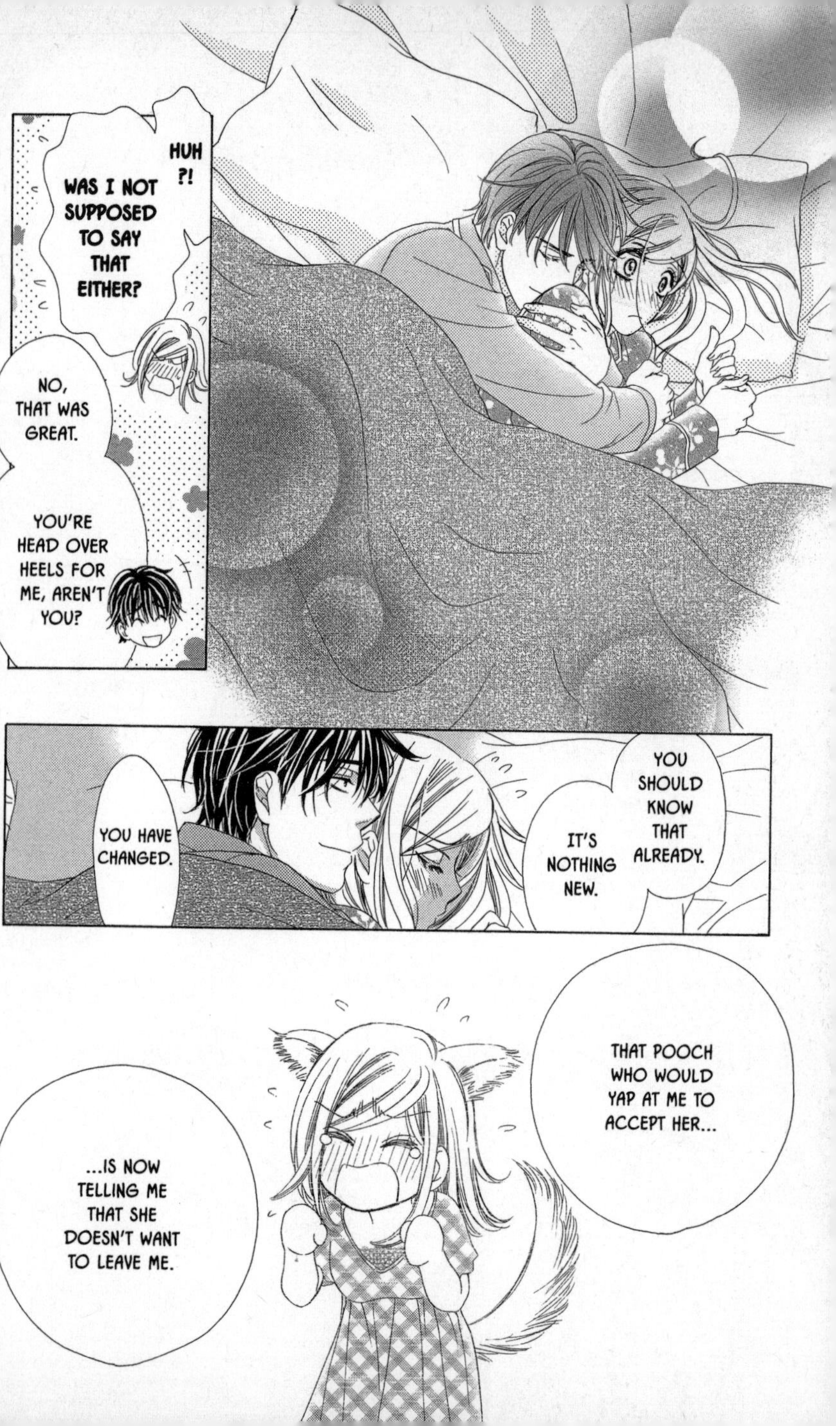
HUH ?!
WAS I NOT SUPPOSED TO SAY THAT EITHER?
NO, THAT WAS GREAT.
YOU'RE HEAD OVER HEELS FOR ME, AREN'T YOU?
YOU SHOULD KNOW THAT ALREADY.
IT'S NOTHING NEW.
YOU HAVE CHANGED.
THAT POOCH WHO WOULD YAP AT ME TO ACCEPT HER...
...IS NOW TELLING ME THAT SHE DOESN'T WANT TO LEAVE ME.

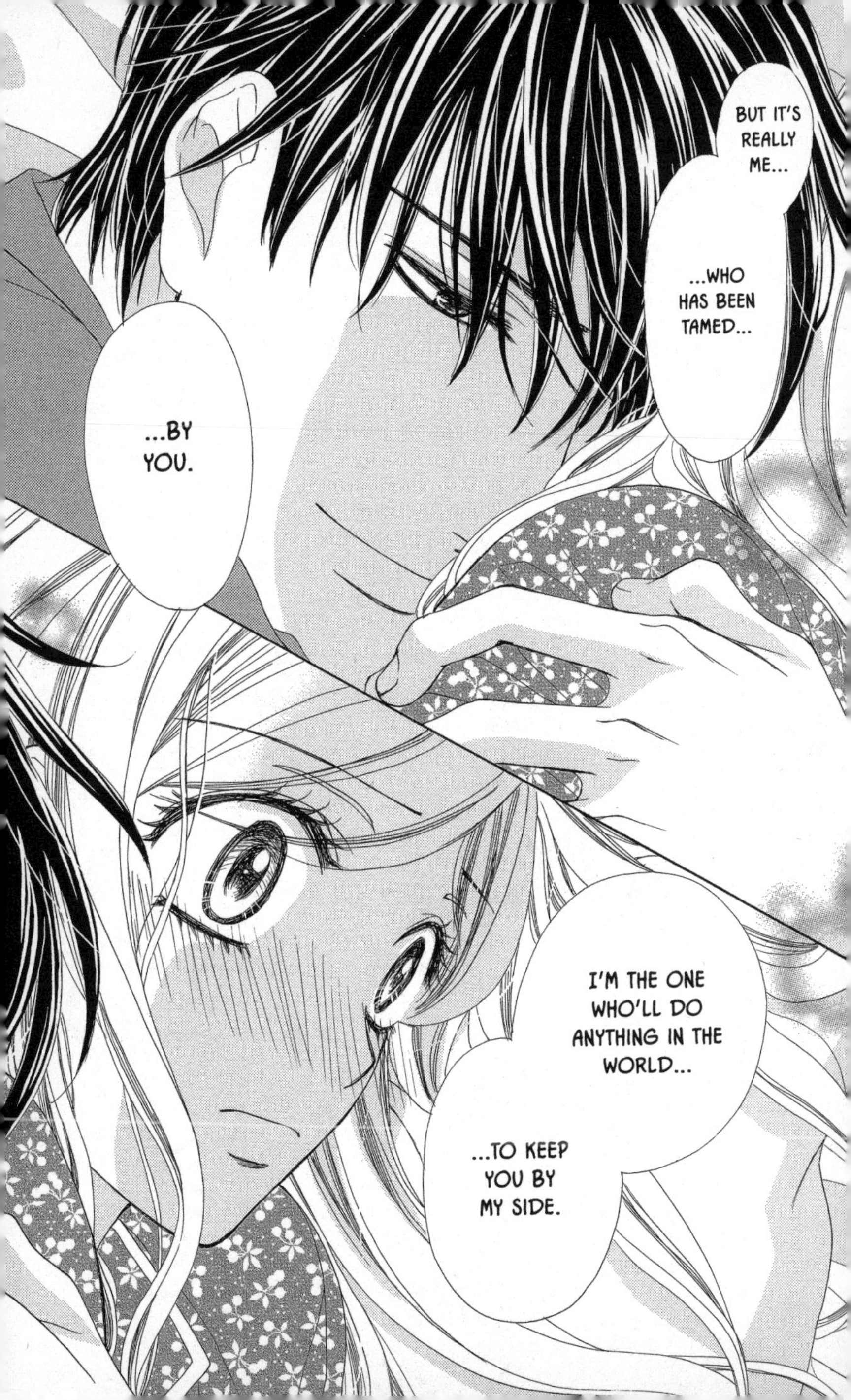
BUT IT'S REALLY ME...
...WHO HAS BEEN TAMED...
...BY YOU.
I'M THE ONE WHO'LL DO ANYTHING IN THE WORLD...
...TO KEEP YOU BY MY SIDE.

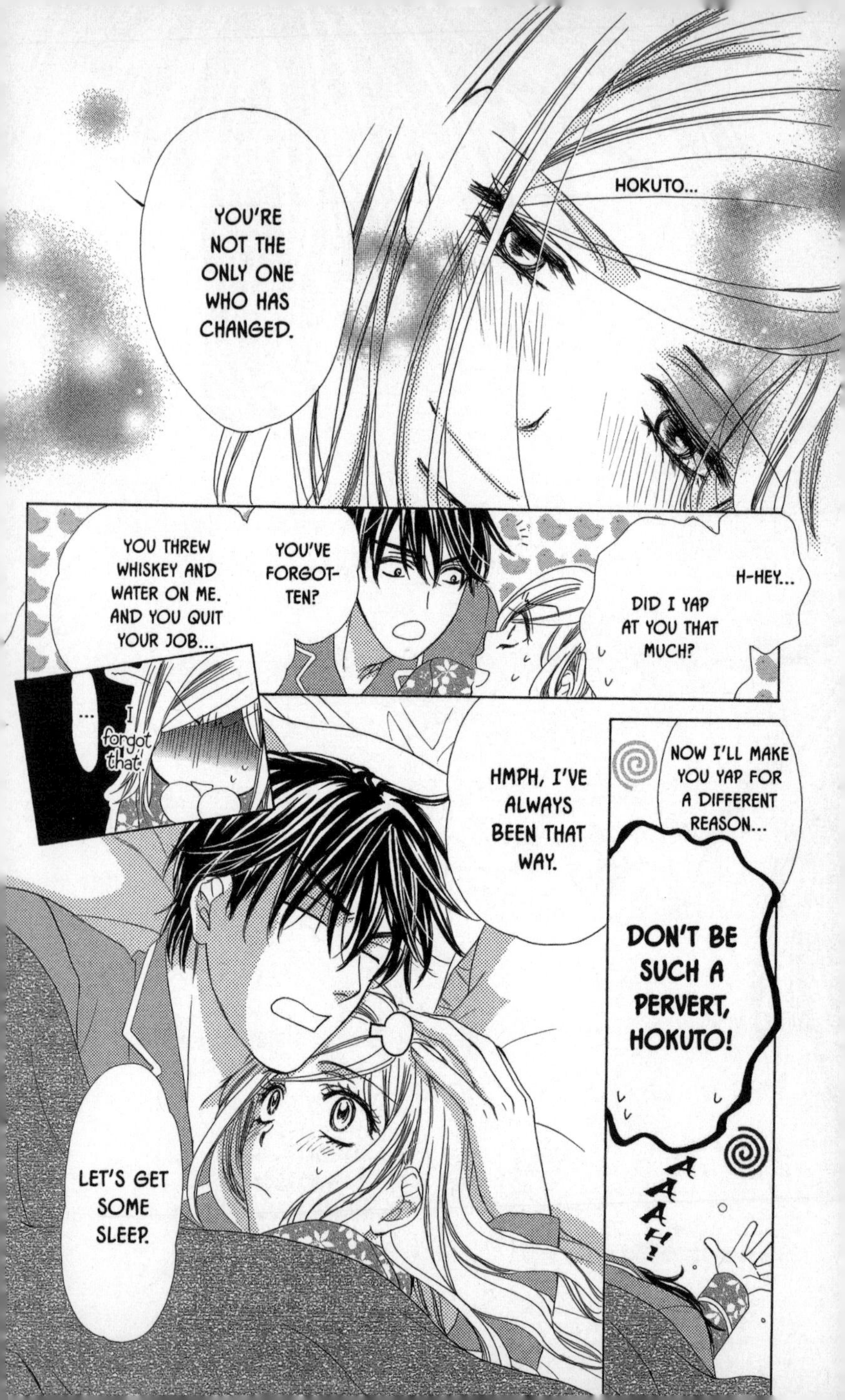
HOKUTO...
YOU'RE NOT THE ONLY ONE WHO HAS CHANGED.
H-HEY...
DID I YAP AT YOU THAT MUCH?
YOU'VE FORGOT-TEN?
YOU THREW WHISKEY AND WATER ON ME. AND YOU QUIT YOUR JOB...
...
I forgot that.
HMPH, I'VE ALWAYS BEEN THAT WAY.
LET'S GET SOME SLEEP.
NOW I'LL MAKE YOU YAP FOR A DIFFERENT REASON...
DON'T BE SUCH A PERVERT, HOKUTO!
AAAH!

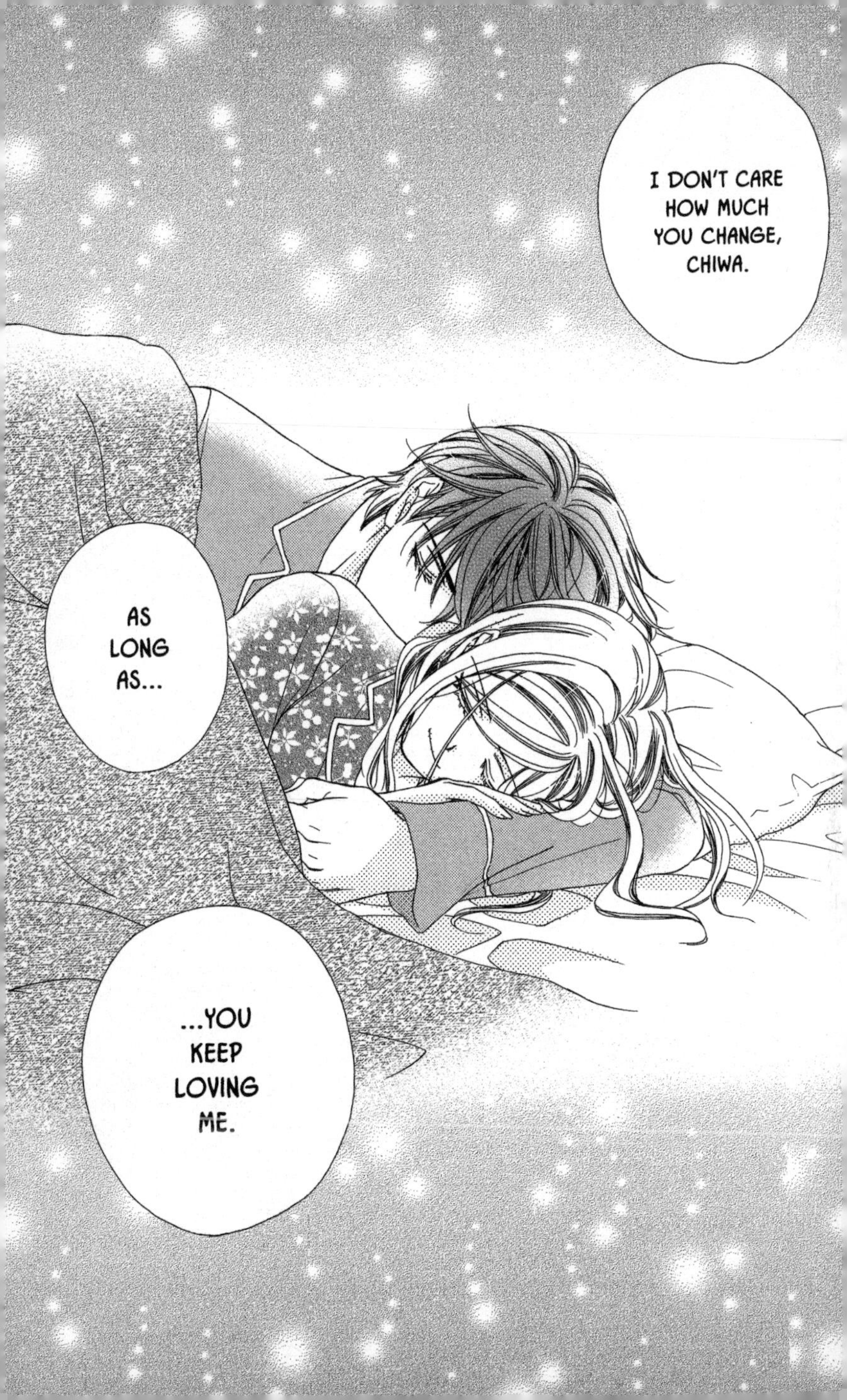
I DON'T CARE HOW MUCH YOU CHANGE, CHIWA.
AS LONG AS...
...YOU KEEP LOVING ME.

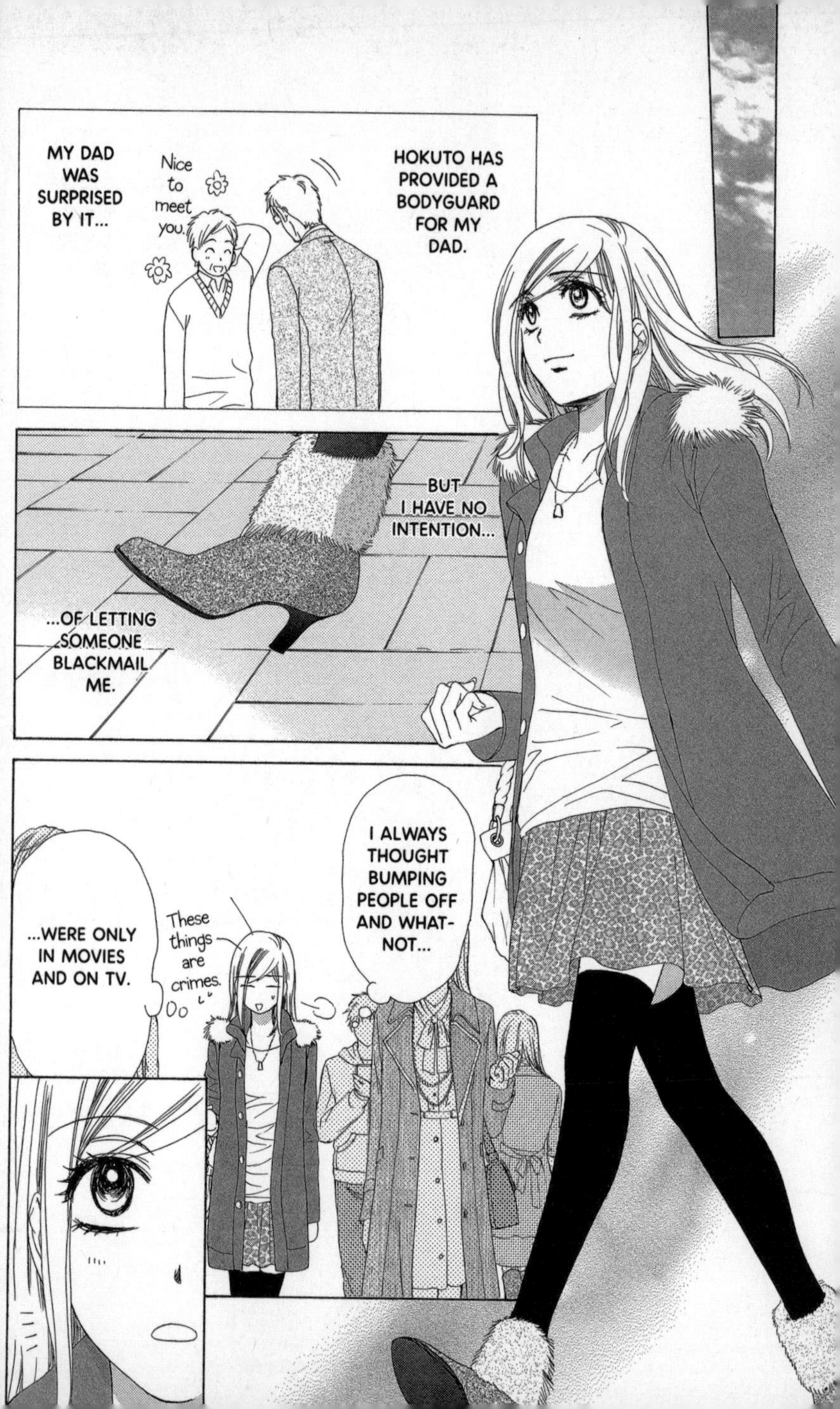
HOKUTO HAS PROVIDED A BODYGUARD FOR MY DAD.
Nice to meet you.
MY DAD WAS SURPRISED BY IT...
BUT I HAVE NO INTENTION...
...OF LETTING SOMEONE BLACKMAIL ME.
I ALWAYS THOUGHT BUMPING PEOPLE OFF AND WHAT-NOT...
These things are crimes.
...WERE ONLY IN MOVIES AND ON TV.

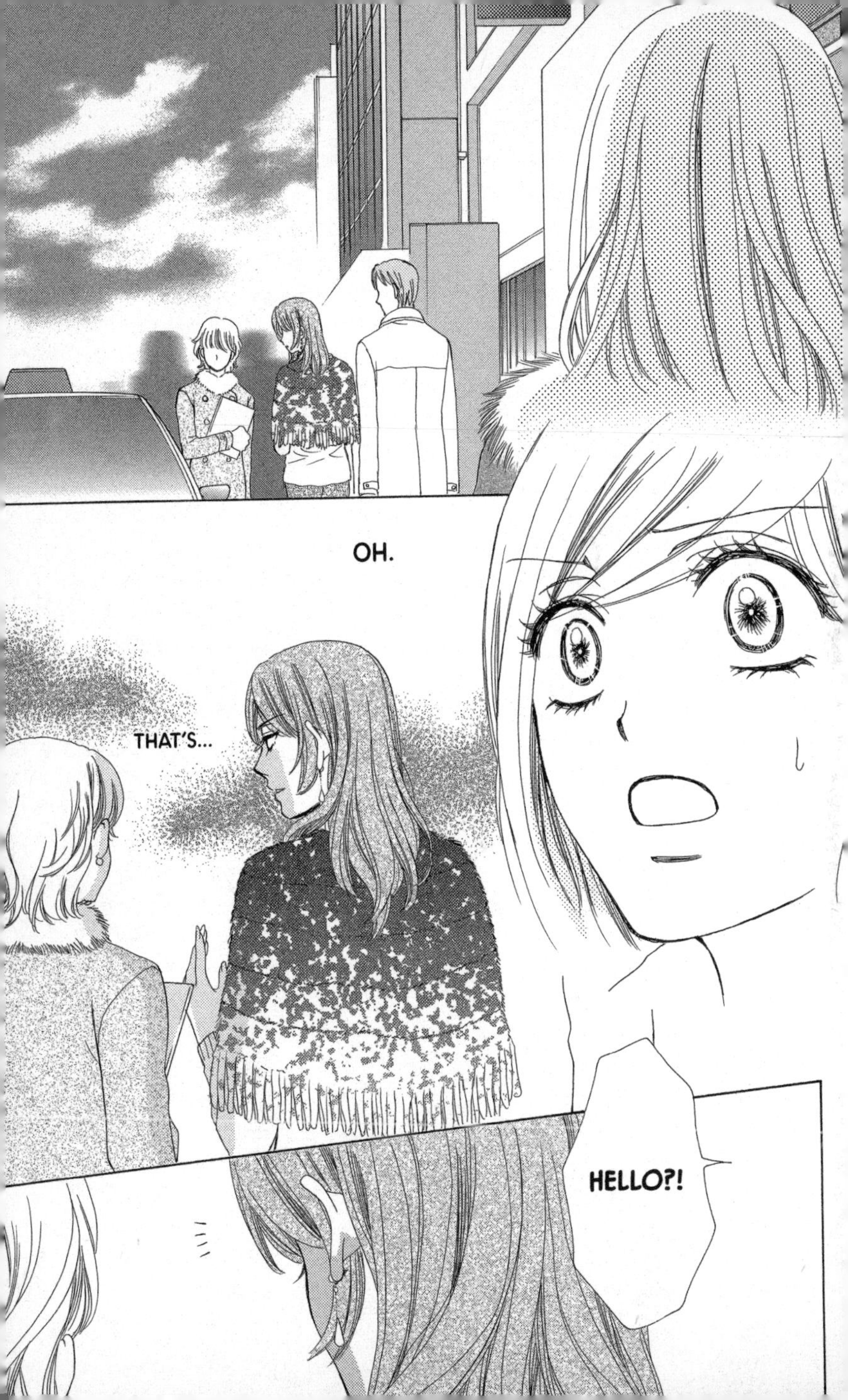
OH.
THAT'S...
HELLO?!

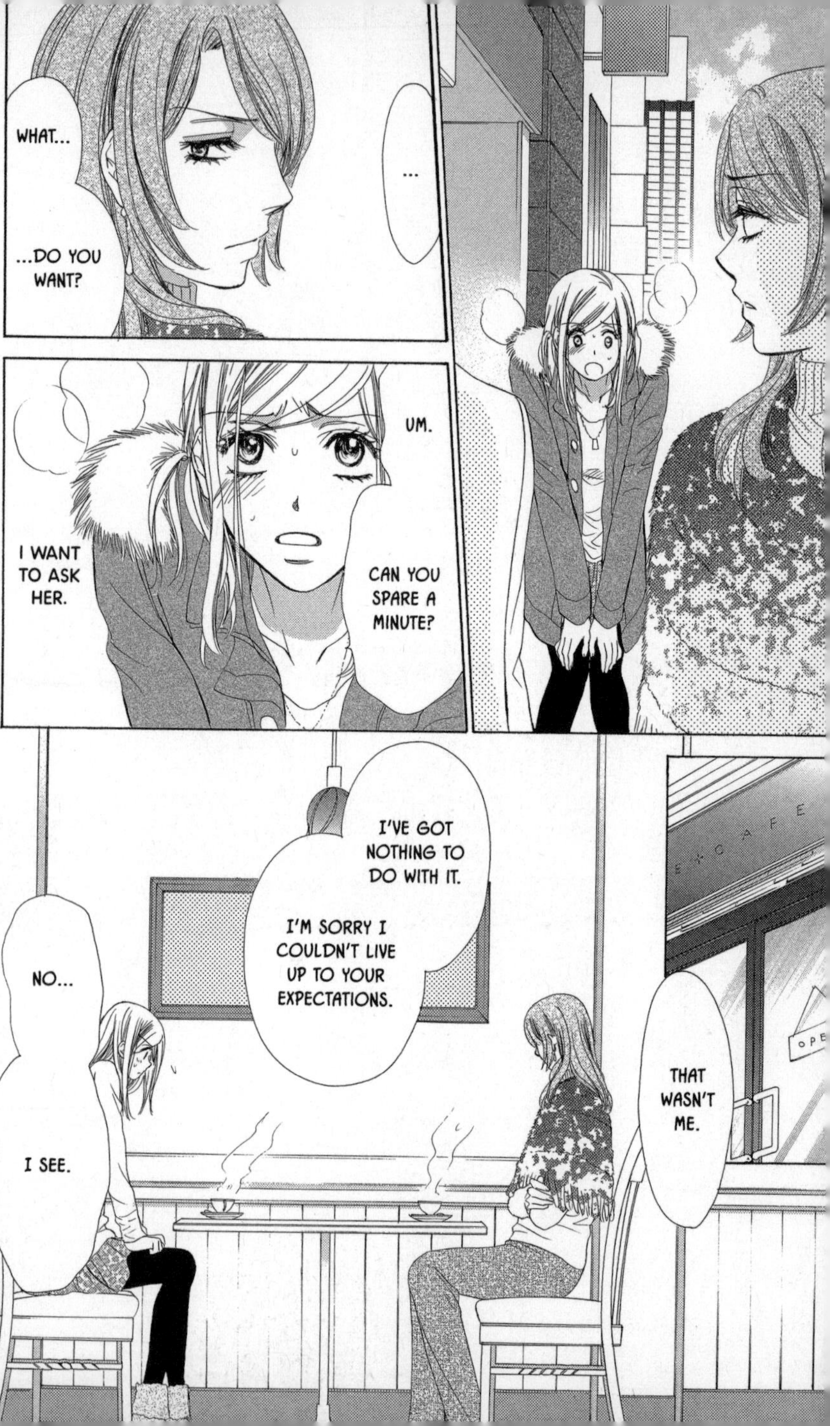
...
WHAT...
...DO YOU WANT?
UM.
CAN YOU SPARE A MINUTE?
I WANT TO ASK HER.
THAT WASN'T ME.
I'VE GOT NOTHING TO DO WITH IT.
I'M SORRY I COULDN'T LIVE UP TO YOUR EXPECTATIONS.
NO...
I SEE.

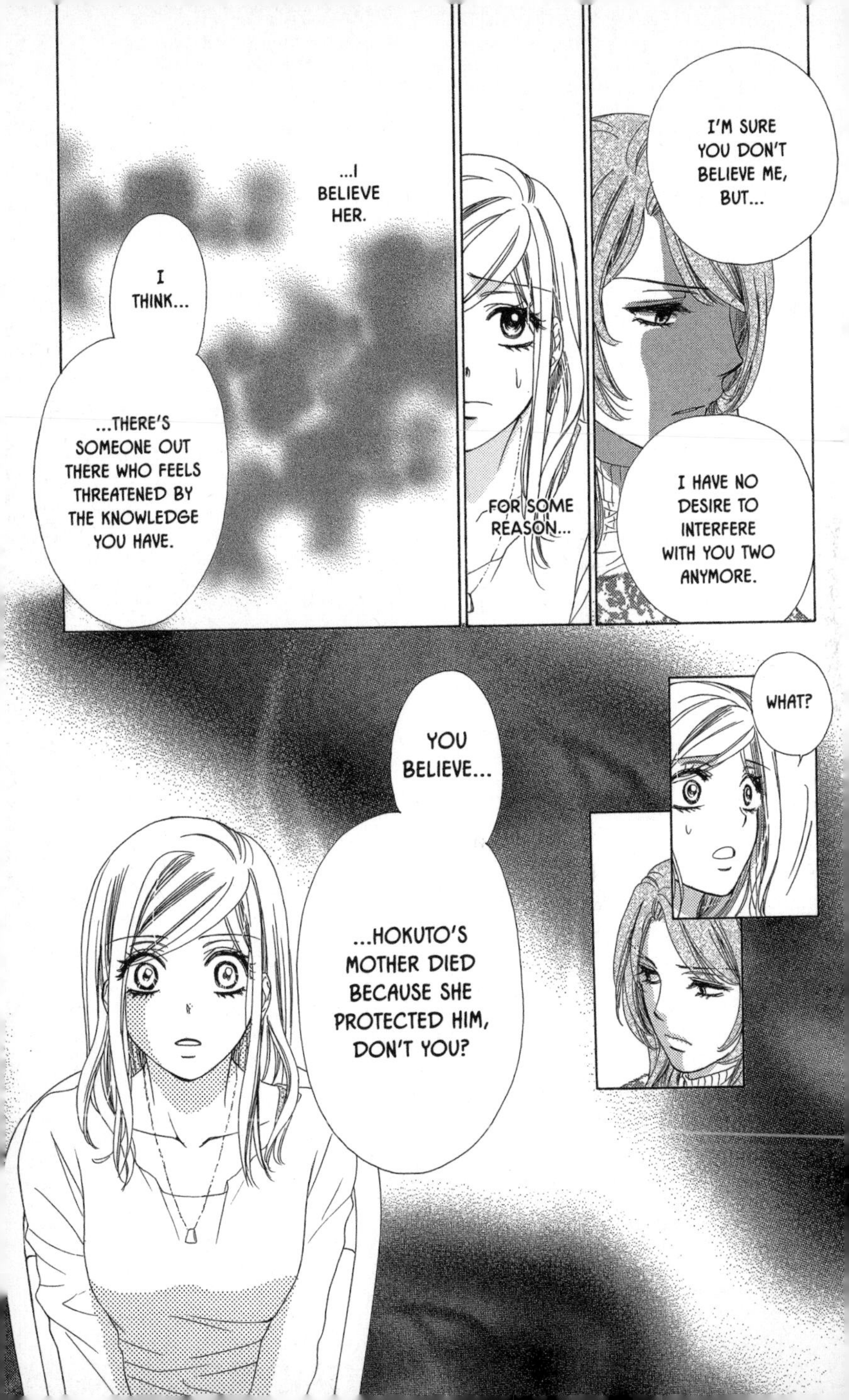
I'M SURE YOU DON'T BELIEVE ME, BUT...
I HAVE NO DESIRE TO INTERFERE WITH YOU TWO ANYMORE.
FOR SOME REASON...
...I BELIEVE HER.
I THINK...
...THERE'S SOMEONE OUT THERE WHO FEELS THREATENED BY THE KNOWLEDGE YOU HAVE.
WHAT?
YOU BELIEVE...
...HOKUTO'S MOTHER DIED BECAUSE SHE PROTECTED HIM, DON'T YOU?

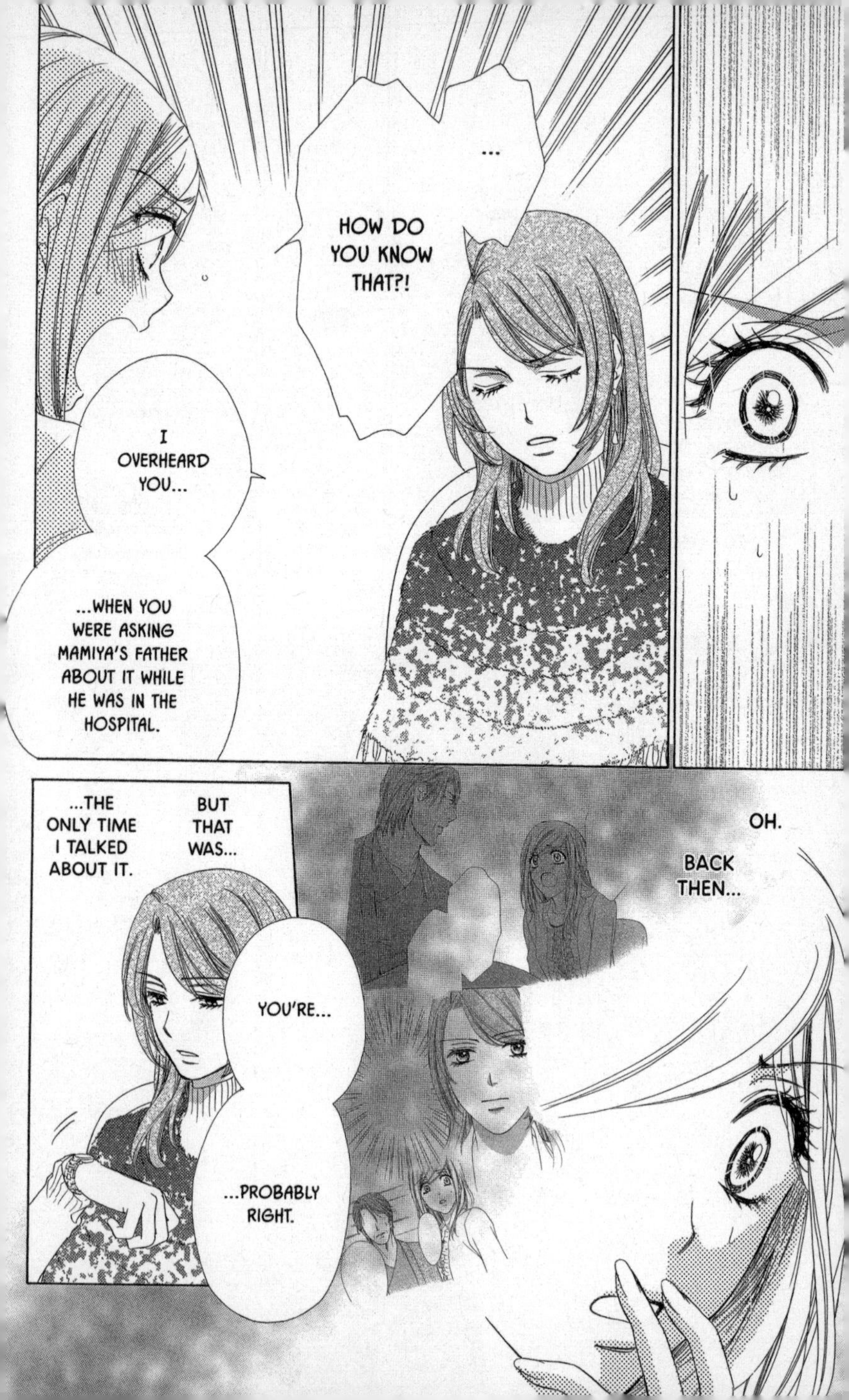
...
HOW DO YOU KNOW THAT?!
I OVERHEARD YOU...
...WHEN YOU WERE ASKING MAMIYA'S FATHER ABOUT IT WHILE HE WAS IN THE HOSPITAL.
OH.
BACK THEN...
BUT THAT WAS...
...THE ONLY TIME I TALKED ABOUT IT.
YOU'RE...
...PROBABLY RIGHT.

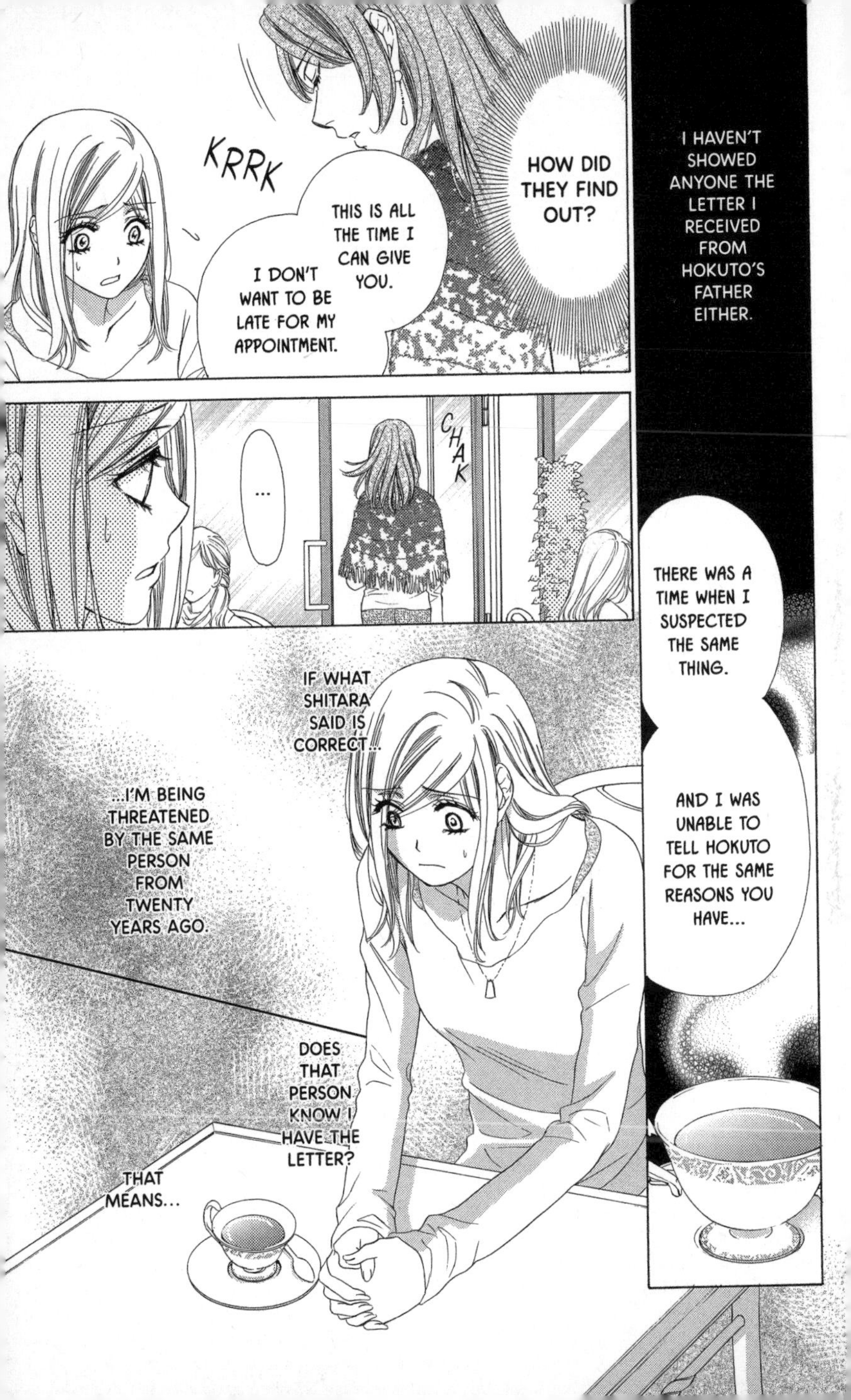
I HAVEN'T SHOWED ANYONE THE LETTER I RECEIVED FROM HOKUTO'S FATHER EITHER.
THERE WAS A TIME WHEN I SUSPECTED THE SAME THING.
AND I WAS UNABLE TO TELL HOKUTO FOR THE SAME REASONS YOU HAVE...
HOW DID THEY FIND OUT?
KRRK
THIS IS ALL THE TIME I CAN GIVE YOU.
I DON'T WANT TO BE LATE FOR MY APPOINTMENT.
CHAK
...
IF WHAT SHITARA SAID IS CORRECT...
...I'M BEING THREATENED BY THE SAME PERSON FROM TWENTY YEARS AGO.
DOES THAT PERSON KNOW I HAVE THE LETTER?
THAT MEANS...

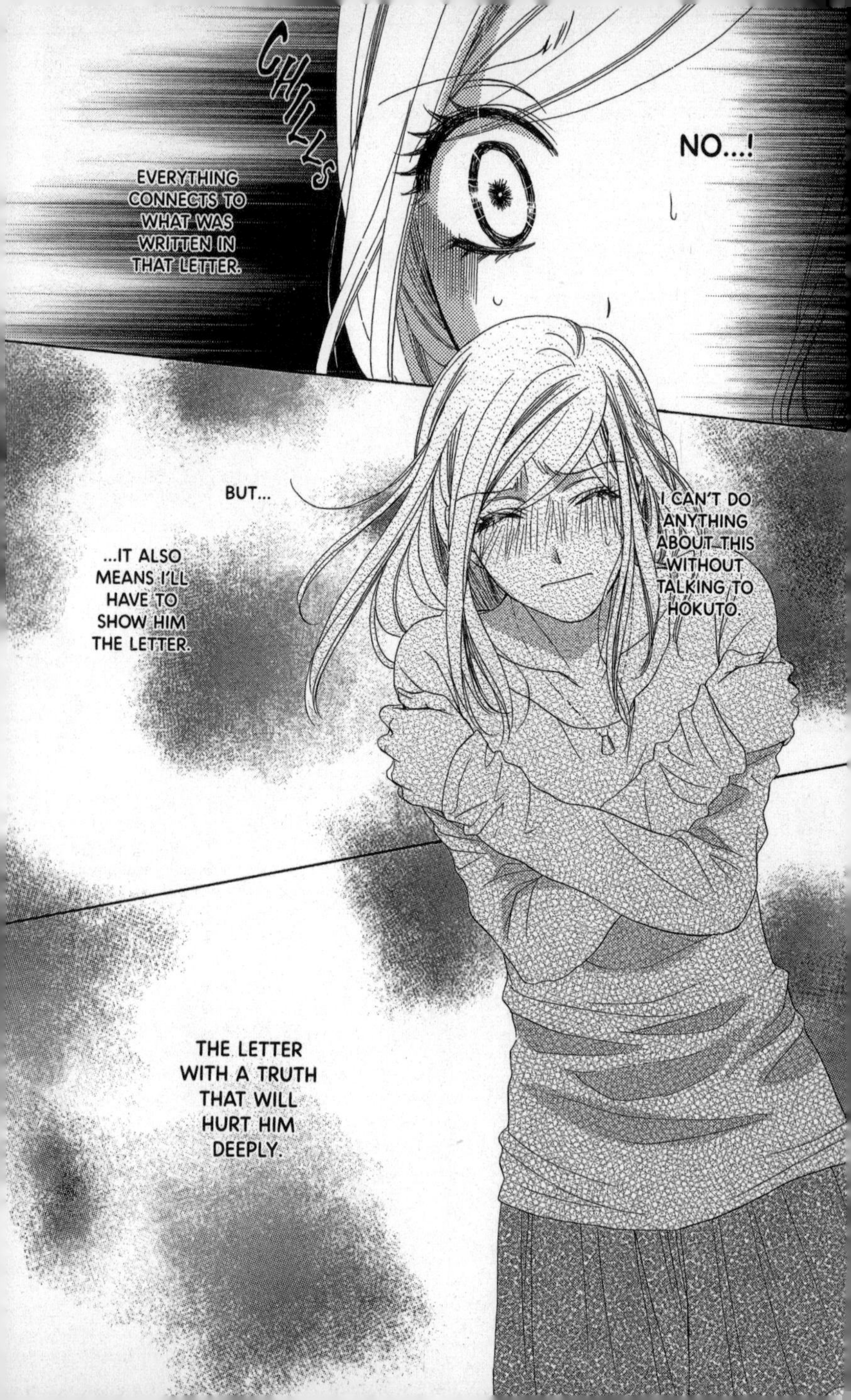
NO...!
CHILLS
EVERYTHING CONNECTS TO WHAT WAS WRITTEN IN THAT LETTER.
I CAN'T DO ANYTHING ABOUT THIS WITHOUT TALKING TO HOKUTO.
BUT...
...IT ALSO MEANS I'LL HAVE TO SHOW HIM THE LETTER.
THE LETTER WITH A TRUTH THAT WILL HURT HIM DEEPLY.

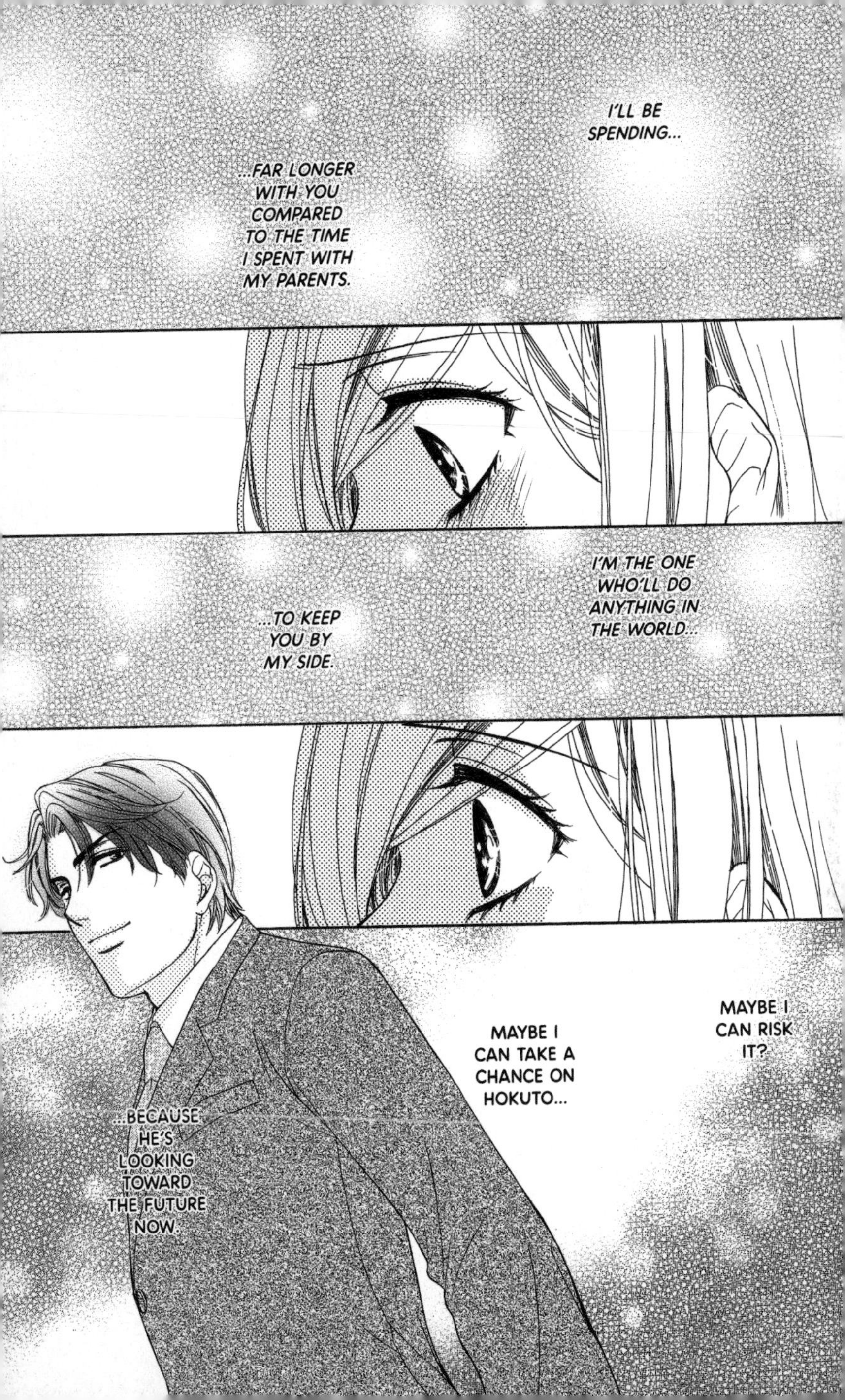
I'LL BE SPENDING...
...FAR LONGER WITH YOU COMPARED TO THE TIME I SPENT WITH MY PARENTS.
I'M THE ONE WHO'LL DO ANYTHING IN THE WORLD...
...TO KEEP YOU BY MY SIDE.
MAYBE I CAN RISK IT?
MAYBE I CAN TAKE A CHANCE ON HOKUTO...
...BECAUSE HE'S LOOKING TOWARD THE FUTURE NOW.

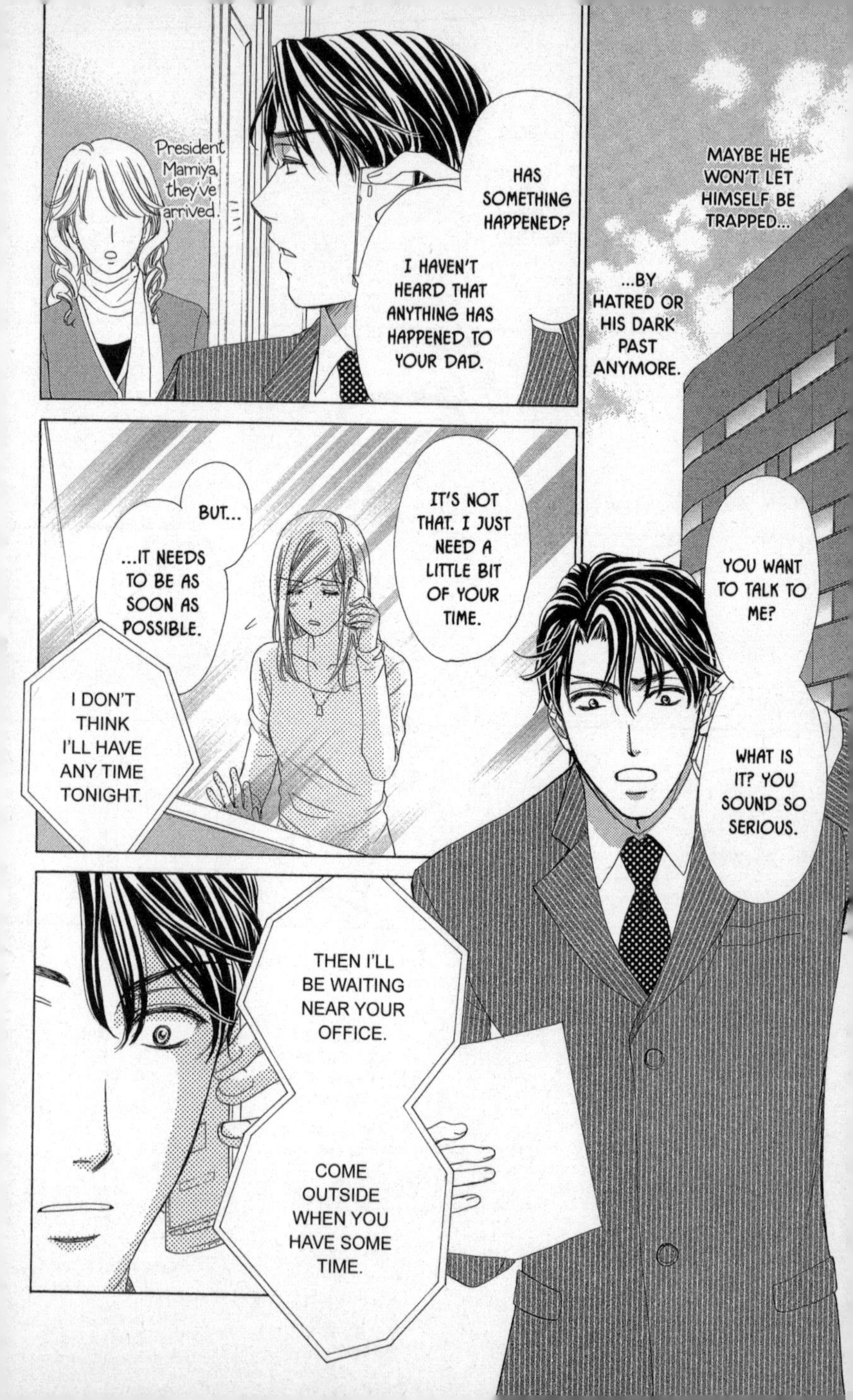
MAYBE HE WON'T LET HIMSELF BE TRAPPED...
...BY HATRED OR HIS DARK PAST ANYMORE.
YOU WANT TO TALK TO ME?
WHAT IS IT? YOU SOUND SO SERIOUS.
HAS SOMETHING HAPPENED?
I HAVEN'T HEARD THAT ANYTHING HAS HAPPENED TO YOUR DAD.
President Mamiya, they've arrived.
IT'S NOT THAT. I JUST NEED A LITTLE BIT OF YOUR TIME.
BUT...
...IT NEEDS TO BE AS SOON AS POSSIBLE.
I DON'T THINK I'LL HAVE ANY TIME TONIGHT.
THEN I'LL BE WAITING NEAR YOUR OFFICE.
COME OUTSIDE WHEN YOU HAVE SOME TIME.

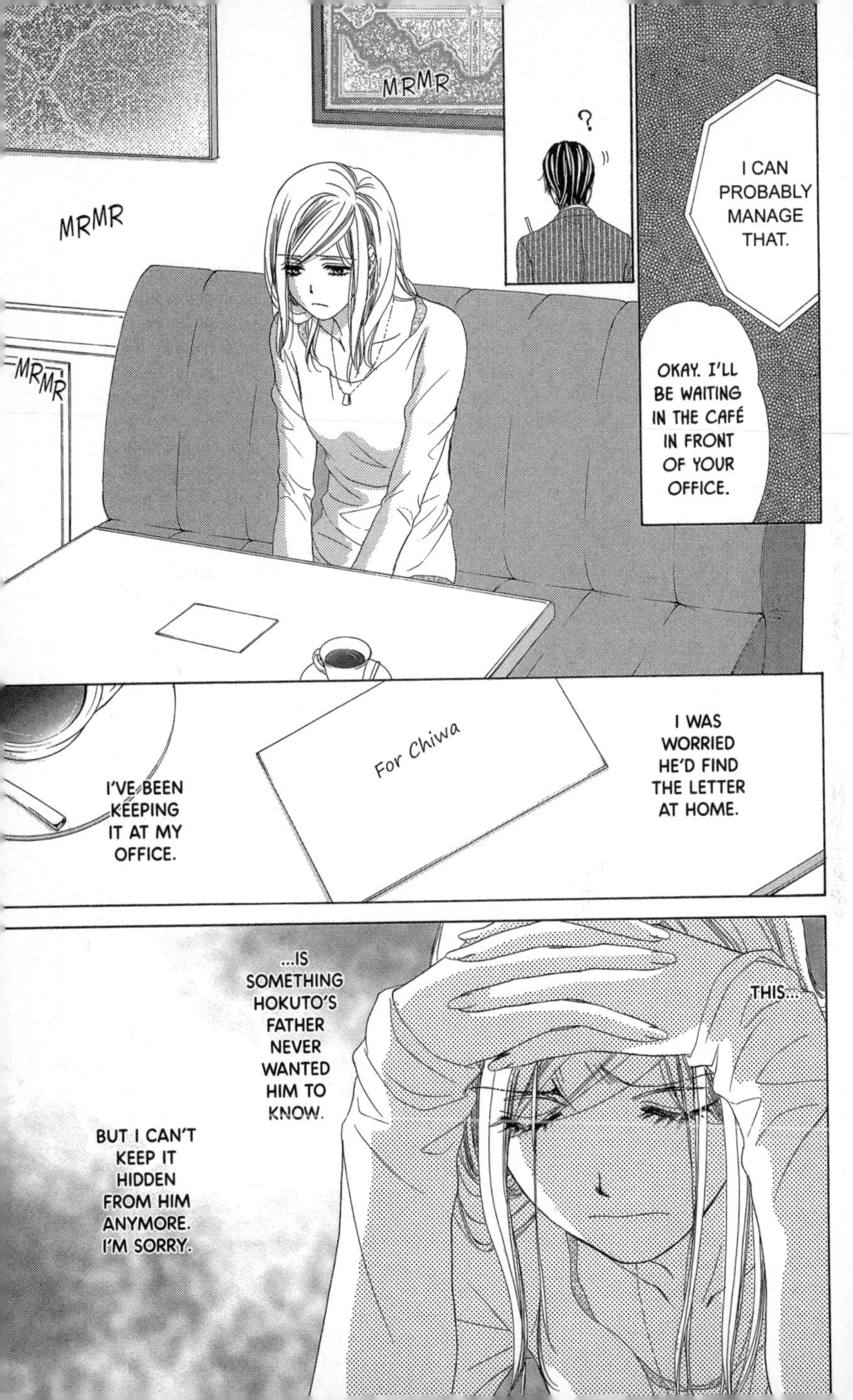
I CAN PROBABLY MANAGE THAT.
OKAY. I'LL BE WAITING IN THE CAFÉ IN FRONT OF YOUR OFFICE.
?
MRMR
MRMR
MRMR
I WAS WORRIED HE'D FIND THE LETTER AT HOME.
For Chiwa
I'VE BEEN KEEPING IT AT MY OFFICE.
THIS...
...IS SOMETHING HOKUTO'S FATHER NEVER WANTED HIM TO KNOW.
BUT I CAN'T KEEP IT HIDDEN FROM HIM ANYMORE. I'M SORRY.

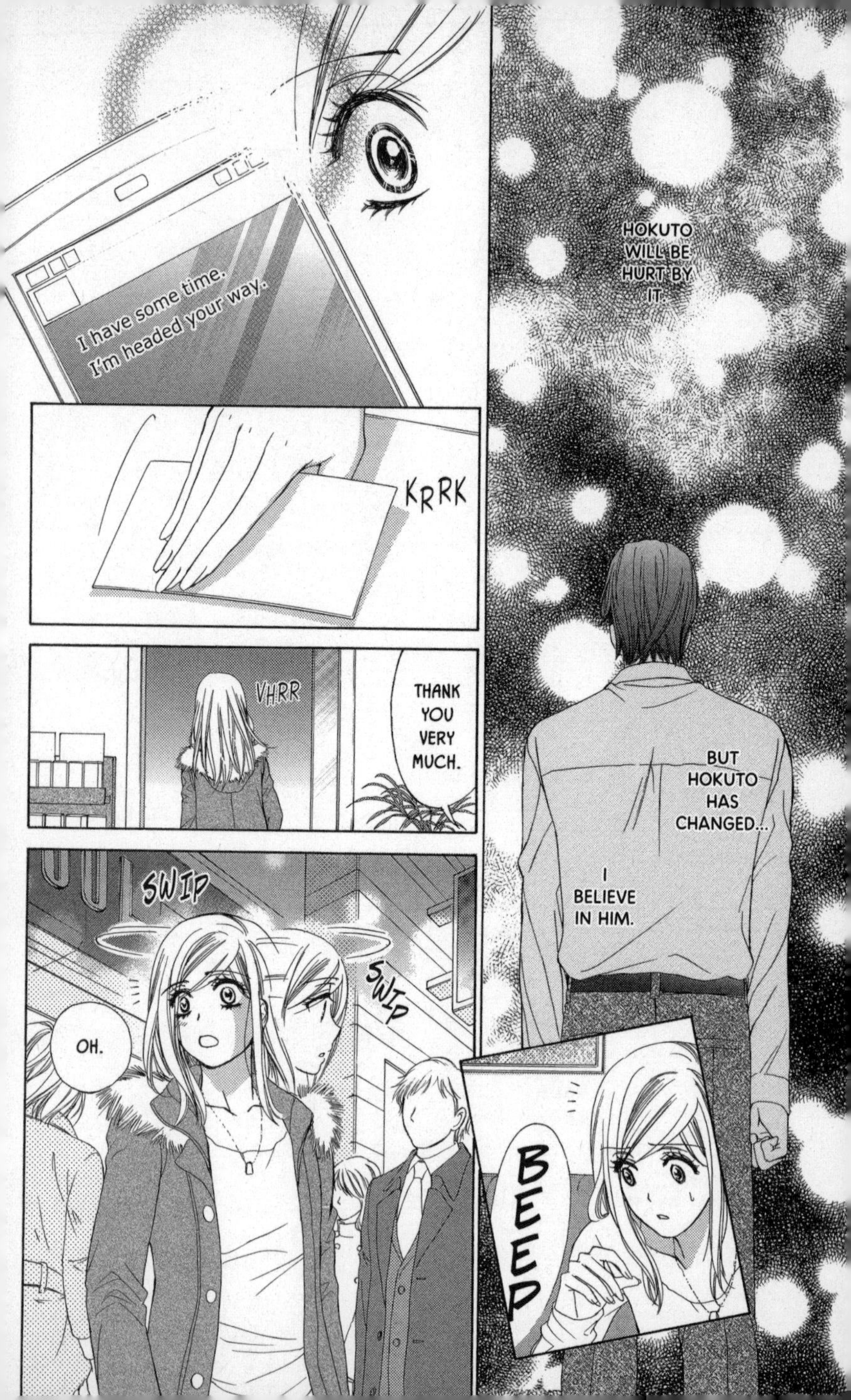
HOKUTO WILL BE HURT BY IT.
BUT HOKUTO HAS CHANGED...
I BELIEVE IN HIM.
BEEP
I have some time.
I'm headed your way.
KRRK
THANK YOU VERY MUCH.
VHRR
SWIP
SWIP
OH.

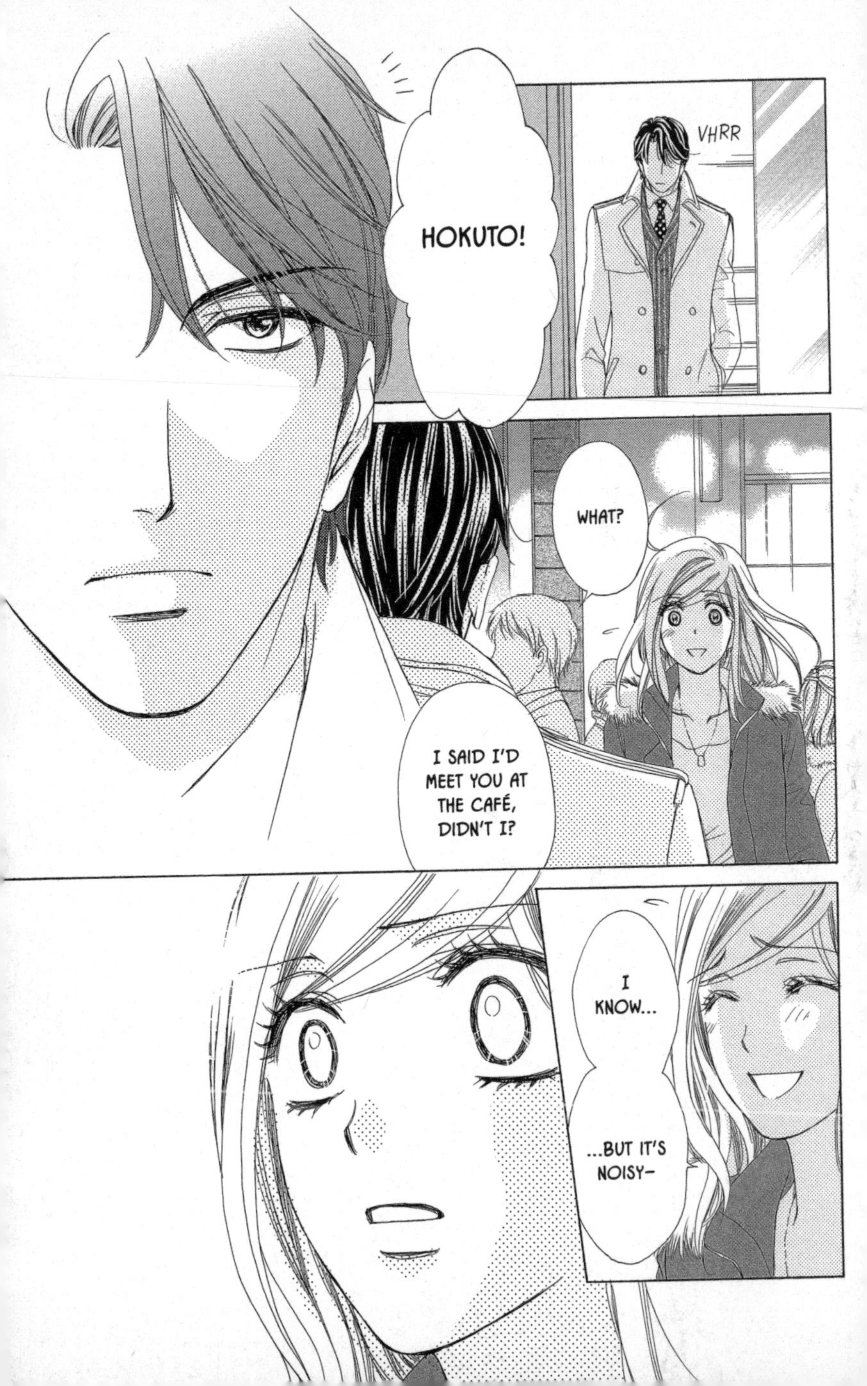
VHRR
HOKUTO!
WHAT?
I SAID I'D MEET YOU AT THE CAFÉ, DIDN'T I?
I KNOW...
...BUT IT'S NOISY–

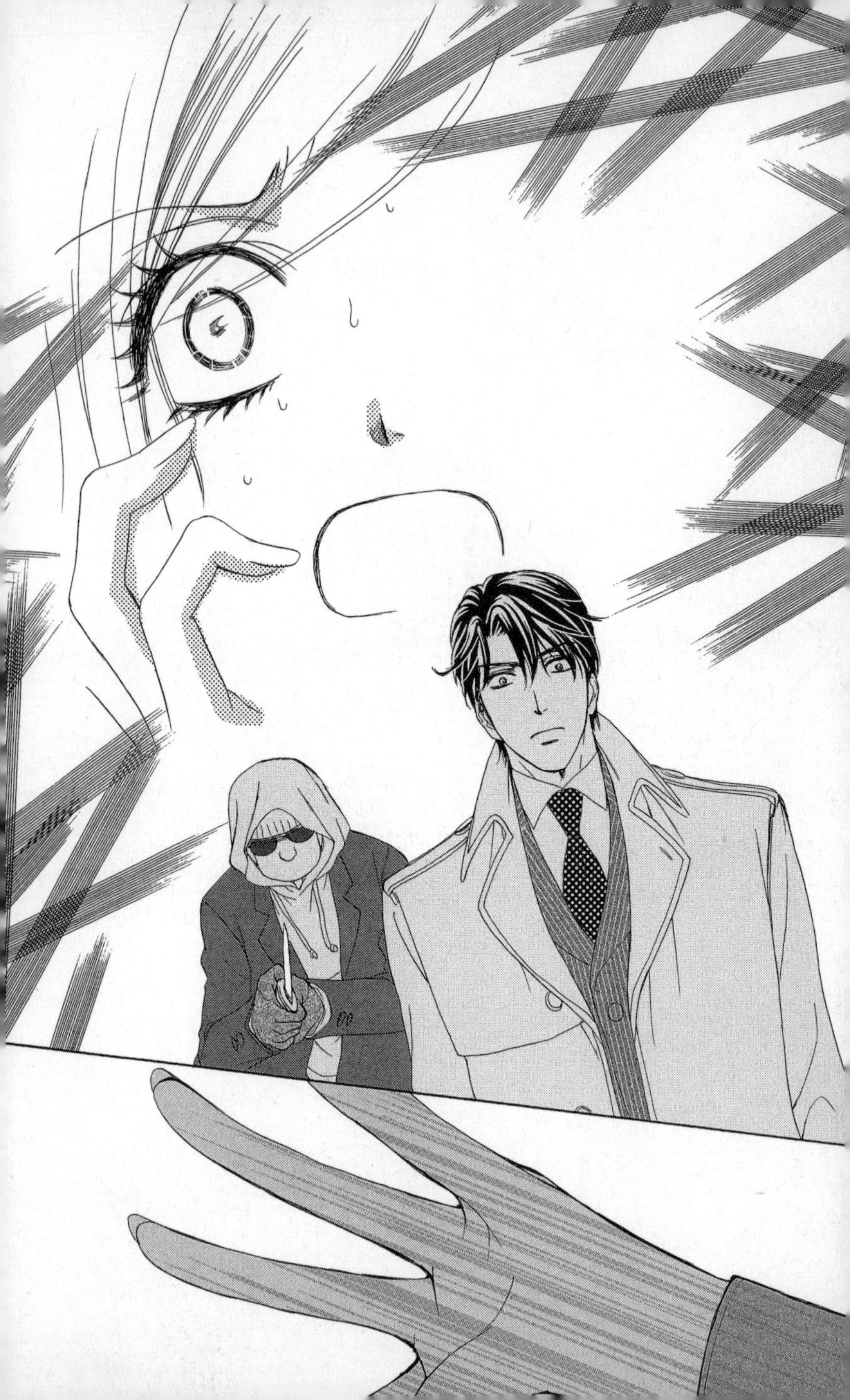

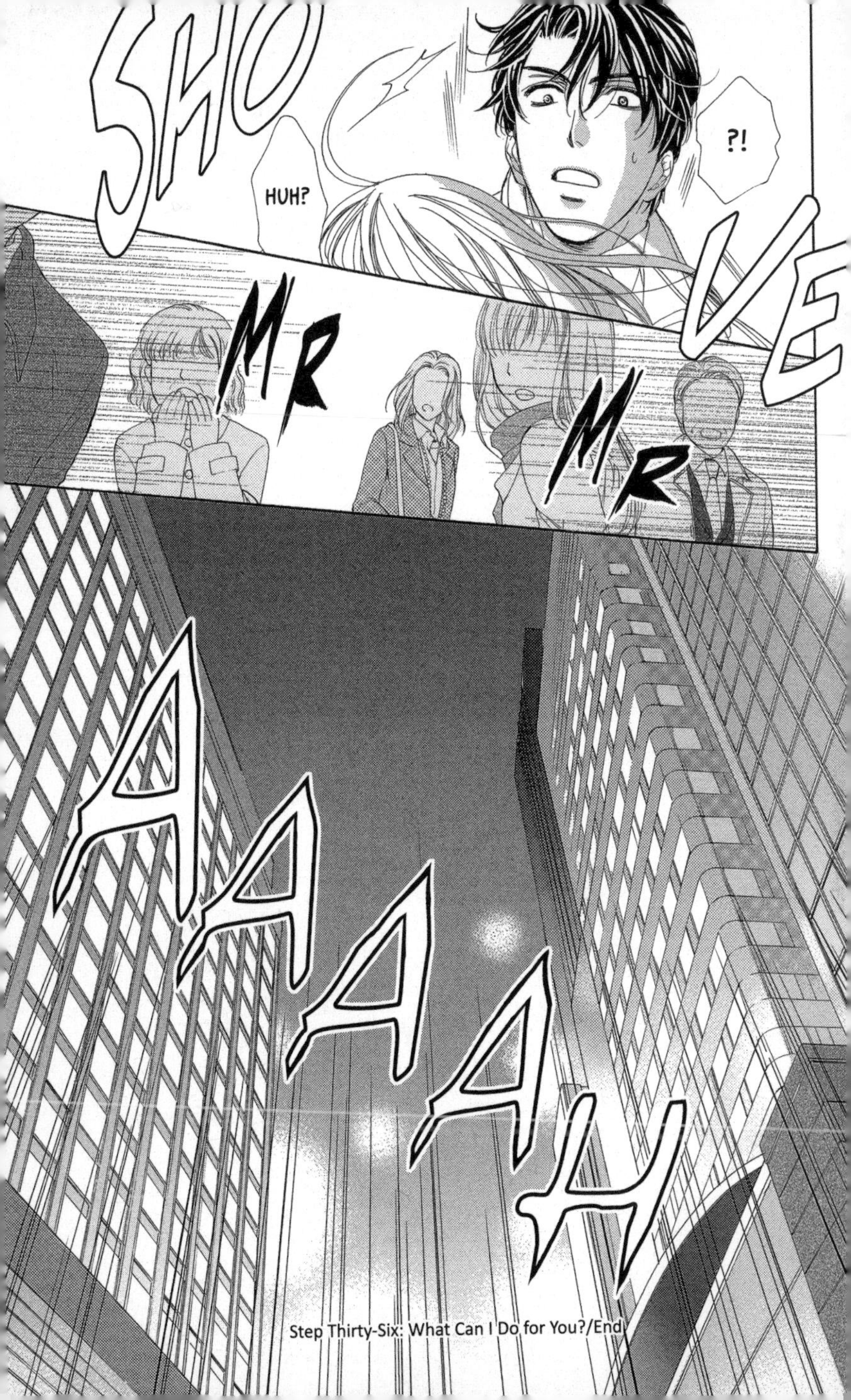
?!
HUH?
SHOVE
MR
MR
AAAAAH

Step Thirty-Six: What Can I Do for You?/End

Special Thanks

Assistants

K. Sano
E. Shimojo
Y. Nagashima
N. Hori

Editor

M. Okada

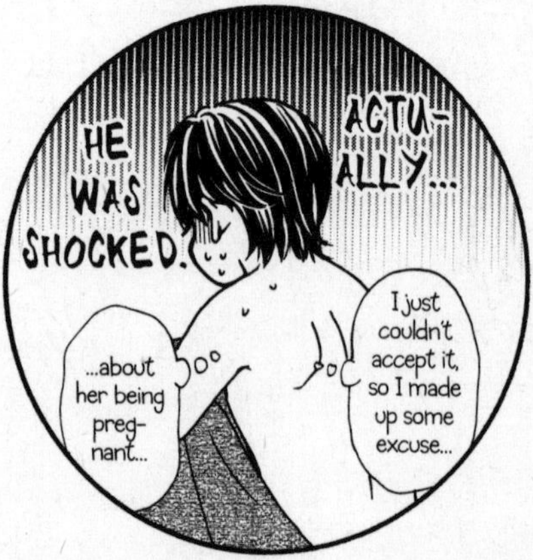
ACTU-ALLY...
HE WAS SHOCKED.
I just couldn't accept it, so I made up some excuse...
...about her being preg-nant...

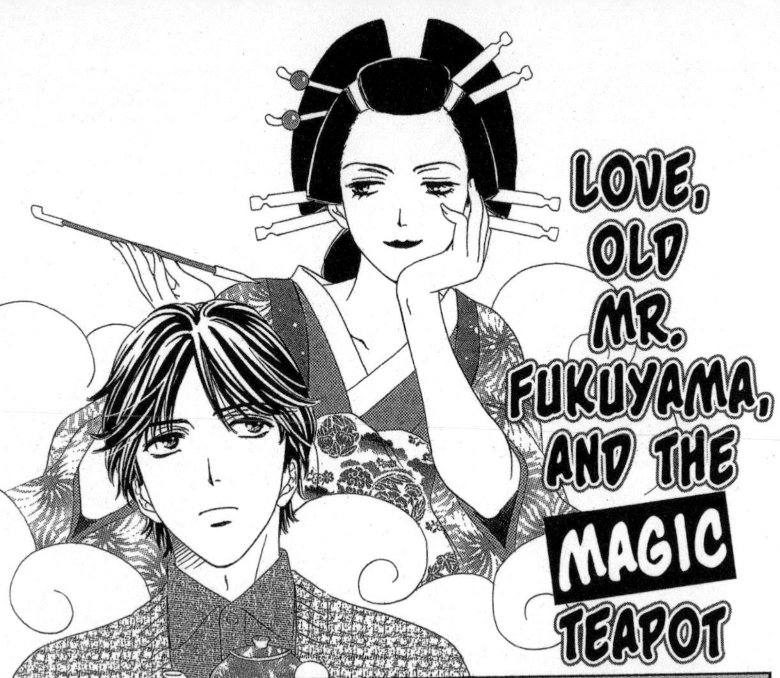
LOVE, OLD MR. FUKUYAMA, AND THE MAGIC TEAPOT

Youthful Once More

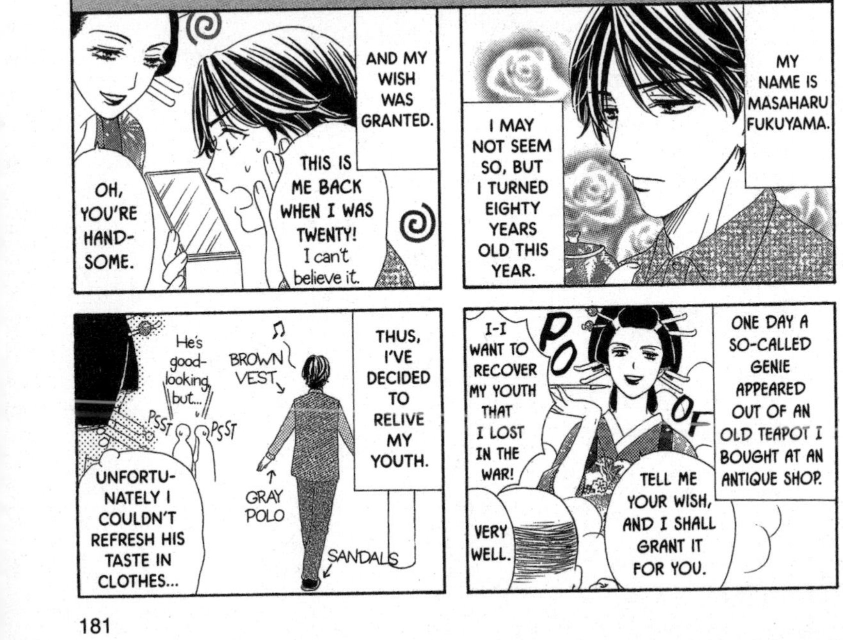
MY NAME IS MASAHARU FUKUYAMA.
I MAY NOT SEEM SO, BUT I TURNED EIGHTY YEARS OLD THIS YEAR.
AND MY WISH WAS GRANTED.
THIS IS ME BACK WHEN I WAS TWENTY! I can't believe it.
OH, YOU'RE HANDSOME.
ONE DAY A SO-CALLED GENIE APPEARED OUT OF AN OLD TEAPOT I BOUGHT AT AN ANTIQUE SHOP.
POOF
TELL ME YOUR WISH, AND I SHALL GRANT IT FOR YOU.
I-I WANT TO RECOVER MY YOUTH THAT I LOST IN THE WAR!
VERY WELL.
THUS, I'VE DECIDED TO RELIVE MY YOUTH.
BROWN VEST
He's good-looking, but...
PSST
PSST
GRAY POLO
SANDALS
UNFORTUNATELY I COULDN'T REFRESH HIS TASTE IN CLOTHES...

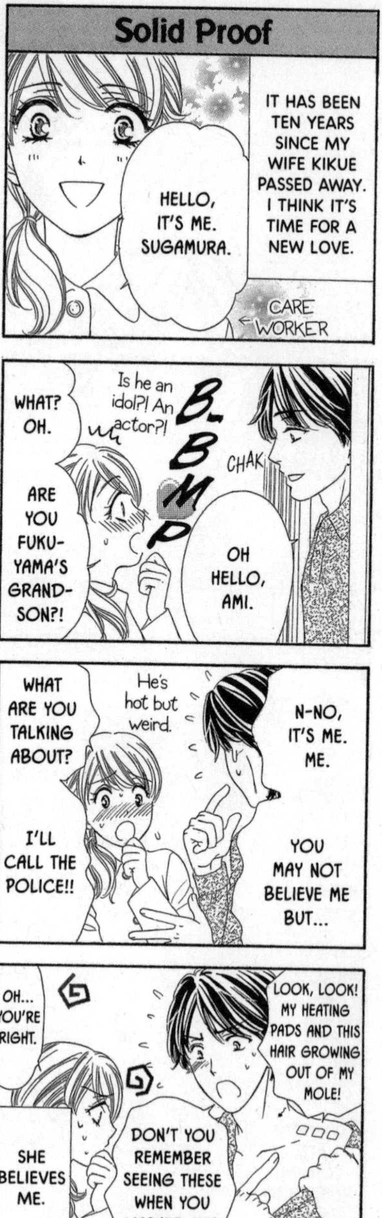
Solid Proof
IT HAS BEEN TEN YEARS SINCE MY WIFE KIKUE PASSED AWAY. I THINK IT'S TIME FOR A NEW LOVE.
HELLO, IT'S ME. SUGAMURA.
CARE WORKER
OH HELLO, AMI.
CHAK
B-B-MP
Is he an idol?! An actor?!
WHAT? OH.
ARE YOU FUKU-YAMA'S GRAND-SON?!
N-NO, IT'S ME. ME.
YOU MAY NOT BELIEVE ME BUT...
He's hot but weird.
WHAT ARE YOU TALKING ABOUT?
I'LL CALL THE POLICE!!
LOOK, LOOK! MY HEATING PADS AND THIS HAIR GROWING OUT OF MY MOLE!
DON'T YOU REMEMBER SEEING THESE WHEN YOU WASHED ME?
OH... YOU'RE RIGHT.
SHE BELIEVES ME.

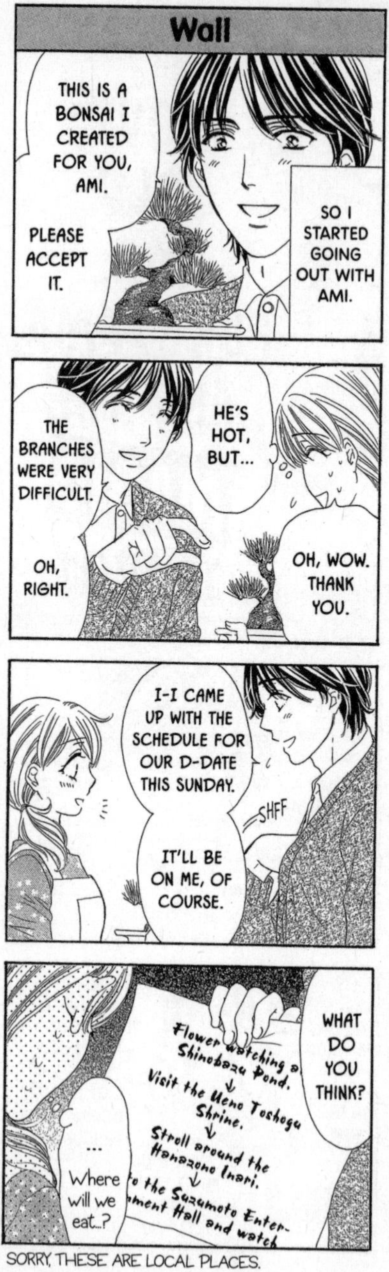
Wall
SO I STARTED GOING OUT WITH AMI.
THIS IS A BONSAI I CREATED FOR YOU, AMI.
PLEASE ACCEPT IT.
HE'S HOT, BUT...
THE BRANCHES WERE VERY DIFFICULT.
OH, WOW. THANK YOU.
OH, RIGHT.
I-I CAME UP WITH THE SCHEDULE FOR OUR D-DATE THIS SUNDAY.
SHFF
IT'LL BE ON ME, OF COURSE.
WHAT DO YOU THINK?
Flower watching a Shinobazu Pond.
Visit the Ueno Toshogu Shrine.
Stroll around the Hanazono Inari.
to the Suzumoto Enter- ment Hall and watch
... Where will we eat...?

SORRY, THESE ARE LOCAL PLACES.

The End of Youth

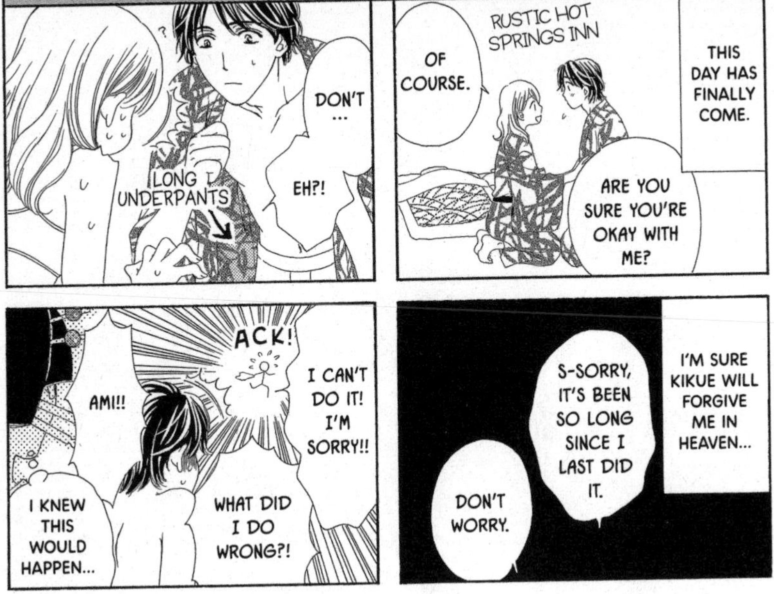
THIS DAY HAS FINALLY COME.
RUSTIC HOT SPRINGS INN
ARE YOU SURE YOU'RE OKAY WITH ME?
OF COURSE.
DON'T ...
EH?!
LONG UNDERPANTS
I'M SURE KIKUE WILL FORGIVE ME IN HEAVEN...
S-SORRY, IT'S BEEN SO LONG SINCE I LAST DID IT.
DON'T WORRY.
ACK!
I CAN'T DO IT! I'M SORRY!!
AMI!!
WHAT DID I DO WRONG?!
I KNEW THIS WOULD HAPPEN...

A strange four-panel manga has been placed in a volume of this series again! These are from 2007... They're old! Just like the one in volume 6, these were published in a special booklet of funnies that came with the magazine. It's an annual tradition (?) for the magazine, and you'll find the four-panel manga from 2008 after this.
Ooh...!

En

Love, Old Mr. Fukuyama, and the Magic Teapot/End

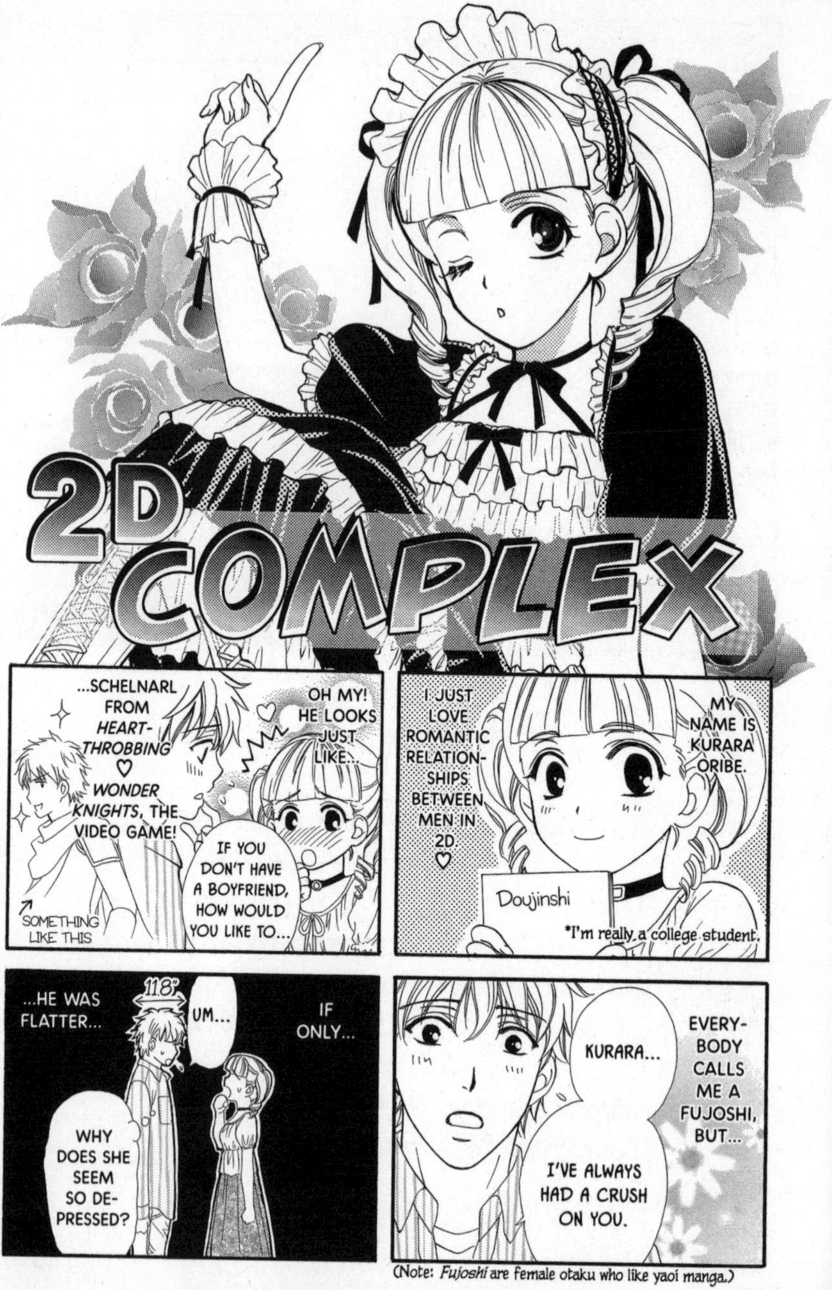
2D COMPLEX
MY NAME IS KURARA ORIBE.
I JUST LOVE ROMANTIC RELATIONSHIPS BETWEEN MEN IN 2D. ♡
Doujinshi
*I'm really a college student.
OH MY! HE LOOKS JUST LIKE...
...SCHELNARL FROM *HEART-THROBBING ♡ WONDER KNIGHTS*, THE VIDEO GAME!
IF YOU DON'T HAVE A BOYFRIEND, HOW WOULD YOU LIKE TO...
SOMETHING LIKE THIS
EVERYBODY CALLS ME A FUJOSHI, BUT...
KURARA...
I'VE ALWAYS HAD A CRUSH ON YOU.
IF ONLY...
UM...
118"
...HE WAS FLATTER...
WHY DOES SHE SEEM SO DEPRESSED?

(Note: *Fujoshi* are female otaku who like yaoi manga.)

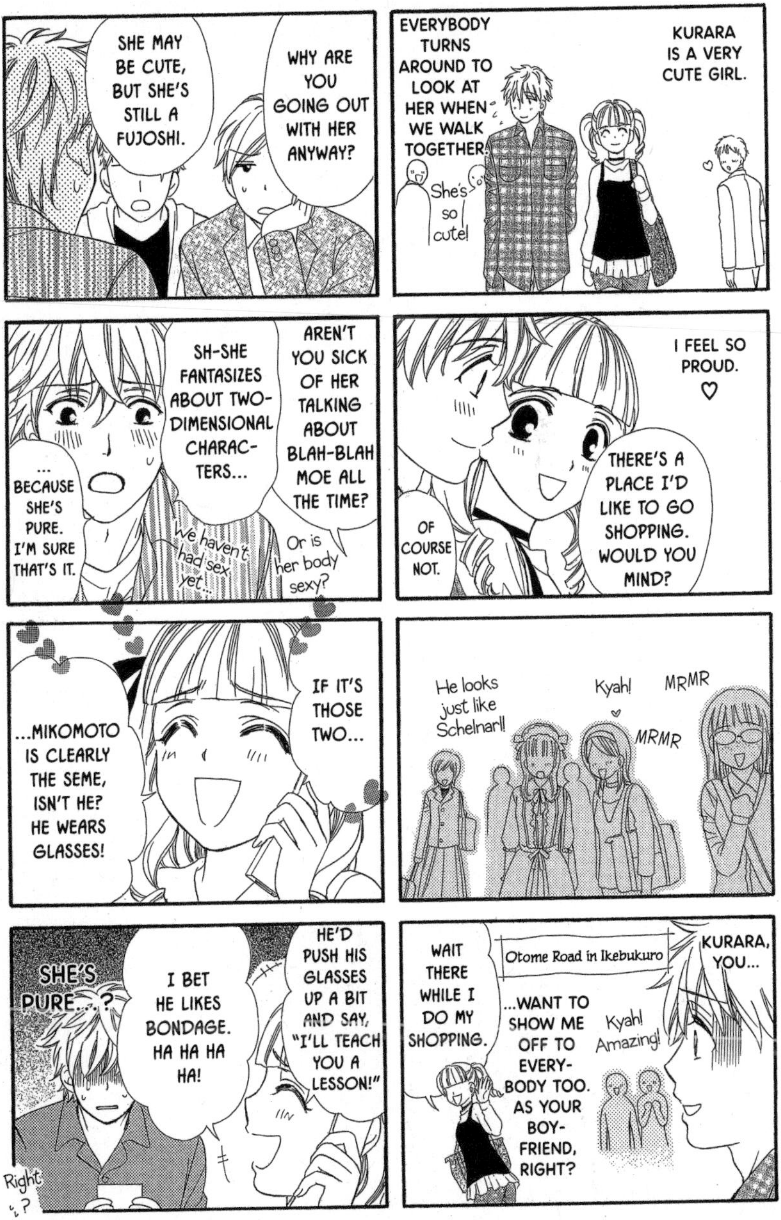
KURARA IS A VERY CUTE GIRL.
EVERYBODY TURNS AROUND TO LOOK AT HER WHEN WE WALK TOGETHER.
She's so cute!
WHY ARE YOU GOING OUT WITH HER ANYWAY?
SHE MAY BE CUTE, BUT SHE'S STILL A FUJOSHI.
I FEEL SO PROUD. ♡
THERE'S A PLACE I'D LIKE TO GO SHOPPING. WOULD YOU MIND?
OF COURSE NOT.
AREN'T YOU SICK OF HER TALKING ABOUT BLAH-BLAH MOE ALL THE TIME?
Or is her body sexy?
SH-SHE FANTASIZES ABOUT TWO-DIMENSIONAL CHARACTERS...
We haven't had sex yet...
...BECAUSE SHE'S PURE. I'M SURE THAT'S IT.
MRMR
Kyah!
MRMR
He looks just like Schelnarl!
IF IT'S THOSE TWO...
...MIKOMOTO IS CLEARLY THE SEME, ISN'T HE? HE WEARS GLASSES!
KURARA, YOU...
Otome Road in Ikebukuro
...WANT TO SHOW ME OFF TO EVERYBODY TOO. AS YOUR BOYFRIEND, RIGHT?
WAIT THERE WHILE I DO MY SHOPPING.
Kyah! Amazing!
HE'D PUSH HIS GLASSES UP A BIT AND SAY, "I'LL TEACH YOU A LESSON!"
I BET HE LIKES BONDAGE. HA HA HA HA!
SHE'S PURE...?
Right...?

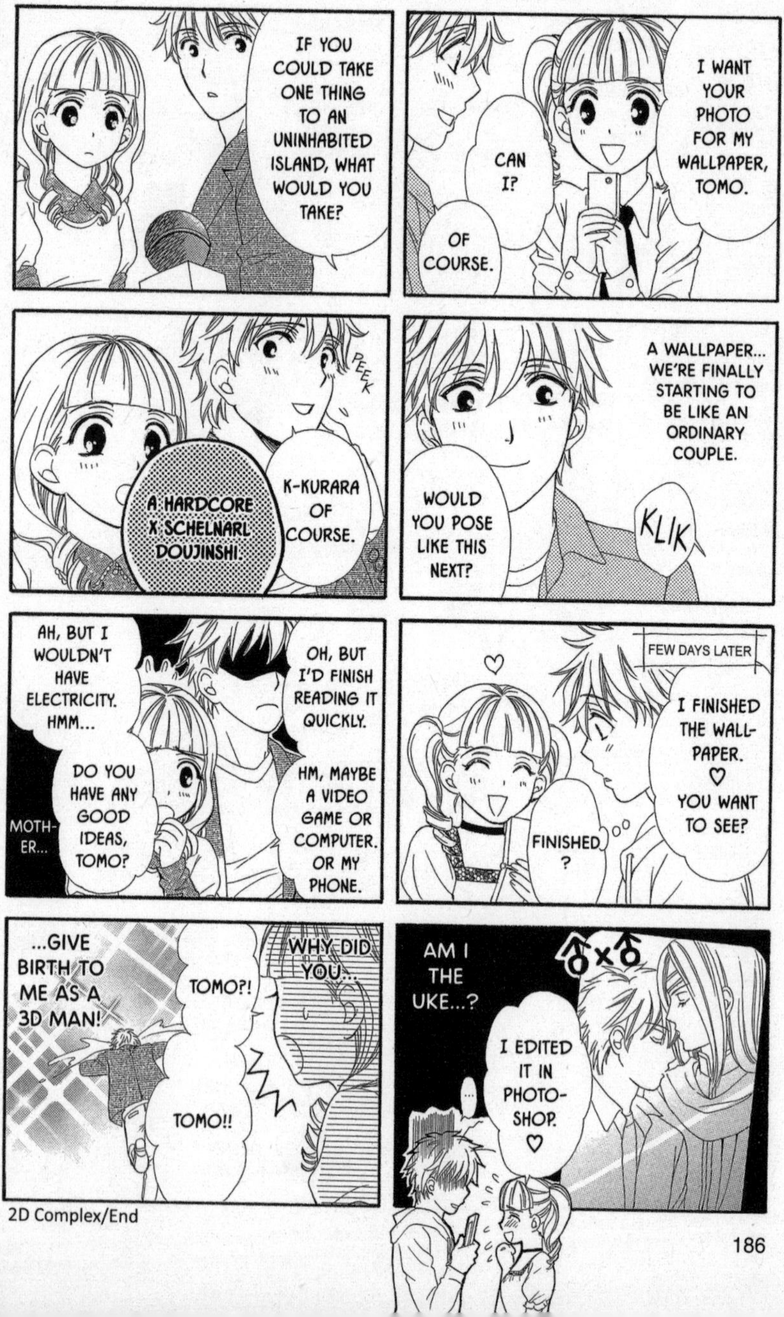
I WANT YOUR PHOTO FOR MY WALLPAPER, TOMO.
CAN I?
OF COURSE.
A WALLPAPER... WE'RE FINALLY STARTING TO BE LIKE AN ORDINARY COUPLE.
KLIK
WOULD YOU POSE LIKE THIS NEXT?
FEW DAYS LATER
I FINISHED THE WALL-PAPER. ♡ YOU WANT TO SEE?
FINISHED?
♡
♂×♂
AM I THE UKE...?
I EDITED IT IN PHOTO-SHOP. ♡
...
IF YOU COULD TAKE ONE THING TO AN UNINHABITED ISLAND, WHAT WOULD YOU TAKE?
K-KURARA OF COURSE.
PEEK
A HARDCORE X SCHELNARL DOUJINSHI.
OH, BUT I'D FINISH READING IT QUICKLY.
HM, MAYBE A VIDEO GAME OR COMPUTER. OR MY PHONE.
AH, BUT I WOULDN'T HAVE ELECTRICITY. HMM...
DO YOU HAVE ANY GOOD IDEAS, TOMO?
MOTH-ER...
WHY DID YOU...
TOMO?!
TOMO!!
...GIVE BIRTH TO ME AS A 3D MAN!

2D Complex/End

A GIRL'S DREAM

The video preview of *Happy Marriage* has been uploaded on YouTube! The voice actors are amazing! If you're thinking of recommending *Happy Marriage* to your friends, please show them the video. It's an honor to have actors voice my characters, but I get really nervous... I felt the same way with the drama CD for *Night Café*.

—Maki Enjoji

Maki Enjoji was born on December 8 in Tokyo. She made her debut with *Fu•Junai* (Wicked Pure Love). She currently works with *Petit Comics*. *Happy Marriage?!* is her fourth series.

Happy Marriage?!
Volume 9
Shojo Beat Edition

Story and Art by
Maki Enjoji

HAPIMARI - HAPPY MARRIAGE!? - Vol. 9
by Maki ENJOJI
© 2009 Maki ENJOJI
All rights reserved.
Original Japanese edition published by SHOGAKUKAN.
English translation rights in the United States of America, Canada, United
Kingdom, Ireland, Australia and New Zealand arranged with SHOGAKUKAN.

Translation/Tetsuichiro Miyaki
Adaptation/Nancy Thistlethwaite
Touch-up Art & Lettering/Inori Fukuda Trant
Design/Izumi Evers
Editor/Nancy Thistlethwaite

The stories, characters and incidents mentioned in this publication
are entirely fictional.

Printed in the U.S.A.

Published by VIZ Media, LLC
P.O. Box 77010
San Francisco, CA 94107

10 9 8 7 6 5 4 3 2 1
First printing, December 2014

www.viz.com   www.shojobeat.com

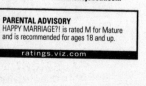

PARENTAL ADVISORY
HAPPY MARRIAGE?! is rated M for Mature
and is recommended for ages 18 and up.
ratings.viz.com

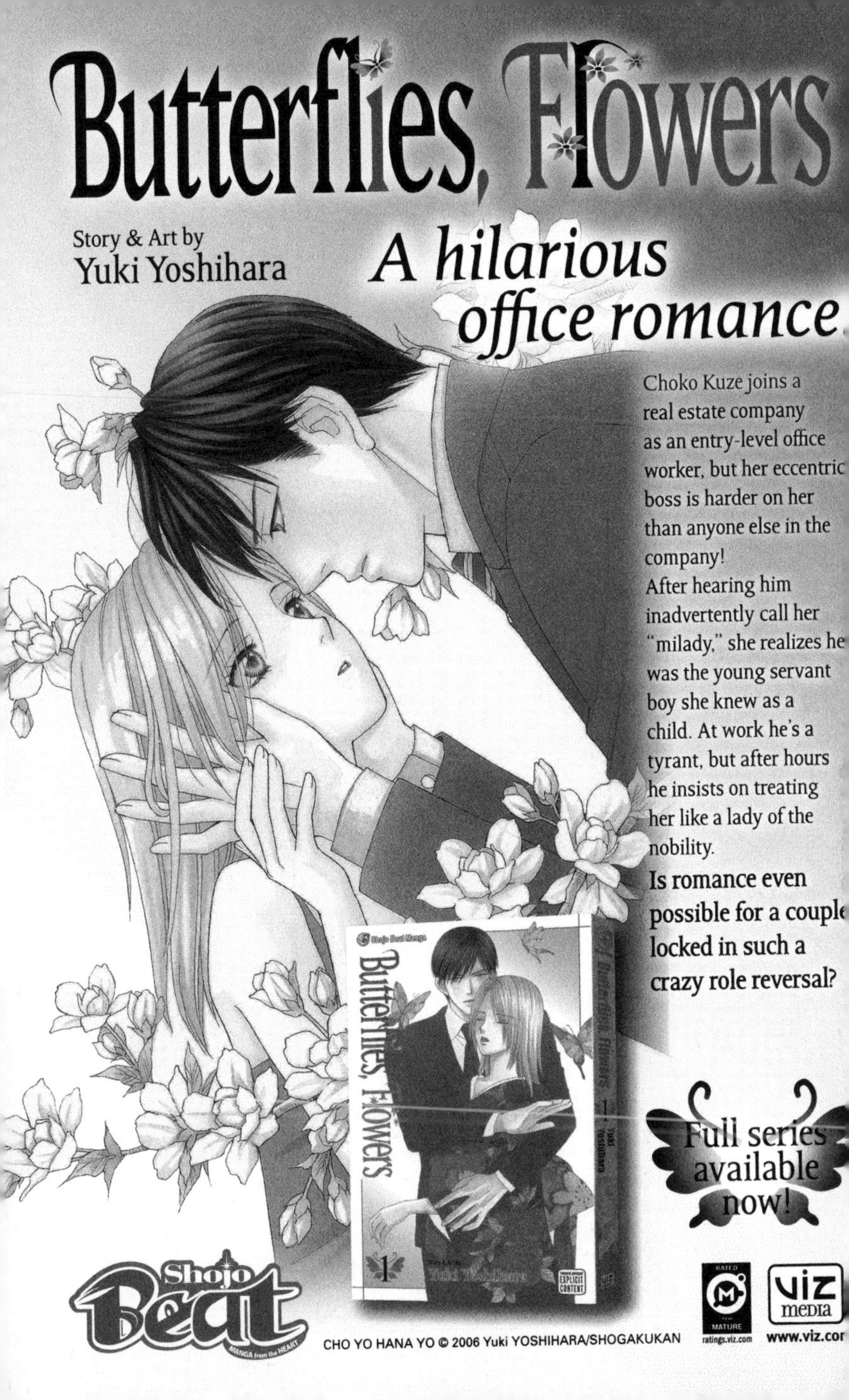
Butterflies, Flowers
Story & Art by
Yuki Yoshihara
A hilarious office romance
Choko Kuze joins a real estate company as an entry-level office worker, but her eccentric boss is harder on her than anyone else in the company!
After hearing him inadvertently call her "milady," she realizes he was the young servant boy she knew as a child. At work he's a tyrant, but after hours he insists on treating her like a lady of the nobility.
Is romance even possible for a couple locked in such a crazy role reversal?
Full series available now!
Shojo Beat
MANGA from the HEART
CHO YO HANA YO © 2006 Yuki YOSHIHARA/SHOGAKUKAN
RATED M MATURE
ratings.viz.com
VIZ media
www.viz.com

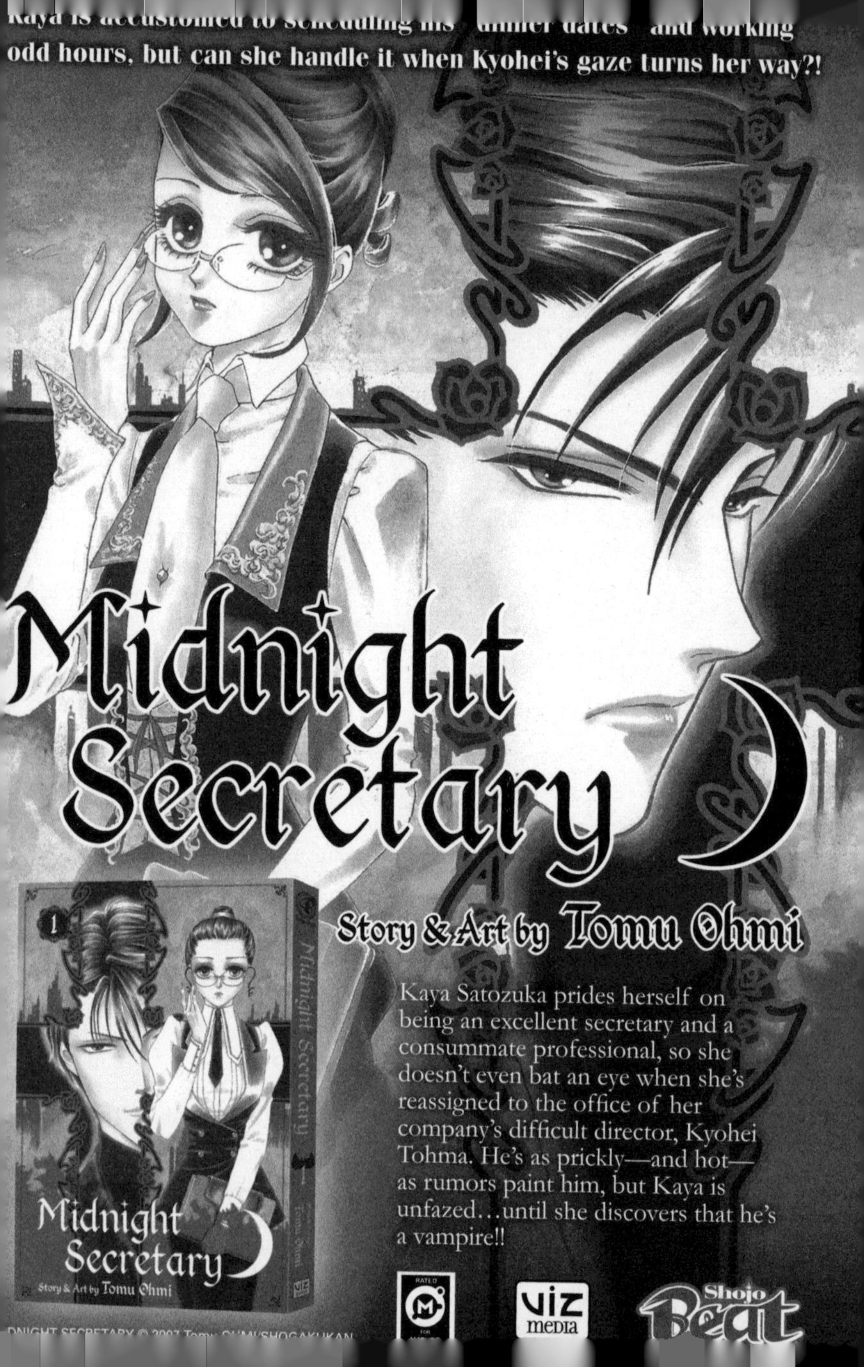

Kaya is accustomed to scheduling his "dinner dates" and working odd hours, but can she handle it when Kyohei's gaze turns her way?!

Midnight Secretary

Story & Art by Tomu Ohmi

Kaya Satozuka prides herself on being an excellent secretary and a consummate professional, so she doesn't even bat an eye when she's reassigned to the office of her company's difficult director, Kyohei Tohma. He's as prickly—and hot— as rumors paint him, but Kaya is unfazed…until she discovers that he's a vampire!!

You may be reading the wrong way!

This book reads right to left to maintain the original presentation and art of the Japanese edition, so action, sound effects and word balloons are reversed. The diagram below shows how to follow the panels. Turn to the other side of the book to begin.

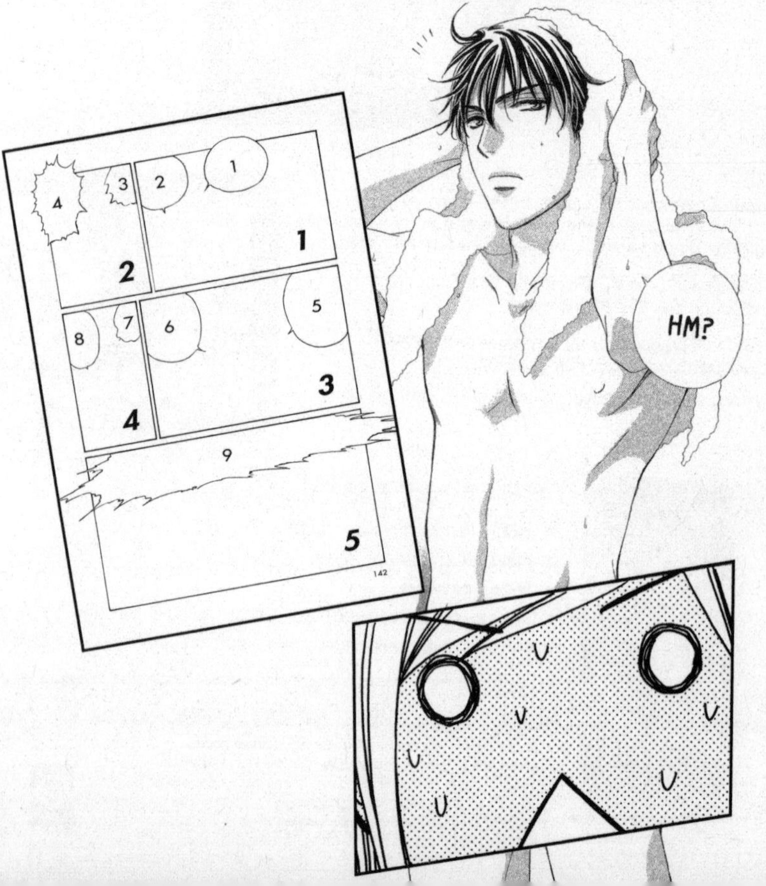
HM?
1
2
3
4
5
6
7
8
9
142